THE N
OF UNHAPPINESS

Also published by Robinson

Why Therapy Doesn't Work

THE NATURE
OF UNHAPPINESS

DAVID SMAIL

ROBINSON
London

Constable Publishers
3 The Lanchesters
162 Fulham Palace Road
London W6 9ER
www.constablerobinson.com

The Origins of Unhappiness first published in the UK
by HarperCollins Publishers 1993
Copyright © David Smail 1993

How to Survive Without Psychotherapy first published in the UK
by Constable and Company 1996
Copyright © David Smail 1996

This combined edition published by Robinson, an imprint of
Constable & Robinson Ltd 2001
Copyright © David Smail 2001

The right of David Smail to be identified as author of this work
has been asserted by him in accordance with the
Copyright, Designs and Patents Act, 1988

A copy of the British Library Cataloguing-in-Publication Data for
this title is available from the British Library

ISBN 1-84119-350-X

Printed and bound in the EU

Contents

Foreword   vii

THE ORIGINS OF UNHAPPINESS:
A New Understanding of Personal Distress

List of Figures   xiv
Preface   xv
Introduction   1
1 Psychology and Distress: The Story so Far   11
2 'When I Was Little': The Experience of Power   24
3 Bodies and Worlds: The Field of Power   56
4 Case Study: The 1980s   93
5 Help   160
6 A Rational Faith   196
Appendix   227

HOW TO SURVIVE WITHOUT
PSYCHOTHERAPY
Preface   237
1 The Treatment of Distress: Current Approaches   245
2 The Experience of Distress   278
3 The Tyranny of 'Normality'   329
4 Troublesome Worlds: People and Power   353
5 What Should We Do? Moral Demands   377
6 What Can We Do? The Problem of Will Power   406
7 What Could We Do? Learning and Change   436
Notes   465

Index   483

Foreword

The two books that comprise this volume – *The Origins of Unhappiness* and *How to Survive Without Psychotherapy* – attempt, respectively, to give a theoretical and a practical account of the origins of psychological or emotional distress, and to suggest what the individual person can be expected to be able to do about them.

Beyond its obvious doubts about the therapy and counselling industry, the title 'How to Survive without Psychotherapy' is, of course, intended as a mildly ironic dig at the whole literary genre of psychological self-help. Therapy and counselling share with self-help a philosophy of human action, deeply embedded in our culture, which is specifically rejected in these pages. While I am far from alone in suggesting the kind of alternative put forward here,[1] it is, nevertheless, a view for which it is extraordinarily difficult to get a hearing. This must be, I think, because it runs so diametrically counter to what we have as a society come to accept as common sense.

We normally think of ourselves as more or less self-determining free agents, able to control our psychological reactions by acts of will based on a rational assessment of our situation. There may be times, to be sure, when we feel the need for a little guidance or assistance with this process, but for the most part we expect to be able to steer the course of our lives in directions of our own choosing. It is on this philosophical foundation that the whole of the psychotherapy industry is built, for fundamental to the idea that a therapist can set you on the right path is the belief that, once you know what it is, you can indeed *choose to take* that path. Thus, when it comes to thinking about our distress or unhappiness, we are liable to see their causes as following from our own bad choices.

This 'voluntaristic' philosophy is one which supports much

more than simply our assumptions about the way that psychotherapy works: it also underpins the entire culture of individualism that, though not without its critics, has come to dominate Western life very nearly totally. If I were merely challenging some basic ideas of therapy and counselling, my task would be much easier. Unfortunately in my hope of being understood, what I am trying to say appears to be undermining some of our most cherished notions of what it is to be a person.

What I *am* saying is of course to be found in these pages. Since they were first published, however, my experience of how they are often interpreted suggests that there can be no harm in using this opportunity to try to clarify further some of the central points (in view of this, this introduction might better be read – or read again – after reading the volume itself).

My central contention is that what we think of as a *person* is the result of an interaction between his or her physical body – what he or she comes into the world with – and the influence of an essentially material environment. From a psychological point of view, this is the environment of social space-time – an environment structured by the operation of *power* both now and in the past. In this way, we are just like every other natural creation and should seek to understand ourselves in exactly the same way that we seek to understand – apparently with great success – everything else we identify in our universe.

Maybe, put like this, nothing seems so terribly contentious. But already there are in fact strong conflicts with our everyday way of seeing ourselves. Although we are happy to acknowledge our biological nature, the influence on our psychological make-up of genes, etc., and although too we have no quarrel with the idea that environmental influences shape much of our conduct, we still reserve for ourselves powers and abilities that are of a different order from those we are prepared to allow the rest of creation. To suggest (as I do) that a person may be defined as a point in social space *through* which outside powers and influences flow, rather than an entity *within* which powers and influence originate, seems to challenge unacceptably our idea of ourselves as agents who, having seen the need for one or other kind of action, can *will* it. It is, after all, an hourly, let alone daily, experience that we assess our circumstances and situations, make decisions on what to do about them and then put the appropriate conduct into action. The idea that we are (as I maintain) merely the hosts of processes which flow through us rather than the architects of procedures we choose seems to outrage common sense.

The difficulty here, I think, lies in our being unable to break free of the overwhelmingly compelling nature of our experience. Were a snooker ball to be endowed with awareness of its own physical state, but not of the higher-order human world surrounding it, I imagine it would not be long before it began to think of itself as *intending* to roll this way or that. It would 'feel' an *internal* impulse (for where else could it feel it but internally?) to take off, say, towards the left-hand corner pocket. And, significantly for the central concerns of this volume, if it found itself rebounding between the pocket's jaws, it would curse *itself* for having missed.

In very much the same way, we, while necessarily unaware of the influences that act upon us from a distance, have no way of escaping the bodily awareness of being involved in activity. Since much of the time we quite literally cannot see or even guess at the origins of such influences, we have no choice but to assume that they stem from the same place where we feel them: *inside* our selves, and that our activity is the direct result of such feelings.

From this assumption of 'inside' a whole stream of psychological errors flow.

Our everyday psychological language is full of terms which imply this kind of interior causation: intention, choice, decision, responsibility, purpose, and so on. It seems to us that as individuals we have privileged access to an 'inner world' which is the origin of much of what we value most about being human: our creativity, our morality, our will power and our spirituality. Our experience of the operation of these processes is so undeniable that we regard with the greatest suspicion any observer who dares to cast doubt on their validity.

For the most part, approaches to therapy and counselling have not significantly or fundamentally challenged the psychological assumptions buried in popular culture. Even the concept of 'the unconscious' simply shifts the whole 'inside' apparatus of will and decision, substantially unchanged, into a yet deeper and even more mysterious interior. The principal exception to this was the behaviourist movement in modern psychology, which adopted such a cavalier attitude to the contents of our cherished 'inner worlds' that it eventually sacrificed its own credibility and became harmlessly diluted into the bastard creation – 'cognitive-behaviourism' – which now dominates contemporary clinical psychology.

I do not mourn the demise of behaviourism – it was a crude and simplistic dogma which obscured far more than it clarified. But it did have a point, and that was to emphasize the causative impotence of 'inner world' phenomena. While it is not the case that our experience of 'inner' does not exist, nor that it is without significance, nor even that it is not a defining feature of our humanity and the source of our greatest spiritual satisfactions, it *is* the case that, in and of itself, it has no *power*.

When it comes to trying to explain how and why people do things, what actually moves them to action, reference to interior processes (like deciding and willing) has very little relevance. It is absolutely not that 'inner worlds' are of no interest, it is just that – paradoxical though it may seem – they are of only tangential interest to a psychologist trying to understand the origins of unhappiness. To avoid misunderstanding, I have to emphasize, therefore, that I am not claiming that the phenomena of the 'inner space' so beloved of 'humanistic' psychology are *invalid*, only that they have very little to offer as *explanations* of what we do and why we suffer.

My position is made no easier to maintain by the fact that psychology is only one, albeit central, plank of a vast cultural apparatus that views interior processes such as cognition and will as self-evident. The natural bias of modern literature, for example, is towards accounting for people's actions in exactly the same kind of interior psychological terms. The depiction of the helplessness of the individual in the face of powers stemming from *beyond* the self (as, for example, in Greek tragedy) tends to strike the modern reader as alien and far-fetched. And yet in many respects this latter kind of model seems to me far more accurate than the kind of 'psychological' notions which dominate our personal, social and political culture.

The individual in distress finds him- or herself *in the grip of* forces which are simply not amenable to the operations of will. While all therapists and counsellors worth their salt know this to be the case, they still have not managed to work out an explanatory theory which takes proper account of it. The Greeks at least knew that the workings of what they saw as fate had an inexorability which would not be touched by any simple 'therapeutic' manoeuvre.[2] People simply *cannot* be lifted out of their social context and 'treated' as if they had the power to change themselves.

I feel sure that it is my recognition of this circumstance more than anything else which has led to my books receiving, on the whole, a more appreciative reception from sufferers than from professional helpers. There is a school of therapeutic thought that seems to react with panic and despair to the idea that our social world causes damage which just *cannot* be repaired. How could one promulgate such a 'nihilistic', 'depressing' notion? Interestingly, though, people who have been at the receiving end of such damage do not themselves seem to find its acknowledgement so distressing – indeed they may react with enormous relief at finding the burden of 'responsibility' lifted from them.

I realise of course that I cannot expect to be thanked by counsellors and therapists for putting forward a view of their trade which seems to undermine its very *raison d'être*. I'm sure, too, that fear of loss of livelihood, though important, is not the only reason for my relative unpopularity with professional helpers: many of them are moved also by the best of motives to do what they can to reduce human unhappiness and are outraged at any suggestion that their powers to do so are strictly limited.

But surely the observation that the world *is* damaging, that we very frequently *cannot* help ourselves, that, once emotionally scarred by our experience of (most often) the abuse of power, we tend to *stay* emotionally scarred – surely that observation scarcely runs counter to our knowledge of everyday life?

In my view there is something extremely superficial – demeaning even – about the current fashion for counselling, as if the kinds of 'problems' for which counselling is so readily offered, including even catastrophic loss of life, are mere inconveniences, bumps on the road to a comfortable consumerist 'life-style' which can be ironed out by a few fifty-minute chats with a professional.

There are many knowledgeable, experienced and dedicated therapists and counsellors who indeed know that such is not the case. What still seems to be lacking, even so, is an account of unhappiness which pays proper attention to its *social* origins. It is as a contribution to such an account (and in the hope that it may be of help to people *beyond* the therapy industry) that these books were written.

Notes

1. A relatively accessible academic overview of similar approaches, some of which have no doubt strongly influenced my work, is to be found in Ian Burkitt's *Social Selves*. Sage, 1991.
2. I have elaborated on the relations between 'psychotherapy and tragedy' in a chapter so entitled in Richard House & Nick Totton (eds), *Implausible Professions*, PCCS Books, 1997.

The Origins of Unhappiness

A New Understanding of Personal Distress

List of Figures

1 The raw materials   62

2 The person as interaction between body
  and environment   63

3 The field of power   74

4 The generation of distress in the 1980s   128

5 The microenvironment of therapeutic space   162

6 The microenvironment of 'psychopathology'   164

7 Therapy in perspective   165

Preface

This is the third in what has turned out to be a series of four books attempting to locate psychological distress in the world which gives rise to it rather than in the individual. The first, *Illusion & Reality*, focuses on the subjective experience of distress, arguing that such experience (so-called 'neurotic symptoms', etc.) is much more an accurate reflection of the state of the person's world than an indication of some kind of 'intrapsychic' pathology. In the second, *Taking Care*, attention is turned to the social context in which distress is generated and maintained, suggesting that it is only by concentrating on the public world, as opposed to private experience, that we can hope to make any significant impact on our psychological ills. (Both these titles are now available in a combined volume, *Why Therapy Doesn't Work*, also published by Robinson.) The present volume has two main concerns. The first is to bring into sharp focus, and to state more formally, a theoretical basis for the observations contained in its predecessors. The second is to use this theoretical basis for an analysis of our contemporary predicament.

There is therefore a certain formality about some chapters (in particular Chapter Three and the Appendix) which invites closer attention to detail than may be usual for books written, as this one is, for the general reader. But, as I suggest in the Introduction, theory is important, and it is above all the elaboration of a *theoretical* position which gives this book whatever importance it may have. Certainly, I regard *The Origins of Unhappiness* as pivotal in my writing, clanfying as well as developing what has gone before and shaping what was (and still may be) to come.

What was to come turns out, so far, to be the fourth book in the series: *How to Survive Without Psychotherapy*. In some ways this latter work is less a development of my views than a companion piece to the present book; it seeks to elaborate the significance of some of the issues dealt with here at a fairly abstract level – for example, 'power', 'free will', 'change', etc. – in a way which can speak directly to, and hopefully make some sense of, the person's experience of distress. *How to Survive Without Psychotherapy* was the first book I have written to be systematically informed by, so to speak, a consciously stated theoretical position – i.e., the position developed here.

Because of the importance of having such a position stated as carefully and clearly as possible, I am very glad to see this book back in print. Its previous shelf-life was not very long, and were it not for Constable's readiness to resurrect it, there would be a serious hole in my published work: one which, I think, would make it much more difficult than I hope it need be to understand what I'm getting at.

The second principal concern of this book – to provide an analysis of our contemporary predicament – constitutes my first attempt to cast what I am getting at in an absolutely concrete form. In many ways this completes the project started, perhaps in a less consciously deliberate way, in *Taking Care*: i.e., to 'turn inside-out' our conventional understandings of distress. Rather than give an account of the 'psychopathology' of the 1980s in terms of the inadequacies of individuals to live up to the demands of the times (which is how nearly all of them experienced it), I try in Chapter Four to establish that the 'pathology' is not *personal* but *social*. It is the pathology of a social environment in which powerful influences impinge on the individual person such that he or she *cannot escape* their noxious effects.

There was always a risk in writing Chapter Four as the 'case study' of a decade that what is a central part of the book would swiftly become dated. So far, at least, this does not seem to be the case. The kind of insane Business 'rationality' which I instance in that chapter has so far blossomed unchecked, seemingly the more popular and successful the more it derealizes our world and alienates us from our embodied experience. The debased language of Business has so permeated pretty well every corner of our culture that we now speak it without even noticing. There is today an even more mindnumbing contrast – in Britain, at least – between, on the one hand, the bizarre world of celebrities and fat cats, media hype and 'proximalizing' political rhetoric,[1] and, on the other, the world of ordinary citizens: crumbling infrastructure, declining public services, the poverty of many and insecurity of most. More than ever, the ideology of power is one of *make believe*.

The management of reality – ever more devious exercises in spin-doctoring – succeeds only because it is sponsored by power. Good social creatures that we are, our reluctance to disbelieve those we credit with authority still blinds us to our own experience, and even as the monetarist and 'free market' fantasies of the last twenty years bring half the globe to its knees, we obediently buy into (not to mention vote for!) the visions we are offered of a promised land, if not already here, then to come. Even as leaders of the 'free world' prattle of a nonideological 'third way', the influence of Business ideology achieves unprecedented heights, and the ordinary citizen is deprived of a language in which even to *think* criticism. It is not easy to find sane voices at this time to explicate our predicament, though some there are.[2]

It is no surprise that, given this context, current approaches to psychological distress tend to split into the biological on the one hand and the magical on the other. Biological psychiatry, which at times in the 1970s looked to be a dead duck, is back with a vengeance. Were it not for our anything-goes era of 'post-modernity', the cheerful coexistence of these drug-and-body-based, apparently scientific certainties with the equally successful approaches of 'alternative' therapies would be bizarre. But they do of course share an important function, and that is to obscure the reality of our predicament.

Our predicament is the world – the social environment – in which we live, and our suffering arises from our relations with it. It has always been in the interests of power to obscure this simple truth, for it has (almost?) always been in the interests of the powerful to run the world to their own advantage while persuading the rest of us that their sole interest is the public good.

Power co-opts any potentially critical force it cannot simply obliterate, and in this situation, psychology soon becomes its all-too-willing lieutenant, busily constructing the filters which distort our understanding of the origins of our unhappiness. Because of the commercial take-over of universities and the Business infiltration of the institutions of health, disinterested research into the ways in which our environment damages us becomes increasingly difficult (though still not impossible) and the development of a sophisticated understanding of how social environments operate to our psychological detriment are likely to take place, if at all, only beyond the margins of what is authorized as respectable.

Psychology, in its clinical aspect, has in the past adopted a far more explicitly 'social-environmentalist' approach than it does now, but even then, in particular of course with behaviourism, its treatment of the social environment was superficial in the extreme - merely as a field (not even a network) of crude rewards and punishments. It was my intention in this book to help resurrect a thorough-going environmentalism, to suggest ways in which a more adequate understanding of the distress-creating environment may be developed and, above all, to do so in a language accessible to non-specialists. However the success of my efforts may be judged, these aims seem to me no less important and valid now than they did when the book was first published nearly six years ago.

David Smail
Nottingham, December 1998

Notes
1. For example, endorsing strategies of disciplinary surveillance (as in OFSTED school inspecnons), victim-blaming via the notions of 'community' and 'responsibility', resorting to 'naming and shaming' as an alternative to legislation, etc. All these are ways of trying to shift accountability for the public good from government (which is in fact in a position to exert appropnate power) to individuals (who are not). See Chapter Three for an elaboration of 'proximalization'.
2. See for example John Pilger's *Hidden Agendas*, Vintage, 1998; also John Ralston Saul's *The Unconscious Civilization*, Penguin Books, 1998.
3. See for example Richard Wilkinson, 1996. *Unhealthy Societies: The Afflictions of Inequality*, London & New York: Routledge.

Introduction

In order to develop a view of emotional distress which is both helpful and true, one has, I believe, to turn prevalent understandings inside out. Instead of looking inward to detect and eradicate within ourselves the products of 'psychopathology', we need to direct our gaze out into the world to identify the sources of our pain and unhappiness. Instead of burdening ourselves with, in one form or another, the responsibility for 'symptoms' of 'illness', 'neurotic fears', 'unconscious complexes', 'faulty cognitions' and other failures of development and understanding, we would do better to clarify what is wrong with a social world which gives rise to such forms of suffering.

This is not to say that we are not psychologically and emotionally damaged by our experience of life, but that neither the causes nor the 'cures' of such damage can usefully be treated as 'internal' matters. I would not claim that we do not at times conduct ourselves 'pathologically', but I do claim that we are all, at the outset, innocent victims of *social* pathology rather than harbourers of some kind of psychological abnormality.

Though unorthodox, the position I am taking here is, of course, not new: psychology and psychiatry have always had their critics, many of whom have emphasized the role of society in the generation of distress. Nor am I by any means the first to see the need to defend the individual against the incipient moralism of so-called 'psychotherapeutic' approaches, which, however subtly, manage to 'blame the victim'.

Former critiques seem to me to have fallen short, however, in three main respects. First, they have tended (entirely understandably in view of their starting point) not to draw the radical conclusion from their own arguments. From Alfred Adler to R. D. Laing, the voices raised in criticism of individualistic approaches have themselves spoken from an essentially psychotherapeutic standpoint, and if they have seen the causes of distress as social, have shied away from acknowledging *fully* what this must mean for a therapeutic practice which still, for the most part, 'treats' individuals. Second, the theoretical elements of the accounts given by such critics tend similarly to be rooted in the perspective of one kind or another of individual psychology; indeed, most have their origin in Freudian psychoanalysis. Third, the vision of society offered concentrates most heavily on the person's immediate context – usually that of the family – so that the link between wider social influence and immediate personal experience is left obscure. It is largely concern with these three issues which provides the framework for my present undertaking.

In this, as in my previous books, *Illusion and Reality* and *Taking Care*, I have emphasized the limitations of 'psychotherapy' as an 'answer' to emotional distress, and indeed question 'psychology' itself as an undertaking of any real relevance to issues which seem to me essentially political in nature. However, more than in those books, I have here attempted (largely in Chapter Five) to place psychotherapy and counselling in a context which shows their positive (if modest) contribution as well as their limitations. I do not wish to be seen as rejecting therapy and counselling out of hand, though I do think one needs to be mindful of their intellectual blinkers as well as relentlessly critical of the grandiosity of their claims.

Working for three decades as a clinical psychologist in the National Health Service builds a viewpoint rather different from that of many other critics of the psychotherapeutic and psychiatric orthodoxy. My own view is that, more than just a relative difference in perspective, it is actually an advantage to have gained one's experience in the setting of public health rather than private practice, and in a profession (clinical psychology) which is, unlike medicine, relatively free of the responsibilities as well as the abuses of power. It is easier, I believe, to get at the 'truth' concerning people's difficulties if one wields over them not even a possibility of the kind of coercive power available to, for example, psychiatrists and social workers. Contact with 'ordinary people', furthermore, gives one a particularly clear sight of what it is and is not possible to achieve in struggling with adversity; that is to say, the difficulties and distress of people who are not especially privileged and well resourced throw into sharp relief the poverty of conceptions such as 'insight' and 'responsibility'.

The attempt to sketch out a theory of societal influence which forms the core of this book is the fruit of my experience as a clinical psychologist. I have become less and less able to see the people who consult me as having anything 'wrong' with them, and more and more aware of the constraints which are placed on their ability to escape the distress they experience. I have long been aware that their suffering can in no helpful sense be regarded as their 'fault', but it is only relatively recently that I have been able to establish for myself a theoretical perspective which actually seems to make sense of how the individual experience of distress is related to the operation of social influences at the very margins of our awareness. Over the last few years it has increasingly seemed to me that talking about, and refining aspects of, this theory with the people whose experience has helped to form it is, in fact, often found illuminating by them, even though it doesn't end their troubles. It is this which made the book seem worth writing.

What has, perhaps, made the elaboration of this theoretical framework possible more than anything else has been the social, political and cultural events of the last ten years or so. What in the mid-seventies may have seemed to some a relatively unusual, perhaps rather provocative claim – that the causes of our psychological ills lie in our society – seems to me now barely controvertible. The experience of people who suffered from the 1980s, placed in the context of a radical critique of 'therapy', seems to me to open up possibilities for an understanding of distress which has never been clearer. By taking a decade as a 'case study' (Chapter Four) I hope that I may be able to set up sufficient resonance with readers' experiences to make the rather more abstract theoretical account of Chapter Three come to life, as well as to illustrate the 'inside out' nature of my whole project.

I have written the book very much with the general reader in mind. Trying to write a book which neither assumes specialist knowledge nor panders to some – very likely imaginary – conception of popular taste does, however, present its difficulties, and to the extent that there may indeed be two stools, one runs a risk of falling between them.

A century of academic and professional involvement in psychology and psychotherapy has trained generations of researchers and practitioners to expect their intellectual fare to be delivered in certain kinds of package and certain kinds of style. The packaging is reflected in the way bookshop shelves have become compartmentalized into specialist areas – 'psychology', for instance, is usually split into myriad subsections which must surely be mystifying to anyone not trained to find his or her way around (it's bad enough for those who are). The style of presentation is probably also something which deters the general reader: all those footnotes and unexplained references to 'evidence', which is taken for granted as within the reader's reach.

The layperson, on the other hand, seems often to be expected not to want to be taxed by his or her reading matter. Complex issues and doubtful theories may thus be presented confidently and declaratively, rather in the 'psychologists have shown' style; notions are presented as facts, and the reader is in general expected to *receive* rather than to *enter into* the text.

My experience of talking to clients of the NHS about their, often profound, personal and emotional difficulties has convinced me that 'ordinary people' are perfectly capable of expressing and understanding any theory about their problems you care to name. They are not particularly reassured by simplistic answers, they are not impressed by pomposity, and can detect intellectual and professional bullshit a mile off. On the other hand, of course, they are often not in possession of the educational equipment necessary for deciphering the formal theories and methods underlying the procedures they are subjected to, or for an elegant exposition of their own insights.

There is, of course, a big difference between talking to people and writing for them, and I cannot pretend that this book will prove effortlessly comprehensible to everyone. It is not, I hope, a simplistic book and it may at times make demands on the reader's intellectual resources, but it does not assume possession of resources beyond those available widely to anyone who reads and thinks.

Trying to elucidate for a general readership the nature of distress and the context in which it occurs has, in contrast to beavering away within the narrow sphere created by the academic/ professional division of labour, some interesting consequences. It makes one question one's assumptions and clarify and sharpen the principles and practices which have become the unquestioned routine of one's day-to-day work. All the familiar, dust-laden clutter of received ideas has to be dragged out from the murk of the ivory tower and submitted to a critical scrutiny which takes very little for granted. Conceptual issues have to be clarified and made comprehensible to a commonsense intelligence and their relations with each other made intelligible; practices have to be explained and justified.

So far as the present work is concerned I have found myself having on the one hand to spell out a quite detailed theory of societal influence while on the other to tackle philosophical and ethical issues which rarely seem to make much of an appearance outside a very small and rather claustrophobic academic world. It is one of the sorrier consequences of the compartmentalizing induced by a 'market' in intellectual activity that theorizing should become the exclusive province of specialists in universities (social scientists and philosophers) capable for the most part of being understood only by each other.

One cannot in my view consider the issues with which this book deals without a carefully formulated framework in which to make observations and a speculative appraisal of the meaning of what one observes. To this extent both theory and philosophy are highly relevant to the everyday lives of all of us, and if I risk the scorn of academics for trampling on their grass, I make no apology: it's high time that we tried to break down the cultural barriers between those who make a business of thought and those who are not aware that they are thinking. I say this not out of any Philistine contempt for intellectuals, but because of my awareness through talking to 'ordinary people' in distress of how relevant to their difficulties intellectual considerations are, and how capable they are of making good use of them.

One cannot, then, hope to understand the nature of emotional distress without facing some of the philosophical issues which have always preoccupied people who speculate about what it is to be, and to suffer as, a human being. There can be little doubt that we all do think about these issues in one form or another, but few people encounter 'philosophy' in its formal, academic aspect, and if they do are unlikely to find its rarefied atmosphere one which they can tolerate for long. It is with some hesitation that I have (particularly in Chapter Six) introduced themes in this book – for example, concerning 'truth', 'ethics', 'free will', etc. – which are the staple diet of academic philosophy, mainly because I am aware that to do so will seem to the professionals absurdly ambitious. However, these *are* issues which cannot be evaded when we come to think about the causes of our ills, and if 'ordinary people' are to expand their understanding of them beyond self-blame and pop psychology, they are going to have to get to grips with philosophy too.

I have tried as far as possible to avoid making the text too didactic and academic. I must confess that this has not been difficult. I feel much happier with ideas, conceptions, ways of understanding as organic, changing things to be used in the living of life, rather than as intellectual property which has to be registered, pored over and obsessively criticized. I have always found reading books less like compiling mental catalogues than like eating meals. Some are indigestible and quickly excreted, others (the best) are enormously nourishing and enjoyable, but the details hard, after a time, to hold on to. Like food, ideas become part of one's physical make-up; they are essential to one's continued existence, but one cannot necessarily remember where and when one acquired them.

I would much prefer this book itself to be regarded as a reasonably nutritious meal than as, for example, a potential text for A level psychology. In the interests of readability, I have in any case not peppered the text with as many references as I could have done, and have kept footnotes to a minimum. Many people, past and present, have contributed to the ideas in the book, and where I am aware of their contribution I have acknowledged it in the text. There may be others whose thought has been so well digested that I can no longer distinguish it from my own; if any of them are living, I hope they will take this as a compliment rather than an act of plagiarism.

I hope this approach to documenting the provenance of the arguments to be set out in the following pages will not be regarded as too cavalier. It may perhaps lead to a suspicion that those arguments are of doubtful intellectual parentage. However, I would claim that, though they cannot be identified with any particular 'school', they are not without a pedigree. 'Schools' in psychology, and in particular what I shall call 'brand name' approaches to psychotherapy and counselling, have always seemed to me too cosily like clubs which offer the reassurance of association with 'people like us' rather than being forums for intellectual liberation and discovery. The idea that a particular group of professional experts could corner the market in 'psychology' seems patently absurd. On the other hand, one cannot but be part of a tradition, and I would be far from wanting to disown the influences which have shaped my approach.

I would, for example, be more than happy to be associated with those critics of orthodox psychiatry and psychology who have striven to place the burden of responsibility for distress on the social context rather than the individual (their names will occur

throughout the text). More broadly, I think there may be a lot
to be said for trying to refract some of the inspired ideas of
European (in particular French and German) thinkers through
the kind of commonsensical prism one tends to acquire from
British empiricism; my understanding (which I freely acknowledge
may well not be theirs) of both Michel Foucault and Jürgen
Habermas has, for example, contributed greatly to what follows.
More broadly still, I wonder how possible it is to escape from
one's intellectual and cultural origins even if one wanted to:
though, as David Jenkins points out,[1] Christendom no longer
rules European culture, it is virtually impossible not to be bound
by Christian ethics.

I offer no simple answers in this book. Though this seems to
irritate some people, who, so far as I can see, tend to equate a
lack of answers with 'pessimism' or even 'depression', it seems
to me only sensible. If there were any simple answers to the kinds
of problems I shall try to elucidate, they would surely have been
found long ago. There has certainly been no shortage of
suggestions, and it is precisely the fact that these suggestions have
signally not worked that leads one to try again to clarify the nature
of the difficulty. To proffer solutions for problems we are barely
beginning to understand does nobody any service. This, in fact,
is something about which nearly all clients of psychotherapy would
agree: being told 'the answer' to your predicament (the most
frequent strategy of well-meaning friends and relatives) is usually
experienced as profoundly unhelpful, and is exactly what drives
people to seek professional help.

Before we can even think about what an appropriate 'answer'
might look like, we need to penetrate the ideological obscurity
which surrounds the whole question of emotional distress. Success
in this latter project, though, might have some interesting effects.
It would probably not reduce to any perceptible degree the
psychological pain endemic in our world, but it might help to

1. See David Jenkins, Bishop of Durham, & Rebecca Jenkins, *Free to Believe*,
BBC Books, 1991.

lift from people the curse of 'abnormality', so that they could at least live their lives as themselves, and understand their own experience as valid.

It is precisely the *validity* of people's experience that I have tried to demonstrate by the use of 'case material' in the following chapters. Above everything, it seems to me, the judgemental clinical eye of psychology and psychiatry needs to be replaced by a respectful appreciation of character, i.e., of the manifold, resourceful, ingenious and, most often, courageous ways in which people of all kinds and conditions come to engage with their fate. I have done my best to give an accurate impression of how the material influences of the social environment ultimately impinge upon and are received by a range of characters who are modelled upon people I have encountered in my work. For obvious reasons I have fictionalized these characters, and not one of them could be identified as anyone personally known to me, though all of them are, I hope, widely recognizable as sharing predicaments typically affecting many people, including, of course, many of those likely to read this book.

CHAPTER ONE

Psychology and Distress –
The Story So Far

So far as psychology is concerned, business is booming as never before. What used to be the esoteric preserve of a minor branch of the Academy and a handful of slightly eccentric doctors is now a growth industry whose principal products – counselling, psychotherapy, psychometric testing, etc. – are familiar to everyone. One can't travel far through life before encountering some aspect of psychological thinking or practice. If not before birth, through concerned parents' perusal of the child rearing manuals, then soon afterwards as the infantile object of postnatal care. And if not then, the older child will certainly not escape the influence of 'developmental' and educational psychology once he or she starts school. In later life, psychology comes at you from every direction: from magazine questionnaires on your love life to personality tests which decide whether or not you get a job.

The concern of this book is with the experience of psychological and emotional distress, and here, of course, psychology is in its element. Apart from psychoanalysis, which formed the exclusive practice of a tightly regulated, largely medical club, fifty years ago psychology's involvement in the treatment of 'mental disorder' was virtually nil. In the years following the Second World War, however, the scene was transformed, and a field which had been considered more or less the sole province of medical psychiatry is today wide open for pretty well anyone with a plausible psychological idea to stake his or her claim to putting it into practice. Nor are the theories and techniques of psychologists who succeeded in storming the fortress of psychiatry contained within the strictly 'clinical' sphere: they spill out into the domestic and working world of 'ordinary people', who are as likely to encounter programmes of 'stress management' at work as they are 'relationship counselling' at home.

Some benefits no doubt stem from this transformation. Not so long ago people struggling with emotional pain and distress had little choice but to give themselves over to the mysteries of medical treatments, which they were not permitted to question, but which as often as not left them drugged or electrically stunned into bemused conformity with what they took to be the laws of science. Now, a whole range of 'treatments' and procedures exists, which offers comprehensible accounts of psychological problems, the fundamentals of which can be learned at evening classes. People can now take an active interest in their own psychology – indeed they can hardly avoid doing so – and even if the official channels of help still leave a lot to be desired, the labyrinths of professional mystique are not as impenetrable as they were.

Psychiatry, to be sure, still holds sway in the field of emotional distress, and seeks with habitual arrogance to define what may and may not count as 'mental illness' and what are its appropriate treatments, but its grip is loosening. Apart from the 'psychodynamic' therapies which derive from the psychoanalytic school, there are many other kinds of therapy for the sufferer to choose from: 'behavioural' approaches, 'cognitive' approaches, Client-Centred Therapy, Transactional Analysis, Gestalt Therapy, Rational-Emotive Therapy, and hundreds of other varieties of therapy and counselling, which are flourishing in a rapidly deregulating market.

As the result of all this we may, perhaps, have developed a rather more tolerant and flexible understanding of our personal and emotional difficulties; they may be less tinged with incomprehension and dread than they were when murky conceptions of 'madness' and 'mental breakdown' formed the limits of most people's knowledge. People who can talk about the 'stress' affecting them may be less estranged from themselves than those who could view their psychological interior only as a dark and well-kept medical secret. But what does the psychological boom really indicate? Is it a response to increasing pressures within society? Is it the fruit of a developing scientific understanding of distress? Do we really know ourselves better, and are we curing our psychological ills more successfully than before?

It is interesting that there are, in fact, no satisfactory answers to these questions. There is certainly no evidence that the wider availability of psychological theories and techniques is leading to a decrease in psychological distress, and the burgeoning of such approaches is not founded on any scientifically established evidence of their validity and effectiveness. Nor is there any indication that the relative 'user-friendliness' of psychological approaches leads to people's being able to understand themselves any better than they ever have. We are looking, I would suggest, not so much at a breakthrough in enlightened understanding of distress as at the success of an enterprise.

Psychology, you would think, is a pretty serious and pretty complicated undertaking. Given the importance of its aims and implications, the complexity of its subject matter, and the moral and philosophical intricacies involved in the study of a species by itself, one might expect to find on entering its territory an intellectual structure at least as complex and imposing as nuclear physics (certainly such seems to have been the expectation of some of its earlier explorers like Freud and Jung). What one does encounter, however, is more like a bazaar.

There are, it is true, pockets in academic psychology where painstaking observational work is undertaken and ingenious experiments performed. However, in that aspect of psychology most likely to touch the lives of the 'ordinary person' – psychology as applied to emotional distress – there is less a unified discipline than a motley of competing factions, each trying to demarcate its own domain, patent its own procedures, and prevent intruders from entering its territory.

The pattern was set by psychoanalysis, which at times in its history looked more like a secret society than an intellectual or scientific undertaking (Freud's distribution of rings to the inner circle of his chosen disciples provides an indication). In fact, psychoanalysis developed from being an exclusive club into a cross-national business which sought and seeks to restrict its practice to initiates, and only in the most distant respects could be said to resemble a branch of knowledge. I do not want to suggest that there is anything particularly disgraceful or necessarily even undesirable about this, but only that it runs completely counter to academic tradition, and marks therapeutic psychology out from nearly all other forms of scientific pursuit in a way which must cast doubt on any claim practitioners make to scientificity. One wonders how physics might have progressed had Newtonians refused to truck with Einsteinians, and so on.

In this way, psychoanalysis became the first in a line of 'brand name therapies' all of which to a greater or lesser extent took exclusivity as a criterion of their validity. Gestalt Therapy, Transactional Analysis, Rational-Emotive Therapy, and many others, all emphasize the distinctiveness of their beliefs and procedures, institute training courses with restricted entry, and accredit recognized practitioners; they all but register their trademarks.

In most cases the theory and practice of brand name therapies are far from being the patiently accumulated knowledge of an industrious academic community, but represent rather the hastily elaborated ideas of one more or less charismatic figure who developed personal therapeutic style into a pseudotechnical blueprint for all (who join the club) to follow. In every case we need only look at the basic theoretical constructs to read off the particular preoccupations of the leader. Psychoanalysis reflects Freud's somewhat mechanistic concern with the gloomy engine-room of psychic deviance; Analytical Psychology speaks to Jung's fascination with religion and the more esoteric aspects of cultural anthropology; Carl Rogers builds Client-Centred Therapy in response to his belief in the self-creativity and fundamental benignity of human nature, while conviction in the power of positive thinking guides Albert Ellis to Rational-Emotive Therapy.

It does not seem to occur to the researchers who sedulously compare and contrast such approaches in the hope of establishing scientifically which is 'right' that, representing as they do the whole range of human resourcefulness in confronting personal pain, they are all equally right and equally wrong. So far as Freud, or Jung, or Rogers developed some useful ideas about how to make sense of life, they may help you make sense of yours, and if you wish to consult one of their followers, you would be wise to enter the booth which seems most congenial to you.

For what are on offer in the psychotherapeutic bazaar are not so much – indeed, are not at all – substantiated theories of psychological damage or demonstrably effective cures of emotional pain and confusion, but a range of more or less homespun philosophies of life and the attendant strategies they spawn for trying to cope with it. Just about every conceivable formula is on display, ranging from the entirely biological (distress is a question of nerves, synapses and body chemistry, its cure a matter of appropriate physical readjustment) to the entirely spiritual (psychological equilibrium depends upon the balancing of various kinds of purely internal mental forces). The majority consist of a plausible mixture of outside influences and the internal processing of them – for example, of traumatic events and their subsequent therapeutic reappraisal – such that few people are likely seriously to baulk at submitting themselves to their ministrations.

There was a time when 'scientific' doubts about the efficacy of psychotherapy, broadly conceived, placed something of a brake on its acceptance, certainly within official medical spheres, but also to an extent within the wider culture. That barrier has now collapsed, and it occurs to hardly anyone to question the desirability of therapy and counselling at times of distress – indeed, the therapy industry has succeeded in gathering round itself an aura almost of moral piety: to call the efficacy of 'counselling' into question comes close to committing a kind of solecism.

In view of the absence of clear and convincing evidence for the efficacy of *any* approach to psychological 'treatment', this state of affairs requires an explanation. In essence, I think the explanation is quite simple: 'psychology' in this area flourishes so spectacularly a) because we so *want* it to be effective, and b) because it's impossible to demonstrate that it *isn't* effective.

It is not really possible to elaborate these two points satisfactorily without anticipating too fully arguments to be spelt out in the rest of this book, but perhaps I may at this point sketch what I mean in broad outline.

THE DESIRE FOR EFFECTIVENESS

Despite there being an extremely wide range of theoretical ideas and practical procedures, many of them markedly incompatible with each other, there are nevertheless some general features which almost all approaches to therapy and counselling have in common. The most obvious of these is that the explanation and treatment of psychological distress are negotiated through the social transactions of two people: the 'patient' and the 'therapist'. It seems almost so self-evident as to be beyond question that if you are suffering for reasons you can't immediately understand and rectify, you are best advised to consult an expert who will be able both to explain your difficulties and to offer an appropriate remedy for them. If in trouble, it seems indisputable that one's only recourse is to someone who can help, and if relatives and friends have been, as they so often are, unable even after their best efforts significantly to ease your pain, then a *person* must be sought who possesses the necessary knowledge and expertise to do the trick; there is scarcely any other way one could conceive of the trick being done. It is this paradigm of help – deliverance through a personal relationship – that underlies and legitimates the role of the counsellor, the priest, the physician, sorcerer and astrologer.

Very often the need for solidarity with a person who is *perceived* as possessing power in relation to the individual's predicament outweighs any rational assessment of how effective that power actually is. Magic flourishes at the turn of the twentieth century no less vigorously than it did during the seventeenth. People still consult healers and astrologers, fortune-tellers and spiritualists in the confident belief that they possess effective powers of explanation and cure, and medicine itself is replete with procedures and practices for which there is no scientifically demonstrable justification. There is a great deal of comfort to be gained from association with someone who is able to convince you that s/he knows what s/he is doing, even if s/he doesn't.

The phenomenon of comfort is one which I shall explore in some detail in Chapter Five, but for the present I wish merely to register that it is more than anything the comfort derived from associating with an 'expert' perceived as powerful which sustains the practice of 'therapy' from the point of view of the 'patient' or 'client'.

It is important to recognize both the strengths and the weaknesses implicit in this state of affairs. 'Comfort' is certainly not a spurious or somehow invalid phenomenon. If you are comforted by the optimistic vision of your fortune-teller (and it would be a foolish fortune-teller who was not optimistic), there is no reason to denigrate fortune-telling simply on the grounds of its lack of scientificity. Lots of things can be comforting without being scientific - love, for instance. On the other hand, if, as 'experts' often do, your expert claims to have special insights into the nature of reality, and material powers deriving from those insights, then the *grounds* upon which your comfort is derived may well be bogus, and you may find yourself having been seriously misled in your anticipation of future events, etc. Though comfort may be what you get, comfort may not have been what you were looking for so much as some kind of change in your relations with the world.

It is not at all difficult to see why counsellors and therapists should want to conceive of therapeutic theory and practice in the way they do: it is simply in their interest to do so. Far from being an accusation of duplicity or lack of integrity, this is no more than a statement of the obvious, but it is an important one. When considering why we do things, we often tend to leave interest out of account, as if there was something shameful about it. We like to feel, perhaps, that a therapist or counsellor should be animated by nothing other than a desire to help and an absolute confidence in the purity of the knowledge vouchsafed to the profession. But therapists and counsellors need to make a living in the same way as everyone else, and cannot be expected to be attracted to interpretations of their work which call its validity into question in any fundamental way.

Freud's modification of the view that sexual seduction during childhood was the most significant cause of neurotic disorder in later life, into one which saw such seduction as no more than the child's wishful fantasy, need not be understood so much as a moral failure on Freud's part (which is how Jeffrey Masson interprets it[1]) as an example of the way in which interest works upon us all. Hypocrisy gets in the way of clear understanding: none of us is free from the pressures which lead us to justify our practices in accordance with our enterprise, and 'truth' cannot be totally detached from interest. Psychotherapists cannot be blamed for believing that the help they offer is effective in the way they commonly conceive it to be (i.e., as more than 'mere' comfort), but at the same time their claims may not be objectively valid.

The person in pain must have someone to turn to – for a socialized being no other recourse seems reasonably possible. And the space which that person's need creates is very likely to be filled by a therapist or counsellor whose sincere belief in therapeutic efficacy is coupled with his or her own personal need

1. Jeffrey Masson, *The Assault on Truth: Freud's Suppression of the Seduction Theory*, Fontana, 1985.

to survive in the world. These two factors alone would be enough to guarantee a place for 'psychotherapy' in modern society. But there is a third, very powerful factor which may well be mainly responsible for having given 'therapy' the impetus to thrive as robustly as it has.

This is what one might call the societal influence: i.e., the interest of a social system in there becoming established a view of and approach to psychological pain which conceives of it as a problem caused and cured *within the immediate ambit of people's personal lives*. Since it is this influence which I shall attempt to describe and to challenge in the rest of this book, I shall not say very much more about it at this point, but it is important to note both how pervasive and how rationally unsupported the view of emotional pain as individual 'psychopathology' has been.

The notion that there is something 'wrong' with the person in distress which has to be put 'right' is absolutely central to the medical and psychological disciplines which have grown up over the past 150 years. For this to become the received view, distress had, of course, to be defined as 'pathology' or 'abnormality', so that the focus on painful human experience became narrowed down to the single individual and what had gone wrong either biologically inside the body or 'psychologically' in some kind of nonmaterial (and essentially mysterious) interior space.

An immense amount of effort and ingenuity has gone into identifying, categorizing, isolating and treating these physical and mental faults; they have constituted the *raison d'être* of entire professions; they have received enormous attention from social planners and political policy makers; they have consumed vast sums of public and private money. And yet the evidence that despair, confusion, misery and madness can really usefully be conceived of as varieties of 'pathology' is slender in the extreme, and, even at its most persuasive, rests on the ideological interpretation of otherwise ambiguous research findings rather than on any intellectually compelling demonstration of its validity. (Medically trained psychiatrists, for example, are likely to assert that 'schizophrenia' is indisputably a form of 'mental illness', while many nonmedically trained psychologists will point to the lack of any consistent evidence for this view.[2])

A society which, even if inadvertently, creates distress in its members is highly likely to develop institutional systems for distracting attention from the more unfortunate consequences of its organization and absorbing their worst effects. It seems obvious that preventing the level of critical analysis from extending beyond the individual to the nature of the society itself would be greatly to its advantage. In circumstances such as these, rational evidence is likely to be the last thing anyone takes any notice of.

THE IMPOSSIBILITY OF DEMONSTRATING EFFECTIVENESS

The second factor I identified above as contributing to the robust survival of counselling and therapy despite the general lack of evidence for their efficacy was the fact that it is impossible to demonstrate that they are not efficacious.

There are undoubtedly very many people whose personal experience of psychiatric and psychological treatments – as recipients as much as practitioners – would lead them indignantly to reject what they are likely to take as my implication that such treatments do not 'work'. The problem, however, is that one is not in this area dealing with procedures which have a precise – or even an imprecise – criterion of success or failure. Psychotherapists and counsellors cannot even agree on what they are *trying* to achieve, let alone on whether or not they have achieved it.

Whatever criterion of psychotherapeutic success one takes, the question can always be posed as to whether or not there would not be more appropriate criteria. Do people have to *feel* better after a course of treatment, or do they have to *behave* differently?

2. In this latter regard, see Mary Boyle, *Schizophrenia: A Scientific Delusion?*, Routledge, 1990.

If they *say* they feel better, do they have to demonstrate in the actual conduct of their lives that they *are* better? Do those close to them have to agree that they're better; what if people *say* they're better and their families say they're worse? Does being 'better' have to show up biologically in some way, for example in the measurement of physiological indications of 'stress'; how might one interpret a situation where subjective satisfaction in fact goes with high levels of stress? What is a 'mentally healthy' way of life – for instance, is compliance better than opposition, or assertiveness preferable to meekness?

Such questions can be multiplied endlessly, and though they are ceaselessly addressed by workers in the field of outcome research in the psychological therapies, they are never resolved. Their lack of resolution seems to be taken by most as a tiresome indication of the complexity of the issues, or the lack of adequately sensitive and sophisticated statistical methods of data analysis, and so on, but what seems not often to be squarely faced is that they *cannot* be resolved.

For the problem psychologists and psychotherapists are addressing is not really a technical one of how to cure an illness or adjust an abnormality, but how to live a life, and that is simply not a closed question of the kind which can expect a simple answer. For example, whether *feeling* better is or isn't preferable to *behaving* better is not a technical, but an ethical issue, and there is no court – scientific or otherwise – in which it can be professionally decided. It is therefore possible to go on practising *any* kind of treatment, since *any* kind of outcome will be *arguably* 'right' (and, of course, equally arguably 'wrong'). Unless 'therapy' or 'treatment' has absolutely no outcome at all, which it would surely be absurd to maintain, it is likely that in a preponderance of cases (those in which no obvious damage has been done) it will be perfectly possible to point to effects which are arguably beneficial.

If psychologists, therapists and counsellors were simply offering their services on the basis that they constituted an interesting experience, there would really be no problem about all this, but of course they are not: they are, usually explicitly, offering a professional-technical service which lays claim to demonstrable effectiveness. Their difficulty is not that such claims have, to date, not been supported, but that they couldn't be, because there are no criteria for the satisfactory living of life.

It is worth noting that this is not the predicament of professional workers in disciplines which might be seen as not all that dissimilar, in some ways at least, from psychology. Teachers, for example, can be held to account according to specifiable criteria of what constitutes learning: either pupils have acquired the knowledge and abilities the teacher purports to teach, or they have not. More like astrology, however, psychology is able to maintain its credibility on the grounds of the plausibility or impressiveness of its procedures rather than on the achievement of concrete results (this is a point which emerges compellingly from Keith Thomas's *Religion and the Decline of Magic*).

What is suggested by the foregoing is that the success of the psychological professions is achieved through the *performance of functions* which have little to do with the explicit rationale offered by the professions for their activities. They have not, in fact, constructed a scientifically established account of psychological 'disorder' from which may be deduced effective procedures of 'treatment'. They have, on the other hand, developed a luxuriant set of conceptions and practices which: a) provide people with more or less plausible perspectives on their difficulties and dispense comfort to them while they try to grapple with their predicament; b) constitute a flourishing business for an army of practitioners; c) establish intellectual and professional legitimacy for the view that emotional distress and confusion are in essence personal matters of individual development and relationship and hence are not seriously to be laid at the door of 'society'.

To a worldly eye there is nothing in this to get terribly outraged or upset about: it merely suggests that, like any other human undertaking, psychology is not all it appears to be, that its motives are mixed and its practitioners not always fully aware of, and able to make explicit, the nature of their enterprise.

There is, however, a serious casualty of this state of affairs, and that is the rational understanding of distress. Emerging from the labours of thousands of academic and professional psychologists, psychiatrists and others, there is, after over a century, practically nothing in the way of a clear account of what gives rise to the kinds of difficulties which drive people to consult the experts, nor is there any agreement on what might reasonably be expected to lead to their reduction. There seems little possibility of the 'brand name therapies' coalescing into anything remotely like a workable theory of distress, or of substituting the incoherent breadth of competing approaches with a deeper consensus on the nature and genesis of our ills.

It would take an optimist of outstanding proportions to expect a mere book to make any difference to this state of affairs, but nevertheless I think some of the main reasons for it are discernible, and need to be stated at every opportunity. The principal of these is that psychology has consistently overlooked the most essential ingredient of distress: the ways in which *power* is exercised over people. It is with exploring the significance of this omission that much of the rest of this book will be concerned.

CHAPTER TWO

'When I Was Little' –
The Experience of Power[1]

It is indeed surprising how little psychologists have had to say about power. You might think, after all, that a discipline which concerned itself with motivation, which set itself the task of discovering the mechanisms which set people ticking, would be quick to observe the kinds of organized and directed pressures which bear down upon us and shape our activity through the application of various degrees of force – coercion at one extreme, incentive or persuasion at the other. But power is rarely mentioned – indeed, it seems in general to attract a kind of fastidious reticence which prevents its becoming explicit in our everyday relations with each other. It is simply not decent to refer to the power manoeuvres which attend our social intercourse.

'Decency' might almost be defined as the ability to shroud the nakedness of our interest. There is, it seems, something very necessary about the typical pretence of the diplomat – the naked pursuit of power is inadmissible, and we repress it. A test of what is decent is no doubt whether or not it is mentionable in polite society. These days it is often more indecent to refer openly to our fundamental appetites for control and domination than it is to our sexual appetite. Sex, certainly, can be discussed without qualms at dinner parties, even down to the revelation of quite intimate personal experience, but openly to impute to an

1. A shorter version of this chapter was delivered in May 1991 as the Eighth Hartop Lecture, University of Durham, and published as an occasional paper by the Durham University School of Education.

individual or group an interest in the acquisition of power is to invite the kind of shock, indignation, incredulity or ridicule which is a sure indicator of the functioning of repression.

This is not to say, of course, that consideration and examination of power is repressed everywhere – politics and sociology, for example, are quite explicit about their interest in the workings of power. But maybe this is because such an interest may be presented as *disinterested*: power is considered at one remove from the person considering it, either as, in the case of politics, a collective activity aimed ostensibly at the public good, or as, in the case of sociology, the study of a process more or less detached from its actual operation. Psychology, on the other hand, is concerned with our personal motives and aspirations and our direct relations with each other, and in these spheres the repression of power seems to operate more insistently.

As a rough, and no doubt far from conclusive, test of this impression, I examined a while ago the indexes of all the psychology texts I could find in the local university bookshop. Out of nine texts, only three listed 'power' and *none* listed the principal medium of its application in our society – money. (There is considerable irony in the fact that, at a time in our history when the successful pursuit of money has attained the status practically of a supreme moral injunction, we remain almost totally silent about what this means for our intra- and interpersonal conduct.)

Even though one very occasionally comes across a psychologist tactless enough to expose our interest in money and power (see, for example, Dorothy Rowe's honest and unsentimental account of what life without money can be like in *Wanting Everything*, HarperCollins, 1991) psychology as a whole tends to function a little like diplomacy: its methods and precepts have been established as much as anything to provide a discreet medium *for* the workings of power, which are themselves left unexamined. Psychology's rendering as internal to the individual constructs such as motive and will, desire and insight, its isolation of the person from a social world and its 'therapeutic' emphasis on his or her own responsibility for personal shortcomings, all serve to provide us with a kind of sanitized technology of conduct which turns totally blind eyes to the crushing and rapacious machinations of power which envelop us as soon as we emerge from the womb.

For power is the social element in which we exist. It is almost impossible to think of a human experience which is not shaped by power, does not carry either a positive or negative charge of power. We are thrown at birth into the most highly charged and potentially shocking field of power which it is possible to imagine. At no other point in life is the disparity of the power between the individual (the infant) and the adults (usually parents) around it likely to be so great. Stamped right at the root of our experience is a message of overwhelming significance – that we have to deal with a world which is immeasurably more powerful than ourselves.

If the field of power around us at that point (and, no doubt, for a while afterwards) is, so to speak, *positively* charged, our whole experience may be built upon an essentially uncritical confidence in the ultimate goodness of the world. If, on the other hand (as too often is the case), we receive a negatively charged shock of, for example, near abandonment or bitter isolation, the rest of our lives may be haunted by a latent 'phobic' dread and vulnerability to panic, or perhaps the insatiable drive for security, which feeds on a ruthless pursuit of wealth or a remorseless concern to expose and exploit the weakness of others.

The world forces on us at the earliest point of our experience strategies for dealing with it which I doubt we ever really abandon. It is not that such early experience constitutes some fundamental kind of mistake or error of judgement which will later need 'psychology' for its correction, but that we are, as it were, immediately seized by the shoulders and spun by irresistible forces to take up our stance towards them. This is no mistake, but confrontation with a relentless reality which exacts from us 'decisions' and 'attitudes' which are truly basic. Do we love or hate, fight or flee, trust or fear, confront or dissemble, confide or hide?

Because such 'decisions' and 'attitudes' really are basic, and formed at a time when language is still a mystery to us, they are formed uncritically. We cannot hold them up to ourselves and examine them; they become rather the inarticulate foundations on which we build the rest of our lives and to which we have throughout a passionate and inexpressible commitment. The world announces itself to us as we open our eyes, and what it says we *know* from that day forth.

Some of the most difficult and puzzling features of psychological distress belong to the time before we could talk, and hence lie fallow in our emotional repertoire as *feelings* laden with inexpressible but extremely powerful meaning. Such feelings burst into life whenever the vulnerabilities on which they rest are nudged into activity by suitably structured constellations of events which act, so to speak, as 'reminders'.

For example, I suspect that the 'psychodynamic' view which relates 'panic attacks' to early experiences of abandonment is often very close to the mark. To observe such an attack – either in oneself or others – is to see someone caught up in a literally dreadful experience of 'abandonedness'. The person feels suddenly drained of supporting power – deserted by power – with no ally and no haven, alone in the middle of a completely alien world.

How insightlessly unfortunate that view of 'childcare' which suggested that babies who disturb their parents' peace should be left to 'cry themselves to sleep'. What failure of empathy could see such 'sleep' as anything but exhausted panic and despair, could fail to imagine the agony of a powerless little creature whose world, from its perspective, had quite literally deserted it? And how inevitable that such an experience, especially if repeated a few times, should come to lie in wait as the not inappropriate response to all those occasions in later life when the threat of abandonment is reiterated. Such threats stir into life what the individual *knows* from his or her earliest experiences.

'Confidence' starts out as confidence in those all-powerful others around the infant to protect it and meet its needs. If, through its experience, the infant comes to know that in certain respects no such confidence is justifiable, that there are certain circumstances in which it will be abandoned to its panic, then the vulnerability to panic stays submerged like rocks beneath the sea of its social world for the rest of its life. And that sea is tidal. If things start to go wrong – at work, say, or with a spouse or partner – then as the waters of relatedness ebb, the rocks begin to appear, and as the person begins to feel more and more exposed (often in an 'exposing' place like a brightly lit supermarket under the gaze of hundreds of strangers) panic once again takes over.

We have all been children, and we all know that to be a child is to be at the mercy of adults. For many of us the experience of childhood was almost inseparable from the experience of fear, in relation to some adults at least. In many ways it is extraordinary that we don't take more account of this at least in our psychology and our pedagogy, but then again we always tend to take most for granted experiences which are more or less universal. 'When I was little' are the words with which many of the people who have talked to me about these issues introduce, in the most matter-of-fact and unemotional tones, stories of terroristic oppression by adults which make my blood run cold. I am struck by what a world of meaning lies within those words, despite (or perhaps because of) their being uttered not with any conscious poignancy, but as a kind of unreflective formula, identifying a mere chronological period rather than a state of being.

But state of being it was, being little and being powerless: not only dependent on others for all the material necessities, not only without access to more or less all effective means of power and influence, but also physically at the mercy of those who wielded all this power. The whole of our early experience is acquired in a state of 'littleness' through which most of us come to accept without question – even without noticing it – a world which is shaped and structured through and through by powers we have virtually no alternative but to obey.

'When I was little' is thus frequently the introduction to a tale of (often, of course, unintended) indifference, callousness, exploitation, neglect, tyranny and mystification which leaves the listener speechless with indignation but which is told with a tolerance and unconcern themselves testifying to the mundaneness of it all, the sheer banality and universality of the abuse of the powerless. As adults we would be outraged by treatment which as children we accept – and are expected to accept – without demur. As a child you may be publicly assaulted in ways which would, if you were an adult, undoubtedly lead to the imprisonment of your assailant. We are able to demand respect from children for actions towards them which if they were a few years older would be regarded as criminal.

I am not wanting to suggest that this state of affairs – i.e., the inevitable disparity in power between child and adult – is *necessarily* wrong (though there is no doubt that it is very often abused in the ways I've indicated) but merely that it is so, and that the experience of the child – characterized most centrally in its 'littleness' – imposes a certain kind of orientation towards power. That orientation is largely an uncritical one, its character determined in advance by the terms in which we customarily legitimate relations between the powerful and the powerless. In this way the 'proper' attitude of children towards adults, the little towards the big, is 'respect', and the striking thing as people relate the sometimes horrifying tales of their childhood is the respectful tones in which they do it.

Mrs Johnson, for example, had for fifty years kept to herself the scenes which were enacted between her father and herself from when she was a girl of about six or seven (her mother died when she was five). As she told her story she became tearful and angry for the first time at how, according to an alcoholic whim, he would stand her in front of him as he sat in his fireside chair and roar abuse at her for half an hour or more. He used to yell obscenities at her which she could only just bring herself to repeat, and when she finished talking she was still superstitiously fearful of her long-dead father's revenge for the betrayal. 'I've never told anybody that before,' she said, 'out of loyalty'. 'Loyalty' – the word was mentioned in passing, and is indeed unremarkable enough unless one stops almost deliberately to reflect upon it. For what can exact such loyalty? Only the operation of an utterly unjust and indiscriminate power to which we become enslaved by virtue of not much more than our relative littleness. The child cowers under the demands of such power as under the vengeful eye of a jealous and implacable god.

Such power acts as a stamp on the child's experience, it impresses its content on the growing organism with a force which marks that organism – the person – for ever. Power exacts respect and 'loyalty' towards whatever it presents as its central demand. The stances the child takes up towards the issues life presents it with are shaped and authorized by power. The parental word is the word of God. (Just think, for example, with what feelings of unease you try to disregard even trivial parental nostrums and injunctions which you now know to be nonsense.)

In Mrs Johnson's case, her father's fireside entertainment set the pattern for her relationships with men for life: she had two marriages and a couple of other long-term relationships with men who without exception turned out to be capricious and sadistic in one way or another, and who quite literally abused her as her father had done. She was an extraordinarily perceptive and sensitive woman, highly intelligent, though not well educated, and I had no reason to doubt her when she said she loved the man she was currently with. He was considerably younger than she, sometimes charming, but he regularly taunted and derided and occasionally hit her. She was typically perceptive about him and understood him, and she loved him *because* she understood him (much, no doubt, as she used to – had to – understand her father). She could not love or be interested in a man whose character had not, so to speak, been authorized by her father's example; her whole life was bent towards loving and understanding the agonized, drunken, terrifying man with whom she spent alone so many of her early years.

We often overlook, I think, the close relationship of love to power. We prefer to think of love as unsullied by the indecency of power, or even opposed to it. And yet, when we are little, the form our loving takes is exacted by power. The relatively helpless infant and child can no more choose the characteristics of those he or she is dependent on than can the family dog, and, uncomfortable as it might be to suggest it, our learning to love contains a strong element of choiceless dependence.

There is, of course, unselfish love, but that is not the variety which attaches itself to our desire. The kind of love we crave, and the lack of which drives us to despair, the love which cements our relationships positively or negatively destroys them, the shape, that is, which childhood experience gives to our loving, is always stamped by the impress of power. For the most part (unless, that is, our early experience has been cast in a 'sado-masochistic' form) we are not interested in or moved by the love of the powerless. We neither love nor wish to be loved by people we see as having no power. We may be hypnotized or enslaved by the powers we detect in a lover – echoes, quite probably, of the nameless ingredients of a parent's rule – and enraged and betrayed if they are withdrawn from us, but even the adoration of someone who has no such hold over us is just an embarrassment. The tramp who sits next to you on the park bench may be as wise as Solomon, but you are unlikely to attach to his words the importance you would to those of a complete idiot who happened to be sitting in an expensive office and had letters after his name.

The nature of the power relation between oneself and others is the unreflected-upon determinant of a whole range of feelings and attitudes one may have towards them. Whether you hate or pity, blame or excuse, desire or dismiss is likely to depend on the extent to which you see the other as having a degree of power in relation to you which you may either fear or covet. It is easy to be cool and dispassionate towards those one cares nothing for, i.e., who stand outside the immediate field of power in which one is situated, but as soon as people move into that field they are likely to become the objects of a nervous, prickly appraisal which anxiously scans them for threat and opportunity. It is particularly difficult to see that what we often take to be matters of fact – for example, objective descriptions of people around us – are really distorted rationalizations shot through with defensiveness and soaked in self-interest.

Perhaps the main advantage of the situation of the psychotherapist or counsellor is that it minimizes the operation of certain kinds of power-saturated dependency which make simply understanding another person difficult. Blame can only give way to compassion if an unusually asymmetrical power structure is established between the people concerned. Similarly, 'professional' interest in someone can only replace desire or dislike if the more usual interdependences and mutual demands of social intercourse are deliberately suspended, as they are in situations, like psychoanalysis and the confessional, where only one person talks and the other listens.

But the positive or negative charge of power cannot be separated out from our relationships, therapeutically or otherwise, as by some alchemical centrifuge. We can, of course, attempt consciously to give our relations with others a certain power structure (as in the therapeutic relationship) but we cannot after the event somehow detach experience from the impress of power, and, perhaps through some purported process like 'cognitive restructuring', give it a different shape from that which it originally possessed. For example, I think it unreasonable to expect someone who, like Mrs Johnson, has suffered profoundly under the sway of parental tyranny ever to come to experience that force which gave shape to her whole life as anything other than, literally, dreadful. One can, to be sure, invite her to criticize the exercise of that tyranny, and though this might seem to her at first like inviting the wrath of God, she may come after some time to see it for what it was and begin to feel less uncomfortable about the grief and anger attached to her early experience. But she is not going to be persuaded that the orientation to life that experience impressed upon her is somehow a mistake.

The fallacy of the Freudian concept of 'transference' is precisely that it suggests that the impress of power can, through the psychoanalytic technique of 'interpretation', be centrifuged away from one's experience, leaving one able to exercise a detached judgement concerning constructions of events which are somehow real in comparison with the distortions of a past which one was, until they were 'interpreted', 'transferring' on to them. What is experienced under the impress of power is, on the contrary, only too real, and imparts a certain expertise in the possibilities the world has to offer which one is, in a sense, fated to work out for the rest of one's life. Greek tragedy is far truer to the nature of our experience in this way than is psychoanalysis and much of the therapeutic industry which derives from it.

It is the relative obscurity of the historical origins of people's experience which makes their subsequent difficulties often initially so puzzling. Problems which seem at face value to permit of quite simple solutions – perhaps through the almost minimal application of a bit of 'will power' – may seem almost maddeningly resistant to 'treatment' until one begins to see that they have foundations back at a time when the person was in no position to understand or grasp critically what was happening to him or her. Almost none of our experiences are defined *just* by the present, and, more than naive, it is simply false to assume (as does the idea of 'transference') that knowledge of the dimensions of the present alone is sufficient to spell out a rational account of our conduct.

Eating problems – as anyone who has ever had one will know – are a good case in point. Being too fat or too thin, even if only in your own eyes, is not just a matter of needing to eat less or more and adjusting your diet accordingly. For the ingestion of food has a history which is replete with meanings given it under the impress of power. The bulimic woman who secretly stuffs herself at one moment and sticks her fingers down her throat the next becomes subject to an anguish which has its meaning in shadows of her past far too dark for her understanding to penetrate now, and not amenable at all to commonsense injunctions concerning diet.

Take Susan, for example. She is, as she herself acknowledges, vastly overweight and desperate to lose some. She can see as clearly as anyone the simple dietary logic which guarantees the realization of her aim but she simply is not able to put it into practice. Diets end in binges which can involve the guilty consumption of colossal amounts of food, sometimes for quite extended periods of time. Even the achievement of losing weight doesn't seem to help. Perhaps she slowly but surely loses weight for six months. She's delighted with herself, begins to feel she's really cracked it. Then she binges for a week, puts on nearly two stones, and consequently seethes with remorse and anger at herself. The conceptual equipment she brings to the problem is no different from that of most people, and consists mainly of ideas about will power and control. If she's failed she must try harder. *This* time she's so disgusted with herself that she just knows she's not going to lapse again. But she does.

One thing Susan does notice is that she binges more often when she's lonely and missing the warmth of a close relationship. She usually manages to lose quite a bit of weight if she has a boyfriend, but this is a rare event not least because she is convinced that any man who shows an interest in her must be some sort of pervert.

A plausible version of her early relationship with her mother emerges only slowly because at first it is presented as conventionally idealized. Far from being selfless provider, however, it seems that in fact her mother both rejected and neglected her in early life, having a passion for horse racing which took up all her spare time and money. But she was not a feelingless woman and not without a guilty awareness of her shortcomings as a mother, for which she tried to compensate by rather unexpectedly stuffing her daughter with sweets and chocolate from time to time. It seems unlikely that she could find in herself much love for her daughter, but as adults so often do with children, she managed to convey to her the feeling that she would be able to love her more if only she were a *good* girl. And when love was delivered, it came in the form of chocolate.

So what Susan knows about herself – what had been stamped in before she could even think – is that she is not good enough to be loved, but that a form of love is obtainable through the guilty and inconsistent administration of 'treat' foods. Because historically what was, in fact, an irresistible power over her was presented as an issue of her own choice (to be or not to be a good girl) she now construes the inability to help herself over bingeing as a matter of weak will, and the guilt she feels when she stuffs herself, and the hasty secrecy with which she does it, she no doubt also learned at her mother's hands.

It is hard when contemplating the parental tyranny by which so many people have been, and are, subjugated to avoid a tone of indignation, and many of those who have explored this area in psychology and psychiatry – like, for example, R. D. Laing – have been accused of 'blaming' parents for their children's distress. Such accusations are usually misplaced, the discomforted reaction of people unable to distinguish blame from explanation. In fact, it is perfectly possible to see most writers in this area as correctly identifying parents and families as the instruments of oppression without there being any implication of moral condemnation. While it may well be important for individuals themselves to condemn those at whose hands they have suffered (principally as a way of ceasing to condemn *themselves*) it would be utterly inappropriate for the outside observer, who has, of course, incurred no suffering of any kind, to get hot under the collar about what can clearly enough be seen to have taken place with fateful inevitability.

For the causal chain in the transmission of power does not end with parents; the field of power does not coincide with the

boundaries of the family. Of course, from the infant's point of
view, it *does*, and in the early days of its existence the infant may
have no conception of any field of power wider than that of the
mother herself (or, if Melanie Klein is right, even of parts of her
body). Someone, however, who stands outside the family
boundaries as an observer seeking to understand the processes at
work could not possibly *blame* parents for what happens to children
because he or she can see that the parents are themselves subject
to pressures and influences, not to mention histories, over which
they in turn have no control.

On the whole, psychology has concerned itself very little with
the field of power which stretches beyond our immediate relations
with each other, and this has led to very serious limitations on
the explanatory power of the theories it has produced. So far as
the psychotherapies are concerned, most deal with the context
of the immediate family itself – looking, for example, no further
than 'Oedipal' conflicts or sibling rivalries for explanations of
patients' troubles – and some even concentrate most heavily on
the here-and-now of the relation between patient and therapist.
Concentration on such microenvironments as these may have
some plausibility in terms of reflecting patients' experience of their
world, but it is very little use for understanding how they come
to be the way they are.

A few theorists of therapeutic psychology have paid more
attention to societal influences: Alfred Adler, Karen Horney, Erich
Fromm, H. S. Sullivan and Laing all looked out into the wider
world for explanations of what was happening to their patients.
And all have remained on the fringes of their discipline – not
without an honourable mention, perhaps, but certainly without
widespread or established approval and lasting reputation. As is
suggested in greater detail elsewhere in this book, the reason why
such views, though fashionable in their time, have otherwise
suffered relative neglect has less to do with any fundamental
inaccuracy (quite the contrary) than with, first, the questions they
raise about the efficacy of 'therapy', second, the already mentioned

discomfort they arouse in those who confuse explanation with blame, and third, the questions they threaten to raise about the nature of the society we live in.

For one of the services performed by orthodox psychology within what Michel Foucault has called the 'discourse of power' has been to reinforce the tendency already established in human beings to look little further than their noses for the causes of their unhappiness. Although most of us are ready to accept that our distress stems from 'circumstances beyond our control', we usually identify such circumstances as those we can see, and have little interest in pursuing their origins out into the further reaches of the social network. Psychology, in encouraging us to restrict our gaze to the microenvironments which provide the context of our personal experience – the ambit of our physical being – wittingly or unwittingly aids the process whereby the machinery of social injustice is kept out of sight.

In fact, of course, our lives are most powerfully controlled by forces that are completely out of sight. It is in many ways a truism that those things which you 'can do nothing about' are the ones which tend to affect your life most profoundly. Our world is structured, then, by powers at varying degrees of distance from us. Those closest to us – proximal powers – are the most salient, the ones which preoccupy us most, the ones focused on by psychology, the most amenable to our personal intervention, and the weakest. Those furthest from us – distal powers – are the least salient, the ones we tend to spend least time thinking about, the ones focused on by sociology and politics, almost entirely impervious to merely personal influence, and the strongest.

A decision made in a boardroom in New York is likely to have a greater impact on a larger number of lives than anything a mere parent can dream up, and yet, of course, its impact will not be *experienced* as anything like as great by each individual considered separately. Most of us don't even know the origin of decisions which may be shaping our lives radically, or indeed that any such decisions have been made, but a father's drunken rage may be experienced as an event of cataclysmic proportions. It is almost impossible for a single individual to shake off his or her personal perspective sufficiently to see how insignificant are the events of the field of power which is immediately open to experience, and yet to give an adequate explanation of how things come to pass even in that individual's world it must in the end become necessary to take account of the distal powers which operate, so to speak, over his or her horizon. It is not that proximal powers don't have the more immediate, and potentially devastating, *effect* on the person – indeed they must do, since it is only through the operation of proximal power that the person can be affected by *anything* – it is rather that the operation of those powers depends in turn on influences much further afield.

Father's drunken rage does not originate within some kind of moral space located inside Father, one, for example, which he can choose to activate or suppress; Father is not a bundle of open possibilities from which he makes, capriciously or otherwise, a selection (though, of course, it will seem like that to the child at the very edge of whose 'power horizon' he stands). Father's alcoholic rage, in fact, has to be accounted for by the influences which operate upon him: some, no doubt, to do with his personal history and some with the circumstances operating on him over which he may have no control (the fact, for example, that he has just been made redundant).

So unused are we to looking for the causes of our distress in the operation of distal powers that one needs to place particular stress on the necessity as well as on the *empirical* justification for doing so – it does not just depend on some theoretical quirk. The influence of political decisions on our lives is perhaps familiar enough, and, though no doubt some would cavil, the effects of unemployment, poor housing, social deprivation and decay are widely accepted as causes of emotional distress and damage. The more distal the powers, the more universal their influence within a given society, and the more likely we are simply to overlook them. As an outsider it is sometimes possible to detect in people's experience the operation of powers which insiders may not notice. I have, for example, been struck by how the doctrines of the Church in Ireland have a sway over the minds of even dissenting individuals such that the 'symptoms' of psychological disturbance are only fully comprehensible through reference to the power of the Church. Laws governing marriage and the reproductive process, for instance, give a significance to marital consummation which renders the act itself vulnerable to forms of 'pathology' rarely encountered in Britain but which often tend to be thought of by the Irish as essentially 'personal' problems.

Even to begin to get an intellectual hold on 'the discourse of power' it is necessary to see how misleading is the almost irresistible perspective given by our personal experience, the perspective determined by our power horizon. The less power one has, the nearer to oneself as centre is one's power horizon. The small child is pressed right up against its towering parents, and comes to see beyond them only when it starts to go to school. Moreover, the little cannot escape a *passionate* relation to the big who overshadow them. The child's involvement with its parents – its love for them, as perhaps also its hate – is closely correlated with the space they occupy in its field of power (in later life the intensity of this emotional involvement with the parents may be maintained by their material rather than their physical dominance; it's much less easy to feel dispassionate towards rich as opposed to poor parents).

Our analysis of our wellbeing (or the lack of it), and what can be done about it, will, unless we make an almost impossibly conscious effort, depend on the limits of our perspective, and that perspective can often be very misleading. The child thinks its parents have the powers of gods. The tea boy, perhaps also the sales manager, thinks that the managing director has insights into the workings of the wider world completely unachievable by him, and hence imputes to him powers he very probably hasn't got. We frequently offer authority for a view by citing the opinion of someone who stands further from the centre of *our* field of power without realizing that in fact they occupy much the same 'power space' as we; though he may seem a long way from you, the perspective available to your boss is determined by much the same institutional limits as is yours.

As long as a social system operates power against the interests of the majority of its members, it will attempt to keep the machinery of power out of sight – well over the power horizon of the ordinary citizen. Even where we operate with power differentials which in principle at least are open to inspection, we still tend to be curiously unaware of their existence, often reticent about and possibly even incapable of describing them. The typical middle-class person, for example, occupies a world of powers and opportunities much less available to the average working-class person – indeed the difference in their availability is partly definitive of class. The manager is trained for and inducted into a world where (relatively) distal powers are mediated linguistically and procedurally by means largely unavailable to the worker. The former knows structure, form, office, protocol, the means of distal communication and influence. The latter knows objects, tools, people, impulses, the making and breaking of social bonds in the proximal world of immediate influence. The former deals in generalities and abstractions, the latter in specifics and feelings. *Of course* middle-class life may be lacking in warmth and immediacy. It can afford to be.

When Mrs Wright, a highly respectable and socially conscientious woman, finally succumbed to despair at the damp and generally sordid condition of her council house, she ended up abusing the housing manager down the telephone and threatened him with a duffing-up by her two large sons. The world of pithy letter writing and veiled hints about personal access to MPs, public health departments, etc. – the paraphernalia of association with power – was completely beyond her ken, and all she achieved by her phone call was a menacing visit from a council minion who frightened her into continuing to suffer in silence.

Although this is all obvious enough, we are still often blithely unaware of the difficulty one person may have in understanding or communicating with another where there is a significant power differential between them. The relatively more powerful are, for example, fond of attempting to solve the problems of the less powerful by offering them advice. However sincerely and helpfully meant, this usually overlooks the fact that the more powerful (most often middle-class) person moves with unconscious ease in a world which contains procedures, resources and knowledge which it would take the less powerful (usually working-class) person years to acquire – by which time, of course, there would no longer be any need for advice.

One way to break the tendency to give well-meant but unhelpful advice of this 'let them eat cake' kind is to invite its donor to imagine going up a social stratum rather than down and trying to conform with the advice he or she would no doubt receive there on how to conduct him or herself. It is widely accepted, for example, that acquisition of the kind of 'taste' necessary for admission to the loftiest circles is a matter of 'breeding' (i.e., life-long application), and few people who share the social stratum I occupy would know how to 'go on' at an aristocratic house party, however clear or kindly the on-the-spot instruction they might receive. It takes time, just for a start, to learn to ride a horse.

In fact, of course, one rarely finds those higher up the social pyramid anxious to impart the secrets of their distinction to those lower down; they are, that is, no more likely freely to distribute what can be called their ideological power to those less well endowed than they are to give away their money.

A woman interviewed on BBC radio news observed: 'The people higher up don't let us little people know what's going on.' The occasion was the fruition of some planning iniquity which had at a stroke diminished her quality of life and that of thousands of other 'little people' while enriching that of one or two 'big people'. And that, of course, is in every sense the secret of ideological power: to control the perception little people have of big people's interests, usually merely by obscuring their view. The power horizon of ordinary people is set not only by the limits of their own sphere of operations, but by the ability of the more powerful to screen their own interests and activities behind veils of 'disinformation', strategically constructed silence, and manipulation of the machinery of knowledge, enquiry and what counts as truth. More will be said about these processes in the following chapter, but it is essential to bear in mind if one is to make any sense of the experience of power that it is not only brute force (coercive power) and financial muscle (economic power) which can be wielded to keep 'little people' in their place – the projects of the powerful may be obscured ideologically just as discreetly and effectively as the material signs of their wealth may be hidden behind hedges and walls.

Therapeutic psychology has been remarkably silent about the actual experience of relative social insignificance – the awareness of being among the 'little people'. This latter is, of course, essentially the experience of class, and while a great deal of sociological attention has been focused on the class issue, I can think of no approach within the so-called psychotherapies which takes seriously the way class position is reflected in the self-consciousness of the individual. The reason for this, no doubt, is once again the fact that therapeutic psychology prefers to overlook difficulties which could not plausibly be dealt with within the confines of the 'therapeutic relationship', and though individuals are often exhorted by their therapists to 'esteem' themselves more highly (it is, of course, mainly those in the lower-class brackets who are going to be disadvantaged by their position), class is fairly inescapably a social phenomenon, and not one over which individual people can be expected to exercise a great deal of control.

For precisely one of the most central features of class occupancy, looked at from its ideological aspect, is its indelibility. The ideological preservation of class advantage, as opposed to its foundation on merely economic power, makes use of indices of distinction which physically mark the person with almost ineradicable signs of superiority or, more important for the understanding of psychological pain, inferiority. Pierre Bourdieu's *Distinction* (Routledge & Kegan Paul, 1984) offers brilliant insights into this process.

Power is maintained within class groupings through the process of distinguishing the superior from the inferior by means of signs which cannot easily be faked. In English society particularly, the possession of money is by no means enough to gain admission to the higher reaches of class distinction. 'Breeding', to pass as genuine, has to show the signs of having been acquired naturally, rather as native speakers of a particular language can usually be distinguished from those who have learned to speak it as a secondary acquisition. What demonstrates the entitlement of the upper classes to their position are the ease and familiarity, the assurance with which they move about a world which is at every level and in every domain peppered with indications as well as tests of their distinction. And it is no accident that the indications of class are so hard to fake – for if they were not, they would, of course, be useless as indications of anything. The aspirated aitch is a good example: if not practised unconsciously from birth, there is nothing more likely to catch out the upper-class impersonator and give him or her away than dropping aitches from where they 'should' be or tacking them on (a particularly telling indication of attempted fraud) where they should not. This is like building a caste mark into the person's brain, a hidden bug in the 'program', which will beep embarrassingly every time he or she tries to slide through the gates of a higher class preserve, which ideologically presents its advantage as birthright.

The lot of the class fugitive, the person who attempts to become free of a disadvantaged background by acquiring the ideological as well as the economic powers of the 'big people', is in many respects an extremely uncomfortable one, and it is perhaps not surprising that it is people in this position who are often possessed by the most virulent snobbery and contempt for the weak and inferior. To venture out of your class and attempt to pass yourself off as an article more refined than it was originally branded is a bit like living undercover in a hostile country, and even the most successful class fugitive is vulnerable to exposure as an impostor by, for example, a buried regional accent suddenly peeping through a treacherous vowel sound. Even if the presentation is near perfect, there are in the background aunts and uncles, cousins and old schoolmates who know a bogus eminence when they see one and may not hesitate to say so. So aspiring social climbers more or less have to turn their backs on their past, fear as well as despise their origins and reject the culture and society to be found there as worthless in every respect. (It is ironic that the impossible vision of a 'classless society' is proffered precisely in the 'yuppie' culture which is so characteristic of the class fugitive. Whatever such a society might actually look like, it would surely not be one in which the insignia of 'lifestyle' are so relentlessly cultivated by the very people who proclaim its classlessness.)

Class disadvantage is a form of injury inflicted on the person at birth. Even those who, in contrast with the class fugitive, heroically stand their ground and fight for social change, who use their experience of oppression to try to modify the system rather than to acquire the secrets of exploitation themselves, even they cannot escape the injurious effects of caste marking. The most admirable working-class leaders often betray a kind of apprehensive awareness of somehow being out of bounds. The uneasy handling by union leaders of the language of the 'educated middle class', so easily lampooned by the unkind satirist, is no doubt an unavoidable consequence of the secondary acquisition (as opposed to the 'inbreeding') of intellectual powers, but the peppering of their speech with expressions such as 'with respect', the bodily posture which is either defiantly stiff or defensively hunched, testify to a fear of the power they challenge which, though certainly not groundless, probably exists less as a response to any immediate reality than as a built-in part of their own experience of themselves as people. The confident slouch of the hands-in-pockets, old Etonian cabinet minister speaks not so much of a current possession of power (on some measures the union boss might possess as much) as of a confidence in social worth which was sucked in with his mother's milk.

People's sense of worth, what one might call their basic self-confidence, stems essentially from two sources: first, their relations as literally little people with the big people who occupied the proximal field of power during infancy and childhood, and second the sense of metaphorical littleness or bigness they later discovered themselves to have been accorded by the more distal powers of a social world which sorts people according to the ideological criteria of class.

The interaction between parental influence and class position often determines the extent as well as the nature of class injury. The latter more easily becomes a permanent disability where the individual's self-regard did not receive its foundation in the loving support and approval of the all-important adults around him or her in childhood. When exposed later to the baleful stare of a remorselessly categorizing and evaluating social world, people who have neither been stamped by positive class distinction nor energetically endorsed, supported and encouraged by parental power find themselves trembling before an exposure from which there is no sanctuary. There is nothing they can call upon 'inside' them – that is, nothing in their history – to place a screen of comfort or protection between themselves and the dismissive judgement of the world; they have no *knowledge* of themselves as worthwhile which they could use to challenge the institutionalized snobbery which keeps them in their place.

The actual experience of people in this position is very rarely accompanied by any awareness of the ideological manipulations of power or illuminated by any critique of the social structure. Their situation is experienced as purely personal, and most would be quite incredulous at explanations of what they feel being couched in terms of social or even historical influences. At the root of their experience is an acceptance of the valuation placed upon them – their worthlessness *is* their personal worthlessness, and they wither before the public gaze as a plant withers before the icy wind. The sense of exposure is indeed central to the experience of someone in this situation: isolated, cut off, surrounded by hostile space, you are suddenly without connections, without stability, with nothing to hold you upright or in place; a dizzying, sickening unreality takes possession of you; you are threatened by a complete loss of identity, a sense of utter fraudulence; you have no right to be here, now, inhabiting this body, dressed in this way; you are a nothing, and 'nothing' is quite literally what you feel you are about to become. The overwhelming reaction to finding yourself in this situation is the need to flee, to find refuge in some 'safe haven' like your home or your car, anywhere protected from the unremitting hostility of public space.

Like so many of those who suffer most from life's unkindnesses, Mrs Lawrence is an intelligent, insightful, gentle and sensitive woman. People respect her and like her, and her husband and children love her, though they and her friends tease her about both her sensitivity and the slightly quirky individuality which the combination of insight and honesty gives to her view of the world. Now in early middle age, she was born and brought up in a notorious urban slum. Her father was a bright, vain man, who spent all he earned on his own clothes and his own comfort – taken mostly in the form of women and drink. He was dissolute rather than brutal, and took absolutely no notice of either of his daughters, though he exploited their cowed and needy mother mercilessly, raging at her contemptuously whenever she complained about her lot, which was often. She gave no support to her daughters, but called upon them to support her, and all her life Mrs Lawrence has had to look after her mother as if mother were in fact daughter.

Mrs Lawrence talks wistfully of the tree-lined avenues where she would like to live, but 'knows' that she has no right to do so – even to wish it is a kind of punishable hubris. An unshakeable knowledge of what she 'is' is carried around with her like a submerged but ever-present grief. She can name the central quality that sums up her nature and her worth, and she is certain that it is patent to anyone who stops long enough to give her the time of day: she is 'rough'. If you dispute this (for 'rough' is about the last description you would apply to this gentle, delicate, emotionally discriminating person), she will smile patiently but a little pityingly at your failure to comprehend.

One of the ideological blocks standing between Mrs Lawrence (and many like her who have shared a similar world) and an enlightening sociopolitical critique of her experience – or the way she interprets it – arises out of a personal acquaintance with social degradation. Despite the romanticizing of life in the old slums by some who seem happy enough not to live in one, people who have, or who live in one of the new slums which have replaced them, have often seen and experienced enough to know that there is a sort of state of ultimate degradation from which even 'roughness' may be positively distinguished, and which, it seems to them, brands its occupants as finally and utterly morally irredeemable. Frequently, the possibility of degradation has a kind of uncanny quality about it which may positively haunt a whole family and turn 'ordinary disasters' (like, for example, a daughter's unintended pregnancy) into nightmarish catastrophes so deeply imbued with shame that recovery seems scarcely possible. It is this state of degradation which tends to get seen by those once traumatized by it as what is meant when people talk of 'poverty', 'working class' or 'socialism'. Any political concern with the environmental damage wrought on those at the bottom of the heap by a social system run by those towards the top tends then to be displaced by an uncompromising moralism about the avoidability through personal effort of apathy, squalor and general moral degeneracy. People raised within sight of ultimate

degradation are frequently concerned only to dissociate themselves
from it, and have no distal view of the reasons for it; they can
speak of the desperation to keep out of it only in the proximal
language of personal struggle.

Take, for example, Mrs MacFarlane. She is the second oldest
of five children born in a quarter even less favoured than Mrs
Lawrence's birthplace. Her two brothers (one actually a half-
brother, the result of her mother's indiscretion with a neighbour)
were boarded out with grandparents, while she and her two sisters
shared the back bedroom of the parental home, she and her older
sister sharing a bed. Her mother was an anxious and superstitious
woman prone to panicky rages, irrational bouts of over-
protectiveness interspersed with a kind of helpless indifference,
whose consequently whimsical behaviour was as important to
predict as the weather but considerably more difficult. Her father
was dispirited, sometimes violent, sometimes warm and kind, often
out of work (when he would become depressed and drink a lot).
Sometimes, most usually when his wife was pregnant, her father
would pay occasional visits to her sister's bed and 'play about'
with her, though Mrs MacFarlane maintains that he never involved
her in these activities.

Mrs MacFarlane had only the most rudimentary education,
not least because her mother singled her out to stay at home
and perform those errands which her own attacks of anxiety
precluded. However, she expresses herself unusually articulately,
reads quite a lot and talks very perceptively about those around
her; it comes as a surprise to discover how little formal education
she has had.

For almost as long as she can remember she has been running
a kind of sexual gauntlet, pursued as a juvenile and adolescent
girl by dirty old men and equally dirty young boys as she walked
her little brothers along the banks of the local canal; now as a
twice-married woman in her mid-thirties she is still (along with
most of her female colleagues) regularly cornered in his office
by the manager of the cut-price chain store where she works.

Mrs MacFarlane has three children by her first marriage, one of whom has an incurable condition which requires medical equipment not provided by the state and which she cannot afford to buy. Both she and her husband have jobs (hers part time) which together bring in less money than they could get on social security, but her equation of 'poverty' with degradation prevents her from regarding her family as 'poor', and indeed she has, together with her husband, who is a kind and supportive man, fought with all her strength to avoid the kind of degradation she felt so acutely as a child. (One of her least pleasant memories is of how, as a part of her parents' requirement that she should clean the house at weekends, she had to collect up the spent condoms from beneath their bed.)

She is one of those rare people who have a kind of innocent clear-sightedness which rests on a combination of irrepressible honesty and great intelligence. In many ways her intuitive sensitivity is far too finely tuned for the world in which she has found herself, and there is within her a latent conceptual power, an unrequited love of truth that needs desperately to be met by an outside world which understands it. The nearest she has got to finding such a world so far has been the disciplined and morally ferocious irrationality of fundamentalist evangelical Christianity; this has succeeded only in providing her with her first husband (whose violent rages and homosexuality in the end became too much for her) and copious amounts of superstitious guilt about the perfectly natural feelings the sect proscribes but which she is far too honest to deny.

Mrs MacFarlane had not learned to criticize her circumstances; she had simply accepted her proximal reality as the actuality of an unchangeable world, and (with medical encouragement) had interpreted the protests of her nervous system as an indication of weakness and instability rather than as an entirely natural response to painful difficulties. She has the 'naturally' deferential attitude to doctors which hundreds of years of the English class system ineluctably imparts, and her relations with them are reminiscent of the relations she enjoys with God: she is overwhelmed with gratitude for their kindness, utterly demolished by their impatience or ill-concealed contempt, and consumed by superstitious dread whenever her irrepressible perceptiveness sees through the sham of their authority. So she has 'panic attacks' which she douses with tranquillizers. But she certainly doesn't lack the personal resources necessary to gain insight into so-called 'neurotic' defensiveness and to act upon it, and indeed she is a quite unusually courageous person.

In fact, she has come a long way in understanding, controlling and losing much of the fear of her panics, and insight into the real reasons for her frustration and pain gives her glimpses of a possible future which sometimes cause bursts of excited hope. To realize that hope, however, would mean making changes which, added together, are just about insuperably difficult. Just to obtain the level of education she would need to lift herself into a social stratum where she would find answering echoes to her own potentialities would mean her having to turn her back on her past, earn the frightened contempt of her brothers and sisters, threaten her husband's self-esteem almost unbearably for him, and in general enter areas of social, emotional and intellectual unfamiliarity of truly terrifying proportions. And all this quite apart from the prohibitive financial restraints on her becoming able to embark on any kind of programme of self-improvement.

She has already encountered in her own life the essence of Freud's dictum about neurotic misery giving way to common unhappiness but her attempts to act on a growing understanding of her situation have not met with unqualified success. Having been pinned up against his office wall by her sexually harassing manager once too often, she told him where to get off and for a while felt a lot better for it. The end result, however, was a loss of vital overtime and a campaign of more or less subtle victimization if anything less supportable than the unwanted sexual attentions. Despite her obvious intelligence and warm friendliness she failed to get a slightly better job in a marginally up-market chain store largely because her local accent was not considered compatible with the refinement of a saleslady. She cannot afford evening classes.

Mrs MacFarlane bears no trace of snobbery, indeed she shows no particular awareness of social classification of any kind, and is warmly acceptant of most of the people she encounters from day to day. The kind of treachery 'class fugitives' display towards those with whom they shared their origins plays no part in Mrs MacFarlane's reasons for voting for a political party which is in fact either totally indifferent or hostile to her interests. Her political sympathies reflect, rather, a wish to emphasize her moral distance from rock bottom. Not only does she vote Conservative, but she associates the whole language of the politics of the left, its references to 'the working class', 'socialism', etc., with a degraded and dissolute world from which all moral decency has disappeared. She is caught in an ideological mystification which indissolubly associates the cure with the condition and so prevents her from criticizing the grounds of her own unhappiness.

Class injury takes another form where loving and concerned, but socially deferential, 'respectable working-class' parents bring up their children to honour middle-class values – especially educational ones – at the same time as drilling them in the art of 'knowing their place' and generally not getting ideas above their station. Products of this combination often find themselves occupying space that they feel is not rightfully theirs, living the life of a displaced person but without ever having known quite where they were displaced from.

James is a young man from just such a background. He is intelligent, sensitive and gifted. As a boy he went to the local grammar school, which he hated. He terrified his parents by becoming 'school phobic', making them despair that all their sacrifices to improve his lot in the world were about to be brought to nought by a failure of co-operation and gratitude which they just couldn't understand. But they succeeded in cajoling and bullying him into school, where he led an isolated life trying to hide from a ubiquitous middle-class gaze which as soon as it spotted him identified him as not belonging. He developed an intense interest in art, and is a very accomplished amateur painter. At seventeen he challenged his parents' supine acceptance of a social order which worked almost entirely against their interests, and even persuaded his bewildered father to join the Labour Party. But after that he ran out of steam. To be a father to his father took too much out of him for him to be able to sustain the courage to face his own world, and he has never found a job which he could tolerate. A sense of unreality and not belonging, of fraudulence and artificiality, a bitter hatred of the rat race combined with an utter lack of faith in his ability to make any impact on it leads him into deep depressions. It is not that he cannot see into the roots of his difficulties, indeed he has developed an intelligent and highly articulate critique of the world he finds himself in. The trouble is, he doesn't believe in his right to make such a critique and is sourly contemptuous of his own motives in doing so, which he sees as founded solely on weakness. He hangs on to the idea that he is 'ill' as the main bulwark between him and suicide.

James was as a child ushered into a world he was not 'bred' for, without ever being taught by his parents to believe in himself. They believed only in the world they wanted him to come to inhabit, and it never occurred to them that if he was to gain the confidence to enter it, they would have to believe in *him*. It was certainly not that they didn't love him, and they still do, though they are pained and mystified by the 'illness' which stops him profiting from all the advantages they themselves never enjoyed. And he loves them, even though the world he is now displaced into is one beyond their ken and he and they have little to say to each other.

The love James received as a child was a love largely stripped of power. Rather than gaining impetus from it, if anything it smothered and hampered him. His parents launched him into an alien world, and having pushed him off in his lonely little boat, they stood waving from a distance as he drifted gradually out of sight. This kind of isolation is often at the centre of depression. Alone in the expanses of alien territory, totally without the confidence which comes from an early infusion of parental solidarity, all the person wants to do is run for cover – dive under the bedclothes and stay there.

One may speculate whether in more ordered and stable societies – at other times, perhaps, or in other places – power relations would give rise to the same kinds of pained and confused experience I have pointed to in this chapter. Where the rules of even a positively tyrannical social order were understood and accepted as more or less immutable, its institutions might be less likely to give rise to the kinds of psychological difficulties encountered so often in 'developed' Western societies. For the operations of power in these societies are, of course, no longer feudally entrenched, but have become 'problematized'. Part of the reason for the repression of power referred to earlier is that power in all its guises has become deeply suspect, synonymous with corruption, double-dealing and oppression. The *problem*, however, is that precisely because of its repression, we are unable to confront explicitly in our relations with each other the operation of a force which cannot be excluded from them and which constitutes indeed the medium within which we exist.

We can only *pretend* to be indifferent to or detached from the wielding of power. Any society in which some must care for others, in which knowledge must be transmitted, laws enacted and enforced, will inevitably give rise to a power structure which its citizens have to operate. And some citizens, equally inevitably, will at various points in their lives and for various reasons have more power than others.

'Decent' people in our society repudiate power because they have, at least, an unexamined and unconscious sense of how much it has been abused. As far as possible, they won't truck with power. This means that all those forms of relation in which power does, whether we like it or not, play a part (as between adults and children, men and women) become confused, problematic and anarchic. This has two unfortunate consequences.

The first is that social cohesion becomes eroded to a point where everyone has to make up his or her own rules when it comes to conducting such problematic relationships. If it is not in some sense 'clear' how adults should relate to children, then a chaotic and unarticulated range of approaches to such relations will be found – anything from the use of children as sexual commodities to a kind of indifferent abandonment of them to their own devices which necessitates their growing up themselves as best they can. The difficulties and uncertainties of relations between the sexes – to be explored a little further below – need no emphasis since they are practically universally experienced by anyone trying to conduct a marriage or a 'partnership' or even simply trying to exist alongside the opposite sex in the current world.

The second unfortunate consequence of the repudiation of power is that it leaves the field completely free to those who are less squeamish; in fact, of course, nothing is more welcome to the 'discourse of power' than for the ordinary citizen to dissociate him or herself from it.

Some readers may by now be wondering uneasily whether I am about to suggest that the problematization of power calls for a 'return' to some kind of settled, authoritarian social order where everyone knows his or her place, and where, for example, class position and the condition of childhood are so tightly and universally defined that, however oppressed the occupants might be, at least their situation precludes the kind of uncertainty and confusion which gives rise to psychological distress. Obviously, however, it is the ultimate failure of these kinds of social institution which has led us to where we are now, and there can be no turning back.

Equally, though, the 'psychologizing' of 'interpersonal relations' and the development of a 'counselling culture' which suggests that the answer to our social ills lies somewhere *within* our hearts and minds, the refusal to truck with the problems of power, simply play into the interests of those at the top of our social pyramid who – whether consciously or not – are only too pleased not to have their methods come under closer scrutiny. What we need is not an unlimited supply of psychological therapy so much as the rehabilitation of politics: the realization, that is, that power can be used for good as well as for ill, and should be.

CHAPTER THREE

Bodies and Worlds –
The Field of Power

We know, reflect upon and judge our world through personal experience of it. In the previous chapter I tried to illustrate the importance of social power in the shaping of ourselves and our lives, and in particular our distress, mainly by considering how its influence comes to be lived out in our personal experience. Fundamental though such experience is to our understanding of ourselves, it is, however, not the whole story: our personal view is not wide enough to take account of all the factors which contribute to a given state of affairs, and for a more complete understanding we need to stand back and consider arguments and evidence which may not be immediately given to us personally. This is, no doubt, what is meant in part by being 'scientific'.

Though some of the themes to be discussed in this chapter were introduced in the last, I want here to take a step or two back from immediate experience and to offer an account of the individual's relation to a world structured by power from a slightly more abstract and theoretical standpoint. Such an account is needed, I believe, in order to give greater depth and breadth to our understanding of the ways in which personal distress is generated in a world over which we as individuals have very little control. (Much of what follows is summarized more formally in the Appendix to this book.)

TRADITIONAL APPROACHES

Those branches of psychology – the so-called 'psychodynamic' approaches – which have concerned themselves centrally with 'mental disorder', or emotional distress, while differing widely in the types of theory they put forward to explain the 'clinical phenomena', tend to share a basic methodology. This starts out with individual adults in distress (usually encountered first in some form of one-to-one 'treatment') and works back from there to postulate supposedly fundamental psychological mechanisms or processes which have led to the 'clinical picture'. In this way the reflective clinician – Sigmund Freud, say, or Carl Rogers – is confronted by a number of complex, socially highly developed individuals who in fact exist as, so to speak, finished articles in a social and cultural setting which they share with the clinician. What the latter then looks for are characteristics which mark these individuals out from other people not considered clinically 'abnormal', and which might point to processes whereby they came to be the way they are. The focus is thus the person ('patient', 'client') and what is assumed to be going on, or to have gone on, 'inside' him or her.

The clinician's consulting room becomes a microcosm supposedly containing all the explanatory material necessary for an adequate theory of 'psychopathology'. The clinician occupies the centre of this microcosmic world as a kind of nonpathological scientific wizard, able to identify and expose the processes leading to the patient's disorder and manipulate them such that the abnormalities are repaired. What tends to get left out of account, since it is so difficult not to take for granted, is the situation – the world – in which *both* clinician *and* patient find themselves. This is a bit like goldfish constructing a theoretical explanation of their condition solely from the data available to them in their bowl: some important and useful observations would doubtless get made, but rather a lot would be left out. The implications of this for the process of psychotherapy itself will be considered in more detail in Chapter Five.

In the end, of course, our scientific understanding is always going to be limited by the horizon of our field of vision: no 'complete' explanation, could there be such a thing, will ever be available to us of anything. But failure to look out of the consulting room window to the world beyond has led to some unnecessary shortsightedness in much psychological and psychotherapeutic theorizing. At least three common mistakes come quickly to mind:

1. Taking insufficient account of a wider world – of the microcosm's being located in a macrocosm – makes it more likely that the clinician will 'pathologize' patients, i.e., will be focally aware of what makes them 'different' rather than of how patients *and* clinician are at the mercy of and shaped by forces which dwarf the events and preoccupations of their individual lives. This error is very nearly universal in the most widely accepted approaches to 'mental illness'. It helps establish a cultural dimension of normality-abnormality which has the most profound and wide-ranging implications for social organization – for example, in determining who are considered competent members of our society and what should be the appropriate means of their 'treatment' or 'management' if they are not. It encourages us to distinguish between each other on the grounds of personal competence or 'mental health' rather than forging solidarity between us in our struggles with the problems presented to us by a hard world.

2. The somewhat claustrophobic concentration on the 'inner lives' of people who have both the self-concern and the resources to seek out individual psychotherapy tends to lead – as it did, for example, in the case of Freudian psychoanalysis – to an elaborate structure of theoretical concepts, many of them wonderful and some of them weird, which the clinician has to postulate in order to keep pace with the complexity of the phenomena which a thoughtful, well-educated and, literally, resourceful adult can present. Hence the appearance on the

theoretical scene of 'unconscious minds', 'ids', 'egos', 'complexes', 'personas', 'animas', and so on. Hence the emphasis in many psychotherapies on internal worlds, inner resources, responsibility and choice, the power in one guise or another of positive thinking. The trouble is that, though no doubt they point to features of human conduct and understanding of great importance, such theoretical constructs have a vagueness, and a tendency to proliferate, that obscure the more fundamental processes which operate beyond the microcosm; they may have a kind of magical seductiveness, an attractive pseudoauthority, but they do not have the generally applicable precision which can be used in any acceptably (nondogmatically) systematic way. This is one reason why no real science of psychology has emerged, but only a collection of competing, semi-patented, 'brand name' approaches.

3. Restriction to the microcosm of the consulting room leads clinicians to overestimate the importance of their own activity in 'curing' patients' problems. This overestimation of the therapist's role has led at times to expressions of therapeutic self-importance almost embarrassing in their absurdity and no doubt damaging to those – particularly patients – who have been either bullied or seduced into taking them seriously (Jeffrey Masson's *Against Therapy* is an enlightening source of examples).

Freud, for instance, issued pompous advice to his patients that they should not make major changes to the circumstances of their lives while 'under analysis', and the theoretical centrality of the 'transference relationship' in psychoanalysis – the notion that the analyst becomes, so to speak, the symbolic centre of the patient's universe – inflates the figure of the analyst in relation to the wider environment such that it overshadows absolutely everything else that happens in the patient's life.

More subtly, the exclusive concentration on what happens in the therapeutic microcosm tends to overemphasize the curative powers of the therapist even where the latter is not represented theoretically as anything other than averagely human. In his

Client-Centred Therapy, for example, Carl Rogers gave central importance to the quality of the relationship between patient and therapist – the well-known triad of 'warmth, empathy and genuineness'. However, while there is no doubt that, in accounting for what goes on in the consulting room, attention to such factors is an advance on the mysteries of the 'transference', still left out of account is the fact that the therapist is only a very small part of the world in which both therapist and patient find themselves.

BEHAVIOURAL APPROACHES

Not all approaches within the broadly 'clinical' field have been quite as entangled in the complicated phenomena of the consulting room when putting together a theoretical account of distress. Apart from those which have taken their main impetus from medicine and which incline therefore to an essentially biological account of distress (and so end up with the pills, potions and electric shocks of psychiatry), the most important are the behavioural approaches. At bottom, behaviourism suggested that we react the way we do because of what happens to us in the environment surrounding us. There is in my view a lot to be said for this transparently simple claim. The trouble is, it was always connected by behaviourists to an extremely blinkered view of what people, environments, 'stimuli' and 'responses' actually were, and adopted an unbelievably simplistic dogma concerning what it means to be 'scientific' while insisting with positively inquisitorial fanaticism that scientific is what we all had to be. As is well known, behaviourism attached itself limpet-like to the doctrines of Ivan Pavlov, the Russian physiologist, who generalized the reactions of experimental dogs to the various predicaments devised for them in his laboratories into a 'conditioning' theory of learning which eventually found its way into clinical psychology in the West (and, indeed, is still to be found there, even if modified out of almost all recognition).

The advantage of behaviourism was that it attempted to escape the complications of making the inside of an adult human being's head the starting point for a theory of psychological functioning. Instead of diving straight into the complexities of 'thought', 'imagery', 'will', 'instinct', etc., behaviourists were attracted to the simpler course – long established in the Anglo-Saxon philosophical tradition – of trying to understand human conduct as an interaction of person ('organism') and environment. The fact that behaviourism almost immediately got swept into painful oversimplifications of the processes involved was partly no doubt a function of the utilitarian scientism of the time, but that it eventually became lost in rationally indefensible authoritarian dogma should not deter us from trying to rescue the theoretical tradition which, even if only momentarily, it kept alive. This is what may perhaps be called the environmentalist tradition: the idea that a human being is the product of a body and a world, i.e., two essentially material structures, out of which the more intangible phenomena of psychology emerge.

THE IMPORTANCE OF THE ENVIRONMENT

My aim here cannot be to set out a grandiose theory of 'psychology'. What I do want to do is to sketch out the features of an environmentalist-materialist approach which are most essential to an understanding of emotional distress and confusion (especially, of course, distress and confusion which are usually thought of as 'abnormal' or 'pathological' in some way). There is not a great deal of point in theorizing for the sake of it; the reasons for its being necessary at this point are a) because, as I've indicated, the current orthodoxy ignores almost totally issues such as power which are crucial to our understanding, and b) because a reasonably accurate theoretical account leads to deepening insight into the phenomena concerned and to new ways of thinking about and handling them.

We start out with nothing more complicated than a human body in a world (environment) as shown in figure 1. In other

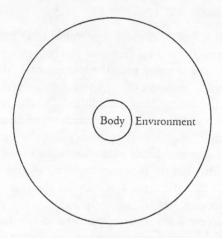

FIGURE 1: The raw materials

words, to account for the inarticulate distress of someone trying to understand and give a coherent picture of the misery he or she feels, one will always refer back in the end to features either of human biology or of the environment(s) in which those biological processes are or were once taking place. (Medicine, of course, places nearly all its eggs in the biological basket, whereas in what follows I shall be putting much heavier emphasis on environmental factors.) In common with the behaviourists, we have no need to import as *basic* components into our theoretical structure such entities as immortal souls, unconscious minds, ids, egos, faculties of will, instincts, or any other of the nonmaterial, 'internal' features of people which it is so difficult not to credit them with as we encounter them as 'finished products' in our everyday lives.

A human body abstracted from its environment is not a person: it is merely a collection of all the biological bits and pieces which go to make up bodies. A person only comes into being when a body is placed in a social world which interacts with it.

As is suggested by the hatched area in figure 2, a person is by no means identical with the material structures of his or her body, but is a construct of the interaction between body and

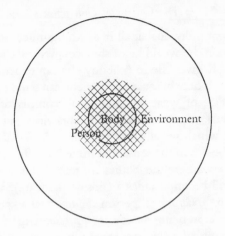

FIGURE 2: The person as interaction between body and
environment

environment. A person is partly body, certainly, but is also partly
environment. For example, a body may make vocal noises – it
certainly has the potentiality to utter, but the *language* which a
person comes to be able to speak, and in a sense 'possesses', is in
the social environment entirely outside the body. Part of what
it means to be a person is being able to communicate, and that
I speak English certainly seems like being part of 'me' as a person,
but it is not enclosed somehow inside my skin – it stretches out
into the world around 'me'. Or to put it another way, the world
outside extends its social institutions and practices into 'me': 'I'
am the hatched area which is neither body nor world, but a
complex interaction of both.

THE POVERTY OF INDIVIDUALISM

All this may strike the reader as tiresomely abstract. There is,
however, an issue of the very profoundest importance to be
recognized at this stage before it becomes overlaid by some of
the considerations to ensue. This is that an 'individual' person

is, in fact, not individual at all in anything much other than the actual space in the world he or she occupies and the experience this inevitably gives rise to (nobody else can experience exactly what you do if only because nobody else can stand exactly where you are). Part of what an 'individual' consists of is precisely nonindividual, social conventions, practices, meanings and institutions which we all share in common. We are, of course, individual bodies in the sense that mine is a different body from yours (but even here our bodies are remarkably similar – a fact which it will be important to consider later on). When, then, we come to examine a person's individual experience (our particular interest being, of course, *distressing* experience) we are likely to be misled if we conceive of its causes and cures purely as an 'individual' matter. We need always, that is, to keep an eye on those aspects of our so-called 'individuality' which are in fact features of a world we have in common.

I do not wish – indeed am not competent – to consider in any detail the specifically biological contribution to personhood of the body-world interaction. There can be no doubt that the nature of our embodiment – whether, for example, as male/female, light/heavy, tall/short, strong/weak, quick/slow, and many much more subtle distinctions than these – contributes crucially to our interaction with the world and experience of life. In these respects also genetic structures cannot but be of fundamental importance. However, while I in no sense see our biology as irrelevant to an account of our personhood, the contribution of the environment does seem to me overwhelmingly more significant for an understanding of the kind of phenomena of distress with which I am centrally concerned. From this aspect it seems to me most important to try to redress the balance in favour of environmental factors which even 'environmentalist' approaches such as behaviourism have failed to establish.

For the behaviourist, in fact, the 'environment' consists of little more than bundles of positively and negatively charged 'stimuli' or 'reinforcements' which spring into life, so it seems, from a

completely unanalysed, (presumably) social world whose contents
and concerns are left utterly mysterious. It is this world above
all which needs elucidation.

The Nature of the Environment

From the standpoint of the individual, the environment consists
of a practically limitless field of influence and a much more limited
field of opportunity. There are, that is to say, a whole range of
influences which bear down and ultimately impinge upon the
individual, and a limited range of actions available to him or her
by means of which he or she may exert some influence back into
the environment. Influence may thus impinge on the person
intransitively (i.e., 'stopping with' the person and resulting, perhaps,
in suffering or pleasure) or *transitively* (i.e., being transformed
through the individual into personal action of some kind). The
environment is ordered according to the dimensions of space and
time and organized by power. One could say, indeed, that the
environment *is* social space–time and that power is the essential
principle giving it motion and structure.

A person's 'state of mind' is thus explainable in principle through
an understanding of the influences operating in the environmental
space in which he or she is located. It is important not to overlook
the dimension of time: not only is there a current set of influences
bearing down upon the person, but there have also been former
sets of influences, so that the person is shaped by a history as well
as by present circumstances (time may be represented by extending
the circular diagram in figure 2, page 63, into the cylindrical one
in figure 3, page 74). Environmental influence has, then, a
dimension of time which runs most essentially from past to present,
and a spatial dimension which, as anticipated in Chapter Two,
I think is best characterized as proximal/distal. For the sake of
clarity I shall consider these dimensions of space and time
separately, though, of course, in practice they cannot be totally
abstracted from each other.

ENVIRONMENTAL SPACE

In everyday life the influences operating in the environment cannot but be experienced as close up against the person. Indeed, ultimately they form a part of bodily experience as sensations. Our experience of life is given to us through our immediate relations with others at home, at work, at school, and in our social and recreational activities. There is therefore an inevitable 'proximity' about our most immediate and potent experience. However, the reasons for the events which happen, so to speak, right up against our skin, may – in most cases will – be located much further away in the environmental power structure. One may or may not have insight into these. Education, access to accurate analysis by those better placed than ourselves, and so on, may help to clarify the distal reasons for our proximal experience, and such access therefore becomes in itself a form of power because it gives us a degree of (only potential) control over what happens to us.

For most people, 'reality' is the proximal world of their immediate experience. They tend to be indifferent to, or even impatient with, analyses of their experience which refer to distal events or influences because these may seem – may indeed be – so uncertain and speculative. They therefore tend to attribute 'the cause' of how they feel to the proximal experience of events or the actions of people close to them which are in fact determined by distal influences well out of their sight.

Geoff has worked for eighteen years in a factory now owned by an international conglomerate of vast proportions. In a hurry to get home after a late shift he runs past the security guard (whom he's known and chatted to in the canteen for the past eight years), who shouts something after him. He gives the guard a wave, jumps into his car and drives off. As soon as he arrives at work next day he is questioned for an hour about his refusal to stop for a spot check on the previous night. At first he jokes about it with the security personnel as he has a spotless record and is confident of his reputation. However, he is finally marched into a manager's office and told formally to account for himself. He is told that disobeying an order to stop for a check is a sackable offence. After an uneasy week's wait he is summoned before an official he has not seen before and summarily dismissed. 'I'm not interested in what you've got to say,' this official tells him, 'so far as I'm concerned you're just a number. You're fired.' This minor functionary, hired no doubt to spare local managers a hatchetry which might prove counterproductive, is described by Geoff as 'the top man from London', and his account suggests that local union officials view his power in similarly awe-struck terms. At any rate, Geoff feels himself up against forces far too powerful for him to challenge, and all his distress centres round the mystifying treachery of the security guard he had considered a friend, the cruel and unjust impugning of his honesty by a firm he had worked for for so long, wild frustration at being unable to establish his innocence, and a nagging sense of guilt at finding his character blackened. Like many people who have in one way or another been abused by power, he feels literally dirty. After three months of sleeplessness, anxiety and distress, he finds another job: 'longer hours and less money, but at least I've got my self-respect back'. Geoff gets little comfort from the knowledge that the factory was running at a loss and needed to 'rationalize' by shedding staff as cheaply as possible (summary dismissal being the cheapest and quickest method). His 'self-respect' was inextricably bound up with his proximal relations at work and could not be rescued through an abstract understanding of the distal operations of international finance.

THE POWER HORIZON

The idea, introduced in the previous chapter, that each of us exists within a 'power horizon' is extremely important to an understanding both of the inaccuracy of much of our moralizing and psychologizing – professional as well as amateur – about why people act as they do, and of the use to which such inaccuracy may be put by those wishing unscrupulously to augment their power. In accounting for our experience of the world, and not least for the pain and distress which comes to be registered physically on our bodies, we tend to tell ourselves endless, often conflicting stories. We revise and revise again our constructions of what we see as the 'motives' of those around us as well as the (usually more creditable!) motives we detect within ourselves. Just as Geoff was stuck with trying to account for the motives of his friend the security guard, we all tend to rummage around inside the supposed 'inner space' of those we encounter in everyday life until we find a 'reason' for what they do which gives us at least temporary satisfaction.

Psychology and philosophy themselves postulate countless variants on the theme of 'motive', 'impulse', 'will', 'responsibility', etc., all of which similarly seek proximal causes for actions which, in fact, can only be accounted for within a very much wider environmental power structure. It is scarcely surprising that accounts of human motivation are often attended by references to its mysterious nature, since as long as one insists on locating the reasons for their actions *inside* people, mysterious is what they're bound to remain: in fact, there *is* no inside of a kind which will accommodate lurking motives. The 'mystery' of the human soul and its supposed motivational component is in my view no mystery at all, but rather the projection inwards (i.e., into an 'inner space' which actually doesn't exist) of an *outer* mystery which is indeed very real.

Both our own actions and the actions of those around us may be mysterious not because we cannot penetrate the depths of each other's inner worlds, unconscious minds, etc., but because we simply cannot see over the power horizons which limit our view of the causes of things. We are thus restricted to telling ourselves stories, making guesses, speculating and surmising about happenings in our proximal worlds which have distal causes well out of sight. Such distal causes set off complex concatenations of events which reverberate throughout large segments of social environmental space and end up registering on our senses through the mediation of one or several people close to us. Much of the time, therefore, we remain in the dark not only about the reasons for the conduct of others, but equally about our own conduct.

Nobody (other than an entirely hypothetical deity) has a limitless power horizon, though people differ widely in the depth of the power horizons which enclose the various spheres in which they lead their existence. As I have already noted, it is frequently in the interests of those with a greater vista of power deliberately to limit as far as they can what others are able to see. One way of doing this is to make use of the nearly irresistible appeal of proximal explanation. Thus the government minister eager to discount the socioeconomic causes of urban rioting will invoke an (utterly mysterious) 'criminality', or absence of 'parental discipline', to account for it. Much closer to home, we are likely in our domestic disputes with each other endlessly (if usually profoundly unsatisfactorily) to attribute personal spites (to others) and virtues (to ourselves) as reasons for our friction which in fact has causes located far off in the networks of power.

I shall be considering issues to do with the kinds of professional help which may be of use to people in distress in Chapter Five, but it is worth noting at this point that a particular difficulty confronting people who wish to change how they feel is that their feelings are often likely to be related to events which, because they are taking place over their power horizon, they cannot even see – and even if they could they would be likely still to find it quite beyond their powers to do anything about them. And when one takes the dimension of time into account, things get even more difficult.

ENVIRONMENTAL TIME

Most approaches to psychotherapy and clinical psychology rely on one version or another of a theory of 'insight' which assumes that once one has identified the origin of one's 'pathological' conduct or experience, one can make the adjustments necessary to return to normality. That in their clinical experience this does not in fact seem to happen has led some theorists to acknowledge the inadequacy of merely 'intellectual' insight, and to proclaim instead the superiority of 'emotional insight'. A change of mind, it seems, is less effective than a change of heart.

However, I think the situation is considerably more difficult than would be suggested by any approach relying on one form or another of the concept of 'insight', which seems to me a good example of the kind of essentially unanalysable and magical process to which therapeutic psychologies so often appeal. Events which have happened in the past to make someone the kind of person he or she is do not just present the kinds of problems of access of distal events happening in the present; they are completely beyond reach.

The illusion of accessibility to the past – greatly and to my mind illegitimately exploited by 'cognitive' psychologies which place heavy therapeutic emphasis on the reinterpretation of history – is probably maintained by an unexamined assumption most of us have that the past somehow exists in the present as memories in some form of internal space. It may easily seem to us that we can reach into this space, shuffle its contents around and so set in train a chain of readjustments which will lead to a radical difference in the way we feel now.

Interestingly, it is felt that such retrospective adjustments are possible only in those matters of what one might call character which are typically subject to moral scrutiny and debate; nobody is likely to assume that the more solid and indisputable achievements of past learning – such as language acquisition or the possession of particular practical abilities – are open to the same kind of interior tinkering. While it might be thought that I can examine my past and revise my reasons for being hostile or anxious, nobody expects me to be able – however expedient it might be – to forget my knowledge of English and acquire one of Chinese merely by recalling the circumstances of my learning the former and reflecting on the desirability of knowing the latter.

In fact, a person's experience at any point along the dimension of time is acquired as part of a bodily interaction with the proximal effects of distal causes. The experience itself may seem to exist insubstantially but somehow accessibly in one's head, but in truth it is organically embodied: becomes, that is, physically part of ourselves. The past leaves its marks upon us in various degrees of intensity and durability – as I suggested in the last chapter the impress of power can be extremely long-lasting – but we have no real say in the matter, and cannot choose what forms of embodied experience we wish to retain and what to erase. Once I have learned to ride a bicycle or play the piano I cannot choose to forget, though of course such abilities may fade with the course of time.

THE REHABILITATION OF 'CHARACTER'

The idea that we are in large part the products of a past which we can do nothing to change – not to mention a present whose influences are well out of reach – suggests to me that it would be valuable to resurrect a concept of 'character' which has largely disappeared from psychology. 'Character' gave way to 'personality', which in turn splintered into various subsets of 'behaviours', 'cognitive styles', and so on, which appeared increasingly to permit of professional intervention: a human being becomes split into manipulable bits and pieces, which can be adjusted and reassembled in accordance with some normative ideal. One can see, of course, what's in this for psychology, but as an accurate conceptualization of what it is to be a person, it leaves a lot to be desired.

In fact, people are the people that they are by reason of the things which have happened to them and the nature of the world in which they are currently having to live their lives. We are characters shaped by a past world and struggling with a current world which, absolutely inevitably, we can understand only imperfectly. Shuffling the contents of our heads may have all sorts of rewards and fascinations, but it will do very little to make us other than we are.

The difference between what psychology can achieve and what it has always hoped to achieve is the difference between self-discovery and self-invention. We can up to a point discover what kinds of characters we are, but we cannot choose to be the 'personalities' we should like to be, any more than we can choose to be Olympic athletes or concert violinists. In maintaining this I am, of course, running directly counter to that very considerable section of the psychotherapy and 'personal growth' industry which promises one form or another of self-choice. Such a promise can only be made, however, through wilful ignorance of a power-structured world in which even the concept of free will is no more than a necessary illusion.

It becomes important at this point to consider in a little more detail the nature of the powers which organize that world.

TYPES OF POWER

Sociologists tend to agree in differentiating three types of power which give order to our relations with each other[1]: coercive, economic and ideological power. Individuals thus find themselves at the centre of a network of social influences which are applied either as brute force, money power, or through the manipulation and control of the meaning systems by which we make sense of the world. While the point is usually made that these three forms of power are essentially independent of each other – i.e., that it is possible to possess one form without having access to either of the other two – in practice they are, of course, often related. When all else fails it is power over the body – physical coercion – which virtually guarantees the achievement of the aims of the

1. See, for example, W. G. Runciman, *A Treatise on Social Theory*, Vol. II, Cambridge Univeristy Press, 1989.

powerful (though the *means* of force, especially on an international scale, may well be dependent on wealth).

While brute force might be the ultimate sanction, the more subtle application of ideological power is likely to be far more effective in controlling large segments of society: if citizens can be brought to believe that their government consists of public-spirited men and women who have at heart only the welfare of society as a whole, things are likely to go far more smoothly than where a 'band of brigands', to borrow Robert Tressell's phrase[2], fails to conceal its designs from an exploited populace and has consequently to resort to brutal repression. The more a government can control the beliefs and perceptions of significant sections of society, the less likely will be its need for control over their bodies.

The Field of Power

The processes, or meaning systems (in this and much of what follows it may help the reader to refer to figure 3), which mediate a person's experience, for example, his or her beliefs about the nature of the world and the social events occurring in it, are derived partly from physical interaction with the environment – the pleasurable sensation of benign influences and the painful sensation of malign ones – and partly, probably mainly, from interaction with the socially established categories of meaning which are firmly in place in the world well in advance of the individual's occupancy of it. To make sense of what we directly, physically experience, we are heavily dependent on the explanations and meanings afforded us by our culture. Our personal assimilation to, and adaptation of, these meaning systems is roughly what is meant by our 'psychology'. It cannot be emphasized too strongly (since it is an error so often made) that this psychology, all those linguistic and nonlinguistic systems for

2. From his *The Ragged-Trousered Philanthropists*.

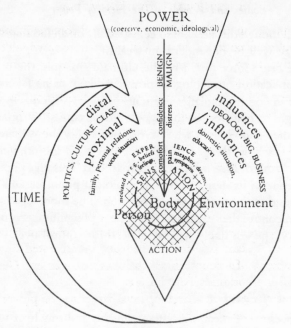

FIGURE 3: The field of power

making sense of the world – thought, memory, dreams, perceptions, feelings, etc. – do not exist independently of the environment of which indeed they are partly constituted. Our psychology is not ours to manipulate at will and we cannot detach it from the social powers which hold it in place.

This means that having, for example, recognized the importance of people's beliefs or 'attitudes' as regulators of their conduct, we cannot somehow isolate them like the printed circuits of an electronic machine and slide them in and out of people in the expectation of achieving 'behaviour change'. For an attitude is not a personal possession in the way that a toe, or an ear, or an appendix is; it is linked to and partly produced by a network of social forces which may stretch out to the most distal cultural powers. It is control of those powers *outside* people which ultimately achieves control of people themselves.

The explanation of individual experience and conduct is, then, to be sought in a complex set of social interactions in which the most likely pattern is for extremely powerful distal events – political or economic perhaps – to reverberate through a network of influence and interest until they work themselves out in the proximal relations which make up the context of the individual's personal life. These in turn will be mediated physically as sensations (pain and pleasure) and psychologically via the meaning systems acquired by the person in social space-time. Geoff's distress was attributed by him mostly to his immediate contact with people where he worked, stretching out only as far as the 'top man from London', and partly to an inarticulate (ideologically determined) sense of personal inadequacy and guilt. In fact, of course, if certain events in far distant boardrooms had not reverberated down through systems of accounting and chains of management, Geoff would still be working where he was.

It seems self-evident that the social structure of power is pyramidal, that essentially the story is one of control of the many by the few. I have already remarked that one of the most important tasks of ideological power is to obscure the workings of this process, and it is indeed striking how difficult it is to obtain any reasonably clear picture of where power originates in society. The mass media are, of course, very little help, not least because they themselves *constitute* ideological power and are owned and controlled by people and groups whose whole purpose (whether or not they are aware of it) is to contain ordinary mortals' understanding of the social processes of power within as proximal a compass as possible.

Moralizing and psychologizing are the stock in trade of those whose interest it is to narrow the power horizon of the average citizen, and so the language used is a relentlessly proximal one of motive and blame rather than cause and effect. The mass media wield their ideological power in an effort to define reality, not to explore and expose its nature. Even scholarly sociological enquiry seems not to be able to penetrate with any clarity the obscurity shrouding the upper reaches of the pyramid of power. Exactly who the powerful are tends to be dimly suggested in fleeting glimpses – as of the chimneys of an enormous mansion rising just discernibly from a copse at the end of a miles-long avenue closed off by discreetly placed electronic gates – or faint flickerings of insight as one senses the extraordinary linkages between political power, big business, large-scale corruption and international crime.

However all this may be (I lay no claim to an especially extended power horizon!), it would seem likely to be a mistake to assume that, in view of its undoubtedly pyramidal structure, power is essentially a personal matter. For tyrants must always remain nervously vulnerable to the very fact of their singularity, whether exerting distal power through the possession of vast personal fortunes or the command of private armies, or the merely proximal power of physical bullying: their power is in truth no more reliable than the proverbial assassin's bullet allows it to be. Power is much more usually, and effectively, gained and maintained through association with others and through an institutional structuration of influence which affords real stability to the powers possessed. Thus, while power in terms of the quantum available to each individual is indeed likely to be distributed pyramidally, it is also the case that people located higher up the pyramid are more likely to be embedded in a relatively stable structure of power involving other people than are those at the bottom. In other words, the really powerful individual, far from being the kind of isolated, power-crazed megalomaniac depicted in the popular literature of paranoia (by Ian Fleming, for example), is in fact more likely to be someone who is located in a network of institutionalized, formal (legally established) and informal (private 'clubs' of one kind or another) powers and privileges.

Those who truly stand in isolation are the people at the bottom of the power pyramid, so stripped of any kind of institutional or socially shared power that they are reduced in the final analysis to the utterly proximal powers afforded by their mere existence as embodied individuals: for a man this may mean recourse to brute force, for a woman to the bartering of her sexuality. (There is a kind of microcosmic theoretical purity about the relation of the prostitute to her pimp which illuminates a great deal of the less palatable aspect of the wider social organization. Reduced to the very dregs of the proximal power available to her, the prostitute is still vulnerable to the sheer muscle power of the pimp who effects a takeover of her business.)

THE MEDIATION OF POWER

Power is transmitted through networks of associative groups, each group seeking to maximize its interest and preserve its advantage. The coercive power of totalitarian regimes is maintained through armies and the secret police; big business operates through a managerial bureaucracy; various kinds of cultural advantage are preserved through a range of educational, scientific and technical, professional groups and institutions; class advantage, as I illustrated in the last chapter, is maintained by a caste system of distinction. Each such grouping or section of society tries to maintain its position by developing exclusive methods of training and selection for admission, specialized procedures and activities mysterious to the uninitiated, esoteric languages largely unintelligible to outsiders, and so on. To belong to such a group usually confers a degree of power on the individual which he or she would not otherwise have, and so he or she develops almost instantaneously an interest in the group's continued existence and a commitment to contributing as much as possible to its stability. The rigour with which even supposedly disinterested social institutions – for example, in education or science – discipline their members, and the readiness of the members themselves to submerge their individuality in adopting the procedures and jargon of the group, testify to their mutual dependence in maintaining an interest which places them at an advantage in relation to the mass of society.

Keeping control of meaning is of central importance to the preservation of power, and this, of course, is the essence of ideology. As Michel Foucault argues so persuasively in *Discipline and Punish*, the construction and maintenance of an apparatus of largely ideological power is a very much more effective way of organizing and controlling mass society than is simple recourse to brute force, and it is through a positive fog of ideology that most of us have to stumble our way towards the truth. There are, of course, a thousand ways of keeping ideological control (or, as Dorothy Rowe puts it, of bamboozling people): officially through the established institutions of religion, education and 'therapy', unofficially through mass media, which are able to shape the very 'reality' we can see and talk about. Enormous power can be gained through the appropriation of meaning itself: to impose a language on all which is interpretable by only a small élite is the ultimate in the exercise of ideological power. Priests and doctors have at different times and to different extents come close to perfecting this technique, but most professional groups are more or less adept at it.

It is important to note that the power of ideology stems from the *social* nature of meaning. To control meaning is to gain power through *associating* with some people in ascendancy over other people. Altering or adjusting 'meanings' as they exist individually as beliefs, attitudes or perceptions in your or my head is of comparatively little significance. The difference between ideological power and impotent magic is that the former is public and social and the latter is private and individual; the former gives real power over people, the latter only a spurious, wishful illusion of power. It is equivalent to the difference between learning a real language (which gives access to real social powers and possibilities) and inventing a private one (which merely locks one into autistic, essentially crazy self-communion). It is in many ways the tradition of magic that survives in those brands of psychology and psychotherapy which advocate tinkering with the individual's personal systems of meaning within the microenvironment of the consulting room; unless the *social* significance of the individual's psychology can be taken fully into account (a question to be addressed further in Chapter Five), such tinkering will achieve nothing of substance.

Almost no adult individual is totally powerless, if only because, as I have indicated, he or she may have recourse to the powers afforded by embodiment. While such power may at times reach a zenith of quite spectacular violence, it is still in the overall scale of things extremely puny, and will be called upon with any regularity only by the socially least advantaged members of society. The power afforded by the simple act of association with others is very much more effective, and for this reason alone the more powerful are always likely to seek to limit the extent to which the less powerful are able to form associations of any kind. The most obvious example is the inclination of employers in a capitalist society to limit the process and powers of unionization, but it is in the interest of any group with claims to power (for example, the professions) to keep dependent on it (for 'advice', 'treatment', or whatever) people who are as far as possible isolated from each other.

The more 'private' and 'individual' people become, the more detached they will be from the possibility of acquiring associative power – indeed such power is likely to become available to them only through association with some sort of 'professional', a lawyer or therapist, for example, or in the confined domesticity of their personal lives (hence, no doubt, the central concern most people have in present-day culture with 'relationships'; hence also the eagerness of some politicians to extol the sanctity of 'the family' and to represent it as the largest viable social building block). For most people these days, 'solidarity' – the participation in associative power – is limited to a 'relationship' with just one or two people. This, of course, provides the optimally extended base of the power pyramid for exploitation by its higher levels.

THE MYSTIFICATION OF POWER

The need for association with powerful others, first experienced in the child's relations with the adults around it, is observable most poignantly in those instances where it is most exploited. It is, for example, easy to react with contempt or incredulity to the apparently utterly trivial preoccupations of the popular press, but, in fact, it thrives upon the provision of a mystified version of the need for associative power – 'mystified' because the power actually yielded is very nearly nil. For associative power becomes itself a marketable product. 'Celebrities' and 'personalities' permit their own, often quite considerable social power to be exploited through encouraging a degree of intimacy with the 'little people' who read in magazines and tabloids of their private concerns, conduct and relationships. The reader is allowed to become the confidant of the 'celebrity', perhaps recreating thereby an echo of the warmth once gained from the trust of a parent, and so comes into possession of 'knowledge' which offers a pathetically false promise of increased social standing, especially presumably among those not so favoured.

The seductiveness of such marketed power is that it appears to be freely offered by the celebrity – the reader is invited into his or her confidence. The 'star' who 'tells' willingly whom she is sleeping with gives her confidant privileged access to her world as to a friend. Where, on the other hand, such intimacies are revealed through the treachery of a former butler or extorted by trickery and the telephoto lens, the knowledge gained seems more like the knowledge of a spy: shameful but potentially useful. Exploitation of the phenomena of power by association is, of course, well recognized by those who need to maintain and augment their ideological capital by patronizing the powerless and cultivating their interest. Almost everyone can feel part of the Royal Family if the ideological machinery is tended carefully enough, and if the paparazzi didn't exist, the rich and famous would have to invent them.

The power actually conferred by mystified association with the powerful is, of course, nonexistent in the sense of the individual's becoming a real intimate of the 'celebrity'. However, it may perhaps do a very little to augment social solidarity between those 'in the know', if only because it gives them something to talk about together. A fan club, for example, might offer people opportunities for association with each other much more valuable than the association each might *feel* they had with the object of their veneration.

Religion seems sometimes to work like this, and, when it does, provides a good example of the contrast between the inaccuracy of personal beliefs based on proximal experience and the more complete account offered by a distal view. I have, for example, encountered several people for whom attachment to one form or other of fundamentalist, 'born again' Christianity has resulted in greatly increased happiness and indeed in their ability to gain some control in areas of their lives where they had been feeling particularly helpless and lost. Not surprisingly, they tend to attribute such improvement to their newly cemented relationship with Jesus, rather as if they had found an especially powerful friend ready to lend them a receptive ear at any time of need, and poised to put at their disposal his virtually limitless resources should the request be sufficiently earnestly made. This seems to me a false belief not only in respect of there being no such friend, but also in there being no real efficacy to the *belief* that one has such a friend (on its own, i.e., out of a context of association with others, such a belief would constitute madness).

While those forms of psychology which have failed to detach themselves from their roots in magic would be ready enough to acknowledge the power of beliefs of this kind, it seems to me much more plausible that their potency lies in the social solidarity which *sharing* them brings about. In every instance that I can think of what has made the difference to the previously isolated and despairing, now born-again-Christian person has not been any special relationship with God (which is merely the story people tell themselves) but an empowering association (solidarity) with a group of like-minded others who are prepared to endorse that story.

'SELF-CONTROL' – INSIDE AND OUTSIDE

The great error – one might even say the fundamental flaw – of psychology has been to consider individual meaning-systems as somehow belonging to and in the control of the people of whom they form a part. Over and over again the assumption is made that things like beliefs and attitudes are located *inside* a person and that, while they may indeed be seen as guiding his or her conduct, they are also, in some way which is almost always left mysterious, subject to operations of his or her will. Thus, if the person sees fit – perhaps through a process of having gained 'insight' – he or she can in some sense 'decide' to alter beliefs or attitudes which have now come to be seen as inappropriate or inconvenient.

Despite having a long and honourable pedigree, particularly in British philosophy, the idea that we are *not* in fact in charge of ourselves in this way is for most people still very difficult to grasp, mainly because it has become ideologically so obscured. Furthermore, those approaches to psychology, such as behaviourism, which have challenged the view that we have total moral control over ourselves have so over-simplified the issues as to discredit the core of their own intellectual enterprise.

What one has to do, it seems to me, is emphasize once again that the 'person' is not a bounded entity separated off from the world in which he or she exists, but an interaction of body with world, consisting partially of both. People cannot control their beliefs and attitudes because people *are* their beliefs and attitudes. Beliefs and attitudes, as well as the nonverbal meaning-systems like dream and metaphor which order our experience, are *constituents* of our personhood: there is no further 'person' who can somehow step outside this constituency, adjust it, and then step back in again.

What seems like our 'inside' – what psychologists so often refer to as the 'self', 'inner space', etc. – does not exist in any material sense. Nor does it 'exist' in any immaterial sense – it is, rather, a way of referring to our self-consciousness. Exactly as we can talk to, as well as about, others we can talk to and about ourselves (though perhaps with differing degrees of honesty) concerning our experience of the world. We can talk about the various ways in which we interact bodily with the world, we can sense things about it, we can dream about, describe and reflect upon it with varying degrees of clarity, accuracy, skill or grace, but we do not necessarily control it thereby. What makes a difference to the way we are, what changes us or permits us to change, is not the voluntary manipulation of inner resources (for there is no 'inner') but the influence of or access to *outer* resources and powers. Neither 'self' nor world can be influenced or changed by anything other than the exercise of power.

This is not to say that we do not as individuals possess personal resources – clearly any such claim would be ludicrous – but that it is seriously misleading to characterize such resources as 'inner', since as soon as we start unreflectively to entertain such a notion, we lay the foundation for a moralistic calculus of 'personal worth' and so on. What people tend to see as 'inner resources' are most usually *outer* resources which they have acquired over time. The idea of an 'inner world' is in this way the transmutation of a temporal phenomenon into a spatial metaphor.

My propensity to meet threat without anxiety ('confidence' or 'courage'), no differently from my ability to speak French, is something I have learned or been enabled or empowered to do at some previous point of my existence. I can no more summon confidence up from some kind of inner space than I can a knowledge of French if I have not acquired them from the outer world at some time in the past; and just as one might find it rather strange to think of 'my French' as existing in 'inner space', it is precisely as strange to think of confidence or courage in this way.

The kinds of entity with which we tend to populate our 'inner worlds', whether personal qualities and strengths, weaknesses, 'personality traits' or 'symptoms' of 'psychopathology', are traceable to and perhaps most often understandable as the historical acquisitions or impositions of the proximally mediated influences on our lives. They may also be held in place by current environmental influences either of our particular personal circumstances or by cultural aspects of that part of the environment which forms a constituent of our personhood and which therefore we share with others – these latter aspects I shall return to presently.

A benign psychology would in my view (and no doubt often does, though not always sufficiently self-consciously) point out to people how much their own self-attributions of personal weakness and blame, of having interior flaws or moral failings, are actually the result of an ideological mystification which obscures an entirely exterior deprivation or exploitation. Where such deprivation or exploitation has taken place far enough in the past for its origin to be beyond the easy reach of memory, or indeed in that prelinguistic period of life in which memory cannot properly be said to be operating (and where events get 'remembered' only as indecipherable metaphors or unexplainable 'feelings'), then their manifestation in the present will often be, perhaps irresolvably, baffling. Sometimes, however, the nature of the ideologically distorted, inward projection of an outer deprivation is very obvious.

Among the more affluent sections of society it is not considered eccentric – it is not even considered a question of 'personality type' – to enjoy a degree of privacy in one's life. To have domestic space in which to live undisturbed by others, in a house set back from noisy roads, with a reasonably secluded garden enclosed by a suitably high hedge or wall, to own a car capable of transporting you quickly and privately behind its smoked-glass windows through the public space which separates your house from places of work or recreation – these are not considered the unusually quirky needs of somehow vulnerable personalities. Indeed, they are rarely considered as 'needs' at all (nothing so interior!) but rather the obviously valuable requisites of a normally comfortable life. We do not impute the 'need' for a hedge to any kind of neurotic personal deficit. And yet what happens to people when the opportunity to enjoy this kind of privacy is denied?

One thing that quite often happens is that they get diagnosed as 'agoraphobic'. Presumably those of us who enjoy privacy do so because we feel uncomfortable if exposed to the public gaze at times and in situations where we want to be 'off duty'. For people who *cannot* be off duty such discomfort may be almost perpetual. It is not, after all, uncommon for life to be lived (especially by women) in a house or flat constantly invaded by the sound, if not the sight, of others, set among hedgeless gardens (if any) and wall-less streets; for walks to the shops or bus stops to be exposed to the gaze of every idling youth, every casual mechanic working on his car, every curious consciousness possibly lurking behind every net curtain; for each bus that has to be taken itself to constitute a mobile aisle of inquisitive eyes. The screaming discomfort which such situations often engender is not 'diagnosed' as a lack of privacy to be 'cured' through the provision of an adequately constructed and tended physical environment, but is projected inward as 'agoraphobia' and 'treated' with drugs and psychotherapy.

Mrs Arkwright moved from a bleak public housing estate – open, asphalt, streaked with graffiti, litter and dog shit – where her existence anywhere beyond her own front door had been one of perpetual tension if not outright fear, to a new house she and her husband had bought in a pleasant residential suburb a few miles away. From the moment of her move her 'agoraphobia' started to diminish until after a few months it became most of the time absent from her awareness. At first, though, she was puzzled and mistrustful of herself, almost ashamed. 'Do you think there's something peculiar about me?' she asked soon after moving house. 'It sounds funny to say it, I know, but it's so nice to walk down roads lined with trees.' She was genuinely afraid that what she took to be a personal weakness before – feeling anxious when walking down 'dog muck lane' – had been replaced by another personal weakness in the form of a somehow reprehensible or abnormal sensitivity to landscape. When asked to think about *why* the trees had been planted in the streets of her new neighbourhood, she was lost for a clear answer; it was as if she could only think of them as having come to be there by accident.

The more negative, though nonetheless essential, task of a psychology which sets out to explode the myth of 'interiority' is to point out that our strengths are no more to be held to our credit than our weaknesses are to our discredit. Whatever may make an individual admirable or effective as a human being does not arise from some unanalysable well of interior moral superiority, but, in all likelihood, from the good fortune of having had *imposed* upon him or her (for example, through the proximal influence of education) abilities and characteristics which become part of an embodied repertoire of resources.

That we almost always experience and talk about as inside those constituents of our personhood which are actually outside leads to profound confusion not only in our self-understanding, but also in our ideas about how to change ourselves and influence the environment. Such confusion is bound to follow on the radical mistake of supposing that social structures outside ourselves are actually moral or psychological structures inside ourselves. For then we either take upon ourselves or apportion to others the blame for faults or shortcomings which, in fact, lie outside us (and them), very probably in the world we share in common, and which can only be set right by attending to that world.

'FORM'

As social beings we live according to shared rules of meaning which are constructed to take account of, organize and explicate the immediate sense of the world (sensation) given to us by our bodies. Language is an example of one such set of rules – we cannot, in our shared experience of the world and our need to communicate intelligibly about it, step outside the linguistic rules which we have created for precisely this purpose. As I have indicated, though language forms an intensely personal and fundamentally important part of 'me', it is not 'inside' me, but exists in the social space I share with others.

Practically all the rules and concepts which give shape and meaning to our experience (many of them, of course, themselves constructed linguistically) are of this kind: they are not our personal inventions, but are acquired by us in the process of becoming *people*, i.e., as we interact bodily with the social environment which surrounds us. For the sake of brevity and quick reference I shall, with an apologetic nod to Plato, call such rules and concepts 'forms', not least because it is such rules and concepts which, precisely, give *form* to our experience. Without there being public forms which (nearly always) pre-exist our bodily experience of the world, resonate with and give meaning to it, we should live in a completely unintelligible, unarticulated and nondiscussable fog of confusion.

To take a very obvious example, but one nevertheless very important to our emotional wellbeing, one's sense of oneself as male or female is inseparable from the 'forms' of masculinity and femininity which are culturally established quite independently of us as individuals. To talk unreflectively of 'my' masculinity runs the risk of conceptualizing it as 'inside' me as some kind of personal possession. In fact, of course, how far I may be considered masculine or not depends upon a 'form' of masculinity which is entirely outside me. A great and often very damaging mistake is made when *a disintegration of the 'form' is interpreted or experienced as a breakdown in the individual personality*. Psychotherapy and clinical psychology, not to mention psychiatry, are the greatest perpetrators of this error, and in turning impersonal difficulties into personal problems have helped shape a culture of individualism where it has become almost impossible for people to differentiate inside from outside and to attribute the pain they so often feel about them-'selves' to its appropriate source.

Political movements are less likely to make this kind of error. Feminism, for example, in its political aspect, correctly sees that for women to gain a more equitable share of social power requires a change in the 'forms' relating to femininity and masculinity; feminists do not suggest (and insofar as they occasionally do they are mistaken) that each individual woman needs to change her 'self'. Psychological approaches to personal distress, on the other hand, are likely to fail to recognize that distress is often the pain of an individual who finds that he or she is unable to meet the requirements of 'form'. A person may, for example, be brought up in a field of proximal power which impresses a gender role of a certain kind, only to find that when he or she moves into a slightly more distal field of power (on escaping from the family, for example) there are new 'forms' of gender which make un-fulfillable, and perhaps even for the greater part unintelligible, demands (an extreme example would be a demand for homo- to be replaced by heterosexuality, or vice versa). The 'problem' here lies in the change in the outside world, not in some kind of personal inadequacy.

While psychologists no longer expect their clients to be able to alter their sexual proclivities at will, they still often assume that people do have access 'within' them to forms of conduct more appropriate or 'adjusted' than those they are currently displaying, and that all that is needed is some kind of (again, unanalysed) moral effort, perhaps inspired by a flash of 'emotional insight'. Apart from anything else, what is not recognized is the often very disturbing *unfamiliarity* which such a change of practice requires. In order to 'behave appropriately' the individual in such circumstances has to submit or be submitted to procedures of learning which nobody – least of all psychologists and therapists – understands and which require him or her to venture out into completely uncharted territory. 'Forms' are acquired bodily through the impress of power *from outside*. To acquire new 'forms' (i.e., to 'con-form' to new demands) when old ones have disappeared or disintegrated may or may not be possible, but in any case this is an issue about which 'therapies' and 'treatments' have had, so far, almost nothing useful to say.

Where an individual's experience cannot receive its meaning from an appropriate public form the result is likely to be experienced as either poetry or pain: the first a struggle to *create* form, the second the expression (or sensation) of its lack. There do exist, however, 'forms' for such pain itself, and those most usually invoked are blame and guilt. People who find themselves isolated with feelings, impulses, ideas or thoughts which find no ready echo in formal, public concepts or meanings are likely to succumb to a guilty sense of failure. They are also likely to find a psychiatric/therapeutic industry only too ready to produce a formal diagnosis for their difficulty.

Pam, suffering from 'depression', for which at times she has been variously 'treated' with electric shock and 'antidepressant' medication, at last finds the words with which to describe her predicament (though they do not, of course, solve it): 'It's as if I have feelings I don't know how to describe, because I was never told how to describe them. There were certain things we were just not allowed to be when we were little – there was no such thing as anger or hatred. I still don't really know what they are. I just know I have feelings, or I suppose they're feelings, which I don't know how to talk about. There's just a hole where I'm supposed to be feeling.' When in that hole, which happens quite often, Pam just sits helplessly with tears pouring down her cheeks. There is nothing really wrong *with* Pam. For one reason or another her parents failed to communicate some essential forms of feeling to her. They didn't (no doubt for the best of motives) want her to be hateful, so they never taught her how to hate, or what hatred was, and thus left her all alone with a feeling which is just a terrifying mystery to her, and about which the only communicable thing she *can* feel is guilt. But the failure, such as it is, is not and never was *inside* her. It was a failure of form. Failures of form may come about, as in Pam's case, through a failure of proximal powers to mediate them, or through the cultural absence or disintegration of forms capable of giving sense to individual experience. Our experience is unintelligible if we are not taught a language with which to describe it.

What makes some manifestations of 'psychopathology' so puzzling is precisely the fact that there are for one reason or another no adequate 'forms' through which they can be rendered socially intelligible. 'Madness' is not, as it is so often said to be, the person's 'loss of contact with reality', but rather reality's failure to make contact with and to explicate the personal experience of the sufferer. What makes somebody 'mad' is not some mysterious internal process or biological fault 'inside' him or her, nor indeed an internal breakdown of personal rationality, but the failure of outer form to give communicable meaning to his or her experience of a world which is and was precisely as real as any other. Though well recognized by some who have worked in this field (and explicated most profoundly and brilliantly in my view by H. S. Sullivan[3]), it seems extraordinarily difficult for this perspective on psychological distress and 'madness' to become sufficiently firmly established to develop productively. Over and over again the orthodox theoretical stance favours some kind or other of 'internal' pathology. It is as if horticulture had never progressed beyond a notion that the growth and health of plant life depended on the internal adjustment of each individual specimen rather than upon the conditions in which they grow.

'Psychopathology' can sometimes be rendered nonpathological through being given meaning by a 'form' not previously available. I have in this way once or twice seen how the conduct of someone supposedly suffering from an 'obsessional–compulsive neurosis' can become entirely appropriate if environmental influences shift in such a way as to accommodate it. For example, a man who worries more or less incessantly about whether he is accidentally

3. See his *The Interpersonal Theory of Psychiatry*, W. W. Norton, 1953.

transmitting a fatal disease to his nearest and dearest suddenly comes into his own (and becomes a lot happier) when he is given the job of safety officer where he works. It is rather as if he has suddenly found the role that life had in some mysterious way prepared him for.

Our private experience is, then, not only given meaning, but may also actually be rendered sane by finding shape in public form. My eccentricity may be like a key in search of a lock. It may, of course, never encounter one, in which case I may always feel isolated, sad or guilty. If, on the other hand, it *does* find one, I may become, perhaps joyfully, *associated* in a world which suddenly has a use for what I know.

The more systems of meaning, 'choices' of 'lifestyle' and moral conduct come to be seen as individual matters of 'personal responsibility', and so on, the more society becomes quite literally disintegrated. Social cohesion, shared meaning and purposive association become splintered into a mass of private idiosyncrasies, united paradoxically only by a common interest in self and structured by little other than market forces. Occasions designed ostensibly for communication or co-ordinated action (meetings and conferences, for example) become merely opportunities for the serial utterance of isolated views: all people share is a chance to speak out into a public space eerily devoid of receptivity, flat and without echo. To gain fleetingly a 'high profile', to be famous for fifteen minutes, to air your view, to flit momentarily across a television screen, is about the most use of public space one can ever hope to achieve. The radio phone-in which strings together a heterogeneous range of unrelated and totally inconsequential opinions provides a model of our shared world.

There is, in my view, little doubt that it is in the interest of the distal powers of a virtually global economy which depends on ceaseless growth, mediated more proximally by the complex disciplinary machinery of a managerial bureaucracy, to manufacture a mass consumership intent on its private satisfactions, trained to attribute its discomforts to 'internal' faults and failings, and detached from public 'forms' which might make possible an accurate critique of its situation. We are, however, entirely social creatures unable to live without common meanings (unless as a collectivity of mad people, which seems unlikely), and there are risks attached to exploitation on this scale.

There is a distinct danger that if 'form' disintegrates to the extent that the resulting famine of meaning becomes unbearable (as it might, for example, if our shared commitment to consumerism were frustrated by economic collapse) the fractured social collectivity would suddenly coalesce around 'forms' of a more sinister kind than those so far considered. By this I mean forms which are not so much social as biological, i.e., which are less the result of meaning through bodily *interaction* with the world than of our shared bodily structure alone. It does not seem implausible to suggest that a culture could become so impoverished of meaning (in respect of satisfactorily socially elaborated 'forms') that people would be thrown back simply on the demands and dictates of their physical needs and the basic, if not primitive, biological structures of sensation and emotion which fuel them.

Fright, anger, superstition and suspicion are prominent among the basic biological characteristics which we have in common, and it is surely no accident that when social cohesion can no longer be maintained through common allegiance to culturally sophisticated and highly developed categories of meaning, one witnesses the emergence of aggressive, magical and paranoid forms of social order – as for example in genocidal racialism, religious fanaticism and other forms of association round fundamentally irrational but emotionally highly charged systems of meaning. These do not stretch out in any attempt to engage with the complexities of a real environment, but rather reach back to cohere around the primitive physical engines of emotion which we all share – and *because* we all share them in such a basic way, such coherence can give rise to a sudden intensity which can be, as terribly destructive as it is, for those caught up in it, extraordinarily exhilarating.

CHAPTER FOUR

Case Study: The 1980s

The previous chapter attempts to sketch out a primarily theoretical account of the way in which the operation of social power may come to be reflected in individual experience – in particular the experience of distress. I hope that somewhat abstract discussion may have laid the ground for, and made more easily comprehensible, the concrete consideration to be offered in this chapter of how the processes involved may be played out in the actual events of a given time and place.

My central thesis is, of course, that individual, so-called 'psychopathology' cannot be understood out of the environmental context in which it occurs, and indeed cannot accurately be attributed to any pathological process *inside* people. It is, in fact, more correctly characterized as a pathology *of* the environment. One very obvious implication of this is that the 'symptoms' of 'pathology' will fluctuate and vary according to what is happening in the social environment, and it will not be possible scientifically to develop a system of classification which attempts to pin down for all time the nature of human psychological aberration. A purely biological approach, as, for example, in psychiatry, does attempt to do just that (and present-day efforts to arrive at a watertight classification of 'neurosis' and 'psychosis' are as energetically pursued within psychiatry as they were a hundred years ago). But variations in the expression of human distress are nowhere near as constant and reliably stable as are, say, the variations in botanical species which permit of the kind of classificatory system so envied by Kraepelin and his heirs.

The theoretical approach outlined in the previous chapter

makes it clear why this should be so: we do not so much have
a relatively constant physical environment providing a home for
a luxuriant variety of widely differing psychological specimens,
but rather a highly unstable environmental context seething with
often unspecifiable social influences in which people, at their core
more or less identical biological atoms, are tossed and turned,
shaped and constrained in an infinity of ways. When we, the atoms
in this social cauldron, give vent to the pain its vicissitudes cause
us, it is not because there is anything 'wrong' with our essential
make-up, but because there are, or have been, things in our
environment which would better not be there.

In seeking to understand these processes one may point, as I
have attempted to do in the last chapter, to the relatively stable
manner of their operation – the way, for example, in which
proximal relations mediate distal influences – but one cannot give
a lasting scientific description of their content, as this is constantly
in flux. Psychiatrists and psychologists have at times paused to
wonder over the fact that 'symptoms' of 'mental illness' change
over different generations – that, for example, the 'hysterical'
blindnesses and paralyses which apparently afflicted so many people
a century or so ago have now virtually disappeared – but they
have not fully absorbed the significance of this phenomenon. It
is not that the nature of personal pathology has undergone some
kind of mutation, nor that such 'symptoms' are not somehow
'real', but that changes have taken place in the kinds of social
influences which bear down upon us.

One cannot, then, hope to say anything eternally true about
the actual phenomena of our distress, the content of our pain.
We can only fight a kind of running battle to keep track of it.
For this reason, in trying to put flesh on the theoretical bones
mainly considered so far, I shall take as 'clinical material' not a
range of exemplary 'cases' intended to stand for all time as typical
instances of 'disease', but a *decade* – the 1980s – identifiable, I
believe, for a set of social-environmental influences which mark
it out from those immediately preceding it (though not perhaps

so distinctly from other decades earlier in this and in the last century). Because of the relativity of social space-time, I also have to limit my case study to a place – Britain. How far the observations to follow have relevance to other times and places I must leave it to others to judge, and whether the 1990s will be significantly different from the 1980s must also remain to be seen.

The fact that it is most essentially the environment which is the source of our troubles does not mean that it does not affect us, at distinct points of space and time, in ways which have a certain discernible regularity. While men and women in distress should not, for the reasons I have given, be categorized as instantiating 'psychopathology', they may nevertheless show recognizable similarities as being victims of a similar fate. In this way 1980s Britain can be approached from two aspects which I shall consider here separately: the environment itself, and its principal effects on the people who inhabit it (the characters it affects).

I THE ENVIRONMENT

There are people far more able and qualified than I to give an account of the wider sociological perspective on how 'postmodern' culture, politics and economics burst upon Britain towards the end of the 1970s (see, for example, David Harvey's admirable *The Condition of Postmodernity*). Much of the more limited perspective that I can offer has been gained through the eyes – not to mention the sensibilities and pain – of the characters who provide the models for the second part of this chapter. From their proximal struggles with a world which most of them saw as the creation of their own inadequacy, I have, I think, been able to discern the operation of more distal influences giving rise to a common culture.

The furthest that reflective people who have lived through this decade were likely to see as they tried to make out the shapes of influence at the edge of their power horizon was the silhouette of Margaret Thatcher and her entourage of apparently unusually ruthless and determined enthusiasts for economic liberalism, the results of the abolition of 'welfarism' and 'socialism', and the restructuring of Britain according to a philosophy of self-reliance and the relentless pursuit of personal interest. However, even the most cursory glance at the literature of social criticism stemming from the USA – or even merely superficial attention to events in the American political arena – quickly lengthens the perspective.

Margaret Thatcher and her government were merely representatives of a culture which had been flourishing in the Western world long before it made its presence so forcibly felt in Britain. The political influence was not the origin of this culture, but the concentration of power which gave it impetus. The Thatcher government were not the originators but the engineers – the managers – of powers which had already thoroughly dominated the other side of the North Atlantic for some time, and were now blowing across it in a gale. Indeed, what brought Thatcher's downfall just after the close of the decade was not her failure as a politician but her failure as a manager. She was too much of an individualist, and had become an obstacle rather than an enabler of the powers whose path she had up till then done so much to smooth. She was replaced by a man who was barely a politician at all in the sense of having a personal vision or a passionate commitment to an ideal of societal organization – he was quintessentially General Manager (UK).

It is extremely difficult even for the reasonably well-educated, well-informed person possessed of access to some of the more distal powers which social advantage confers to penetrate the murky depths of power which the politics of Western democracies screen. All one can tell with any certainty is that economic conglomerates whose power cannot even accurately be measured (if only because they operate beyond the boundaries of any one authority competent to do the measuring) set in motion interests which are fertilized and nourished by the social conditions in which they take root.

Huge cross-national companies dependent for their survival on ever-increasing expansion float round the global market like giant economic icebergs, crashing into and fusing with each other, while the waves they make are absorbed, and eventually controlled and directed by armies of producers, consumers and enablers (managers) who will typically be located in those parts of the world best designed for their function.

The processes of production and the kinds of alienation and exploitation they involve – and which so preoccupied sociologists and political economists of the last half of the nineteenth century and the first half of this – have to a great extent drifted out of the sight of the citizens of affluent Western nations. This is, of course, by no means because they have ceased to exist, but because they have been exported to parts of the globe where labour can be bought more cheaply and conditions of production controlled less scrupulously. While so far as Britain is concerned this has had little visible effect on the ideology of class, it has certainly made some difference to the actual class structure. People ideologically labelled 'working class' became during the eighties far less likely than formerly to be members of an organized, self-consciously unionized industrial workforce, and were, in fact, either likely not to be working at all (becoming part of an 'underclass' existing outside the formal economic structure) or to be engaged in some form of industrially unproductive work, quite possibly in a role to be seen as to an extent 'upwardly mobile'. There was also on the labour market a steadily increasing number of people who had gained formal qualifications in subjects (social sciences, business and media studies, etc.) which led them to expect employment in some form of managerial or other 'white collar' capacity.

The population of countries such as Britain thus became more preoccupied either with the business of consumption, from the point of view both of fulfilling the unwritten duties of consumer and of maximizing the opportunities for others to do so (swelling the ranks of the 'service industries'), or with mediating the complex social powers which the global as well as national economies demanded. While these two roles – those of consumer on the one hand and mediator on the other – can be separated from each other only with a degree of artificiality, I shall for the sake of clarity consider them here one at a time.

The Mediators

The impress of distal power shapes and engages with the interests already structuring social organization in such a way as to carry through its projects with the minimum of resistance. The social revolution which took place almost anonymously in Britain in the eighties took advantage of the proximal needs, aspirations and self-perceptions of a relatively (in global terms) affluent and well-educated populace in order to render the country as a whole far more responsive than it had been to the imperatives of big business. To move money quickly and easily, to dissolve obstacles in the way of rationalization of working practices, and, perhaps most essentially, to expand the scope and influence of the market, meant the wholesale and ruthless removal of as much as possible of the pre-existing social institutions and ideology identifiable as incompatible with these aims. This was to be the Business Revolution, and in order to achieve its aims not only would existing business people be enthusiastically recruited to the cause, but nonbusiness people would have to be – sometimes, but in fact surprisingly seldom, more reluctantly – re-shaped and retrained into *becoming* business people.

A significant part of the ideology of 'postmodernism' or 'postindustrialism' was designed to loosen allegiance to 'outmoded' intellectual, philosophical and ethical systems which threatened to impede the permeation of every level of society by business concepts and practices. The bluntly calculating language of accountancy – the 'bottom line' of costs and benefits – had first to oust and then to take over the function of 'old' concepts such as 'goodness' and 'truth'. There can, I submit, be almost nobody reading these pages who was not in some way or other during the eighties caught up in or affected by the extraordinary upheavals which attended the ideological as well as the more crudely material triumphs of the revolution. To some extent or other we all helped to mediate these processes; we had no choice.

To replace with the values of the market, within the space of a decade, the ideology of a social system which at least purported to be based on the values of truth, justice and equality traceable back to the Enlightenment was no mean achievement. Its accomplishment demanded three main thrusts:

1. The application of raw (coercive and economic) power at the distal region of the political system. Here Mrs Thatcher obliged with a ruthlessness scarcely experienced in the memory of postwar generations. The breaking of the unions following the repression of the miners, the remorseless 'rationalization' of heavy industry and the engineering of mass unemployment, the dismantling of the structures of welfare and protection for the poor and the weak, and the deregulation of any system which offered either economic or intellectual privilege of any kind (for example protection against economic competition; professional freedom of self-determination), set in motion the conditions for a radical insecurity more than sufficient to induce the co-operation of the entire population in realization of the aims of the brave new business world.

Since my central aim is to explicate the way distal power becomes mediated proximally as psychological or emotional distress, I shall not consider its origins and dynamics in any greater detail here. This should not, however, lead us to ignore its enormous importance; without the application of such distal power the following discussion would have been neither necessary nor possible.

2. The construction of a high-level, articulate and defensible intellectual rationale. It is here that we encounter the intelligentsia of 'postmodernity'. I must admit that I find it difficult to discern the nature and significance of the role of those who managed to lay the foundations of a superordinate philosophy which

scornfully swept aside the Enlightenment values we have
supposedly misled ourselves with for the past two hundred years.
I would not for a moment suggest that those who attacked our,
apparently, pathetic notions of abiding truth (Richard Rorty),
reality and objectivity (François Lyotard), or individual integrity
in thought and idea (Jacques Derrida), somehow colluded with
distal powers to become apologists for their aims. Nor, to tell
the truth, am I sure how much their activities really mattered,
especially as part of the achievement of the Business Revolution
was to discredit and dilute the value and power of intellectual
activity itself. However this may be, the result of the new
pragmatism was to help remove from the ideological pipeline any
awkward little lumps or bumps likely to prove resistant to the
smooth flow of endlessly recyclable, critically unstoppable, always
expansible market rhetoric. A world without truth is an adman's
dream, and, when it comes to respect for truth, there was left
following the revolution almost no distinction between the most
exalted strata of the academy and the most banal fabrications of
television advertising.

In large part, I suspect, the intellectual respectability which
'postmodernism', 'deconstruction' and so on, gave, perhaps
unwittingly, to the operation of the market was generated by the
influence upon Academe of the market itself. Under market
pressures, 'truth' either becomes diluted into the endlessly
multipliable uncritical jargons of a half-educated mediocracy (see
below), or else it becomes impacted and squeezed into the
fearsome locutions of those superintelligent, hypererudite
academics who, to succeed in a university knowledge industry
where there is simply not enough truth to go around, must spin
ever more ingenious and rarefied critical visions out of a strictly
limited stock of basic themes. Hence, for example, the popularity
among literary theorists of the speculations of psychoanalysis or
'poststructuralism' which, respectively, suggest that meanings are
not what they appear to be, and that ideas are not attributable
in any significant sense to the people who had them. It is not

so much that such conceptions are necessarily wrong or intellectually valueless, but that, to sustain and elaborate the academic market, good faith is likely to give way to the cultivation of novelty. Intellectual debate at the highest level becomes but a high-flown variation on the 'new blue whitener' theme invented to boost the flagging sales of an already perfectly adequate detergent.

The upshot of all this, anyway, was that during the eighties the academy became no longer the refuge of disinterested seekers after truth, nor somewhere to go in search of resistance to Business values. This may, in fact, have been a much more serious loss than might be suggested by the rather equivocal position occupied by intellectuals in the power structure of the Business Revolution. It seems probable that part of the, perhaps unconscious, appeal to many people of the revolution itself was its irreverence towards various kinds of 'professionals' – not least university teachers – who had formerly been able to take advantage of a deferential respect they undoubtedly (because they are human) did not always earn. Whatever the occasional pomposity and impracticality of their occupants, however, the universities had nevertheless been the guardians of some of the most central and essential 'forms' of post-Enlightenment society. The dilution of the concept of truth and the redefinition of knowledge as a ready-made commodity in which people may be trained (rather than as something to be *discovered* by people who have the ability, the time and the necessary patronage to look for it) threatened to make higher learning into a mere extension of shop-floor instruction and to remove from it the possibility of developing any kind of critique of the business culture.

Business must dispense with truth if it is to avoid limits on its expansion and to be able ceaselessly to invent new needs. It has, indeed, a concept ready made to slip into the place of truth – fashion – which far more adequately suits its books. It can, furthermore, happily substitute training for the pursuit of knowledge since its aim is a) to maintain a technology of management by managers who do not reflect upon their role, and b) to instruct a mass consumership in the technology of consumption. It will, it is true, need to preserve an essentially scientific/technological élite in Research and Development, but it has no use for the humanities except as markets. It will also prefer oblivion to history, since fashion can be recycled more quickly if everything seems 'new'. All in all Business can do without higher education, and if given half a chance, as the 1980s demonstrated, will do.

3. The installation of a social apparatus of proximal mediation: i.e., of those whose task it was to convey the influence of the distal 'revolutionary' powers to men and women in the street. In order to slide into place anything so one-track minded and ethically and intellectually impoverished as the Business Culture, there are required towards the practical and ideological base of the social pyramid multitudes of willing workers. It would be utter madness to suppose that revolutions such as these are achieved through the connivance of a vast officialdom in the *conscious* exploitation of the mass of the citizenry. What is needed, rather, is the enthusiastic co-operation of well-meaning – even altruistic – people in a project they are fully able to believe in. Once someone is convinced that his or her 'motives' are of the best, he or she can be happily recruited to literally any kind of cause (it may be paradoxical but it certainly isn't even improbable that concentration camp guards really *could* be nice people).

The explanation for the paradox – for the involvement, that is, of benign people in malign activities – is, of course, to be found in our mistaken attribution of the reasons for things to the interior motives and impulses of the people who enact them. As far as the Business Revolution was concerned, there were at the end of the seventies armies of people whose best intentions could easily be invoked as their various interests were engaged in the revolutionary cause. Many of these people already formed part of the business world; others, products of an expanded tertiary education system, were massing at the boundaries of established professional territory, not quite possessing the élite credentials for entry, but close enough to be convinced that given a chance they could do at least as good a job. Self-confident, eager for opportunity, ready to serve and poised for what could only be seen as a thoroughly deserved slice of upward mobility, this vast class of mediators suddenly found itself, once the gates of the established social institutions and professions gave way, rushing into the positions which were waiting for it. The rule of the mediocracy had begun.

A Business society built solely on the imperatives of economic rationality and consumerism could not be run by a hypocritical cadre composed of people consciously compromising the 'old' values of goodness, truth and justice. It had rather to make use of people only half instructed in the traditional culture, sufficiently blissful in their ignorance to install the simple-minded precepts and practices of monetarism and the 'classless society' with absolute conviction. Attachment to knowledge, scholarship, ethical reflection and analysis, logical or epistemological scrupulosity, was a definite impediment to the Business world, and those foolish enough not to relinquish such attachments voluntarily were likely to find themselves the objects of intensive training courses which, whatever the 'package' of 'skills' they pretended to impart, were really forms of instruction in the financial, commercial and promotional languages of Business.

Business language, Business mores, Business fashions and 'lifestyles' surged during the eighties into every stratum of British social life. University lecturers found themselves abandoning corduroys and pullovers for smart dark suits and flowery ties; previously anonymous clerks and typists turned, overnight it seemed, into the power-dressed houris of the television series *Dallas*. Doctors found themselves studying business systems rather than case histories; teachers became preoccupied less with lessons than with 'income generation'.

To those who enjoyed their new activities, perhaps their participation seemed like an act of personal choice – certainly many seemed to embrace the new culture as if they'd been waiting for it all their lives. To many others, however, the new era dawned as in a dream, an almost-nightmare in which they donned their shoulder-padded jackets and forced their ethical conceptions into the ledgers of accountancy with a sense of stunned unreality: they seemed to *want* to do these things (else why would they be doing them?) but felt nevertheless painfully out of tune with themselves. Yet others found themselves unable to cope with the demands of daily life and looked around for help.

Most interesting of all, almost nobody seemed aware that the world had radically changed and that a revolution had taken place. It was just life, from day to day. This does not mean that the revolution was achieved without anguish. Bloodless it may have been. Largely unremarked upon it certainly was by the vast majority whose view extended little further than the ambit of their own domestic lives. But it was certainly not achieved without cost in terms of distress and personal disintegration.

The composition of the 'mediocracy' closely reflected the principal concerns of the culture. Alasdair MacIntyre[1] wrote compellingly right at the beginning of the decade on the significance of managers and therapists to a social world which had abandoned virtue, and Robert Bellah et al.[2] again highlighted the role of these two groups in maintaining what they call the utilitarian individualism of American culture. Certainly management on the one hand and therapy and 'counselling' on the other are among the most prominent components of modern mediocracies. One should also note the important ideological role of the advertising and promotional industry, as well as the essential disciplinary function of what Christopher Lasch[3] has called the 'tutelary complex': those whose job it is to set and maintain the normative standards of society, including counsellors and trainers of various kinds and extending deep into the fields of education

---

1. See his *After Virtue*, 2nd ed., Duckworth, 1985.
2. *Habits of the Heart*, Hutchinson, 1988.
3. *The Minimal Self. Psychic Survival in Troubled Times*, Pan Books, 1985.

and social work. All such people stand between the individual and the world in order to mediate his or her experience of it in accordance with the aims of a Business Culture. For the most part these aims are twofold: to establish the ideology of the culture and to extend the market.

MANAGEMENT

The 'manager's right to manage' was a prominent slogan of the early part of the decade, and certainly the managers' role in forcing into place the disciplinary and instructional apparatus of the revolution was crucial to its success. Traditional methods of assessing vocational ability and professional competence, embedded institutional practices of hiring and firing, long accepted (even if unspoken and unwritten) rules concerning the rights and duties of employers and employed were suddenly replaced by new definitions of competence, formal systems of appraisal, restrictions on information and communication, and authoritarian lines of accountability. These 'new' systems of discipline and surveillance, backed by the very real threat of unemployment, were usually introduced as the spin-off of reorganization and change, and extended across the entire working world forms of uncertainty and insecurity which had previously been the lot only of an exploited industrial workforce.

Virtually no place of work escaped the upheavals of reorganization: large public institutions in health and education, small family businesses, public and private companies of every size and description seemed to be overrun by management consultants advising on change and trainers instructing in its accomplishment. The besuited managerial group having a 'time out' weekend at an expensive country club could equally well turn out to be the board of a large engineering firm, a group of NHS administrators, or the senior academic staff of a university department. Everyone who wasn't made redundant underwent a change of role or a change of rank, everyone was taught the new language of efficiency and effectiveness, quality control, appraisal and time management. Everyone, no matter who or what, was sent on a course. I met a telephone engineer in a Dublin guesthouse who was just completing a five-day course on 'the management of change' – he was, he said with a wonderfully ironic smile, due to take his retirement in six weeks' time.

If the aim of this managed upheaval in the lives of almost everyone was intended to realize the claims of its superficial rhetoric – that 'time' could be 'managed', for example – it could only be considered a disastrous failure, for the most likely sequel to 'training days' was organizational chaos. If, on the other hand, its actual achievements – of disconcerting, disorientating, and rendering the workforce receptive through sheer vulnerability to the new business ideology – if these were its real intentions, then it was an immense success. The sublime confidence with which the managerial mediocracy imposed its debased language of 'performance indicators', 'Total Quality', and so on, on people who had all their lives spoken, albeit uncritically, a far more ethically nuanced language left them conceptually completely off balance.

The captives of the mediocracy thus struggled (often with surprising good will and docility) to force the previously unarticulated complexity of their experience into the linguistic moulds imposed by the hyped-up banalities of Businessese. To a puzzling extent they seemed unaware that rather than being offered a 'whole new way' of 'developing their management skills', or whatever, they were in fact being robbed of the linguistic tools to express the violence being done to their understanding. Their docility – indeed their often apparently eager compliance – in this process is, however, only puzzling if one forgets that people judge intention on the basis of proximal relations, not distal objectives. Managerial mediocrats are often very nice people, completely unaware of the sources of the power they are mediating, and it's hard to take exception to their activity if you locate the reasons for it somewhere behind their kind and obviously well-meaning eyes.

The mediocracy maintains the credibility of its managerial rule, as well as the ultimate viability of its enterprise, by exploiting the knowledgeable. It cannot, of course, become knowledgeable itself without ceasing to be mediocre. The exploitation of knowledge is achieved in two main ways. The first is through the importation into the business enterprise of outside consultants; the second is through the direct exploitation of 'inhouse' technical or professional knowledge.

The explosion in the use of management consultancy and training organizations during the eighties was at first sight hard to understand, not least as their employment seemed to run counter to the expressed management aim of cost-cutting. One thing that systems consultants, advisers on information technology and trainers in all kinds of personnel management functions were not was cheap. However, a closer examination of the relations between mediocratic managers and their consultant advisers reveals some interesting ideological gains for the former. In fact, technical consultancy was one of the principal tools through which the mediocracy could maintain managerial control without disclosure of its own ignorance. Technical and professional knowledge becomes 'mystified' as something which no manager could be *expected* to have, but which needs to be subject to management control through the exercise of economic power. Managerial 'expertise' thus becomes quite detached from technical know-how, which it makes economically subordinate – its servant rather than a necessary requirement of its own function. Not only, then, is mediocratic management protected from recognition of its own mediocrity, but it places itself in a relation of control over the technical knowledge which might otherwise threaten it. Business, in other words, can take over professional knowledge without having to go to the trouble of actually acquiring it.

One of my reasons for dwelling on this phenomenon is because of the 'pathology' it gave rise to in the eighties. Among the casualties of the working environment were to be found competent and successful professional and technical employees of both public and private concerns who had previously scarcely been represented at all in the typical clientele of clinical psychology. People who had formerly occupied positions of respect and influence suddenly found themselves sidelined by a mediocracy which first usurped their managerial function and then maintained its position by importing (at enormous, and what appeared to be unnecessary, expense) hired 'experts' to perform the very same technical/professional functions, but on its own terms. Even where professional expertise was not subjugated through the device of consultancy, many people performing technical functions vital to the concerns of an organization but incomprehensible to the mediocracy managing it found themselves in a painfully ambiguous role of indispensability coupled with low status. In the second part of this chapter I shall introduce one or two of the characters typical of this newly exploited class.

It should, of course, be absolutely no surprise that the management of a 'reality' which must be opened up fully to the dictates of the market would ally itself to a propaganda machine. Business and advertising naturally belong together. What was perhaps surprising in the eighties was the extent to which promotional ideology infiltrated its methods and its language into every corner of the culture. The first coup was indeed the redefinition of reality itself. A 'real world' was defined as one in which the ruthless relations of the market reigned supreme. This was the world where nothing was for nothing and the weak went to the wall. Any world constructed on alternative ethical lines was stamped as outmoded, deranged or dangerous. The 'real world' was a hard, cold world of self-made success, virulent moralism, uncompromising individualism and pitiless contempt for sociality of more or less any kind. Having thus defined the world it wished to colonize, Business culture left it to the mediocratic promotional machinery to package it seductively and fill in the ideological details, and suddenly the language was full of market hype.

Not only were social issues and problems of every kind approached through the 'attitude change' mythology of advertising – everything from the training of the unemployed to the fight against AIDS – but even the most sober representatives of high culture found themselves declaiming the virtues of their wares in the manically urgent language of the supermarket. Works of art, scientific theories, affairs of state, medical treatments, courses of higher education, would all be 'sold' with the same tired combinations of fatuous hyperbole. Everything was major, new (usually 'major-new' as a kind of compound attraction), unique, massive, important, 'important-new' and exciting. 'Stunning' and 'awesome' appeared a little later. Mediocrity was clothed as 'excellence'. Scarcely any social or vocational practice or pastime could be envisaged which did not seem both designed and expected to engender a kind of frantic excitement; the prescribed mode of mediocratic life was one of the mediation and consumption of euphoria, and anyone who attempted to engage in any other kind of activity, or speak a milder or more considered language, stood in danger of finding him or herself beyond the boundaries of the real world.

The Orwellian irony of 'the real world' is particularly poignant in the light of the promotional impetus of the eighties towards make-believe. For while on the one hand it was a 'real world' of economic rationality and throat-cutting competition, on the other it was one of wildly proliferating market diversification which had to be promoted and stoked by multimedia propaganda. Everything from the political manipulation of demographic statistics to the spells and potions of the 'alternative health' industry was aimed at making people believe not only that the harsh consequences of economic exploitation didn't really hurt, but that the world was positively bursting with opportunity and choice.

Make-believe also performed the job of disguising the inevitable results of emptying the public purse into private pockets. As public assets were stripped and public services depleted of the personnel necessary to run them safely and efficiently, curiously transparent attempts were made to paper over the all too obvious cracks. Examples that spring to mind are the VDUs that appeared in railway stations giving arrival and departure times of trains the spuriousness of which only became apparent to the infuriated traveller after he or she had been wildly misled a couple of times. 'Visitors' Centres' would issue hopeful tourists with 'information' on local events and transportation seemingly inspired by simple fantasy. Anybody who, however well-intentioned, could make money out of an expanding market in promises and appearances did. Prominent among the practitioners of make-believe were also, of course, the therapists and counsellors.

THERAPY AND COUNSELLING

If managers can be seen as the Machiavellian mediators of a disciplinary insecurity which provided the basis for Business Culture, therapists and counsellors were foremost among its gullibly well-intentioned ideologues. This might in some ways be unfair to managers. Though some certainly were, and prided themselves on being, Machiavellian – their role models the unscrupulous manipulators of *Dallas* – most were probably convinced that they were performing a necessary and socially useful task. In the case of therapists and counsellors there can be little doubt that very nearly without exception they were utterly certain that their profession was solely concerned with the humane relief of suffering, and if 'sincerity' (that typically 'internal' eighties substitute for external reality and truth) could be taken as a valid index of social role, then the activities of counselling and therapy would indeed have to be acknowledged as above reproach. I have met hundreds of psychotherapists and counsellors of many kinds from all sorts of professional, semiprofessional and amateur backgrounds, and I cannot think of one I would accuse of conscious charlatanism. They provide, in fact, a marvellous example of the way our motives can remain pure while our interests are engaged in the pursuance of enterprises of which we are completely unaware.

It is very easy to come to believe that one has a special gift for counselling. 'I'm a good listener'; 'People seem to find it easy to tell me their troubles'; 'X said it was the first time she'd ever told anybody about that': these are the kinds of experience which set many of us on the road to becoming counsellors. Because we observe the pleasure and relief with which people react to our listening attentively to their troubles, we feel we have discovered within ourselves some special gift of healing. In truth, however, such is likely to be the experience of *anyone* of reasonable intelligence and good will who can shut up long enough to allow someone else to talk. What we take to be a personal prerequisite for our vocation is merely a universal human potentiality. What it does do, however, is provide us with the inner conviction we need to embark upon a career in which we may with the highest moral probity profit from the distress of others. (At this point I think I sense some rising gorges among my readership. Let me therefore emphasize as strongly as I can that I am *not* denying all validity, moral or scientific, to counselling and psychotherapy. I shall be considering their positive potential in the next chapter.)

We must distinguish, then, between the well-meaning but ingenuous beliefs of therapists themselves about the significance of their role, and their actual functions as part of the mediocracy. The first such function is precisely that of appropriating and marketing aspects of care and concern which should constitute a part of the everyday ethical life of any humane society. In the developed Western world there are likely to be very few people who perceive any incongruity in the professional provision of sympathetic listening, and indeed there may well be an enduring social necessity for the kind of dispassionate confessional role formerly more the province of priests. With psychotherapy, however, this role becomes specifically commercialized, and we are made most acutely aware of this when it comes to the opening up of new markets.

During the eighties there was a positive explosion in the expansion of the therapy and counselling industry in Britain. The deregulation of the health care market allowed professional groups, voluntary workers and a wide range of the 'brand name' schools of psychotherapy and counselling to gain access to 'treatment' which had previously been the preserve of medicine and one or two of its satellite professions. As part of this process the market was extended in several new directions, and 'counselling' – previously considered a minority practice of doubtful validity – suddenly became the self-evidently necessary antidote to occasions of distress which up till then people had just had to muddle through as best they could. A particularly good example of this extension of the frontiers of the market into the previously noncommercial territory of ordinary social intercourse was that of 'disaster counselling' and the development of the concept of 'post-traumatic stress disorder'.

The need for the provision of aid and comfort to those involved – victims and their families, professional rescue workers – in 'major incidents' such as transport accidents and sports stadium disasters can scarcely be seen as a matter for debate. What may be questioned, however, is *how* such aid and comfort may best be achieved, and what was remarkable during the decade under consideration was the entirely uncritical way in which the prevailing winds of Business swept aside the traditional 'coping mechanisms' of family, neighbourhood and Church to put forward as the most obviously proper response a professional network of counselling.

As the letter pages of many a professional journal testified, therapists and counsellors disputed heatedly each others' qualifications to attend the scene and advise on the aftermath of such events, while commercial groups rapidly formed to lay claim to special expertise. A whole literature concerning the particular psychological characteristics and consequences of disasters sprang into existence practically overnight, research grants were applied for, and treatment programmes hastily constructed and advocated for anyone who could conceivably be counted as a victim (even down to people who had been disturbed by witnessing events on the television). Not one of those professionally involved in this activity, I am perfectly ready to be persuaded, had in their heart anything but sympathetic pain for the injured and bereaved, and an ardent wish to help. But equally few, it seemed, stopped to consider that by their very activity – by standing between individuals and the world to mediate their pain and grief – they were a) claiming for Business a previously noncommercial social function, and b) offering a service for the effectiveness of which there was no particularly convincing evidence.

A social services pamphlet issued in response to an aircraft disaster defined 'normal feelings' likely to be experienced by relatives or friends of victims, for example: 'fear of "breaking down" or "losing control" ', 'guilt for being better off than others, i.e., being alive, not injured . . .' It outlined likely physical and mental sensations, for example: 'Privacy – in order to deal with feelings, you will find it necessary at times to be alone, or just with family and close friends.' It offered some practical 'dos and don'ts', for example 'DON'T bottle up feelings. DO express your emotions and let your children share in grief', and gave guidance on when to seek professional help, for example: 'If after a month you continue to feel numb and empty.'

Now my point is not that such advice is wrong or misguided – much of it indeed is obvious common sense – but that it breaks down public 'forms' of appropriate social conduct and offers them back to the individual reconstituted as commercially available professional knowledge. Unintentionally, of course, it alienates people from their own bodily sensations and mediates their experience by making its meaning dependent on professional interpretation. The person becomes unable to say to him or herself: 'This terrible experience has numbed me', but must say rather: 'What can this strange numbness mean? I must seek the explanation from an appropriately qualified expert.' Once the need (in this case for 'counselling') has been created, the consumership then establishes a demand. No longer confident in their ability to handle their own distress as part of a traditional social process, people demand the presence of counsellors as a right.

There may be readers who find my argument far-fetched. It is obviously helpful, they might say, for people in such dreadful circumstances to have available professional reassurance and help: that cannot be taken as an indication of some commercial conspiracy to rob them of an understanding of their own feelings. To this I would respond that of course I imply no conspiracy – conspiracy is far too 'proximal' an activity to account for the kind of process I am trying to clarify. What I can say, on the other hand, is that in my role as clinical psychologist I am daily confronted with people who depend on me to read the significance of their own feelings, and it must in some sense be in the interests of professions such as mine to increase their number.

It was not only an expanding market in the mediation of experience which therapists were able to take advantage of in the eighties. There was also a marked increase in the possibilities for mediating relationship. The somewhat staid Marriage Guidance Council transformed its 'image', renamed itself 'Relate', extended its sphere of operations and became altogether a much more businesslike organization. (Whatever your 'business' in the eighties, it was *de rigueur* to refurbish your image and adopt a new logo.) Marital counsellors, sex therapists and dating agencies became the respectable end of a market whose business was procuring, in one way or another, emotional and sexual 'fulfilment'.

'Relationships' had, in fact, to bear a heavier and heavier strain as they became billed as the main source of warmth, intimacy and satisfaction in a world which was otherwise more coldly competitive than it had been for decades (I have written about this at some length in my book *Taking Care*). It was, then, not surprising to find a growing army of professional advisers at hand to counsel those who found the strain too great and, once again, to imply thereby that the business of relationship was no amateur matter. Relations between parents and children received similar attention – the decade which 'discovered' child sex abuse, and set up around it an extensive network of professional surveillance and correction, also constructed programmes and packages of 'parenting skills' which could be bought off the peg.

The function (as opposed to the conscious intention) of this mediocratic caste of therapists and counsellors was not only concerned with expanding the market for mediation of experience and relationship. It also provided shock-absorption for a society in which emotional and psychological, as well as physical, damage was a necessary part of its economic and ideological policies. Unemployment, ceaseless radical change, diminished status and insecurity all took their toll in the workplace and strained the domestic relations of people whose only recourse was 'counselling'. Counsellors performed the ideological function of representing as proximal causes of distress which were in fact distal, and then offered comfort and advice to those who identified themselves as falling short of the norm in 'coping skills', the 'management of stress', etc. What was essentially distal economic coercion was represented proximally as a remediable personal failure, and counsellors occupied the space vacated by reason in this conjuring trick to create a substitute 'credibility'.

The bridge over the credibility gap was at times exposed as a rhetoric too obviously shaky for anyone to trust – for example the suggestion that lack of a job reflected merely the unwillingness to look for one – but more often it was held in place through a suspension of rationality which could be maintained only by a curious kind of sentimentality. Personnel managers of large firms instituting programmes of redundancy could, for example, seriously set up as a humane measure the provision of counselling to those affected. An insult added to an injury was thus presented – and surprisingly often accepted – as a 'package of care' for which the redundant employee should feel grateful.

An aspect of their role from which nearly all counsellors are able (via the mystified notion of 'motivation') to dissociate themselves is thus one of increasing the likelihood of the very social evils whose effects they are supposedly there to mitigate. They do, certainly, offer forms of comfort which are often gratefully received by those in distress (the shock-absorbing function), but they also, through an ideology of personal change which suggests that people have a choice over their predicaments, make the occurrence of such predicaments more probable. Just as the 'redundancy counsellor' legitimizes putting people out of work, so the 'debt counsellor' makes more likely the irresponsible extension of credit, and the 'disaster counsellor' renders more conceivable the operation of a 'risk economics' (another phenomenon of the eighties) which calculates the 'acceptable' limits of expenditure on safety.

The Consumers – Markets on Life's Way

Consumerism is, of course, not just a phenomenon of the eighties, but the necessary ideology of an economic system which depends for its survival on limitless expansion of the market. The logic of this system, its adamantine rationality, is inexorable, and its triumphant progress has spanned much more than a mere decade, but the special contribution of the eighties was perhaps to slacken the few remaining ethical brakes on the raw injunction to consume which lies at the root of, at least, affluent Western societies.

Even if the shreds of alternative ways of life remaining from religious and political systems which had placed convivial sociality higher than economic self-interest constituted by the beginning of the decade little more than a kind of desperate hypocrisy, they were in any case swept away by the assertions of a 'new right' which proclaimed its philosophy of competitive individualism with absolute confidence. There was, said Mrs Thatcher, no such thing as society. For individuals and families to grab what they could for themselves was presented, and widely accepted, no longer as selfishness or greed, but merely as the obvious and inevitable

– and in a sense therefore the most sensible and virtuous – thing to do.

In this way the 'forms' which (again, even if crumbling) had been held in place by traditional institutions of ethical guidance became openly discredited, and in their place were enshrined the values authorized by Business. Parallel with a stern new morality of cost-effectiveness and rigorous competition there grew up a kind of redeeming therapeutics aimed at the rehabilitation of greed. Counselling became available for people who felt inhibited about money, for example, sufferers might be encouraged to gaze lovingly at a ten-pound note, expressing their desire for and appreciation of it in a therapeutic group of others similarly afflicted. Life had for most people long been structured and shaped by the need for money and the craving for consumer goods. So far as Britain was concerned, the eighties simply made such concerns official and provided a formal ideological framework in which they could flourish.

The most important social function of the vast majority of the population of a country such as Britain is to consume. It is true, of course, that so far our lives as social beings are ordered, perhaps even fundamentally, by public 'forms' of morality which arise more from our common humanity than from the dictates of consumerism, but such 'forms' have become tacit, unofficial, and survive only as the embodied practice of a collectivity of *individuals* who no longer have access to any coherent, clearly articulated, statement of them. The only values which are made manifest to someone living an everyday life are Business values.

During the eighties we became a monoculture in which just about every conceivable form of activity was appropriated by Business. Whatever was itself not business was sponsored by Business. The very language was adjusted in such a way as to strip people of any role other than that of being clients of Business. At various junctures, for example, both 'passengers' (on the railway) and 'patients' in hospital were redefined as 'customers'. Activities which had formerly had a special identity of their own became disorientatingly subordinated to Business – anyone who travelled on a cross-Channel ferry, for instance, will know how the concept of 'voyage' was converted into a kind of floating retail opportunity. Even isolated individuals became walking advertisement hoardings as more and more ordinary items of clothing were manufactured to carry a written commercial message. Empty churches became converted into supermarkets. The person's lifecycle came more obviously than ever to be marked less by the social and spiritual significance of events than by their market implications. From cot to coffin, the stages of life derived their meaning as much from the typical pattern of purchasing they involved as from any consideration of what Ivan Illich has called 'conviviality'.

Just as the yearly cycle is marked by a series of consumerist celebrations – birthdays, holidays, Christmas, etc. – so the course of our lives has tended increasingly to be demarcated more clearly by the spending sprees they give rise to than by their significance as social rites of passage.

The childhood preoccupation with 'toys' is a good example of this. Given a chance to talk to and occupy themselves with the adults around them, most children are fairly indifferent to toys. However, in a world in which those adults are themselves busily preoccupied with their own corners of the market, children have less chance of socializing than of learning the arts of consumership in their own specially prepared world of toys. Not only do they receive, from the moment their eyes can focus, a training in the acquisition and rapid obsolescence of consumer goods, but they are also inducted into a world of make-believe which offers virtually limitless market opportunities and which may very well serve to detach them for life from any commercially undesirable anchorage in the realities of social existence. For almost all our lives, our market-induced fantasies of how our relations with others, as well as the main events of life, should be tend to obscure the actuality.

There is, in fact, no recess of personal life, however intimate, immune to the intrusion of the market. Sexuality is a case in point. Early in adolescence the addictive power of male sexuality is commercially harnessed to a marketed female insecurity to create a model of 'relationship' which leaves both boys and girls – and later young men and women – at times incapable of controlling and almost always unable to understand both their sexual feelings and their need for intimacy. At worst, youths are reduced to barely articulate chunks of erectile muscle, quartering the Friday night streets in an alcoholically heightened expectation of finding girls they can fuck in a car park somewhere – girls who, again at worst, signal, probably unconsciously, a raw seductiveness no less market-inspired than the romantic love they actually crave. These can appear as people emptied out of their humanity, enacting like sleepwalkers fantasies in which they have been soaked ever since they were small children. They are, of course, not empty of humanity at all. They are like everyone else, human bodies subject to all the pains and longings which are common to human bodies. The difficulty is that they have learned no ways of giving expression to and elaborating their embodied humanity other than those constructed and promoted by the commercial interests of Business.

Very few people have the confidence any longer to allow their subjective experience of their bodies to guide an understanding of their 'relationships'. A woman who doesn't *feel* as sexually rapacious as the heroines of her husband's videos is often easily persuaded that there is something ('frigidity') the matter with her. She is far less likely to take her body as a valid index of the state of her intimate environment than she is to regard it as a substandard commodity. Many women find themselves conforming with a kind of weary despair to the fantasy-infused sexual expectations of their male partners authorized as 'normal' by a commercial world which relentlessly fetishizes sex. And men, as much deprived of an understanding of their own needs for tenderness as of the arts of expressing it, become totally mystified by their female partners' ultimate disgust with and fear of sex. The market defines as 'abnormal' (and hence in need of further consumer activity) states of social and interpersonal being which are an inevitable part of virtually everyone's experience, but which, like not wanting sex, offer no other market opportunity.

It is, of course, not difficult to identify the particular markets which give definition to the various milestones of our lives. In some of the more obvious festivals of the consumerist lifecycle, social rituals seem, in fact, to have given way almost entirely to commercial ones. Marriage, for example, seems more or less to have disintegrated as a meaningful social 'form': its rules, its function, its moral and societal significance are curiously difficult to define or state. By contrast, the consumerist aspect of marriage as 'wedding' has gained a ceremonial precision as elaborate as that of any arcane religious rite. From the wedding dress to the placecards for the reception tables, from the purchasing of the rings to the bridesmaids' bouquets and the booking of the video, the business of getting married has taken on a demanding, deadly earnestness which all but eclipses any other social meaning the act may have. It is almost not too outrageous to suggest that we are close to being able truthfully to say that the point of getting married is to have a wedding.

Infancy and old age are alike in exempting the subjects themselves from being targets of the market – to qualify for that one needs to have some spending power. It is, of course, not difficult to exploit the pride and pleasure of young parents in their new baby (even competing with breast milk may be not so much a defeat as a challenge), but the market opportunities offered by old age have to be established less directly.

Any doubt about the principal function of the elderly in late-twentieth-century British society will be quickly resolved by a glance at their bedside tables or bathroom cabinets. The arrays of bottles of medicine, boxes of pills, inhalers, creams, powders and unguents to be found there give plentiful evidence of the value of old people to our economy. Not to mention all the other institutions of the health care industry (day centres, nursing homes) which will, as chance would seem to have it, in all probability manage to extract their (if not their carers') last penny just before they die.

'Cynical', did I hear someone say? The predicament of the old gives the starkest testimony imaginable to the spiritual profligacy of our way of life. We have no use for their knowledge, for their memory, for their humour or for their love. We leave them as isolated as we dare in cold and lonely rooms where the most they are likely to have for company is a cat, or a weekday visit from the district nurse. And, just as we talk most animatedly about our holidays, or our cars, or our microwaves, they will tell us, if they get the chance, about their operations, their pills, and the progress of their leg ulcers. My point is not a moralistic one intended to stir up shame or inspire new resolves to care. It is rather to indicate the structure of the boat we all find ourselves in, and in which, individually, we shall all eventually founder.

Because the stages of life are given meaning by the consumerist 'forms' which place them in relation to a particular market, and because distal influences are inevitably experienced as proximal or 'internal' events, it follows that a breakdown in the power of the market will be experienced as *personal* breakdown. There is, in fact, one stage of life where the market does seem, at least partially, to lose its grip in this way. The 'mid-life crisis' is not so much a personal breakdown as the temporary absence of a market structure to distract and absorb the energies of post-child-rearing, middle-aged people who have suddenly found themselves confronted by a world which offers little to preoccupy them other than the approach of old age and death. What inevitably feels like a personal hiatus may thus more meaningfully be understood as a gap in the market.

The untapped market opportunities offered by middle-aged people at the height of their economic strength, but no longer with dependent children to expend it on, have not gone unnoticed in the commercial world, but even so it seems peculiarly difficult to identify and exploit a set of needs powerful enough for people in this position to dedicate their lives to satisfying. In this respect middle age contrasts interestingly with adolescence. The insistent self-concern and blossoming sexuality of the adolescent, though often painful enough, are immediately engaged by a market designed to define and exploit them. Through a wide and highly elaborated range of popular cultural media the young person is invited, seduced and bludgeoned into a garish supermarket which positively explodes with sights and sounds offering meanings for his or her feelings and retailing satisfactions of his or her needs. The middle-aged person, on the other hand, steps into no such emporium of excitement. On the contrary, he or she emerges from a marketplace centrally concerned with parenting and family life, and all the consumerist activities associated therewith, into a suddenly silent, almost empty space likely to fill him or her with a mixture of loneliness and confusion.

In the absence of any guidance from the environment about how to conduct their lives – in the absence, that is, of recognizable consumerist 'forms' – middle-aged people have a limited range of options. One is simply to become relatively inactive, self-absorbed and 'depressed', perhaps looking back nostalgically to happier days. Another is to shake free of market influence and become engaged in activities which have social, political or spiritual significances not (yet) easily appropriated by Business (this, of course, is the aspect of mid life addressed with considerable distinction by C. G. Jung). A third is to recycle the activities and preoccupations of earlier phases of the market – the 'second time around' phenomenon which certainly enticed a significant proportion of 1980s middle-aged males.

The seeming inevitability with which so many men during the eighties found themselves circling back to the age of twenty-five almost as soon as they hit the age of forty was on the whole, however, not matched by their spouses. While these middle-aged men, seemingly in droves, departed the family home to set up all over again with women almost young enough to be their daughters, their deserted wives had for the most part no such opportunity. Largely excluded from a sexualized market place which fetishizes only youthful female bodies, no longer centrally necessary to their grown-up or nearly grown-up children, their only possibilities were bitter resignation or, if strengths acquired in their young days were sufficiently developed, a kind of breakthrough into independence and a degree of spiritual self-sufficiency. If one can envisage one class sufficiently extricable from the web of Business Culture to form the core of a counter-revolution, it would probably be that of middle-aged women.

As things are, the market does indeed show signs of trying to organize itself for the middle-aged, and the more it succeeds in doing so, the less, I predict, will be the incidence of 'mid-life crisis'. So far, however, market provision for this age group does not seem particularly imaginative: not much beyond invitations to invest and manage money, buy time-shared holiday accommodation, private health insurance and personal pension plans. Rather surprisingly, the British consumership, during the eighties anyway, still seemed relatively resistant to the option of reconstructing youth through cosmetic surgery, chemistry and prosthesis, though no doubt there was expansion in that direction. Aggressive marketing, one might have thought, might have bitten the ethical bullet and, through PR and promotional campaigns, more actively have developed an advocacy of mid-life divorce and recycled younger adulthood (or at least make-believe versions thereof). On the whole, however, the middle-aged are still a relatively unexploited group, and as such are likely to continue to feel uncomfortably dislocated from market 'forms'.

Perhaps the most important theoretical lesson to be learned from the weakness of the market's hold on life in middle age is the fact of the ultimate dependence of consumerism on biology. If the person is to become locked into his or her essential role as consumer, then consumerist 'forms' have to be linked to biological need. It is, in the last analysis, the body which is seduced into the market's embrace, and it is ultimately the physical sensations of satisfaction which entice us into the glitteringly packaged world of consumer goods.

Consider a little vignette of the mid-1980s. The scene is an inter-city express from Nottingham to London. It is Saturday. A young family distributes itself round one of the tables. A slightly punky young woman with spiky blonde hair, perhaps in her late teens; a young man maybe a year or two older, thick set, with short-cropped hair, a sleeveless T-shirt revealing tattooed biceps and love-bitten neck; a boy of about five, short fair hair and a hard, shrewd gaze; a girl of about nine, apparently too old to be the couple's daughter, with bleached, in places bruised, skin, and an apparently permanent expression strangely compounding supplication and complaint. The table, the rack above them and parts of the seats not occupied by their own bodies are taken up with holdalls and plastic bags. For the entire journey of nearly two hours the older pair converse not at all except to exchange invitations to eat, drink, smoke or hand tabloid newspapers and magazines to each other. The children squabble a little, complain a little, make the occasional demand. Central among the heap of plastic bags on the table is a huge, cumbersome ghetto-blaster which emits the ceaseless chatter and pounding rhythm of popular radio.

There is no point of the journey when all four of these people are not consuming. The plastic bags contain a seemingly endless supply of crisps and canned drinks, cigarettes and packaged sandwiches, plastic toys and puzzle books. Incredibly, at about Bedford, the bags run dry and all four depart for the buffet car to replenish supplies, leaving the radio gabbling and thumping on the table. They are having a happy day out together – they seem relaxed and there is an affectionate quality to their relations which one senses is not always there (the bruises on the young girl's deathly white skin). Though there is very little interaction between them, they seem not disunited: indeed there is something almost determinedly exclusive in the intentness with which they consume, and they are as if encapsulated from the indignant gaze of those other customers of the railway who are forced to consume with them the DJ's babble and computerized 'music' (nobody dares intrude on the idyll – the tattoos and muscular arms bespeak a possible instability it would be unwise to test).

What is this activity which they seem so contentedly to be sharing while, actually, hardly communicating at all? The word springs irresistibly to mind: they are doing precisely what the radio's commercials so insistently recommend – they are 'enjoying'. The journey is one of uninterrupted enjoyment of tastes, sounds, tabloid scandal, the defloration of tantalizingly wrapped packages, the sucking in of tobacco smoke and the excited exploration of new plastic toys. Like piglets at a trough they are united in solitary enjoyment which graphically links physical craving with the 'satisfactions' designed to stimulate it.

Consumption on this kind of scale is, of course, not a matter of spontaneous choice, but is maintained by the institutions of a highly elaborated culture. Indeed, it would not be too far-fetched to identify the family in the train as members of a 'consuming class' which bids fair to replace in societal importance the old 'working class'. Consumption is, of course, not restricted to any one social stratum, but then neither was work. Just as the economy used not to be able to function without an industrial proletariat exploited for the purposes of production, so now, in countries such as Britain, it cannot function without a semi-employed proletariat exploited for purposes of mass consumption. 'Enjoyment' thus becomes the *social function* of the mass of society on which the Business economy depends.

It is certainly in this 'consuming class' that one observes the clearest dedication to, and most assiduous, if informal, training in, 'enjoyment'. There is, for example, likely to be far more emphasis placed on the importance of instant satisfaction in the consuming than in the mediating class. Consuming class people are more likely than their mediating class counterparts to feel an obligation to provide their small children with instant comforters like sweets, to provide the family with a restaurant-type service at meals (with an emphasis on *choice* both of dishes and of the time at which they are eaten), and to make the chief consumerist festivals like the summer holiday and Christmas into occasions for particularly lavish spending. The mediating class – successors to the 'old' middle class – will by contrast lay more stress on the importance of delayed satisfaction to occupancy of a social position which necessitates the exercise of managerial power.

The logic of a consumerist ideology which aims at exploiting the essentially physical capacity for enjoyment of a mass consuming class culminates inexorably in a process aimed at creating addiction. The ultimate market success is to exploit the properties of the human nervous system such that a stimulated 'excitement' is followed by 'instant satisfaction' in a maximally accelerated cycle. Food, drugs, alcohol, tobacco and sex clearly lend themselves admirably to the process of 'addictification', and the challenge to the market resides only in its refining and augmenting their addictive properties (the reduction of food to its most easily assimilable and basically appealing properties – 'fast food' – is an obvious example). Products less directly biologically linked may be sold on the basis of an association with an addictive bodily process: here one thinks immediately of the ubiquitous use by advertising of fetishized sex which has less and less time for romantic subtleties, employing a rapid series of sharp-focused sexual images which punch straight into the nervous system. Alternatively, products not obviously associated with primary biological needs may be rendered virtually addictive through appropriate processes of research and development. Popular music, for example, by being reduced in subtlety and aesthetic demandingness, electronically standardized, perfected, amplified and delivered through systems which cut out or obliterate competing stimuli, manages to hook the consumer into something approaching biological dependence. (To look at the rows of mesmerized customers flicking through the racks of tapes and CDs in the strangely dehumanized mass record emporia found in any city centre is to be reminded of other scenes of addiction – lines of solitary drinkers in 1950s Glasgow bars, for instance.)

Even cultural products designed for the mediating classes were during the eighties marketed increasingly on the basis of their biological appeal. Art, literature, drama and dance, as any recording of an arts review programme broadcast later in the decade is likely to testify, came to be constructed and appreciated on their ability to affect the nervous system of the consumer. The highest praise critics appeared able to bestow on an artistic or cultural production was that it excited, satisfied, moved, stunned or astonished them. Art is thus finally emptied of any pretension to social significance, and is reduced simply to a passive *experience* of an essentially physical state.

The ultimate Business logic is, then, to reduce the average member of the consuming class to an addict of the mass market, locked by the nervous system into an optimally cycled process of consumption, rendered immune to unprofitable distractions, dissociated from any form of solidarity which might offer resistance to the function of enjoyment. The vision is no doubt apocalyptic, but it is one the 1980s brought closer to realization.

Before turning to consider how some of the characters of the decade fared as it progressed, it may be of interest to use the structure of figure 3 in the previous chapter (page 74) to indicate how the theoretical consideration of environmental influence it outlines may assume the features of a given time and place. Figure 4 is thus an attempt to summarize diagrammatically much of what has been discussed so far in this chapter.

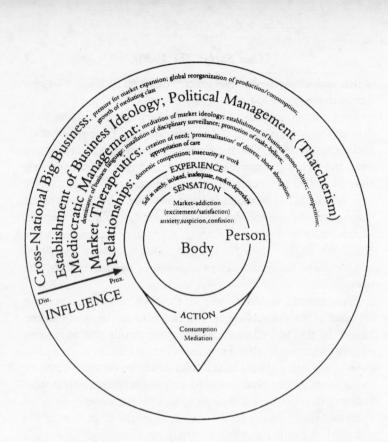

FIGURE 4: The generatioin of distress in the 1980s

II THE CHARACTERS

Character is, of course, not formed in or by a mere ten years, though certainly the *first* decade of life is likely to be immeasurably more important in this respect than all the rest put together. It is as yet too early to see what the contribution of the eighties might have been to the fundamental character formation of the very young, and I do not wish to imply that the people to be considered shortly, most of whom spent their childhoods in very different times, were irrevocably shaped by the eighties. They were, rather, presented with a problem by the events of the decade which coloured their experience and their conduct with a *characteristic* type of distress.

All six of the characters I shall be introducing felt themselves in some way inadequate to cope with their daily lives, and all blamed themselves for their perceived shortcomings. None considered that his or her difficulties could be attributed even partially to social influences typical of a particular time, and all expected to find what solution there might be to their predicament if not simply 'within' themselves, then certainly within the ambit of their most proximal relations.

A point in social space–time which laid *everybody* low would be unlikely to be seen as causing 'psychological' casualties either because the sources of everyone's distress would be so obvious or because there would be no basis for some people's comparing themselves unfavourably with others. Everyone would be in the same boat, and indeed might derive empowering solidarity from taking arms together against a sea of troubles. Would this not suggest, then, that for only a minority to be disturbed by the times, there must be something 'the matter' with the individuals who constitute it – some weakness not shared by those who cope more successfully?

In my view this would be as strange as concluding that there was something 'the matter' with people who caught smallpox as compared with those who didn't. A society which engenders casualties on any noticeable scale must be found wanting. In this respect the eighties were particularly significant since it was in this decade that all pretence of society's being for people was abandoned: it was now up to people themselves to survive the rigours of the 'real world', and no provision was to be made for 'lame ducks'. In fact, those who, without suspecting it, were injured by the times were far from being lame ducks – often, they were people whose sensitivity, social responsibility and sense of moral integrity rendered them particularly vulnerable to the dishonesty, superficiality and callousness of Business Culture.

It was inevitable that a decade which reintroduced a superficial version of social Darwinism would in a sense render some more 'unfit' than others to survive it unscathed, and if there is any common thread among the stories shortly to be told it is probably that of a lack in the provision in early life of the kind of confidence which, later, helps people to be reasonably certain of themselves in times of trouble. Again, however, I would argue that it is only a perverse view of society which would suggest that this 'goes to show' that the essential question is one of personal weakness: it should be the business of the public sphere to make allowance and where possible to compensate for the inevitable variations in and shortcomings of private experience (themselves, it must be remembered, established under the impress of *social* power), not to exploit and exacerbate them. The characters considered below were all making their way through life as well as it customarily allows until they were confronted *either* by some of the more baneful effects of Business Culture or by a disintegration of 'form' traceable ultimately to that culture.

THE ACCOUNTANT

Dave was slightly bewildered and certainly embarrassed to find himself talking to a clinical psychologist. He was a tall, friendly, good-looking man of thirty-seven. He was wearing a smart dark suit, expensive but not ostentatiously so. While he talked he fidgeted with the keys of his Volvo and looked at his watch at about ten-minute intervals.

His principal complaints were of pains in the stomach and feelings of numbness in the chest. 'My doctor reckons it's stress', he said, but it was fairly obvious from the way he said it that he himself was not so sure. He was more afraid that there was something seriously the matter with him physically, like a stomach ulcer or even a heart problem. He was keen to get to the bottom of things, but he was not used to talking about himself and clearly found it difficult to articulate the subtler features of his complaint. There were, for example, some rather odd aspects to his story which he was obviously as puzzled about as anyone else. He mentioned in passing that he was a keen squash player, and though he had worried about its effect on his physical condition, it had not apparently occurred to him actually to give it a rest for a while – in fact he was playing harder and more often than ever. It was as if, while he was afraid he'd got a heart condition, he actually in some sense knew he hadn't.

In total it took a couple of hours of conversation for a more coherent picture to emerge; coherent, that is, from the psychologist's perspective – though he was willing to give it serious consideration, Dave was not yet quite ready to acknowledge that that was the way things really were. His symptoms were in fact related to the imminence or anticipation of events which he dreaded; they were, that is, manifestations of fear. The events themselves were almost solely related to work, and involved largely two kinds of situations, the first in relation to confrontations with staff who were accountable to him and the second in relation to various kinds of meetings he had to attend, often to give a technical presentation of some aspect of the firm's accounting procedures.

As he began to assimilate and accept the notion that his feelings were to do with fear, Dave was able to reveal an additional problem which had been a considerable source of difficulty and shame. He was desperately apprehensive about driving long distances, especially on motorways. His firm had branches all over the country, and about once every month or six weeks he was likely, sometimes at short notice, to be summoned to a meeting at an office or factory perhaps two hundred miles away. He simply 'couldn't' drive on motorways – his back went rigid, his legs and feet ached so much he couldn't use the pedals properly. He sweated profusely, and started to feel terrifyingly cut off and distant, as if he was about to faint. He resorted to all kinds of subterfuges to avoid having to drive: often he could find a colleague to go with, sometimes he could on some pretext persuade his wife (whom he had not told about the problem) to drive him. If the worst came to the worst he would drive the whole way on secondary roads, which he could just about manage. Whichever way he did go, he arrived at his destination ragged with exhaustion and sick at the prospect of the meetings about to take place.

There were no great difficulties in Dave's home life. His wife had given up nursing to look after their three children, and now that the youngest was old enough she was looking for a part-time job. Their marriage seemed stable and affectionate, though Dave was guiltily aware of having become bad-tempered and less approachable over the previous eighteen months or so; he also had a rather brittle relationship with their oldest daughter, who he felt didn't help enough in the home or work hard enough at school. His wife worried about his symptoms, but knew next to nothing about their causes.

The puzzle, of course, was why Dave's difficulties should have come about when they did. And nobody was more puzzled than he. His success in his career, though not quite phenomenal, had certainly been unusual, and he had risen from a very junior to a pretty senior position within the firm in a very respectably short time, and it was not unreasonable to think of a directorship before too long. He had a secure family life and was socially well integrated. All his life he had enjoyed and was successful at competitive sports, and he and his wife had a wide circle of friends whose company they regularly enjoyed. And then, suddenly and for no apparent reason, he found himself living substantial parts of his life in near-crippling fear.

Someone in Dave's position seeking to understand the causes of his distress is likely to be thrown off the scent by the fact that nothing bad has happened. It is particularly difficult for a man whose life has been an uninterrupted story of success to countenance the possibility that success could itself be a problem. In fact, it transpired that Dave's troubles really started when he was promoted at work into a managerial role which involved the 'presentational skills' of 'image-making' as much as technical ability. Instead of being in charge, as he had been, of a large section of the firm concerned with the production of accounts, he found himself in a position in which he had to represent and explain the procedures involved to others inside and outside the firm as well as ensure that his subordinates carried out those procedures efficiently. He had had to transform himself from a technical expert, a role with which he felt entirely comfortable, into a boss and a front man, both of which roles were completely unfamiliar to him. Instead of making sure things got done by doing much of them himself, he now found that he was called upon partly to bully former equals into getting them done while himself having to represent the results to people (his bosses as well as clients) who were not technically qualified to understand them, but lived rather in a sphere of social influence and manipulation which was quite strange to him.

Dave had been the second oldest of five children, and the apple of his mother's eye. His father had worked as a plumber for a large construction company, and his mother was 'just a housewife', though her father had been manager of a small business. Dave, it seemed, had always been the cleverest of the two brothers and three sisters, and his mother had derived great satisfaction from his success in getting to grammar school. His father had been a quiet, passive man who rarely seemed to be at home during the children's waking hours and who apparently took little interest in his family; he drank fairly heavily and was obsessed with vintage motorcycles, with which he spent most weekends alone in his shed. His wife, though not overtly contemptuous of him, somehow conveyed to her son that she had little sympathy for his father in any particular respect, and Dave himself felt about him rather as of a distant and neutral acquaintance.

Dave did not particularly enjoy grammar school because it was distant from his home and he had few friends there, and felt 'a class below' those he did have. He was successful academically as well as at games, and not unpopular, but neither parent took a direct interest in his life there – his father because, in Dave's view, he had no interest anyway, and his mother because, he suspected, she felt overawed and diffident about getting involved in any way with the school. After passing A levels, the necessity to contribute to the family finances meant that he had to abandon hopes of going to university, and instead he joined his present firm as a junior clerk. He learned accountancy at night school and by correspondence course, and his intelligence and likeability soon set him on a successful path.

All went well so long as he was asked to be nothing other than a highly competent accountant leading a team of other accountants. He had little to do with the board of directors other than meeting requests for financial information. When the company was taken over in the early eighties by an international conglomerate, however, things changed. A new 'dynamism' was introduced in order to achieve a 'leaner, fitter' organization. Dave's old boss, who had been to an extent also his mentor, was made redundant, as were several of his colleagues, and those remaining were required to take on considerably more work. The new top management, as Dave came with only minimal encouragement to acknowledge, consisted for the most part of 'bullshitters' who knew little of the technical sides of the business, including accounting, and Dave found himself increasingly often having to frequent the expensively carpeted offices of board members who needed him to tell them what to say. He was called upon to help entertain clients in a world of fine wines and haute cuisine which he had never formerly encountered, and to attend meetings which demanded a 'high profile' of him since he was often the only one present who had any real grasp of the issues. At the same time, as a new-style 'manager', there came to him with the Volvo an obligation to mediate the demands which organizational leanness and fitness required – Dave had to badger and cajole, bully and threaten people who had previously been friends and colleagues into producing results there was in fact no time to produce.

Dave had never been one to thrive on confrontation. His whole life until the point of his promotion had taught him that success was achieved through conscientious work and amiable social relations. Nor was he one for high living; his was a modest background and he had always felt uncomfortable when out of his social depth, and he had never liked being the focus of attention in large groups. Furthermore, a reticence about emotional relations in his family, especially between his mother and father, had always made it difficult for him to talk about his feelings (there had never formerly been much need) and it did not occur to him that his wife would want to know about or wish to help him with the stress he was experiencing at work.

From his perspective it just seemed that he was failing, and possibly about to fail really spectacularly. He was respectful towards his bosses at work and did his best to learn the new game according to their rules, but the more he tried the more unfamiliar the world seemed and the more gauche and incompetent he felt. His knowledge that often what was being asked of him, and what he was having to ask of others, was impossible led him not to criticize the demand but to reflect even more despairingly on his perceived incompetence.

Because he was not much good at talking about his feelings, Dave was not much good either at talking *to himself* about them, and so he just experienced them as physical sensations, plus a nameless terror that overtook him on motorways.

THE SECOND-TIME WIFE

When her first really bad panic attack struck, Annette thought she was dying. It overcame her while she was waiting in the queue at a supermarket checkout. She left her trolley full of shopping and rushed out into the fresh air; she could scarcely remember how she got home. Her heart was pounding, she was sweating, trembling, unable to get her breath and terrified out of her wits. She suffered three more such attacks – all in exposed public places – before accepting her GP's suggestion that they were indications of anxiety rather than physical illness.

Annette's was not a privileged background. The oldest of four children, she had for as long as she could remember been largely responsible for her brother and sisters while her mother devoted herself to trying to accommodate and appease her husband. The latter – Annette's father – was a gregarious womanizer whose income went on entertaining himself, while his wife trailed round after him in a vain effort to gain his attention and keep his fidelity; when she was at home she complained endlessly and bitterly either to him or about him. Once in a while Annette's father would charm his children by taking them for a weekend outing on which money seemed no object, but for most of the time his attitude was one of irritable neglect, and there was barely enough money to keep them adequately clothed and fed.

Her role as substitute mother to her younger siblings meant that Annette missed a great deal of school. Even so, she passed the eleven-plus exam, but her parents thought it both too expensive and unnecessarily 'stuck up' to send her to grammar school, and in any case the older she got the more she was needed by her mother at home. The first experiences of anxious distress Annette could remember were in relation to the responsibility she felt for the younger children (her parents used to lock them all into the house when the two of them went out for the evening).

As soon as she could (though not having it as a conscious aim) Annette made her escape from the family home. She was conscientious, hard-working, highly intelligent, and pretty – all assets contributing to the possibility of escape. She worked at first in a wholesale warehouse where she soon became a supervisor, and she met at sixteen the man she was to marry at eighteen. She married him because he was kind and attentive, but never really felt strongly attracted to him; indeed strong attraction was not something she experienced until quite a lot later in her life.

Annette had a boy and a girl by her first husband, Alan. His kindness and attentiveness started to wane not long after their marriage, especially as he became more and more absorbed in the small business he was running with increasing success. As time passed he seemed to become remarkably like her father, staying out in the evening and becoming involved with other women; unlike her father he had a tendency to occasional violence. The third time he hit her really hard, shortly after their twelfth wedding anniversary, Annette left him, and went with the children to live with Keith, whom she'd met and fallen in love with some months previously.

Keith was a man who knew a remarkable woman when he came across one, though he could not quite work out what was so remarkable about Annette. He was, in any case, devoted to her even though the speed of her mind often left him standing and the almost painful rawness of her sensitivity sometimes totally mystified him. But what he lacked in mental agility he made up for in commonsense practicality and emotional stability, and they set up house together on what seemed to be a strongly positive note. Money was tight, however, as Keith had left his first wife with their two children and was contributing heavily to their maintenance (his wife had finally moved in with the man she'd been having an affair with for five years).

Annette's first severe panic attack happened eighteen months after she'd gone to live with Keith, and a few weeks before they were due to get married. Even after accepting the hypothesis that she was experiencing anxious panic rather than life-threatening illness, she still had no idea what she could be anxious about. Her unusual intelligence and emotional honesty, however, made clarification relatively easy, and it was not long before she was able to say things which had up until then been no more than vague, unspeakable feelings, laden with dread.

Had they been able to detach themselves from their past, Annette and Keith might have been as happy as couples ever are. Their difficulty was that the small council house they came to live in together with Annette's two children was also inhabited by ghosts – ghosts who, moreover, had a disconcerting habit of materializing in the flesh every so often.

Annette was particularly haunted by Keith's first wife, Janice. The fact that his friends and his parents seemed unable to avoid subtly, and sometimes less subtly, comparing Annette with Janice was little more than a source of nagging irritation; much worse were the effects of Janice's unstable relations with her and Keith's two boys. Every so often she would throw Jimmy, aged sixteen, out of the house, so that he would turn up unexpectedly at his father's and have to be accommodated on the living-room settee until his mother could be persuaded by Keith to take him back.

It took Annette some time to acknowledge that she hated Jimmy. As far as she was concerned he was lazy, dirty, cocky and abusive, but Keith would brook no criticism of him. So Annette spent much of her time rigid with anticipation of his visitations, quiveringly sensitive also to the aura which emanated from Janice (for example, via Keith's muffled telephone conversations with her), for on Janice's whim depended the possibility of an extended dose of Jimmy. Janice herself materialized only very occasionally, at funerals and golden weddings, and Annette did not find her particularly disturbing in the flesh – it was her malign background existence which disquieted her. Jimmy's younger brother Annette found much more tolerable, and so evidently did his mother because he visited far less frequently.

Then there was the ghost of Annette's first husband, Alan, who haunted her through his relationship with their children, especially the younger of the two, Katie, who cried every time she returned from a weekend with her dad and spoke often and appreciatively about him, his ever-increasing affluence, and his unhappiness with his new girlfriend. Annette was tortured with guilt over having robbed her children of their father, and though their son, Robert, had little time for him and was strongly supportive of Annette, Katie's ceaseless remarks turned the knife in her wound remorselessly. Annette had almost no direct contact with Alan, but Katie never lost an opportunity to convey to her her impression of his sadness and that he really missed them all terribly and wanted them back. Alan still sent her affectionate cards at

Christmas and on her birthday – a gesture which would reduce Keith to hours of silence.

Annette's experience as a child had left her resolutely determined never to leave her own children simply to fend for themselves, and to provide for them materially as unstintingly as she possibly could. Not only did she feel that she had deprived them of a father, she had deprived them of a *rich* father, and deposited them in a cramped council house haunted by, and prone to more concrete visitations from, step-relatives they as well as she hated.

Quite apart from all this there was, of course, the question of Keith's relationship to her children. Here Annette was torn between her affection and respect for Keith and her guilt-laden protectiveness of Robert and Katie. An intuitively courageous woman with a sureness of ethical touch in almost every other circumstance, when it came to her own children, especially the sometimes mercilessly implacable Katie, Annette seemed paralysed and without authority. She could not bring herself to take disciplinary action, but nor would she allow Keith to. Despite appreciating and wanting to accede to – even encourage – his wish to 'be a father' to them, she felt they had a right to be protected by her on those occasions when they incurred his quite justifiable and usually mildly expressed wrath. Her ambivalence in this respect caused Keith a good deal of exasperation and frustration, especially when he saw Katie 'walking all over' her.

Annette was not 'neurotic', or 'inadequate', or any of those other things which roll only too readily off the professional tongue. She was a competent, clear-sighted, warmly sensitive woman of unusually strong moral integrity, and while, of course, one could find echoes of her childhood in her present situation of extended and entangled responsibility for people (Keith's children) whose dependence had been imposed upon her, such historical vulnerability cannot in my view be taken as anything like a complete explanation of her panic. She could cope with a lot: with responsibility, with lack of material resources, cramped living conditions, people's hostility, even with visits from the (from her standpoint) loathsome Jimmy. What finally brought her to her knees was not so much 'stress' as an absence of 'form' in which that stress could be cast and given meaning.

There are – for people of Annette's age and social standing at least – rules about marriage. The rights and duties of first-time spouses, parents and children indicate, even if imperfectly, not only how those involved should conduct themselves, but also what it is possible to *feel*. But those rules cannot be extended into a second marriage without incoherent complication. However unsatisfactory first-time marriages may often turn out to be in practice, spouses know, for example, that the 'form' of fidelity makes it 'wrong' to maintain an attachment to another man or woman, and the 'forms' of parental and filial love are also reasonably clearly prescribed. People know when they can legitimately feel jealous, angry, affronted, deprived or rejected. But what do you do about the ghost of a former spouse? Is their ghostly attachment wrong, or simply inevitable? What is the feeling it arouses in you? If you could express it, *should* you? How should step-parents behave towards their spouse's child – as they want to, as the spouse wants them to, as the child wants them to? How should they feel about their stepchild? Should they or shouldn't they disguise their feelings? If so, from spouse as well as stepchild? Annette felt certain about her duties in relation to material provision for her children, even though she could not fulfil them as satisfactorily as she would have liked – the 'forms' in relation to that issue were clear enough. What she (and there are undoubtedly many like her) felt completely at sea over was the *meaning* of her feelings about all the relationships involved, and what she should do about them. Like everyone else in this situation, she had in the end to make up her own 'rules', which after her interlude of panic she managed quite successfully to do.

A society which exalts private individualism in the place of public 'form' often places a crippling epistemological as well as moral burden on those left struggling to find their way: they have to find a language for their feelings as well as guidance for their conduct. And if they fail, they may find themselves simply competing with each other in dumb hostility according to the only rules left – those of the marketplace.

THE AIMLESS YOUNG MAN

It never occurred to Paul to attribute his sense that something was profoundly wrong to anything other than his own inadequacy. Despite having had an expensive education, he was at twenty-one unable to find anything he really wanted to do and had been drifting from job to job – mostly unskilled manual work of one kind or another – at intervals of only a few weeks. His 'relationships' were rather similar. He had no difficulty in attracting young women, but, apart from his relationship with his first serious girlfriend, Amanda, they never seemed to last long, usually because he found quite quickly that he 'couldn't be bothered'. There were times when his lack of direction and general sense of the meaninglessness of things made him quite alarmingly despairing, and he had once (at the time when he was breaking up with Amanda) made a serious attempt at suicide. If a flatmate had not come home unexpectedly, Paul would almost certainly have died from an overdose.

On the face of it Paul was typical of the kind of 'case' which convinces psychiatrists of the validity of their medicalized view of psychological disturbance: he came of a 'good family' and had throughout his life wanted for very little in any conventionally material way, and yet he had never settled down with any energy or enthusiasm to any of the roles which, so far, education and work had offered him. By the age of eighteen he had already found himself in the consulting rooms of a range of medical specialists and psychological advisers who had been appointed by his wealthy parents to advise on the lacklustre performance of their son (Paul had an older sister). His failure to profit from the advantages accorded him led easily enough to the assumption that the trouble must be rooted in some aspect of his biology. The combined efforts of the experts had, however, made very little difference even though Paul had followed their advice and submitted himself to their regimens as conscientiously as he could. He was not a rebel, and would have joined conventional society with satisfaction and relief if only he could have found the right path.

Paul's father was a highly successful businessman who spent a great deal of time flying round the globe and very little in the large house which had been the family home for most of Paul's life. He was a volatile man, not emotionally close to either of his children, and whenever he was at home seemed most preoccupied with extricating himself with as much dignity as he could rescue from the stormy, tearful scenes which regularly took place with his wife. In these, she would reproach him with what she saw as his neglect of his family and with the warmth and generosity which she suspected, but didn't know, he showed to a number of other women in his life. Paul's mother consoled herself during the periods of her husband's absence with gin and tonic and a circle of friends centred round the golf club. She showed an effusive concern for her son's problems, but though he was fond of his mother, Paul found her attentions embarrassing and preferred as far as he could to keep out of her way, which, given the size of the house, wasn't difficult even when he was living at home.

His sister was the person Paul felt closest to and could most easily talk to. She had married a local farmer, and seemed perfectly adjusted to the society which Paul found it so perplexingly difficult to take part in. She would listen for long hours to her brother's rather unsuccessful efforts to articulate his despair, and she racked her brains over courses of action he might take. She introduced him to her own and her husband's friends; she took him to dinner parties and found interesting girls for him to meet; she got acquaintances to offer him jobs in banks, building societies and estate agencies, and she did not allow her frustration at Paul's failure to take advantage of these opportunities, or her husband's eventual irritation with him, to dull her concern.

Paul had gone as a boarder to a second-rank public school near enough to home for him to spend most of his weekends there. The educational emphasis of the school seemed to have been placed on getting pupils into a suitably advantageous position in the business world, and on the whole it had a fairly liberal atmosphere: there seemed to have been little of the pressure-cooked sexuality or sadistic élitism often to be found in such establishments. Paul had, in fact, not actively disliked his time there; he had made some good friends and had been successful enough in the things which mattered to his fellow pupils to be not unpopular. His academic achievement had however throughout fallen far short of what his teachers considered his potential, and it was primarily this difficulty, combined with his apparent inability to 'join in' with real enthusiasm, which occasioned his visits to expert advisers. He failed a couple of science 0 levels, and apart from an A in art only scraped through the rest. His parents bought extra tuition for his A levels, but even so he only managed a low pass in one subject.

In talking about this period of his life Paul was not able to throw any light upon it from introspection. He just never felt he really belonged, like someone standing outside in the cold and looking in through the window of a warm, brightly lit room in which a lot of nice people are having a party.

Capitalizing on his artistic talent, and through the exertion of a little paternal influence, Paul managed to get a place on a course in graphic design in a southern polytechnic, and it was there that he met Amanda. He was bowled over, but also bemused by her. She was, it seemed to him, outrageously unconventional in both her appearance and her attitudes, and Paul could keep up with her only through the pretence of sharing feelings and views which he didn't really understand. Occasional Sunday lunches with her father and her brothers (her parents where divorced) were a nightmare. Her father was a left-wing historian who had a bottomless contempt for anyone who didn't match either his intelligence or his politics, and Paul found himself stretched to the very limit of his ability to dissemble in order not to be exposed as a hopeless bourgeois nincompoop.

There was something about Amanda's world which, even though he could place it in no comprehensible context, Paul found profoundly attractive. Despite often embarrassing if not positively scaring him with her forthright rejection of everything that he had assumed until then right-minded people stood for, it was as if he had at last identified something, though he was at a complete loss to say what it was, which he had previously found missing. Something which had simply been a blank in his life no longer was. But Amanda was a year ahead of him at the polytechnic, and when she left to work in London their relationship survived only a few months. He himself left halfway through his third year, after a spell in hospital following his suicide attempt.

He went back to live at home while he looked for work. He had a number of friends locally, most of whom had well-paid jobs in finance and business, but though he went drinking and night-clubbing with them without real discomfort, Paul still felt on the outside looking in, and, after the suicide attempt, was becoming more and more frightened about his 'peculiarity'. He suspected that his parents' marriage was about to break up, and since most of the time he was alone at home with his mother, he was becoming increasingly uncomfortable about her alcoholically sentimentalized dependence on him. He spent a lot of time with his sister, but felt he was a burden to her.

As Paul, with the latest in the line of his professional advisers, grew more able to articulate his feelings, it became clear that one of the things which most frightened him, and which looking back over his life he had always felt a degree of shame over, was his tendency to what he saw as morbid introspection. He would 'think about' things and people, 'notice' how they interacted, watch and judge the sincerity of the expressions on their faces. He would brood about what they saw in his expressions, and would ponder anxiously – perhaps for almost a whole sleepless night – about whether or not what someone said, or how they had looked, had been 'genuine', and how one could possibly ever know what was genuine and what wasn't.

Paul related these concerns cautiously and shamefacedly, as if he expected to be instantaneously certified insane. When he wasn't, he went on to reflect a little more boldly on the significance of his relations with Amanda. She had, in fact, aroused in him the glimmerings of an idea that it might be possible to lead a life of some real significance and value to others. At a low point of his vocational fortunes he had once even mentioned at home the possibility of looking into social work, but the disbelief and derision he met with had strangled the infant thought at birth.

Paul looked doubtful when it was suggested to him that perhaps there was *nothing* the matter with him, but that he had, with the partial exception of Amanda's, so far simply not been able to find a congenial world to live in, i.e., one which would receive, reflect and even elaborate his interests. He was especially sceptical that incoherent thoughts such as his about 'genuineness' could have been developed by others into a whole philosophy of authenticity, but even so he accepted with some gratitude the suggestion that introspection could be an honourable activity, and that world literature had thrived upon it. To the disbelieving amusement of his best friend, he went on psychological advice to buy a novel by Dostoevsky (an author neither had previously heard of), and he read it with mounting interest. He became more confident in his rejection of the village society which until then he had simply felt excluded from, and began to entertain the idea that there might somewhere be a world he would positively want to join. He began to see that as well as not being suited to be, he did not *want* to be a financial analyst, and probably not a social worker either. He decided to take a year out, drew his savings from the bank, and set off for South America with his still somewhat puzzled friend.

During the 1980s, the suicide rate in England among men aged twenty to twenty-four increased by 71 per cent (*The Health of the Nation. A Consultative Document for Health in England*, HMSO, June 1991). In order not to be aimless, you need a world which has some interest in what you've got to offer it.

THE TRAPPED YOUNG MOTHER

It was not until she was twenty-seven that Dawn plucked up the courage to consult her GP about the panic attacks she'd suffered on and off for almost as long as she could remember. They were a source of deep shame to her. They struck in almost any situation in which she found herself the object of attention – particularly among strangers in public places, but also at work or at social gatherings with people she knew quite well. She would suddenly find herself blushing and stammering, her head would spin, her heart pound, she would feel sick and faint. She felt sure at these times that her distress was glaringly obvious to everyone around, and that they would be concluding that she was either mad, bad or stupid, or probably all three.

The frequency and ferocity of the attacks had increased markedly over a period of two or three months before she went to the doctor, so that she had reached a point where she tried to avoid any kind of public or semipublic appearance which wasn't absolutely necessary. She had stopped going out socially, never went shopping on her own, and did everything she could to avoid contact with people where she worked (she worked three evenings a week as a cleaner at a local school).

Dawn's attitude towards herself was one of utter contempt. The one thing she ought to be able to do, she thought, was look after her children and run the household properly; she'd never had a particularly high opinion of herself, but now she just seemed to be utterly useless. She would have agreed wholeheartedly with the view, had she known it, of a young psychiatrist whom she was referred to that she was an 'inadequate personality'. However, it was only when she encountered a rather more sympathetic audience that she began to articulate some of the background to her distress.

Life was certainly a bit of a struggle, but that was no particular cause for complaint: most people Dawn knew were struggling, some more than she, and they didn't seem to be riddled with anxiety and shame. It was true that Mick, whom she was living with, was out of work, but she could just make ends meet without a wage from him, and he wasn't a bad bloke – he was at any rate kind to her children, who weren't his, and he didn't drink or beat her up, as her ex-husband had used to do.

Dawn had her first baby when she was seventeen and another when she was twenty. She'd divorced at twenty-two and met Mick three years later. She thought a great deal about her children and how to provide them with a degree of stability and emotional security she herself had not experienced. She had come from a large family which had always been materially deprived and riven with violent emotional discord. At one point Dawn had spent three months in care when her mother ran off with a man who turned out to be even less palatable than her father, and her education, if one could call it that, had been ceaselessly interrupted by enforced house moves, parental demands, and occasional truancy. She became pregnant when she was sixteen by the first boy who treated her in what she took to be a loving way, escaping gratefully from the domination of her family. She then lived for eighteen months with her inlaws, with whom she got on well, though her new husband soon proved not to be able to sustain his lovingness – in fact, he was a feelingless, conceited bully whose violence amply exceeded her father's.

Violence, in fact, had not been the main problem for Dawn with her father, who had reserved the full force of his fist for her mother, sisters and brothers. Dawn had, as she put it, been his favourite, but his favouritism had assumed a sexual form which she could well have done without. She hated him with a healthy hatred, but had never been able to reveal to anyone in the family the furtive games he had made her play with ten-pence pieces and the nocturnal 'cuddles' he had imposed upon her. One of her worst worries was how she could keep her ten-year-old daughter away from her grandfather's affectionate embrace, for though Dawn had little time for either of her parents, her family, splintered even as it was into warring factions, was the only source of solidarity available to its members, and they still saw quite a lot of each other. The one person who knew about her father's special attention to her was Mick, but he appeared not to attach very much importance to it, and indeed got on with him quite well – they had several times had a few drinks together.

Dawn was a strikingly attractive woman, but seemed to have little awareness of it. She knew that men often showed interest in her, but even so she had never encountered one who treated her with real tenderness, and she didn't see why she should expect to – on the whole (though it took her some time to see the truth of this) men seemed slightly frightened of her and intent on undermining her confidence in herself. Mick, for example, never seemed to miss an opportunity to remind her of all the things he could do which she couldn't.

Buried deep at the core of her sense of shame was the fact that she was only just literate, and she dreaded any occasion which bore the slightest possibility that she could be unexpectedly called upon to fill in a form or read aloud. Any sign she gave of independence towards Mick would be met by him with a demonstration of his indispensability as a mediator with the official world, and he seemed positively to welcome her phobic anxiety as an indication that she couldn't do without him. She had at one stage plucked up the courage to attend adult literacy classes with a friend, but after two visits Mick found a (short-lived) part-time job, which meant that there was no one to look after the children, and so Dawn had once again to abandon her attempts at getting educated.

She was, however, far from stupid. Despite her profound lack of certainty about her own worth, Dawn adopted a stance towards the world which was characterized by a morally insightful intelligence, and a kind of dogged courage which committed her to a defence of her beliefs even when it cost her agonies of doubt and anxiety. She insisted, for example, on being truthful and direct with her children and protecting them as far as she could from the casual abuses of a world which – she understood but could not say – already had them marked down as exploitable objects rather than privileged subjects. She took a lot of interest in their schooling, and though it was Mick who ostentatiously helped them with their homework, it was she who dragged herself in fear and trembling to school parents' evenings to enlist what support for them she could.

Painfully conscious of her tongue-tied clumsiness in coping with the public side of the family's affairs, and aware (not without a strong tinge of resentment) that she depended on Mick for many such transactions, she failed to realize the degree to which she actually took responsibility for things. In fact, for example, Mick was highly unreliable with money, and Dawn had a constant battle to keep what she earned out of his pocket and available for paying the bills.

It was as if all her life there had been a conspiracy to prevent Dawn from realizing that she was an intelligent and beautiful woman who had a great deal to offer the world. But even though the world for the most part showed a cruel indifference to her gifts, she was constrained to offer them nonetheless in whatever form she could, with her limited resources, devise. The fact that she had never had held up to her the kind of loving and truthful mirror which she so tenaciously kept in place before her own children meant that her courage, though it never died, often failed her.

She was, for example, unable to break her dependence on Mick even though in her heart she suspected that it damaged both of them. She needed him as a front man, but she rejected him sexually with a ruthlessness that hurt him deeply (another example of her stubborn refusal to compromise her core feelings: even though she felt sorry for him, she experienced Mick's advances as a violation of her body which she could not and would not permit). He was terrified of losing her but far too vulnerable to let her see the extent of his need, so he kept her with him by undermining her self-confidence and hobbling her to the household by any means he could find. Because he was, in comparison with the other men in her life, in many ways kind and certainly not violent, she could not understand why she didn't love him – indeed, she was far from clear that she did not.

Her whole life had in many ways been a storm, and her situation with Mick was the safest port she had yet found. She didn't expect any better, and certainly in the social and material seas surrounding her there was to be descried no reassuring lighthouse's beam.

THE MID-LIFE MALE

So far as he could see, life had not been especially unkind to Donald, and he was therefore a little diffident over using the term 'depression' to describe his condition. But that was what his doctor had called it, and he had been prescribed antidepressants, so depression, he supposed, must be what it was. He felt unhappy, certainly, but what seemed to be missing was something for him to be depressed about: he couldn't 'put his finger on it', and it was as much as anything with that aim in mind that he found himself talking to a psychologist.

Donald was not an unreflective man, and not one to run away from his feelings, and though he could see that his life, since his forty-second birthday in 1981, had been in a considerable state of turmoil, he could still not understand why he should feel so desolate and so lethargic, nor why every so often (usually when by himself) he should be overcome by uncontrollable bouts of sobbing over, it seemed, some nameless loss.

Losses there had indeed been, but, though he readily acknowledged their significance, they did not seem to Donald to be the type of loss he was looking for to account for his feelings.

Eighteen months ago he had left his wife and two children to live with Frances, but he did not miss them in the kind of way which would explain his pervading sense of pointless sadness. He saw his children – a boy of sixteen and a girl of fourteen – frequently, and they seemed to be taking the separation of their parents well. His daughter, it was true, had not talked to him for eight or nine months following the break-up of the marriage, and her school work may have suffered a bit, but they were, as he put it, the best of friends now, and what he had feared at the time might be a scene of terrible marital wreckage had proved in the event to be from his perspective surprisingly uncomplicated.

It was only in retrospect that Donald could see how it had all started. He had not been aware of feeling discontented with life, though he had felt frustrated and at a dead end with his job. He was deputy head of a comprehensive school, and unlikely, he felt, ever to be anything else. He lacked the element of ruthlessness he saw as necessary to becoming a head teacher, and in any case was frank about not wanting the responsibility: he preferred being prominent among the led to being a leader, apart from which the job of administrating and managing to the virtual exclusion of all else appealed to him not at all. His wife, who held a position similar to his in a different school, had been completely supportive of his stance in relation to his career, though he felt that privately she had probably been a little disappointed in his lack of ambition.

Donald was a gentle, thoughtful, intelligent man, and though he had always felt a little pained and puzzled by the world's cruelties and uncertainties, he had by no means been rendered ineffective by them. He was sociable, even quite gifted – good at sport, he still played team games at weekends, and he also played the guitar in a small folk group which performed regularly in local clubs. He was passionately interested in ancient Egyptian history and society, or at least had been until the onset of his present troubles, which had put paid to most of the activities which he was not actually obliged to do in order to earn his living.

His marriage to Ruth had been – he would have said at any point – happy and successful. Again, it was only in looking back from his present vantage point that he could see anything lacking in it. They had always got on well, and were even now quite good friends despite the injury he had inflicted on her so unexpectedly. They had both concerned themselves deeply with the upbringing of their children, in which project Donald had assumed a full partnership. Ruth was a practical, down-to-earth woman who accepted the minor peculiarities and foibles of others without censure or complaint, and even though she may at times have wished that Donald could have made a little more time to spend just with her, she never made undue demands upon him. But there had been, he now saw, a certain distance, perhaps a lack of passion between them, which had presumably left him vulnerable to later events.

A similar, though very much more marked distance had existed between his own parents. Thanks to the Second World War, he had seen little of his father until he was five years old, and he and his two brothers had been brought up during that time scrupulously but far from lavishly by their mother, a serious, somewhat anxious woman who, though essentially kind, had been rather undemonstrative emotionally.

Both Donald's parents had been keen for him to make a material success of his life and were acutely aware of the importance of education, not least because they themselves had received only rudimentary schooling. He knew that they were proud and pleased when he got into grammar school (though, characteristically, they didn't show it) and the only real friction that arose in the family was when either he or one of his brothers showed signs of deviating from the path which their parents had tacitly mapped out for them – i.e., of succeeding at school and becoming established in a safe profession. They were, Donald felt, quietly satisfied when he became a schoolteacher, though he did not now feel closely involved with them. He was 'quite fond' of them, saw them regularly if infrequently, but felt that he had little in common with them now. He had, however, been quite surprised at the sympathy shown to him by his father in a recent conversation they had had. He had expected to receive nothing but sharply expressed parental displeasure at his marital misdemeanours, but during the course of an afternoon in the garden his father had managed somehow to convey to him an understanding of his position which made Donald wonder whether his father might not himself have been tempted to take similar steps at some time in his life.

It was Frances who had woken Donald from the slumbers he now saw that he had been in. She had arrived as a junior teacher at his school, and though at first he had considered his attraction to her preposterous, not least because she was thirteen years younger than he, when it dawned on him that his feelings were reciprocated, the two of them became consumed in a blaze of passion he had not imagined any longer possible. For some months he staggered around in a daze, almost mad with love on the one hand and racked with guilt and apprehension for the future of his family on the other. The rather superficial attempts he made to disguise the affair from the rest of the world were far from skilful, and Ruth, with her customarily practical eye, accurately diagnosed his state almost as soon as he had fallen into it. She did not rant and rave at him, but she was profoundly shocked and hurt, though at first Donald didn't allow himself to see just how much. He made several half-hearted attempts to break off his relationship with Frances, but his will seemed to have no say in the matter, and in the end he acceded with little resistance to her begging him to move into her small flat with her.

At first there had been a feeling of almost overwhelming joy at finding himself, as it were, back in his twenties with a beautiful young woman for whom he had become the centre of the universe. Donald was overflowing with tenderness and wisdom, almost ecstatic with gratitude to fate that he should have been given the chance of applying the knowledge and insights of his forty-odd years to nursing this new relationship into an enduring creation of love, free of all the petty blemishes and pitfalls so easily fallen into by the younger and less experienced.

Frances, however, turned out to be less malleable an object of his mature creativity than Donald had led himself to expect. Not only did the inconveniences and material privations of their new life together begin to intrude to sully the idyll, but she proved to be dependent on Donald for love and reassurance in a way Ruth had never been, and though he was still inclined to see this as a positive aspect of their relationship – a sign that it was meaningful and alive – he couldn't deny that it often made for difficulties between them, and occasionally he caught a glimpse of the, so to speak, mechanics underlying their passion.

It seemed just possible, for example, that Frances needed an older, wiser man for a security she had been unable to find with younger ones, and that Donald's age had not been, as it had at first seemed to him, merely an irrelevance to a passion that had grown out of pure ideality. It was with some reluctance that Donald had to acknowledge that there were occasions when he felt that Frances was positively nagging him, and he was rather chastened to discover that the intensity of her sexual ardour had also noticeably cooled. Though he was adamant that his leaving Ruth and the children had been an inevitable, almost necessary event, he also confessed that there had been just a couple of occasions when he had a nostalgic twinge for the peace and familiarity of his former domestic state.

The other aspect to Donald's rather depressed apathy was a restless feeling of unfulfillment. He could scarcely face going into school, and indeed had several weeks off work: the meaninglessness of the routine, the pettiness of the relations between his colleagues, the ever-increasing need for him to be a cross between a businessman and a social worker, neither of which did he feel cut out for, left him longing for a life of greater vividness and significance. Much to Frances's alarm and distress, he applied for a job to work abroad with a Third World population, but in the end didn't attend when called for interview.

Frances wanted a baby, and though at the start of their affair he could have envisaged nothing more wonderful, the prospect of it now made him feel surprisingly tired and old, and his reluctance to enter into the project with any real enthusiasm introduced a little further strain into their relations.

There was a café in the town where Donald lived which was a meeting place for older, mostly retired people who went there in couples or groups to chat for an hour or so. Some Saturday mornings Donald would drop in there to sit at a table on his own and listen to them talking – just for a bit of peace and quiet, as he put it.

THE DESPAIRING OVER-FIFTY PROFESSIONAL

By pretty well any standard, Judith's had been a highly competent and successful career. In her mid-forties she had become the acting head of a small department in the arts faculty of a large university, and had not been made professor only because of the financially straitened circumstances of the institution as a whole and the particularly uncertain status of her department within it: there was a possibility that it might be merged with a similar department in a neighbouring university, or, if things got any worse, possibly disappear altogether.

Judith's fear was that she had become incapable of dealing with the demands placed upon her. She accepted the need to change structures and practices which had since the middle of the century tended to fossilize the academic world, and she did her best to comply with the new managerial demands for the more efficient use of information technology, staff appraisal, the need to attract more students, especially from overseas, and so on. At the same time, she could not but object to any sign of a lowering of academic standards, and she fiercely resisted any innovation which did not preserve the high quality of the department's teaching and research.

Judith was puzzled and upset that she found herself so often in conflict with her senior colleagues over issues about which they themselves seemed in full accord, and she was also hurt and disturbed that her junior colleagues seemed equally often to interpret what she saw as her defence of their interests as a failure on her part to guide the department effectively through the troubled waters of change. She felt weak and helpless, suddenly bereft of the personal resources as well as the professional allies she had previously been able unhesitatingly to call upon.

The striking thing about Judith was how little her current conception of herself seemed to match her actual character. Far from being weak, she seemed a strong and resolute person – positively tough, in fact. She had a fine, quick mind, was clear and positive in her perception and formulation of things, and stuck unerringly to her purpose once she had elucidated what was morally and practically the right thing to do. Not until now, at the age of fifty-one, had she ever really felt profoundly uncertain of herself. She was extremely shaken and frightened to find that on some mornings the very prospect of going into the department made her tremble and weep with frustration and despair.

Not only had Judith developed a successful career as a scholar with a modest but not insubstantial international reputation, she had also been a tower of strength on the domestic front. Her husband was also an academic, but much less successful than she, and had an alcohol problem right from the early days of their marriage. He was a kind man, gentle to the point of ineffectuality, and his drinking had resulted not so much in unpleasantness as in Judith's having had to take almost all the responsibility for the upbringing of their three children. This she had done with the systematic resoluteness – and indeed the love – which she brought to all her enterprises, and they were now successfully established in academically related careers in various parts of the country. They had, as she put it, their own lives to lead, and though she saw one or the other of them quite frequently, she made very little in the way of emotional demands upon them, and they knew little of her current difficulties.

Judith looked after her husband with a tender resignation which had become habitual. She probably knew that his role in the university contributed to precisely the 'dead wood' that the new business-minded management was so eager to excise, but she protected his reputation and minimized the effects of his drinking as much as she could. So far as could be seen, she got no emotional support from him, and indeed he appeared to lean with his full weight on her support.

Judith also had an elderly mother to support. Her father had died in the early seventies, and her mother now lived alone in a bungalow Judith had found for her within easy reach of her own home. Since her mother had become increasingly lame, and also noticeably forgetful, there were few days in the week when Judith did not find it necessary to call in for an hour or so to make sure that all was well.

Though she was a loving, and certainly dutiful daughter, Judith's relations with her parents had not been characterized by great warmth. It had not been so much that warmth had been absent, but rather that, from her parents' side at least, it had been conditional. Her parents, both from the 'respectable working class', had made their only daughter very much the centre of their concern, and had brought her up with the combination of strictness, kindness and impartiality which their unswerving allegiance to Methodism dictated. Judith had always felt utterly certain of them, completely convinced of their interest in her, firmly resolved to earn their approval and acceptant of the justice of its being withheld on those (rare) occasions when she fell short of their standards.

It was not until she found herself in a world that failed to appreciate her industrious intelligence, her moral integrity and her willingness to serve a just Authority that Judith began to see that she did not know how to evaluate her own feelings. For until this time her feelings had always been ratified and approved by others – her parents, the Church, school and university – and those of her private feelings beyond or beneath the interest and concern of this external world had lain largely unexamined, and she was far from sure whether what she herself felt in this neglected domain were things that could and should be felt.

Thus she was not sure whether or not the mistrust she felt for the terms of the new language of management – in which, for example, the avowed pursuit of 'Quality' or 'Excellence' seemed to accompany a diminution in what she had always considered quality and excellence – reflected a justifiable criticism, or whether she had merely somehow missed the point. Such an unaccustomed mistrust of properly constituted authority threw her back on reliance on personal judgements which she didn't really know how to make and couldn't bring herself fully to believe in, and so she simply felt incompetent and 'de-skilled'.

The apparent capriciousness with which new administrative (and sometimes contradictory) regulations were imposed upon her department; the indifference of the new breed of business manager to the failure of the much vaunted 'innovations' to achieve what they were supposed to; the incongruities involved in replacing methods of academic assessment and appointment with 'appraisal' systems of much less depth and substance; the resentment of her departmental colleagues at her earnest attempts to introduce these changes to them as much as at her parallel efforts to protect them from the worst of their effects: all these happenings served to hurt more than anger her, since she could find no point of reference in which to anchor her own view of them. She had become the servant of a master she could no longer recognize, in whose good faith she could no longer trust and who, worst of all, appeared not to appreciate the very attributes of her character which had until then been her greatest strengths.

Although Judith could be witheringly scornful of many of the management procedures she was asked to mediate, and although she on several occasions made herself profoundly unpopular at faculty and other meetings by upholding in the face of what she saw as unintentional Philistinism the academic values she had held dear all her life, she could still not bring herself to believe that the system as a whole had in any degree become destructive or malign. It was above all this inability to diagnose a moral failing in the system which forced Judith to diagnose it in herself.

The incongruity of so competent, strong, resourceful and courageous a woman blaming herself for a state of affairs so clearly perpetrated by others would have been obvious to anyone not blinded by the ideology which had taken such a grip on the decade. The sad thing was that so many of those around her, instead of fanning into life the glimmer of her suspicion that all was not well with the system that had overtaken her, should have treacherously concurred in the view that she was 'getting past it'. Like many women and men of a corresponding age and station in life, Judith found her discomfort and isolation rapidly turning into a longing for early retirement.

CHAPTER FIVE

Help

It is the main argument of this book that emotional and psychological distress is brought about most fundamentally through the operation of social-environmental powers which have their origin at considerable distance from those ultimately subjected to them. It would seem to follow from this that distal causes need distal cures, and it will be the task of the final chapter to suggest what kinds of political, ethical and ideological changes might be needed if some of the worst ravages of our form of social organization are to be avoided.

However, though the reasons for our pained and painful experience may be located far away from us as individuals, we live perforce in a proximal world, and just as the powers which hurt us tend to be mediated by those 'fellow passengers' we actually encounter, so the help we get to relieve or withstand their worst effects is likely to be received from people whose lives in one way or another touch upon our own.

The paradox involved in this state of affairs has already been emphasized: the people who *seem* to be the most important in our lives, those with whom we engage daily in transactions of love and hate, victory and defeat, frustration and elation, are, in fact, but the mediators of powers often so distant in time or space that we, the protagonists, cannot even say what they are. This paradoxical state of affairs applies equally within the realm of psychological help, and much of the difficulty with most approaches to 'treatment' – the unsustainability of claims made as well as the nihilistic implications of some of the blanket critiques advanced – follows from a failure to unravel the paradox.

For it is not that psychotherapy and similar approaches are either marvellously efficacious or dreadfully damaging, but rather that they are at best strictly limited in what they can achieve, and at worst seriously misleading, both theoretically and practically, in their approach to distress. However, it is important to add a qualification to this view, which follows from the premise that counsellors and psychotherapists have very little formal power in relation to those they are seeking to help. As Jeffrey Masson's work in particular has established,[1] psychotherapeutic and psychiatric intervention can be very damaging to the recipient, the more so in proportion to the power available to the practitioner. Psychiatry especially has been accorded sweeping powers over the individual at various times in its history, and though these are probably more in question now than at any previous time, they may still be very considerable.

The critique of psychotherapy which follows, as well as the elaboration of how this form of proximal help may be beneficial, are thus based on the assumption that we are talking about practitioners – whether called therapists, counsellors, psychologists or indeed psychiatrists – who have not been accorded or do not use significant formal power over individuals (for example over their bodies or their liberty). This is not to say that such practitioners have *no* power, and indeed part of my task is to clarify what powers psychotherapists do have, and how they may be used for good as well as for ill.

As I argued at the beginning of Chapter Three, the over-estimation of therapeutic power and the failure of theorists of psychotherapy to see beyond the walls of the microenvironment of the consulting room has led to a great deal of misunderstanding about what psychotherapy and counselling can and cannot achieve. If I risk labouring the argument by recapitulating it here, it is because there are, in fact, very few theoretical approaches to counselling and psychotherapy which cannot be fitted into either

1. See Jeffrey M. Masson, *Against Therapy*, HarperCollins, 1989.

or both of two microenvironmental models: that is to say, such approaches try to account for and to 'cure' personal distress which has been engendered in a *world* by both *treating* and *understanding* it within the immediately proximal compass of the patient's intimate relations, particularly, of course, with the therapist.

The first such microenvironment is limited to the space of therapy itself, i.e., the consulting room, and may be represented as in figure 5.

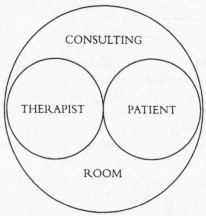

FIGURE 5: The microenvironment of therapeutic space

It is scarcely surprising that where theorists allow their thinking about psychological phenomena to be swamped by their experience of the consulting room they should end up giving the enormous importance they do to the events which transpire between therapist and patient. It is, after all, a world which contains no other occupants. Were the protagonists to be marooned together for a decade or two on a desert island, it might well be the case that their feelings and fantasies about each other, their personal quirks and mannerisms, their expectations, moods and interpretations of each other's conduct would all become matters of large and central significance. However, in a world which permits, indeed demands, that the pair live a vast proportion of their lives outside the microenvironment of their personal encounter, such factors need to be kept in perspective.

The psychoanalyst's emphasis, for example, on the fundamental importance of the 'transference' and on the curative powers of his or her 'interpretations' of it, just like the Rogerian counsellor's concentration on the crucial powers of the 'warmth, empathy and genuineness' of his or her relations with the patient, though, of course, significant in a microenvironment in which little else takes place, are completely dwarfed by the events and relations of the world in which the patient actually lives. Failure frankly to acknowledge this limitation, or even apparently to see that it exists, is, as noted earlier, to court absurdity, and no doubt the touch of ridicule which often attaches to the popular idea of the 'shrink' is brought about by the inflated self-importance of a profession which seems to have forgotten that the world does not end at its front door.

The second microenvironment given consideration by most theorists in the broadly 'clinical' field consists of the personal space in which the patient's difficulties may be said to have developed – the arena of his or her so-called 'psychopathology'. This is often seen as having been most important in its historical aspect, and is once again occupied by a limited number of very proximal influences, as is suggested in figure 6.

It is not, of course, that the mediating influence of parents, siblings and other significant people in patients' past and present lives is not important for an understanding of their psychological development and personal distress. The problem with this microenvironmental model is rather that its obscuring of the influences of a wider world a) tends to give the forces within the microenvironment a dynamism they in fact don't really possess, and b) leads to ideas about 'insight', etc., which extend this dynamism into the patient's present in the form of concepts such as 'will' and 'responsibility'.

In other words, if you limit your understanding of the powers and influences within the world merely to the proximal arena

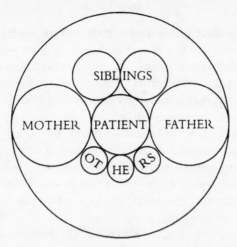

FIGURE 6: The microenvironment of 'psychopathology'

in which your immediate social encounters take place, the *origin* of the activity in that arena will appear to be *inside* the figures who occupy it – for the simple reason that there is no other conceptual space in which it *could* be. It therefore becomes increasingly attractive to believe that activity taking place in the proximal arena is due to the intentions, impulses, desires, unconscious motives, or whatever, located 'within' the principal actors. And once *that* view has been conceded, it becomes convincing to suppose that the individual patient has such impulses and intentions, etc., residing 'inside' him or her and that, perhaps with appropriate guidance from the therapist, he or she can exercise some form of moral choice in changing or adapting them.

Now I am not making what seems to me the dangerous and in fact unsustainable claim that there is 'no such thing as free will'. To do so would invite the kind of fatalism which suggests that 'since nothing I can intend will make any difference, I might as well not bother' or 'I can't help what I do – it's all because I had an unhappy childhood'. Free will, as I suggested earlier in this book and will attempt to elaborate in the final chapter, must exist in the form of a 'necessary illusion' – to act in good faith human beings must *believe in* a concept of free will. For the psychological theorist, on the other hand, it is not a particularly useful concept, and it is likely to be far more fruitful to consider what patients are able to do about their predicament from the point of view of what powers and resources are available to them to make changes in their lives.

In terms of the help therapists and counsellors may be able to offer patients from the very proximal position they occupy in relation to them, the situation is a very much more modest one than that implied, for example, in the microenvironment of figure 5, and might more accurately be represented by the position as suggested in figure 7.

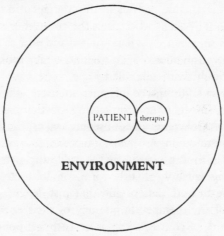

FIGURE 7: Therapy in perspective

The Ingredients of 'Therapy'

There are, it seems to me, essentially three components to the kind of help which can be offered to a person in distress by someone who, though suitably experienced and perhaps qualified in some professional sense, has no powers over that person other than those of persuasion. These are the provision of a) comfort,

b) clarification, and c) encouragement. I shall consider them in turn.

COMFORT

In Chapter Four, I tried to show how easily the therapeutic provision of comfort could be exploited by a Business Culture. This does not mean, however, that such provision is *necessarily* linked to exploitation. It does mean that one needs to take great care to understand the limitations of therapeutic comfort.

There can be few practitioners of counselling or psychotherapy who have not witnessed what often seem to be the almost miraculous therapeutic powers of the 'therapeutic relationship' itself. A patient or client who enters the consulting room for the first time, tense, ashen, eyes dark-ringed and near to tears, leaves after being given an hour of sympathetic listening looking relaxed, pink, eyes bright with rekindled hope.

It is above everything else this phenomenon – the immediate, even physical impact of comfort-giving – which has in my view provided the whole range of counselling and psychotherapy with its principal justification. As always, it is proximal experience which is registered as most powerful by the individual person, and the pain-relieving quality of this form of intimate support is unmistakable to both patient and therapist, leaving both easily convinced of the therapeutic potency of their encounter.

This should, of course, come as no surprise: popular culture is full of expressions which recognize that 'a trouble shared is a trouble halved', that 'two heads are better than one', and that it helps to have 'a shoulder to cry on'. Our whole experience of life impresses upon us the value of proximal solidarity, and the more powerful (or socially highly accredited) the people with whom we are able to establish such solidarity, the more aid and comfort we are likely to be able to extract from association with them. No doubt the mega-rich (or mega-'important') derive great comfort from having in their entourage personal physicians and lawyers (not to mention bodyguards) who are available to share their trials and tribulations at any hour of the day or night.

Our very social existence as human beings, the structure of our bodies and the means through which they are brought into and subsequently sustained in the world *demand* that we have on our side people who will support us. In other words, proximal solidarity is an *essential* form of power without which we would be almost certain not to survive.

There is thus no mystery about the centrality in counselling and psychotherapy of 'the therapeutic relationship', though it has indeed often been mystified and sentimentalized in ways which, though no doubt augmenting professional 'credibility', obscure the very obviousness of the phenomenon of comfort itself. Virtually *any* human transaction is rendered more effective, and certainly experienced as more empowering, if it is conducted kindly and sympathetically.

One must, however, distinguish between the *experience* of empowerment which follows the provision of proximal solidarity, and the processes by which the actual causes of an individual's distress may be removed or modified. Your friend's sympathetic commiseration over your trouble with meeting your mortgage repayments may temporarily make you feel much better, but it won't actually keep the bailiffs from your door.

Just such a confusion between comfort and cure is endemic in the psychotherapies. The person who looked and felt so much better after the first consultation with a therapist will in all probability return a week or two later to say that though the improvement lasted three or four days, it began to wear off after that. For neophyte therapists who have not yet been able to shake off their entanglement in the magical appeal of their profession, this is often a disheartening and worrying experience, and they may find themselves being driven defensively to cover up a sudden doubt about their therapeutic potency. But then they may be reassured as the patient confides a little more, and lo and behold, starts once again to improve under their very eyes. And so it may go on: as long as the patient can maintain contact with the therapist, he or she will feel better, and the longer they are apart, the more painfully will the world re-establish its grip.

What therapists have to realize, of course, is that their contact with their patient is not curing anything, but merely providing a form of empowering proximal solidarity which depends for its effectiveness on its continued existence. There is nothing the matter with this so long as the therapist is able to continue offering support and the patient is able to keep on paying for it. This relationship amounts perhaps to the 'poor person's' equivalent of the personal physician, and for people who have either very few or no other sources of proximal solidarity in their lives it can be of the utmost – even life-saving – importance. The *essential* thing is for counsellors and psychotherapists not to confuse their provision of this service, which may in fact often be the only one they are legitimately able to provide, with some quasi-technical form of effecting 'change' in people.

Received psychotherapeutic wisdom eschews 'dependency' and warns solemnly against creating it in patients; it even assumes a distinctly moralistic tone in disapproving of 'dependency' as an altogether undesirable trait in adult human beings. But this is to miss one of the central points about being human: we are *all* 'dependent' in all sorts of ways, and the question must rather be one of understanding the modes and meanings in our dependencies and with which they occur. It would, of course, be wrong (as therapy could and probably too often does do) deliberately to create forms of dependency in people in order to exploit them financially or in some other way. On the other hand it would be simply foolish not to recognize that our society is a highly intricate network of dependencies which define the very nature of our being.

Inasmuch as the provision of comfort is a, and often the, central component of counselling and psychotherapy, therapists need to disabuse themselves of the conceit that they are achieving anything more grand than giving proximal support to people who for one reason or another cannot get it any other way. The less the availability of such support in people's lives, the more they may depend on its professional provision, and the longer term that provision may need to be. There is no shame, or necessary exploitation, in that. But there is a need for professional comfort-givers to recognize the limitations and dangers of their trade. Several of these come quickly to mind.

First, proximal solidarity is in no way necessarily connected with the distal causes of distress, and is therefore unlikely to be able to modify them. Second, the effectiveness of such solidarity will be in proportion to its extent and duration, and is therefore best provided in the context of the individual's life by people whose availability and commitment are maximally dependable. In this way a counsellor or therapist cannot effectively take the place of family, friends, lovers, etc., and should always be concerned to do everything possible to encourage patients to develop these more enduring sources of solidarity in their lives, thereby rendering therapeutic comfort redundant. Third, though the therapeutic relationship is at its heart a commercial one and should not be sentimentalized, its comfort-giving quality stems from the nature of the participants as people rather than from any technical therapeutic skill. This injects an unusually strong ethical element into the therapeutic relationship, and means that therapists need to consider carefully the implications of withdrawing support from patients for whatever reasons (for example, changing jobs, etc.). Fourth, it needs to be borne in mind that the nontechnical, basically personal nature of the comfort-giving relation means that it becomes peculiarly liable to the kinds of abuses which Jeffrey Masson and others have highlighted.

Priests, doctors and therapists have no doubt all in their different ways contributed to the professional mystification of comfort-giving, but there is really no secret about it. Its essence is to allow another person to *be* without trying to impose upon him or her either a responsibility for being that way or a blueprint for being another way. If you are in pain or distress you are as unlikely to be comforted by the observation that it's your fault as you are by an insistence that you should try this, that or the other solution to your predicament. Ironically, it is often people 'trained' in a helping profession – medicine and nursing are prime examples – who are least good at offering comfort pure and simple, usually because they feel it so incumbent on them to *solve* the person's problems.

But comfort-giving is precisely *not* problem solution, and, paradoxical though it may seem, its very effectiveness depends on its not trying to solve anything. The reason for this will I hope by now be obvious: most of the causes of the kind of distress which puts people in need of comfort are *not soluble* because they are originated by distal social powers which are out of reach of both sufferer and helper.

What we are in most immediate need of as we suffer the torments of a cruel world are *companions* with whom to share our suffering. We need acknowledgement of our condition and affirmation of our experience. We don't need people to press upon us ineffective solutions or blame us for our feelings. The *first* move to be made in confronting outrageous fortune is to stand shoulder to shoulder with others in contemplation of its effects. All too often this is the *only* move which can be made, but even so, so long as it is possible to maintain such solidarity, it is a relief. All you really have to do to establish with someone the beginnings of such solidarity is sit and listen carefully to what they have to tell you, and for that you don't have to be a psychotherapist. But neither, if your are, do you have to be ashamed of it, but merely to bear in mind the modesty of your undertaking.

CLARIFICATION

If comfort is the almost inevitable by-product of virtually any form of sympathetic helping, some version or other of clarification constitutes the core of nearly all psychotherapeutic 'techniques'. The wizardry of the therapist consists in his or her being able to penetrate patients' confusion in order to reveal to them the 'real' reasons for their distress.

It is in this process of clarification that practically all of the mystique of psychotherapy is contained. The arrogance of the therapist who claims to be able to 'tell at a glance' the nature of patients' relations to their parents (as for example Masson reports of Jung, *Against Therapy*, p. 158) is matched in propensity for myth-creation by the popular conception that psychologists can 'read the minds' of anyone their eyes happen to fall upon. We move, so it would seem, in a web of self-created illusion which veils a secret, *interior* space where our (thanks to Freud, largely dishonourable) motives wait to be discovered by a knowing clinical gaze.

Slightly more soberly, the process of clarification is most usually seen as one in which people's moral equivocation over the 'real' reasons for their conduct is resolved through the patient and skilful work of the therapist in revealing their origin. In this way, in psychoanalysis, for example, a patient's current concerns, perceptions and actions may be 'interpreted' in terms of the emotionally (sexually or aggressively) laden situation in which they originated; the sex or aggression is, of course, most likely to be construed as in some sense 'belonging' to the patient. Having thus had revealed to him or her the somewhat murky motives which lie behind the fog created by 'repression', the idea is, of course, that the patient sees, literally (though analysts are not bold enough to put it so bluntly) the error of his or her ways, and becomes at last able to live in the pure reality of therapeutic revelation.

Therapists have, of course, noticed that insight into the origins of 'neurotic conflict', etc., does not always lead automatically to an abandonment of the strategies it has engendered, but they have not on that account put any less effort into the therapeutic work of clarification. In one form or another the notion that people should, once they've seen what they've been up to, be able to adjust their conduct to more favourable or acceptable goals seems to be one that therapists simply cannot relinquish.

The observation that 'intellectual insight' – the more theoretical appreciation that such and such were the reasons for one's present state – did not seem to produce a change in that state led to the concept of 'emotional insight' in which one was supposed really to feel *impelled* to change through the force of the emotional impact of a revelatory experience of insight. But, as I have pointed out earlier, there is no particular reason why a change of heart should from any theoretical or practical point of view be any more or less effective than a change of mind.

The importance accorded by the psychotherapies to an understanding of the origins of one's condition does not necessarily stem from the kind of psychoanalytic creed that one may, through the process of insight, become free of morally dubious enterprises on which one has been engaged since childhood. An alternative, seen for example in various versions of 'cognitive therapy', is that current conduct is a product of beliefs or attitudes which, far from being necessarily grounded in some prototypical childhood experience, may be acquired almost accidentally, and certainly potentially interchangeably. In this case clarification of what patients believe – what are their 'cognitions' about their conduct in relation to their world – is important principally so that one belief can be substituted for another, more adaptive one. In this kind of approach the *origins* of patients' cognitions are far less important than the nature of the cognitions themselves, and it is *this* which needs clarification. In this way, for example, it may be seen as much more important to point out to someone that he or she resists venturing into new social situations out of an expectation of ridicule (and to replace it with an expectation of approval) than it would be to lay bare the origin of the sense of ridicule.

Whatever the debates and differences among the various brands of psychotherapy, however, they all in one form or another find it necessary to enter with the patient into a process of clarifying the 'true' nature of his or her enterprise. This procedure is likely (as in the case of 'insight' therapies) to be seen as in itself therapeutic, or (as in the case of 'cognitive' therapies) essential as a preliminary to installing the attitudinal equipment necessary for alternative enterprises. In any case, the emphasis is understandably enough on the potential of the clarificatory process to result in therapeutic improvement; to form, that is, the main technical procedure through which, within the context of the consulting room, the therapist can work the magic of change.

The point I wish to make about this is not that clarification is in itself necessarily misguided or morally undesirable, but that there are within this general area both epistemological and ethical confusions which may be avoided only if the process of clarification is placed within a coherent theoretical context which takes proper account of its strictly limited *therapeutic* significance.

Of course in the understanding of distress it is important to explain how it came about, but, equally obviously, such an explanation, however accurate, does not lead automatically – or in many cases even conceivably – to a change in the conditions which created the distress in the first place and maintained it thereafter. Even if there were such things as changes of heart following from insights into the moral wellsprings of one's conduct, it is far from clear how that might enable one to conduct oneself differently. It is even less clear what the relation of people's conduct is to their 'beliefs' or 'attitudes', or why, if such things are fundamental, they should be any easier to change than the conduct itself.

All the motivational bits and pieces of machinery which are supposed to clutter our interiors and which therapeutic clarification is supposed to reveal – the unconscious wishes and complexes, the impulses, the attitudes and beliefs – are on the whole left unanalysed by the approaches which postulate them. This is in my view bound to be so because they are cut off from any environmental context which would make their explication possible. They are, in fact, inward projections of distal outer influences which are overlooked by therapists mainly because they so obviously display the limitedness of the therapeutic enterprise. If the causes of your distress are not inside you, but relatively far off in environmental space–time, can you really be expected to do anything much about them?

There is indeed a point to helping people clarify the grounds of their distress; it is not, however, to place upon them the burden of responsibility for it, to imply that it is a matter of their mistaken perceptions, their infantile immorality or their inappropriate attitudes, but to help them achieve an accurate view of how they have come to be affected by the field of power into which they were thrown at birth. From this perspective *the point of therapeutic clarification is to undo the mystifications of power.*

Of itself the process of clarification makes absolutely no difference to the person's distress, since of itself an appreciation of the nature of the influences on one's life carries no *necessary* implication of being able to do anything about them. But there is at least likely to be some ideological advantage to knowing where one stands in relation to the operation of past and present powers, and it may, of course, be that in practice one can do something about some of them.

People may be mystified about the reasons for their distress in three main ways: either they a) cannot *remember*, or b) cannot *see*, or c) cannot *say* how something came about. The concept of 'repression', with its unnecessary moralistic overtones (that the person manages to hide from him/herself a morally unacceptable thought or impulse), would seem to me better replaced by one which, as I am suggesting, emphasizes the contrary notion that something has been concealed from or forbidden to the person.

a) Being unable to remember
Whether or not someone can *remember* the origin of their distress will depend upon whether it falls within their available span of memory. This is the temporal equivalent of the spatial power

horizon. The impress of power is perhaps particularly strong when it takes place before the person is able verbally to reflect upon and rehearse the events of his/her life (i.e., during infancy). As with so many of the concepts in which it deals, psychoanalysis manages often to moralize the faculty of memory by implying that if you cannot remember childhood events it's because somehow you have chosen not to. As I have already suggested, however, a memory which has not been verbally encoded remains embodied as a *feeling* which simply cannot be turned into a coherent account.

In Chapter Two, Susan provided an example of how this kind of incoherent feeling may dominate a 'clinical condition' such as an 'eating disorder'. Susan did not contain within her a greedy, wilful infant who somehow needed to be brought to book, but had impressed upon her *as* an infant embodied practices which she just could not say anything about and upon which she could gain no critical purchase. She literally could not remember the origins of her feelings, and no amount of 'interpretation' could have made her remember them. They could only be reconstructed as a hypothesis which more or less fitted facts which *could* be remembered or otherwise ascertained from data available in the present.

Clarification of events beyond the span of memory is thus a matter of inventing a 'likely story' which accords as closely as possible with what can be known. Its value lies precisely in *weakening* the sense of guilt which is often instilled into small children along with the exercise over them of adult power and which accompanies the feelings that remain at the base of their experience ever after. It may at least be preferable to be in possession of an only partially supported hypothesis that there was a 'good' reason for one's pain than for ever to bear the burden of an original sin one cannot remember committing.

b) Being unable to see
I have already discussed at some length the way in which people may not be able to *see* the reasons for their distress because of

the limitation placed on their view by the 'power horizon'. One often cannot know – and in the past could not have known – the causes of events which originate in distal environmental space and reverberate through the field of power until they are mediated proximally right up against our bodies, simply because those events take place too far off for our understanding to reach. In principle, the explanation for many of the things which end up giving us pain may be quite simple, but will in practice be almost impossibly obscured by the complexity of the transmission of social influence through environmental space.

The point I wish to emphasize is that, though complicated, impossible to see as well as hard to trace, the reasons for much of our activity and experience are not in the least mysterious in the sense that they originate in some murky inner gloom which only the beady eye of the expert can pierce. Much of the time, to be sure, we don't know what we're doing or why, but this is not, as it is so often taken to be, a *psychological* mystery of the 'unconscious mind', but the rather prosaic result of our being unable to identify the environmental influences which operate upon us.

The trouble is that we confuse the *mechanics* through which we react transitively to environmental influence with the *causes* of our actions. We experience events largely through our bodily sensations and we assess their nature and significance through the psychological apparatus – the meaning systems – which individually and collectively we have developed. We then mistakenly assume that what we feel, believe and know about the processes of our reacting to the world is all there is to know about them, *including* their causes.

Geoff, in Chapter Three, thought that he was in possession of a more or less complete explanation of his distress in relation to being dismissed from his job, much of which referred to the feelings and intentions of himself and those around him, but, of course, no causal account of those events could be complete without an analysis of business policies and activities of which he could have had no conception. In many ways the means through which environmental influences are mediated – for example, the events in the nervous systems of individuals caught up in them and their conscious appraisal of them – are mere details (if extremely complex ones) in a causal process of much more fundamental importance. Therapeutic psychology, if it's not careful, gets so bogged down in these mere details that all it does is compound the confusion of those it seeks to help.

People who consult psychological experts frequently want and expect their distress to be ended by being shown how they can work on the processes 'inside' them which, in their and too often also the expert's view, bring it about. If they have a biological bias they will want a pill, if psychological a formula or procedure which will somehow switch off the pain. This is about as sensible as trying to 'cure' feeling cold by suppressing your shivers.

Much of the time I spend in 'clinical' consultation with people is in trying to persuade them that there is nothing wrong with them, and that rather than trying, metaphorically speaking, to suppress the shivering, or blaming themselves for it, they should look around to try to identify the reasons for it. Because it runs so counter to so much of our 'psychologizing' culture, and because also it highlights the limitations of therapeutic power, this is often a surprisingly difficult task. When successful, however, it may help people to feel a little better about themselves if only because, again, it lifts a moral burden from their shoulders: at least they don't have to feel that their condition is 'their fault'.

It is, of course, not often that a clarification of someone's distress which enables him or her better to see into the nature of the influences causing it leads to any greater possibility of his or her being able directly to do anything to affect those influences. It may occasionally be possible for people to identify influences which are proximal enough for them to act upon them directly, for example, by negotiating a new relationship with an immediate superior at work. It may also be possible for someone to develop strategies which subvert the influence of powers which cannot be modified in any more direct way.

For example, many of those in the 'despairing over-fifty professional' bracket could use a 'demystified' understanding of their predicament simply to ignore demands made upon them. Where such demands were the product of make-believe, or of rapidly changing and extremely short-lived managerial fashions, bundles of papers could safely be consigned to waste-bins without the threats they contained or the enervating procedures they required ever materializing.

On the whole, however, few people can through the process of clarification become aware of much more than the fact that the events out in environmental space which constitute the ultimate causes of their distress, even if they can be seen, cannot be touched. This is a matter for despair only for those professional helpers who depend for the justification of their activities on an essentially magical conception of 'psychology' – for example, that the world can be changed by the power of thought. Most 'patients', in my experience, are relieved to have their personal competence, i.e., their moral viability as human beings, restored to them even if they are no more able than before to get at the causes of their troubles.

c) Being unable to say
The third principal source of confusion over the reasons for distress centres round what people cannot *say*. This probably conforms more closely than the other two sources – what lies beyond the span of memory or over the power horizon – to the conventional concept of 'repression'. The latter, however, as I have indicated, tends to suggest that if something cannot be said it is in some sense or other because the person does not *wish* to say it (even if the 'wish' be an unconscious one). My point, rather, is as always to shift the dynamics of this kind of process from the individual to the field of power in which he or she exists.

One of the main ways in which 'big' people exercise tyranny

over 'little' people (and, of course, maintain thereby their relative advantage) is by placing an embargo of some kind on 'little' people's ability to criticize the mechanics of their oppression. A child very quickly learns what it can and cannot say, and if adult censorship is impressed upon it with sufficient ferocity, it may well come to be unable to speak a forbidden text even to itself. (It was, once again, typical of Freud's disciplinary moralizing that the concept of the 'censor' in repression was placed *inside* the person, so that instead of being a victim of oppressive power, he or she becomes the neurotic editor of guilty impulses.)

There is nothing strange about becoming unable to say to oneself what one cannot say (because it is forbidden) to others. 'Thinking', in the sense we most usually give to it, is nothing other than talking to ourselves, and we talk to ourselves in exactly the same ways and for exactly the same reasons we talk to others (the Russian psychologist Vygotsky[2] gave helpful accounts of how these processes develop). We are not split psychologically into two realms in which entirely different rules apply: an outer realm where we use a special language of diplomacy, and an inner realm where we confide to ourselves the real truth. The rules which govern our talking to ourselves, though, of course, we may apply them differently, are exactly the same as the rules which govern our talking to others (and they to us).

It follows, then, that if the impress of power is used sufficiently heavily to reinforce an interdiction upon a particular utterance, we will be as unlikely to utter it to ourselves as to anyone else, especially if, as in the case of the small child, we have not yet been able to perfect the skills of concealment and lying. It is a familiar part of everyone's experience that the social context in which one finds oneself is a powerful determinant of what one feels able to say. It takes an unusually brave person to point out that the emperor has no clothes to an audience who do not wish to hear it, and the fact that after a time even that person becomes

2. See his *Thought and Language*, MIT Press, 1962.

unable to *think* the word 'naked' is an indication, not of creeping cowardice, but that language (and hence thought) are not our personal, interior possessions, but part of a culture we share with others. If, for example, the Business language of the eighties continues to be parroted for long enough by enough of us, and to be backed by the institutions of power, before much longer we shall be able to speak nothing else.

Whoever controls language, then, to a great extent also controls thought. In this way, as Foucault has established, the very nature of knowledge is bound up with the authorization of power. People who are submerged within a particular field of power often have great difficulty in giving credence to ways of speaking and thinking which originate from anywhere outside it. For example, a company man who had as part of his 'appraisal' been given a psychometric test which labelled him a 'thinking introvert' (and therefore rendered him, it was supposed, of doubtful potential as a salesman) became immediately profoundly pessimistic about his prospects, despite having spent the previous fifteen years successfully selling. The context of power in which his 'personality' had been 'measured' and the label fixed authorized a view of him which no amount of experience seemed able to gainsay.

In the same way, a particular context of knowledge acquisition – a university education, say – doesn't so much liberate the mind for a disinterested contemplation of truth as authorize through the impress of power a certain type of analysis and criticism. 'Knowledge' – what we can legitimately expect to be able to say which will command a respectful hearing – cannot be separated from the mechanics of power.

One of the problems faced by a psychologist or psychotherapist concerned to 'demystify' such processes illustrates this very point: he or she is likely to be speaking from a standpoint not authorized in patients' experience. Patients may simply feel that, although they can see the logic of therapeutic advice which runs counter to the received ideology of medical authority, it lacks sufficient 'credibility' for them to be able to act upon it.

However, the fact that something cannot be said, or that only certain kinds of things *can* be said, doesn't necessarily mean that it doesn't exist. Whatever the community might say, the emperor *is* naked, and it may only take a shift in the structure of power which ties everyone's tongue to enable his state to be openly remarked.

It is perhaps not surprising that the therapeutic concept of 'repression' has concentrated so heavily on what cannot be said, since the 'lifting' of such repression is the only form of clarification likely to be of direct and immediate benefit to people. In other words, helping someone to speak a truth which is or had been otherwise forbidden to them may be a source of enlightenment which really is empowering.

Steve, for example, was totally at a loss to explain his irritability at home. This had occasionally developed into outbursts of violent temper during which he had hit his wife or subjected his son to a vicious verbal assault. He was deeply ashamed of these incidents and extremely worried that his marriage would disintegrate as a result. He put it all down to stresses at work and wanted to know if there were any techniques of relaxation or self-control which could prevent further lapses.

As often seems to be the case with people who simply cannot say what is happening to them, an examination of Steve's circumstances was extremely puzzling – there seemed to be absolutely no reason for his state. He had, it was true, had some quite serious problems at work, but these had been resolved months ago. He was devoted to his wife and family, and there was no obvious sign of his own family background having been in any way disturbed. It began to seem as though there must be some demon inhabiting him, some interior fault or 'dysfunction' to account for the terrible disturbances in his otherwise almost unusually untroubled life.

However, reading between the lines of the account he gave of his early life yielded one or two clues to the nature of his difficulties. His description of his parental upbringing as loving and supportive and his boyhood relationship with his sister as 'brilliant' at first diverted attention from a state of affairs which was in truth very different. It was only when he let drop that his father had died of a liver complaint, and that he had not seen his sister for a 'few years' despite her living in the same town, that more persistent enquiry revealed that his father's liver complaint had been cirrhosis and that he had been an alcoholic with a 'very nasty' temper, and that Steve's sister had been the overwhelming favourite of his mother, with whom she had shared a life-long contempt for almost everything Steve thought and did.

Neither his father's drinking nor the bitter rows it provoked with his mother had ever been directly alluded to in the family, and it was only in talking about them to his psychologist that Steve began to acknowledge that they 'must have been a problem'. But before he could voice such criticisms, he had to be, so to speak, offered a language in which to do so. It wasn't, of course, that he literally didn't know the words, but rather that he had not been accorded the authority to apply them to his experience in the way that the psychologist was suggesting. Even with practice, he clearly found the exercise a strange and unfamiliar one.

Having come to grips with the historical embargo on telling the truth to himself about his early family life, Steve found it much easier to assess his current position more accurately, and he was quite quickly able to confront features of his marital situation which until then he had simply avoided talking to himself about (the fact, for example, that for the last six years his wife had completely withdrawn from him sexually). Being a capable and resourceful man, Steve made good use of his new-found power to tell himself the truth, and had no further need of psychology. He was no longer surprised by his bad temper, and discussed quite amicably with his wife what course their futures might best take.

Although sometimes difficult to identify (simply *because* the person cannot say it) interdictions on utterances of the kind which caused Steve his problems are relatively easy to lift. By their very nature they usually involve only the most proximal sphere of the person's relations – often, of course, in the past – and so are held in place by no very great or inaccessible social influence. The power of the therapeutic alliance in such cases may well be enough for the person to use an accurate analysis of his or her situation to act directly upon it.

I cannot say, however, that in my experience this kind of personal dilemma (in contrast to the *societal* control of meaning and authorization of knowledge) is so often to be found at the root of people's problems as the therapeutic literature suggests. Most of us who survive childhood have managed to find ways of saying what our parents forbade us to, and will quite early on have been able to abandon the necessity for the kind of despairing, 'don't-know' muteness one sees in frightened children, perhaps to develop instead strategies whereby we are able to lie to our parents while telling ourselves the truth. (Lying, I have often found, is a skill necessary to the avoidance of oppression, and if people can't do it, they need to be taught.) Far more usual as causes of lasting distress are those which are beyond our reach in space or time.

ENCOURAGEMENT

Most psychotherapies lay very little theoretical emphasis on the necessity for people to grapple with those material structures in the outside world which have contributed to making their lives a misery. Therapeutic change, it appears, is wrought within the walls of the consulting room. Of orthodox individual therapies, only the behavioural approach takes proper account of the influence of an environment beyond those walls, but even in this case such influence is seen as almost entirely intransitive: patients are not so much expected actively to get a grip on the world as to be submitted to processes of 'conditioning', 'contingencies of reinforcement', etc., which will be devised by the therapist. As with the 'psychodynamic' approaches, this again has the merit of preserving the status of the therapist as expert and the process of treatment as technical.

It seems likely, however, that despite their theoretical indifference to the outside environment as a factor in therapeutic change, pretty well all experienced therapists will in practice, though very probably unknowingly, accord it quite a lot of importance. Having established a relationship which provides patients with a degree of comfort, and having clarified as far as possible the nature and causes of their difficulties, the obvious problem remains of considering what they should do about it all.

Again with the exception of the behaviourists, the interesting thing about psychotherapists and counsellors is that they don't even pretend to know what people should do to make changes in their lives. The difficulty, no doubt, is that once again the barely formulated idea at the back of therapeutic thinking is that 'change' is a matter not of changing a *world*, but of bringing about some kind of 'intrapsychic' event which will fill people with new resolve, transform their attitudes, expectations and beliefs, or adjust their perceptions of the past – in short, operate in some way on those internal moral and psychological forces which are supposed to 'cause' our 'behaviour'. Even where behavioural therapists acknowledge that the person is related to and shaped by a world, their therapeutic imagination doesn't seem to stretch beyond a vision of shaping the patient in a new way by setting up the necessary reinforcements.

So when it comes to doing something about the predicaments that people find themselves in, the conventional therapeutic answer seems to be that they should either be exhorted, persuaded or conditioned into taking a new tack. The world will not budge, so the patient must 'adjust'.

If, however, we are not independent moral entities, and if therapeutic microenvironments cannot legitimately be detached from the influences of the wider environment in which they are set, then therapeutically inspired resolve and consulting-room experiments in conditioning are not going to be enough to make any real difference to people's troubles. We need to realize that, rather than the patient being a problem for the world, the world is a problem for the patient. We are the embodied products of environmental space-time. To make a difference to our lives we need to be able to exert what little influence we have on the environment to make it, from our perspective, a little more benign. It is not *we* who need to change, but the world around us. Or to put it another way, the extent to which we are able to change will always depend upon some material change in the environmental structures of power which envelop us (and insofar as these cannot be changed, for example because they are in the past, neither can we be wiped clean of their effects).

The difficulty with this is immediately apparent: how do we, relatively powerless creatures, bring effective influence to bear on the environment? It is this difficulty which accounts for the therapeutic silence on *how* to confront the causes of our distress. Since they have no particular knowledge of the procedures of getting to grips with and modifying the baneful influences of power, counsellors and psychotherapists are reduced to *encouraging* their patients to do the best they can. There will, of course, be times when an experienced therapist may be able to suggest courses of action which have served patients well in the past, but this kind of knowledge remains completely informal and unelaborated, and will continue to do so as long as the therapeutic profession shirks the theoretical task of emptying people of all the intrapsychic contents it has stuffed into them and putting them back into a coherent relationship with the environment. Even the achievement of this aim, one should note, would be less likely to extend the sphere of therapeutic influence than to define more accurately its limitations.

If you wanted to learn to play the violin, you would be well advised to seek out a teacher who knows how to play one, who is acquainted with the *materiality* of the instrument, its sound, its feel, its relations with the body. The teacher should know not only all this, but also how to impart such knowledge to the pupil –

how, for example, to reproduce in another person the body-instrument relations known so well by him/herself. The teacher thus puts the pupil into a new set of relations to a world the pupil has not previously encountered. What such a teacher does *not* do is talk endlessly about how to play the violin, or merely exhort the pupil to play, or assure the pupil that he or she *can* play, or train the pupil to *imagine* being able to play, or offer a course in hypnotic suggestion that the pupil is already a virtuoso.

The project of the psychotherapist (and perhaps as much as anything it is this which reduces it in any ultimate sense to absurdity) is, of course, considerably more ambitious than that of a music teacher. It's hard enough to acquire, refine and communicate the kind of knowledge you need to teach someone to play the violin. What do you have to know to become an expert in living life without distress?

Psychotherapy's 'credibility problem' is by now familiar. The ideological enterprise of psychology and psychotherapy has been to detach person from world so that social exploitation can be represented as personal breakdown. Therapists who unwittingly mediate this process, even when they can see that their patients have been injured by a malign world, and even if they cast around for effective procedures which they can encourage patients to adopt, are likely, because of the impossible grandiosity of the aim, to find themselves falling back helplessly on the magical tradition out of which their profession grew: the belief in personal transformation following upon a form of ritual consultation with a charismatic expert.

However, it has not always been and is not everywhere quite as muddled as this. The importance of the environment in the constitution of human character has been a theme of philosophical and psychological thought throughout history, and it may well be only in the twentieth century that it has become quite so distorted and submerged. In the *Republic*, for example, Plato's concern with the kind of environment which would produce his ruling class is meticulous, and a preoccupation with the arts necessary for shaping a desirable life was, of course, common in Greek thought. In the present day, 'psychology' of this kind has, ironically, passed out of the official discipline of psychology and become the informal practice of politicians and business people who set about engineering the kind of society it is in their interest to produce. It is only in the new, and so far 'low profile', development of 'community psychology' (and even there not everywhere) that serious thought is being given to the relation of the individual experience of distress to the social structures of power which cause and maintain it.

I do not wish to imply that there is no value at all in the therapeutic encouragement of patients to try to grapple with the proximal mediation of their difficulties – I have already acknowledged that there may well be empowering aspects of patient-therapist solidarity. Encouraging patients to challenge people who have so far exacted unquestioning submission, to risk situations which have always been avoided, to learn procedures which have previously been feared, and so on, is likely to be recognized by nearly all therapists as something they spend a lot of time doing. Often such forms of encouragement are likely to be dressed up in a technical guise, as, for example, 'assertiveness training', 'systematic desensitization', 'anxiety management', etc.

But the fruits of such enterprise are as limited as they are because the field of power in which we are caught is relatively so impervious to our attempts to act transitively upon it. There are useful adjustments which people can make – for example the woman who fearfully challenges her husband's domination to find to her surprise that, even if reluctantly, he gives way; the man who finds that abandonment of a macho posture brings relief rather than defeat – but on the whole the distal influences which transfix us through their proximal mediators are not moved by such tactics.

An important part of assessing the changes people can make to their lives is to establish what powers and resources they have available to bring to bear on their environment. It is remarkable how little detailed research has been carried out in this area, and yet in my experience it is *always* the case that useful 'therapeutic' gains are made only by people who have the resources to make them. The more one is able to reach out beyond the immediate proximal influences on one's life to impinge upon the structures which control them, the more chance one will stand of being able to relieve the distress they give rise to. The means which make such reaching out possible are, of course, precisely those which people have down the ages tried to appropriate in order to establish or maintain social and material advantage: money, education, association with powerful individuals or groups. There are also, of course, the personal – even biological – characteristics which may be exploited or bartered in pursuit of such material forms of power – for example, intelligence, physical strength or attractiveness. A therapeutic approach which maintained that you could effectively influence your world without *any* of these (for example, by tapping some form of 'inner strength') would be not only stupidly sentimental, but ideologically very damaging.

Before encouraging someone to set out in an attempt to make changes to their world, one needs, then, to establish what resources they have to back them. If they have none, the enterprise will be doomed, and further encouragement would amount to irresponsible cruelty.

One of the sturdier pillars supporting the mystique of 'psychodynamic' therapies is the notion that therapeutic change, if it is to be accounted valid, has to be an outcome of the therapy itself, an aspect of the alchemical reaction which supposedly takes place in the crucible of the 'therapeutic relationship'. In fact, however, exactly the opposite seems to me to be the case. Whatever the temporary enthusiasms which may be fired in people through solidarity with a counsellor or therapist, the world will inexorably reassert its grip unless they can marshal against it powers and resources which are in themselves thoroughly mundane. Changing (or finding) jobs, moving house, forming new bonds or associations with others, acquiring knowledge or abilities which can be put to use in changing one's circumstances:

these are the kinds of events and activities which make a real difference to the way that people feel. (Perhaps what misled traditional theorists was that so many of their clients already possessed a wide range of such resources, so that the most visibly significant change appeared to be a therapeutically inspired 'decision' to deploy them in new ways.)

For the person whose troubles are caused most fundamentally by events or difficulties in the present, the possession of appropriate powers and resources is a hopeful indication that they may be able to resolve them. If you have the money and the requisite vocational abilities and qualifications, you can, for example, change your job or your location. If you have the money and the brains, you can equip yourself with new abilities through further training or education. If you are not too old, too unattractive or too inextricably materially enmeshed in current relationships, you may be able to form new ones. If you have none of these powers and resources, you will be entirely at the mercy of a world which is quite likely to turn out to be a ruthlessly cruel one.

Change, in short, comes about through somebody being able physically and materially to alter their *position* in the world, to escape malign influences or to find benign ones. The motive power for making such moves is *always* either directly or indirectly traceable to resources which are or have historically been (for example, in the form of education) acquired from outside. The ultimate 'therapy' is thus the acquisition of some kind of socioeconomic advantage, and it is above all this fact which the psychotherapies have helped so effectively to mystify.

Therapists may be therapeutic to the extent that they can help people identify the powers and resources needed to tackle their difficulties and encourage them where possible to acquire them. In this respect therapy is much more like teaching than the esoteric enterprise it is so often made out to be, but with the unfortunate difference that the arts to be taught and the manner of teaching them are not specified. In most cases, then, the therapist is reduced to making fairly obvious suggestions about how patients might tackle things – for example, by joining an evening class, making new social contacts, seeking legal advice about difficult domestic situations, etc. In one form or another this kind of encouragement usually consists of helping people to extend their own influence upon their lives beyond the most immediately proximal sphere in which they *feel* their miseries into the slightly more distal regions where the *mediation* of them may be modified a little. The details of how such changes may be made are left largely to trial and error, and therapeutic expertise falls a long way short of actually being able to offer people a step-by-step blueprint of how to make life more comfortable.

There are, of course, particular times in people's lives when the possibility of change – the opportunity actually to take up a new stance in the world – is greater than at others. Adolescence is one such period. It seems likely that therapeutic encouragement given at a time when the individual has the opportunity to act upon it will be much more powerful than when there is virtually no room for manoeuvre. Society, so to speak, 'licenses' the adolescent to escape one powerful set of influences before becoming too deeply enmeshed in another, and knowledgeable and considered advice at this point in someone's life may be extremely important and useful. In the same way some forms of activity are much more permissible at one stage as compared with another. It is, for example, entirely respectable for a child to be learning to read and write, but far less so for an adult – it usually takes a lot of courage for someone to go to adult literacy classes. For these reasons it is important for anyone in a helping role both to be aware of the 'windows of opportunity' which life offers people for change, and to try, through the process of encouragement, to help force them open a little where they are shut.

There may also be some value in therapists offering their clients solidarity and encouragement in the face of unfamiliarity. Most therapists will have encountered people's frequent reluctance to make important changes to their lives even when they have the necessary resources to do so. Usually this is because the making of such changes would require their entering frighteningly unfamiliar territory. So rather than making what seems to be an obviously necessary and easily possible change, people may persist in an unproductive and perhaps damaging form of conduct which, even if it once served them well enough, has long since ceased to do so.

Mystified by psychoanalysis as 'repetition compulsion', this kind of difficulty seems to have much more to do with the virtually universal adult preference for familiarity. Apart from anything else, one is not socially 'licensed' as an adult to experiment with ways of relating to people or to display obvious uncertainty or idiosyncrasy in one's dealings with them. What may seem charming in a child may well be extremely strange or even offensive in an adult, and once people have learned the lessons of their youth, they are not only understandably reluctant to abandon them, but there may well be real difficulty in the social acceptability of their doing so.

Rather than therapists imputing such difficulties to some kind of neurotic failure of development, it would be more helpful for them to deliberate over the construction of a theory and practice which reflected more truthfully the realities of their position. Though this would destroy much of their mystique, it might also affirm their role as accomplices and encouragers of people who, though in possession of the necessary resources, lack the support to embark on an arduous course of learning and to take real social risks in the process of making changes to the circumstances of their lives.

The activities of comforting, clarifying and encouraging are not in themselves in any way dishonourable. Indeed, these have always been the ingredients of any effective kind of proximal help, whether given formally by doctors, priests and psychotherapists, or informally by friends and families. If we ceased to be able to perform these functions for each other life would become unbearable, even though in performing them we may make only the shallowest impression on the past and present environmental influences which cause our distress. When we come to confront the reasons for our distress, then, the 'therapeutic' functions are both highly essential and completely inadequate, and this is because on the one hand they touch us in the proximal sphere in which our lives are lived, experienced and felt, and on the other because they are incapable of reaching out into the distal regions where lie the origins of our social ills.

I do not agree with those radical critiques of psychotherapy which condemn it because of the involvement in the therapeutic relationship of an imbalance of power. I noted in Chapter Two how in some ways the unusual power structure of the therapeutic situation is what gives it what little advantage it may have over informal helping relations (for example, the rule that one person talks while the other listens). Power is not in itself immoral; indeed no good could be done without it. The power of loving adults is essential to the proper development of children. We shall not overcome the difficulties of our social environment by abdicating from positions of power.

What makes psychological forms of help suspect is not so much the relative power of their practitioners as the falsity of the claims they so often make, along with the paucity of their concepts and the ineffectiveness of their procedures. In exploiting magical thinking they obscure our vision of the reasons for our difficulties and sap our determination to take on the rigours of trying to change them; in assuming a technical guise they conceal their ignorance of any truly effective method while illicitly appropriating forms of help which belong to everyone.

It can be argued, I think very persuasively (as Jeffrey Masson has done), that because any effective and justifiable form of psychotherapy is nothing more than a human undertaking, a form of moral conduct which *in principle* cannot be technicized or taught, it cannot be legitimately given the status of *profession*. Certainly there is nothing in the procedures of psychotherapy, in the forms in which comfort, clarification and encouragement can be offered, which cannot be – and indeed should not be – done by anyone. I think, however, that it is possible for people to acquire a degree of expertise by virtue of becoming familiar with particular kinds of difficulty or distress through lengthy acquaintance with them. Knowledge comes from experience, and it is certainly likely that a practitioner who has encountered particular kinds of problems in a wide range of instances may learn more useful ways of helping than someone who is new to them.

In this respect 'therapy' and 'counselling' are not – as they are so often made out to be – 'skills' in themselves which can be applied to any form of distress which comes along (any more than 'music' is a 'skill' which can be applied to the playing of any instrument you care to name). Far from being a contentless 'skill', effective help is likely always to be part and parcel of a *knowledge* of the kinds of difficulty to be tackled. But knowledge, of course, is precisely what is in shortest supply in the psychological therapies.

Knowledge may be either transmitted or exploited. The great danger in the professionalization of help in the form of 'therapy' is that it hugs what little it knows to itself for commercial gain, rather than passing it on to its clients. Such knowledge may be used to disparage others for their ignorance while they are kept dependent on the knower for its fruits.

Disparagement, certainly, is a feature of the psychiatric and psychological literature. It is extremely difficult to think of any major text in these fields which does not either belittle those who become the objects of its attention, or patronize them by holding before them an ideal of how they ought to be. At the same time, there is, of course, absolutely nothing to justify such professional conceit – no evidence that the authors of such texts know better than anyone else how to live their lives, and none that the application of their methods actually leads to a significant amelioration of distress.

The clinical gaze which sorts and labels those it falls upon into various categories of inadequacy and incompetence, the professional hubris which presumes to know how unhappy people should 'adjust' themselves to their fate, are surely in need of the humility which would come from the recognition that their claims are bogus and their methods bankrupt. Our gaze needs rather to turn out towards the world in a sober appreciation of the infinity of ways in which social forces over which we have no control throw our lives into chaos and generate ever new and intractable varieties of pain.

Psychologists, psychiatrists and psychotherapists – the police force of 'normality' – need to switch their focus from the physical and mental 'interiors' of their patients to stand with them in human solidarity while together they probe the social space around them for the causes of our distress. We surely have by now abundant evidence that nobody knows how people should be, and if they do are incapable of conveying it. The most we can hope to know is how to reduce some of the impact of some painful influences, and this is done by helpfully taking people's sides, not by diagnosing or by lecturing them.

In our private aspect – that part of our personal experience which is not knitted into or given shape by the social 'forms' we share – we are *all* lonely, eccentric and bizarre. As far as we can be, we need to be supported in our idiosyncrasy and reassured that we are not alone in loneliness; we need, that is, an informed understanding of what it is to be human, to have spent our lives located bodily in a position which *nobody* else can share in a world which, potentially, *everybody* else shares. We do not need our imagination to be policed and our feelings to be regulated by moralizing professionals who are no less victims than we of the ruthless forces which too often make our lives so bitter and our hopes so blighted. We need to be seen as characters whose experience of the world, however bizarre, gives us something true to say about it, and something which might usefully be heeded by others. We have nothing to thank those people for who seek in one way or another to pass judgement on the validity of our experience. Our pain is not an indication of what is the matter with us, but of something which is hurting us from outside.

It is sometimes helpful to suggest to people that, rather than thinking of themselves as social inadequates in need of adjustment, as containers of various undesirable components, they consider themselves as they would a character in a novel: as individual, certainly, but as interesting, as signifying something about the world and as having something to say about it. Nobody really expects characters in novels to get themselves sorted out and 'normalized' in psychotherapy. One seeks to *understand* and *appreciate* characters rather than to change them. To the extent that fiction is less inclined to look for magical solutions to the 'problems' set by its characters, it is more 'real' than life.

Many of the people whose distress drives them to consult a professional expert of some kind do so because they are afraid or ashamed of feeling what they feel, seeing what they see or being who they are. It may help them a little to be taken seriously and to discover thereby that their experience has meanings which point out beyond themselves to a complex and difficult world which none of us knows how to handle. Often it will transpire that they have already done all that they could with exemplary courage and concern for others, but for one reason or another have been unable to give themselves (or get from others) much credit for their efforts. For the most part it's not they who need changing, but the world.

CHAPTER SIX

A Rational Faith

The confusion and distress which form so intractable a part of so many people's lives at this time, and which are so often mistakenly ascribed to an 'interior', personal failure, in fact originate in two main varieties of distal influence. The first, described in detail in Chapter Four, stems from the socio-economic pressures of big business. Its effects (on the vast majority who do not profit from it) are oppressive, painful and acutely unsettling. Radical insecurity is its chief characteristic, and it is profoundly inimical to all those forms of activity which show human beings in their best, most productive and constructive light. The conditions which permit peaceful collaboration, concentrated, creative work and disinterested intellectual enquiry are instantly destroyed by insecurity and threat, which create in their place strife, competitiveness, callousness and fear.

The second main variety of distal influence might better be described as a lack of influence: the breakdown of 'form'. The collapse of traditional systems of values, the tendency to individualization induced by market pressures, the disintegration of the public sphere, the privatization of morals, have all been remarked upon by those who sense the gathering of a millennial crisis the outcome of which is completely incalculable. However this may turn out to be on the grand scale, there is no doubt about its effects on the experience of individuals.

In that proximal sphere in which we are fated to live our lives, the *rules* by which we may do so are no longer clear. The only easily identifiable rules that there are – those of the market – are either simply not adequate or positively inappropriate as guides to social and ethical living.

To take perhaps the most obvious example, the extent of the guidance they give on how men and women should conduct their relations with each other – as competitors, exploitable objects of satisfaction, replaceable commodities, etc. – just does not take account of the problems set by being embodied in a world from which, however hard you try, gender cannot easily be eradicated. And so, lacking 'forms' which enter, *as part of their personhood*, into the structuring of their lives, people experience confusion, bewilderment, self-doubt and suspicion. We don't know how to 'go on' any more not because we lack the intelligence or will to live decently and sociably, but because the necessary guidelines for doing so have disappeared.

And they have disappeared for good reasons. I am not about to make a plea for the return of 'Victorian values' (not least because that is in large measure exactly what in the eighties we got), but want rather to point out that it is precisely the unsatisfactoriness of old values which makes any return to previous, apparently more settled times impossible. From the oppressive domination of a corrupt Church to the hypocritical imposition of the suffocating, conformist values of European imperialism, from the stupid pomposity of privilege to the terror-inducing rhetoric of Stalinism, there has one way and another been a long history of life-destroying 'moralities' imposed on ordinary people by systematic power. There seems absolutely no reason to believe that Business Culture has done any better.

Small wonder that power in any shape or form has been and is being radically called into question by those sensitive to the pain it has so consistently inflicted. From the measured, intellectually and ethically often very attractive speculations of eighteenth- and nineteenth-century anarchists (William Godwin, Alexander Herzen, Peter Kropotkin, Proudhon, Leon Tolstoy), through the reflections of social critics of twentieth-century American society (Paul Goodman, Murray Bookchin, Christopher

Lasch, Noam Chomsky), to the protestations of the oppressed minorities of the present time (the familiar triad of gays, blacks and women), the question arises as to whether *any* form of power which creates and enforces social rules can be morally viable and acceptable.

The greatest of all critics of power, Michel Foucault, seemed to see power as inseparable from a technology of normalizing rules, and yet there is more than a hint in the developments of most recent times that power may manifest itself in an unexpected guise – that of, precisely, the *absence* of rules. For with the 'triumph' of capitalism and the 'end of history' proclaimed by the euphoric wing of 'postmodernity', it seems that the society held together by the discipline of scientific surveillance which Foucault so brilliantly revealed is metamorphosing into one which thrives upon the superficial anarchism created by deregulation and 'blue-sky' make-believe. Disciplinary scientism is being replaced by magical liberalism, but both are equally the creation of power.

For power is not synonymous with rules. Power will employ *any* strategy which creates privilege, distinction and advantage. Anything at all which results in the accretion of economic and ideological control will be adapted and adopted by power. A mistake of systematic thinking about social and cultural issues has often been to underestimate the resourcefulness and adaptability of power, which is as resourceful and adaptable as human ingenuity can make it. Marx may well have been right about the inherent contradictions of the capitalism of his day, but power can cope with contradictions. If things get too inconveniently contradictory, you just move the goal posts.

Foucault's particular genius was to show how institutions masquerading as caring were really controlling. It may well be, however, that power can, for a while, best maintain its position by abandoning care/control for a chaotic free-for-all in which the privileged are isolated from the teeming, disorganized mass through sheer invisibility as much as anything else. This would be the extreme development of the contrast between a hidden private affluence and an ungoverned and all too obvious public squalor.

Absence of rules does thus not necessarily bring freedom, and certainly not equality. There are rules and rules: oppressive ones which we would be well rid of, and constructive ones which are the very fabric of our social being. On the whole we have not been very discriminating about which are which.

It has often struck me (as no doubt it has many people) how, for the most part, amazingly well ordered road traffic is. Rush-hour traffic on a busy city ring road, for example, is an extraordinary phenomenon of co-ordination, anticipation and co-operation. All those people of the most varied social condition and personal temperament, with utterly different interests and preoccupations, irreconcilable values, young, old, male and female, all manage to obey the same, quite stringent and tightly defined rules. The odd maverick, it is true, may switch lanes inconsiderately, vehicles may break down, accidents, of course, happen. But given the volume of traffic, the number of people and the complexity of their differing aims in travelling, it is an astonishingly stable and predictable situation. So it certainly is not the case that we cannot and do not willingly conduct ourselves according to rules. What seems to permit us to do so is our being able to appreciate their usefulness and see that they have been constructed in our interest.

But if the Highway Code can command our assent, there seems to be very little, other than 'the market', to organize our conduct on the grander scale, and the absence of a coherent and codifiable moral order is making the experience of living increasingly difficult and painful for larger and larger numbers of people. We have tried an authoritarian God, and that didn't work. We have tried both the majesty of the King and the dictatorship of the proletariat, and they brought us only grief. The project of the Enlightenment – the belief in Reason and Science as the foundation of a golden future – is also widely proclaimed to have failed. Certainly the tyrannical objectivity which became established via a degenerate scientism, even though it still maintains a disciplinary hold on our lives, has become so discredited as to be scarcely any longer viable, and in any case appears to have outlived its usefulness. Aside from Business values, what else seems to be on offer?

Now that the old 'forms' have been exposed as 'grand narratives' which simply couldn't bear the moral weight placed upon them, it is not particularly difficult to identify the ideological influences which compete to take their place. The appeal of fundamentalist religion is particularly in evidence, and seems to offer a rallying point both in societies which offer little hope of material comfort and for sections of affluent Western populations which find the insecurities generated by Business values rather more than they can cope with.

There is clearly a strong element of wishful thinking in the reborn varieties of Christianity which appeal to so many people, but there is nothing like association to give magical wishfulness an appearance of solid reality. The shattering of that part of our personhood which is structured by 'form' is experienced as the kind of pain which cries out to be assuaged by the comfort of association. As a last resort people seem to seek refuge and stability by huddling together on any moral high ground that offers, whether in rigid adherence to 'politically correct' ideologies concerning gender and sexuality, etc., or in the sometimes quite fanatical espousal of surprisingly small-scale moralisms such as vegetarianism, anti-smoking campaigns, and so on.

Nationalism fulfils a function similar to that of fundamentalist religion, but is probably considerably more powerful in view of the ready-made associative strength of nationality. It takes, to put it mildly, quite a stretch of the imagination to believe that Jesus Christ is taking a personal interest in your everyday affairs, but that you are a Serb or a Croat seems simply a matter of fact, and already a sound basis for getting together with other Serbs or Croats. Nothing seems more predictable than that, as other values which give social coherence disappear, nationalism should once again cast its shadows across human society.

If religiosity and patriotism fail to appeal, there is still the option of turning one's back on the public sphere altogether in order to celebrate 'interiority'. Apart from the vulgar privatism of Business, in which the ideal of life is to 'enjoy' both your personal possessions and your commodified 'relationships' in the privacy of your own home, there are the morally rather more sophisticated approaches to life which suggest that its value lies in the cultivation of the self and the riches thought to be contained therein. Whether fostering the 'personal growth' of the humanist psychotherapies, or tending the 'God within' of theologies which, like Don Cupitt's, have 'at last understood that our life has no outside',[1] the emphasis is on the inward-turned gaze which endlessly contemplates selves or souls in order to render them more personally satisfactory.

Apart from such approaches as these, then, we have little to shape our common purpose except the 'magical liberalism' which is loosely and somewhat incoherently associated with Business values. Rules and regulations, other than those of the medi-ocratically imposed discipline which generates competition and insecurity, are out, and they are out partly because of the further insecurity that their absence occasions. In the place of the old 'grand narratives' of medieval and reformation Christianity and the Enlightenment quest for scientific certainty and ethical confidence, we have a motley collection of petty narratives whose relatedness to material circumstances and wishful thinking is so obvious that there seems little likelihood of their achieving more than some temporarily expedient goal (for example, securing national boundaries or warding off the invasion of personal insecurity).

We are left, in fact, with a 'postmodern' relativity of values or 'narratives' from which, in the best market tradition, you pays your money and takes your choice. I have no doubt at all that this state of affairs gives rise to considerable distress, and I hope

1. From the back cover of his *The Long-Legged Fly*, SCM Press, 1987.

that it is by now clear from what has gone before that this is not just a matter of our 'not knowing what to believe in', or of not being provided with some kind of arbitrary moral goal to cement our social life into a common purpose, but is rather a factor of part of our nature as persons having disintegrated. This is, of course, the part of our personhood which is situated in the social environment outside our bodies. Its breakdown is our breakdown because 'we' are not separable from 'it'. But 'it' cannot be reconstructed through an attempted therapeutic reconstruction of our 'selves': if we want to 'feel better' we have to pay direct attention to the reconstruction of that part of our common environment whose disintegration is making us all feel bad in the first place.

At present, our common social environment, where it has not fractured into various essentially magical relativities or nationalistic interest groups, is held together only by the precarious structure given it by Business Culture. If the economic basis upon which that world is built (and whatever one thinks of it, it is at least real) should collapse – as indeed in its present form it surely must – we shall be in a sorry state indeed, with nothing to fall back on but the barbarous attachments dictated largely by our biology.

What we need is not a 'narrative', grand or petty, with which to glue together our fractured social lives, for it is precisely our having seen through such narratives – their arbitrariness and hypocrisy, the smoke screen they have provided for the machinations of power – which has led to their demise. We need rather to *re-establish a relationship with reality* which has all but disappeared into magic and wishful relativities.

For however seduced we may have been by our own inventiveness, by the power of make-believe and the artistry of a huge promotional industry, however dazzled by the endlessly reflecting images of a 'postmodernity' in which it begins to seem that absolutely everything is 'in the mind', it is still the case that we do live in a real world, and more than ever the case that we need to come to a satisfactory accommodation with it.

If the 'project of the Enlightenment' collapsed into the totalitarianism, strife and destruction of the twentieth century, does that really mean that the search for truth, justice and equality which inspired it is discredited, or may it be that it is only the means of trying to attain them which can be shown to have failed?

One of the central messages emerging from the mixture of confusion, despair and excitement which appears to be attending the close of this millennium is that 'form' is passé, that we have nothing to rely upon but our selves and whatever organizing principles can be excavated from their interior spaces. The sober constraints of an 'outside' which, it is felt, is so hopelessly beyond our understanding as to be not worth further serious consideration seem to be giving way to a Nietzschean exultation in a kind of absolute subjectivity which places humankind not merely at the centre of the universe, but practically encompassing it as its container.

But if 'form' is necessary to our integrity as persons, we shall have to continue to pay attention to the nature of the world as its creatures rather than its containers. If the project of the Enlightenment failed to reveal to us a reality solid enough for us to anchor ourselves in reasonably comfortably and harmoniously, it need not mean that we have to abandon the project so much as learn from our mistakes. It is still, I submit, not only relevant, but more than ever essential to pursue two fundamental Enlightenment questions: what is it possible to believe and what is it right to do?

The point of pursuing these questions – knowledge and truth on the one hand and ethical guidance on the other – is not simply to keep academics in business (allowing the intellectual market to corner these concerns is precisely one of the mistakes we have made in the past) but to reconstruct an essential pole of our personhood by placing ourselves in a viable relationship to the real world we actually do live in and which we absolutely cannot wish away.

KNOWLEDGE AND TRUTH

The concept of 'truth' and the forms of knowledge which have been built upon its foundations have not been unsullied by the interests of power. Indeed, far from being the shining centre of enlightened humanity's quest for liberation, truth is quickly turned into a blunt instrument of oppression. Rather than providing the gateway to an understanding we can joyfully pursue together, truth becomes the brutal, cruelly unresisting fact which whips your arms behind your back and marches you helplessly along the narrow paths laid down by those who 'know'.

It is quite remarkable how politicians, when they are about to lie most blatantly, preface their utterance with 'the truth is . . .' The truth they invoke is the truth which constrains the opposition and shuts up objectors, the same truth to whose demands generations of school children have been terrorized into trying to conform, the truth which paralyses dissent and exacts obedience.

The truth pursued in scientific knowledge, most clearly evident in the wonderful intellectual liberation of those courageous seekers who fought their way free of the grim discipline of the Church, soon enough became yet another form of that discipline, this time embodied in the dogmas of logical positivists and other systematic thinkers who like to set rules for what it is possible to believe.

It is really quite difficult for most people even to imagine a concept of 'truth' which is not tied so closely into some kind of discipline as to be more or less identical with it. Truth is what we *have to* believe and what we cannot escape from, either because it is defined and laid down by some absolute Authority or because it is stamped with an equally absolute Objectivity which cannot be gainsaid. Truth, for most people, is either to be possessed or feared as a weapon for controlling or being controlled by others. As an instrument of power, its availability becomes strictly limited, and inevitably it ends up embedded in a whole technology of secrecy. Truth is dangerous.

It is also extremely difficult for most of us to disconnect the idea of truth from that of certainty. What gives it such invincible authority, what makes it such a prized commodity and such a dangerous weapon is its infallibility. Truth is the final arbiter, and before its judgement one can only stand in dumb submission. Philosophers who have been concerned to duck from under the tyranny of one form of 'infallible' truth have nearly always sought to establish another in its place by discovering something new which cannot be doubted (something, naturally, which suited them more than those they saw as their intellectual oppressors). And as soon as a suitable candidate is found for the role of indubitable instrument of liberation, it is immediately appropriated by power as the next weapon of oppression. The science which slew God becomes the all-pervasive net of discipline in which Foucault showed us we are caught.

The same fate is sure to await the efforts of those who seek to replace 'truth' by an entirely new authority which repudiates its ancient claims altogether. There have since Nietzsche been various attempts at suggesting that there *is* no truth, no grounds of certainty, but only our own desire and will, nothing but infinite relativities of perspective, so that ultimately only might determines right. From critics of 'modernity' (like Herbert Marcuse) who have suggested that we may escape to freedom via an unbridled eroticism, to apologists of 'postmodernity' who (like Richard Rorty) frankly make pragmatic self-interest the foundation of our concerns, there has been a great deal of intellectual activity in recent decades aimed no doubt at undermining the despotic claims of certain 'truth'. But there is no revolutionary thought here which cannot be comfortably adapted by power.

It seems strange at first that the compound of Reason and Power which we discover 'truth' to have been made of should be considered by so many present-day thinkers to have been rendered more liberating by dissolving from it the element of Reason. But strange only so long as we forget that those thinkers cannot avoid living in and being shaped by a world which is itself structured by power. If power can operate successfully by dropping its pretence of reason, why shouldn't it do so? As long as 'truth' had the authority of certainty, it was needed by power to underwrite its claims about the nature of the 'real world', but once certainty has been shown to be a philosophical impossibility, truth (which in any case carried with it many inconvenient limitations on power's freedom to do *exactly* what it liked) can be discarded as a rather out-moded and uncomfortable old garment.

An interesting characteristic of the 'old' concept of truth as indubitable knowledge, as the certain ground of what we may believe, is the extent to which it is suffused with magic: a longing for absolute knowledge-power which will give us absolute control. It does indeed seem to be the case that philosophers who pursued the infallible ground of truth were as ludicrously mistaken as tormented alchemists trying to distil gold from base metals. The most powerful lesson taught us by science itself is that there can be no ultimate certainty.

But rather than drawing from this the 'postmodern' conclusion that knowledge based on truth must be abandoned, that truth is after all a useless concept, could we not rather see that what is needed is to receive gratefully a concept of truth divested of magic and to elaborate it in the sober realization that though it will not yield up to us absolute power, it is nevertheless the best tool we have for understanding our world? Having arrived at the possibility of separating Reason from Power, should we not explore the nature of Reason a little further before we give ourselves over totally to be enveloped in unmitigated Power?

At first, to be sure, we may be a little disorientated, for if truth based on reason has no ground in a certain authority, what possible use could it be to us – what, for instance, would make it different from opinion or guesswork? But the answers to questions such as these are, in fact, already quite easily available in scientific thought, and indeed the practice of reason is quite familiar from everyday experiences.

Scientific enquiry proceeds in the recognition that all it ever establishes conclusively is that something is not the case, never that 'the truth' has finally been arrived at. What even scientists themselves have not always seen is that the lesson to be learned from this is not that 'the truth' must for ever elude their grasp, but that there is literally no such kind of 'truth' as this: it is an unattainable, magical ideal. So far as 'truth' has any meaning (and, of course, it does), it lies precisely in what scientists do: that is, in trying to establish that one is not mistaken, that one is not making a claim which can be shown to be false by someone who examines the evidence and arguments more closely and carefully. There is no *ultimate* truth waiting in the wings to pop out one triumphant day and put its seal of approval on our speculations. But this does not have to mean that 'anything goes', that we can think anything we like, or that if you make enough people agree with you by main force you have as good as arrived at 'the truth'.

The truth exists precisely in its separation from the constraints of power. The truth is what we arrive at when we have the freedom and resources to look for it. There *is* no truth beyond that truth. Although, of course, the scientific community can quite easily become colonized by power so that its principles and practices are hardened into disciplinary dogmatisms (this has certainly happened in the social sciences), ideally scientific practice is characterized precisely by the freedom of its community to pursue it. There are, of course, always dangers – particularly apparent once again at the present time – that scientific knowledge will be appropriated into whatever constitutes the current 'discourse of power'. In this way Business, as it takes over universities and removes the protections of academic freedom, threatens to reduce scientific enquiry to sterile technological routines which merely exploit applications of what is known rather than seek to know.

Scientific knowledge is by no means the only kind which pursues truth in ways which are at least potentially disengaged from the oppressive interests of power. Reason is liberated by the absence of threat. Any situation which removes from people the possibility of their being punished for what they think allows them to investigate their world with the kind of dedicated seriousness which displays rationality at its most admirable. This may sometimes happen, for example, in individual or group psychotherapy where the judgemental attitudes which literally constitute our ordinary social activity may be temporarily lifted. It may also happen as a jury tries in good faith and without prejudice to determine the weight to be given the evidence it has heard.

Reason is, of course, not completely detachable from power. To operate effectively it needs access to the resources which fuel its exercise. Even in the absence of threat, the individual's untutored perspective is not on its own sufficient to guarantee a reasonable judgement or true belief. The reasoned pursuit of truth is a communal activity, calling upon the collaboration of others in enterprises which may well span generations. Just as 'truth' is not a commodity which may be individually appropriated and wielded as a weapon, but rather the ever-corrigible judgement of a society, so knowledge can only be pursued in an unconstrained association with others who seek to establish no patent on what they find.

One of the strongest currents in the philosophical tradition concerned with knowledge and truth has tended to suggest that if we cannot say with certainty what the nature of the world is, we must have imagined it. If the world isn't so insistently 'real' that we are all ultimately stunned by the sheer weight of the evidence into acknowledging what it is like, then it must simply consist of ideas in our heads, and anyone's idea is probably as good as anyone else's.

In many ways this realist/idealist debate is reflected in the issue of exteriority/interiority which has been such a bone of contention in psychology, and indeed a central preoccupation of this book. But the philosophical version of 'interiority' is writ very much larger than the psychological one: it is not merely suggesting that there are such things as interior worlds, but that the world itself is interior. The argument implied (though, of course, not stated anything like as crassly as this) seems to run along the lines that if we cannot describe reality in complete and convincing detail (sufficiently incontrovertibly as to be able to beat doubters into submission with 'the truth'), we might as well give up the whole idea and let ourselves rip with the various imaginary versions which we can create out of our own desires, interests and impulses. If 'reality' is not our master, we might as well make it the plaything of our fantasy.

The fallacy of this kind of thinking stems from the essentially magical conviction that if there is 'a reality' we must be able to say with certainty what 'it' is (and that, therefore, if we cannot say what 'it' is, there cannot be one). All this tells us really is that human beings have an overwhelming need to achieve intellectual certainty and an extraordinarily inflated belief in the significance of their own mental productions. There is something remarkably infantile about this. Even if we have grown up enough to recognize that we have to do without a benign and omnipotent God, perhaps we now have further to realize that 'truth' in the form of certain knowledge is also irretrievably beyond our grasp.

There are some interesting, and strangely paradoxical, parallels between our attitude to knowledge and our attitude to religion. Most of us would probably feel that, while religion is the arena of our beliefs and superstitions, which can lay no claim to objective validity, secular or scientific knowledge is testable against a reality which can be known. In fact, however, something close to the contrary is arguable: it is precisely *from* religion that we have taken over and projected into secular knowledge our infantile yearning for certainty. While we may have given up God, we have not given up the concept of 'Truth' on which religious awe and obedience were founded. Indeed, 'science' seemed to offer a safer home for that concept than did the Church. Even more paradoxically, what we now need to recognize is that, to recover a usable concept of truth, we have to reconnect 'science' with the idea of *uncertain* belief, or faith. It thus becomes *more* scientific to *believe*, or have *faith* in the reality of our world, than it does to have 'certain knowledge' of it.

There seems to me no contradiction in saying that the nature of reality is a mystery which can *never* be known with any certainty, but about which we should always try to speak the truth. Even though this contention runs superficially counter to some of our less reflective everyday thinking, it nevertheless does nothing more than state the obvious. Reality *is* a mystery to us, but the fact that we can only know it from our own perspectives and for our own purposes does not mean that it is not 'there'. We all have a sense of its being 'there', and in our everyday lives we, wisely, treat its presence with considerable respect: we don't try to walk through brick walls or fly unaided by machinery over chasms. We seek to avoid pain and we know how to inflict it. We are in no fundamental doubt about the reality of the world in which we find ourselves. Why, then, not try in good faith to develop together a knowledge of what we are in no fundamental doubt about? Why not try to tell each other the truth about our experiences as creatures embodied in a natural and social environment? The fact that in doing so we are necessarily unable to arrive at an ultimate description of the universe which fixes its character for all time and brooks no alternative perspective is absolutely no cause for despair. The proof that we can do this perfectly successfully is, once again, that that is precisely what, at its best, scientific enquiry does do (even if it is not often encountered at its best).

There is no reason why our being unable to demonstrate with complete conviction 'what reality is' should cause us to lose our nerve and deny its relevance and validity altogether. We need only recognize the magical absurdity of *trying* to say 'what it is', and take up a position of relatively unruffled belief in its significance as it manifests itself to us.

We need to do this as much as anything in order to regain a purchase upon the world which has become dangerously loose. Both through our rigid insistence on particular dogmatic versions of 'reality' ('certain truth') and through our more recent tendency to slide into self-interested relativities which scoff at the idea of truth of any kind, we have become prey to manipulations of our world by forms of oppressive power which we are barely able to recognize, let alone control.

We need to rediscover procedures of enquiry and a conceptual language which enable us truly to describe what is happening to us, and to build 'forms' for our experience which are, precisely, rooted in reality and able to receive the assent, *freely given*, of the communities they help to shape. Rather than being browbeaten into accepting versions of 'the truth' which come in the end to be exposed as the hypocritical mythologies of a self-serving structure of power, we need to *discover* the important features of the social *reality* which encompasses us and gives form and content to our experience. We need to be able to describe the world which makes us feel as we do, and to describe it accurately. We have to clarify together the nature of our predicament.

As always, it is much easier to see what is needed than to be able to say how to achieve it. In fact, there probably is no recipe for the reconstruction of society, even though we can see what makes it, as it is, so psychologically damaging, and even though we can specify some of the conceptual changes to our ways of thinking about the world which would be necessary to our making of it a more comfortable habitat. Societies are not made like cakes, and even though clubs of intellectuals and social engineers (like, for example, the Adam Smith Institute) may have their day, their contribution to giving shape to the times is probably far less significant than they think. The vast network of interest which holds our social environment in place is extremely unlikely to be moved by an idea, or even by several ideas mooted in concert; it is much more the case that the network itself generates the ideas which oppose as well as support it. But that is the point: 'the system' is not infallible, and where it gives rise to injustice and pain, it risks being modified by its own negative consequences.

The aim of suggesting procedures for the reconstruction of 'form', and of developing what are in the end philosophical conceptions to help with that process, is not to provide a recipe for social revolution which will strike into the hearts of the oppressed and bring them out into the streets. It is rather to try to clarify issues in ways which may help people diagnose the nature of their predicament and encourage them to take advantage of whatever opportunities may present themselves for improving things.

It should I hope by now be clear that the 'reconstruction of "form" ', even though it raises philosophical issues concerning truth and knowledge which are rarely seen as the concern of 'ordinary people', is not just an arid intellectual game. I have already suggested that a concept of truth sufficiently viable to enable us to describe our common world – the reality in which we find ourselves – in ways to which we can give our assent cannot be developed outside a certain kind of context. This context must be free of threat, must contain other people in an association of good faith, and must have access to the kinds of resources which make such enquiry possible (the tools of education, and so on).

It is not always the case that intellectual activity is seen as dependent on requirements of this kind (though there are eminent thinkers who suggest that it is – in particular Jürgen Habermas). What underlies these requirements is in essence an *ethical* position. In the division of labour which characterizes universities as much as any other institution, 'ethics' has tended as a discipline to be split off from 'epistemology' (theory of knowledge), as if the one had very little significance for the other. This is rather similar to the split noted above between 'knowledge' and 'faith', and just as we need to knit the latter two concepts together again, so, I think, do we need to see that no purely intellectual enquiry is possible, but that any such enquiry must always be guided by a practical ethics. We cannot really consider what it is possible to believe without thinking also about what it is right to do.

This is especially the case in a situation like ours, where we have to do without certain knowledge as our guide. No doubt if 'truth' were revealed to us (by God, or Objectivity, or some other Authority) as absolute, we might not have to worry too much about how to take it, as we would presumably have little choice. However, if we are, as I have suggested, caught up in a reality whose nature is and will remain essentially mysterious to us, the ways in which we conduct ourselves towards it become problematic. We shall need, in fact, our forms of knowledge to be guided by our ethics, and our ethics to be informed in turn by what we know: the two become inseparable.

ETHICAL GUIDANCE

Moral philosophers have tended to be as preoccupied as their epistemologist colleagues with looking for a form of authority which would establish absolute certainty for their field of enquiry. Just as we long to discover truths which may be known for certain, so we scan the horizon for values which may be held with absolute, unquestioning confidence. We want to know the rules, and we don't want to have to think about them.

In the field of ethics, however, the search for certainty has been even less fruitful than has been the case with nonmoral knowledge. Trying to stipulate rules for right conduct by deriving them from some kind of behavioural formula, or offering a calculus for defining 'good', has always ended in incoherence. Such approaches either commit what the philosopher G. E. Moore called 'the naturalistic fallacy' or leave such obvious gaps and implied contradictions that they are useless as any form of ethical guide.

The 'naturalistic fallacy' points out that any definition of 'good' which is not simply circular – i.e., which does not define 'good' in terms of a disguised synonym of it – always leaves it open to a doubter to question whether what 'good' is said to be *really is* good. There seems, in other words, to be something irreducible about moral concepts such as 'good' which cannot be unpacked into more factual, nonmoral equivalents. Another way of putting this is to point out, as did David Hume, that an 'ought' cannot be derived from an 'is'. One can always ask of a factual state of affairs whether it is right: it is never so self-evidently right as to be capable of providing a *criterion* of rightness.

Attempts at ignoring these difficulties and pressing on regardless have not met with great success. For example, the Utilitarian idea that what is good is what brings the greatest happiness to the greatest number (apart from providing the ideology underpinning the kind of soulless moralism Dickens attacks so effectively in *Hard Times*) soon runs into all kinds of impossible complications. The resulting frustration has left moral philosophers with a limited range of options. One is to suggest that moral judgements are really no more than expressions of personal preference. In the dry language of logical positivism, for example, 'X is good' is taken to be an essentially meaningless statement more or less equivalent, as A. J. Ayer suggested, to 'hurrah for X!'

This is by now a familiar situation: if a basis for our ethical judgement cannot be either found in the absolute authority of God or derived from the incontrovertible nature of a self-revealing Reality, then we have apparently to conclude that it resides somewhere inside ourselves as, for example, a feeling or an impulse which can be no more objectively justifiable than a liking for a particular food.

More recently, it is true, there have been efforts to locate the source of our moral sentiment in the *community* rather than in the *self* (see for example Alasdair MacIntyre's *After Virtue*), but even here there are uneasy questions to be asked about *which* communities may be taken as forging the core structure of a moral system. Once again, with views such as this, we face the possibility that right will be determined by might, and that if you happen to find yourself in the wrong community you may be branded as outside the pale of human values.

Insofar as ethics are all about the way we conduct ourselves towards each other, it certainly seems an advance on some positions to suggest that they should be viewed from the perspective of community. What binds together the individuals who form a community, however, is the part of their personhood which they have in common and which may in large part consist precisely of ethical 'forms'. Certainly communities *will* differ from each other in this respect, as for example Iranian Muslim fundamentalists compared with born-again Christians from the USA. Far from being a cause for moral celebration, this looks more like a recipe for disaster, especially when one considers that 'community' of this kind may be but a large-scale version of an infinity of factions, interest groups and cliques seeking to assert the supremacy of the values they happen to share. Is there no more fundamental basis to a common human morality than (to mention but a few) the political, religious, national, class, race and gender issues which some of us share with others?

To locate the 'forms' of morality in that part of our being which is *cultural* is precisely to 'communitize' humankind in accordance with the religious and national clubs into which it is split, and hence to invite competition and strife into the very core of our ethical outlook. But, even if it is understood very differently by different cultural groups, there *is* something that we *all* share and which provides the foundation for a *general* human community: our existence in the world as embodied subjects.

Psychologists and others, particularly those interested in the simulation of human thought and behaviour by machines, often set themselves the conundrum of trying to define the essential properties of 'humanness'. If a robot could be built that looked, sounded and acted exactly like a person, could it meaningfully be said not to be one? This seems to me a contrived and not really very significant puzzle. What makes us human is our embodiedness: the fact that we possess bodies which are in all essentials identical to each other. An experienced surgeon cutting open any one of us will not be surprised by what is revealed, and if it turned out to be a collection of printed circuits, cables and transistors, would have no difficulty in concluding that it was not a human being under the knife.

The ultimate solidarity is the solidarity of pain. Strip people of power, strip them of all those cultural aspects which give them distinction and individuality – so that they are, indeed, stripped of their very 'personality' – and you are still left with a sentient body, even if one incapable of the functions we normally expect of persons.

It is certainly this solidarity-as-bodies that we recognize and acknowledge in caring for the infirm, the old and the handicapped, who are indeed often deprived of some of the powers which contribute to personhood. It is this solidarity which makes us wince and squirm with sympathetic sensation when we see someone else incur a painful injury. We recognize that, as bodies, we are not distinguishable from each other. It is perhaps also this solidarity which makes it possible for a tiny infant to imitate apparently without trying the exaggerated facial expressions of a parent. So similar are we, we can almost feel each other's feelings, and quite often literally do.

Our vulnerability to pain and our recognition of it in others is what binds us across otherwise unbridgeable divides. The image of the dying body of a Somalian child, leaving a pathetic smear of blood on the pavement as someone gently drags it away by the heels, moves – even though impotently – the comfortable Westerner eating a bag of crisps in front of the television. The discrepancy in power and privilege between these two figures is, to be sure, obscene, and, of course, testifies to a global society which has gone terribly wrong, but nevertheless as long as one is moved by the plight of the other, there must be hope.

It is, of course a truism that people embattled against a common enemy, or otherwise fallen on hard times, may co-operate together in forms of solidarity which completely evaporate in more comfortable circumstances. It is often observed that people living in conditions of Third World poverty seem able to be happy in ways apparently not possible in the affluent West, and certainly anyone who has worked with the underprivileged, the sick and the disabled will know how heroically altruistic people in the worst of all possible worlds can be, and what warmth, support and loving self-sacrifice they can be capable of. It seems that, in some circumstances at least, the more people are reduced to the status of suffering bodies, the more they are able to act with and for each other in a quintessentially moral way.

Perhaps it would be the case that, if we were able to live out our lives in proximal relation to each other, undisturbed by the insecurity and competitiveness imposed by distal influences, our embodied solidarity would provide a basis for genuine community. As things are, however, such a possibility does not arise, and it is only ever the case that we are *forced* into such proximal collaboration by malign distal powers which (like war) are too pervasive in their impact to allow the operation of distinction between those affected – competition is *suppressed* by threat rather than made unnecessary by the absence of threat.

For, except in those cases where threat is so overwhelming as to force a kind of solidarity, power's ultimate resort is to reach right into the body in order to sow the seeds of distinction in this last bastion of community. To exploit the difference between male and female (rather than celebrate its mystery), to invent and accentuate 'racial' issues, to valorize the body in terms of its sexual potency and make it the foundation of an industry of pornography, to invest it with symbols of power by any means available – all these are the techniques of a system which, to survive, must find ever new ways of dividing and ruling, objectifying and commodifying. To manufacture physical differences and distinctions which generate shame, insecurity and competition is to distract us from the subjective embodiment which gives us our most fundamental solidarity.

The reaction to this in present-day society is to attempt a magical disembodiment. The response to the colonization of the body's materiality by power seems to be to deny that the body has any materiality at all. If power succeeds, as undoubtedly it has, in pitting men against women, the response is to assert that there is no difference between men and women. The same is the case with black and white, fat and thin, strong and weak, able and disabled, beautiful and ugly. 'Anorexia' is an expression of the plight of women struggling to free themselves from the curse of having to occupy bodies which have become both biological liabilities and the fetishized objects of a male gaze emptied of all enchantment. The attempted solution of the problem through 'anorexia' is symbolic of a much wider tendency to seek to escape from imprisonment in bodies which are the ultimate target of malign power by denying their existence.

The denial of embodiment, literally in the case of 'anorexia', and by implication in the case of those ideologies which prohibit 'politically incorrect' references to physical characteristics, while understandable and perhaps laudable in intent, is nevertheless profoundly mistaken, and likely to lead to a kind of totalitarian distortion of reality which will only create new punitive moralisms and their attendant repressions. The incoherence of the kind of 'loony left' ideology which prohibits the use of words like 'black' or 'fat' or 'disabled' is that it attempts to combat a malign reality by denying that it can be spoken of. This is similar to the ultimately hopeless anorectic conjuring trick of trying to continue living in a body while starving it out of existence.

Our embodiment is real and inescapably material and does make possible differences and distinctions between us which may be and will be exploited by power. But what is inviolable by power, and what founds our common humanity, is not so much the brute fact of the body's objective materiality as its subjective vulnerability. In the final analysis we all feel the same because we are all constructed in the same way. If you prick us, we bleed. It is *this* which is true whoever you are, and however strong or weak, or beautiful, or rich or important you are.

The appeal which Shakespeare placed in Shylock's mouth is echoed in a moral insight which transcends time, place and culture and which serves to remind us that in the subjective experience of our embodiment we are *not* different from each other.

Tzu-Kung asked, 'Is there a single word which can be a guide throughout one's life?' The Master said, 'It is perhaps the word shu. Do not impose on others what you yourself do not desire.'

Confucius, *The Analects*, Book XV.

Then one of them, which was a lawyer, asked him . . . Master which is the great commandment in the law? Jesus said unto him Thou shalt love the Lord thy God with all thy heart, and with all thy soul, and with all thy mind. This is the first and great commandment. And the second is like unto it, Thou shalt love thy neighbour as thyself.

Matthew, 22, 35-39

So act that the maxim of your will could always hold at the same time as a principle establishing universal law.

Immanuel Kant, *Critique of Practical Reason.*

Surely what underlies and unites these three statements, uttered by three very different people for very different reasons and in very different contexts spanning over two millennia, is a recognition that what hurts oneself will hurt others, and vice versa.

It would be unrealistic in the extreme to expect to be able to create a world from which inequality had been banished. It is inconceivable that differences between people and the amounts of power available to them could be eradicated. Although one might hope that in some dimly distant future societies might become established in which power is used more for good than for ill, there seems little doubt that for the time being individuals and groups who have access to power are likely more often than not to use it to maintain their own advantage. This means, in effect, that we cannot expect for the discernible future to live in a social world free of competition, dispute and struggle; equality and justice will have, probably only too literally, to be fought for, and if your more powerful neighbour proves to love himself more than you, you may have, if you are not simply to suffer them passively, forcibly to resist his attentions.

In these circumstances nothing will be gained by *pretending* that everyone is equal or inventing ideologies which proscribe the use of a vocabulary which refers to inequalities which patently do exist. On the other hand, we need to be clear that what makes people unequal is the amount of power they possess or have access to, not some intrinsic quality which somehow becomes attached to their very embodiment.

Perhaps in some semiconscious way nervously aware that *in themselves* they are no different from anyone else, the powerful have often sought to create a myth of personal worth which does indeed extend into their bodies, for example by claiming that 'blue blood' courses through their veins or that 'breeding' is responsible for their refinement and their taste. This can, of course, prove a risky ploy, since if accepted at face value it may backfire as it did in the case of the French aristocracy. Many of the most horrifying excesses of human hatred, in fact, follow from the error of confusing people's power with their embodiment and supposing that you dispose of the former by exterminating the latter.

It may be that underlying the seemingly rather naive Christian advocacy of neighbour-loving, cheek-turning, forgiving others their sins and so on is the insight that it is not another's physical being that threatens you, but only the power he or she possesses. In fact, of course, others seen as threatening may not so much possess power as occupy positions in which they are constrained to mediate it. The prisoner may wish his jailer damned to hell, and could not reasonably be expected to feel otherwise, but in reality the jailer is no less enmeshed in the web of power than the prisoner. To identify evil in the embodiment of the evil-doer is to make a serious mistake, and is one which, of course, the interests of power are happy to have made. There is a danger that any ideological or political movement which implicitly locates wrong-doing or injustice in forms of embodiment actually comes to serve the interests of the very powers it is trying to undo –

varieties of feminism which simply see biological maleness as 'the problem' provide an example.

Once rendered powerless, we are all the same. There is no need to execute the tyrant whose power has been removed, and to do so is merely a pointless cruelty. We need rather to dismantle the structures which make the acquisition of tyrannical power possible (a much more difficult and demanding task). Compassion for each other as embodied beings derives not so much from a sentimental ideal as from a sober acknowledgement of social and biological reality.

Having established that as embodied subjects we are all very much in the same boat, vulnerable to much the same suffering and exposed to similar pains, the conclusion that we should treat others as we would wish to be treated ourselves seems only reasonable. Tragically, as a guide to human conduct, it appears to play little part in the formal, essentially political institutions which structure our society, which for the most part engender and encourage distinction and differentiation. Fundamental solidarity based on our common embodiment tends to be put into practice only informally in the proximal sphere of the lives of the least powerful members of society. Otherwise, it forms a conspicuous part of social practice only in its negative aspect, as a fundamental tenet of torturers and terrorists.

For in a world in which our embodiment is either mystified and exploited by power or the object of a magical denial by those trying to escape from power, it is left exposed to the pitiless devices of those who have calculated its significance only too accurately. While the market promotes a make-believe invulnerability and psychology tells us that salvation is to be found in our mental attitudes, the torturer (by doing unto others what he would most hate having done to him) and the terrorist (who sees that, in our basic equivalence, to injure one is to injure all) make use of ethical truth in the most unscrupulous way imaginable. This looks like a variation on the theme of the devil having all the best tunes.

*

An appreciation of reality which seeks to come to an accommodation with it while acknowledging its ultimate mysteriousness, combined with an ethical solidarity based on the fundamental vulnerability of all people as embodied beings in a social environment structured by power, provides a reasonable enough basis for a clarification of our predicament. It suggests also an *attitude* to people and the world which would be desirable not merely on the grounds of its being 'a good thing' in some charitable but essentially impracticable way, but because caution and common sense would advise it.

Because we cannot know with certainty the nature of the mystery we are caught up in (if, indeed, it has a 'nature'), and because it seems clear that in all basic essentials other people are virtually indistinguishable from ourselves, both we and the reality we find ourselves in need to be approached with respect, humility and care. Having discovered how easily we can mistake our own dreams, fantasies and wishes for ultimate verities which in time disintegrate only too obviously, and frequently catastrophically, we need to construct our knowledge of the world with the utmost circumspection, disturbing it as little as possible in the process in case we do some unforeseen damage.

It is easy to build Utopias in the imagination, and scarcely anyone would deny that the construction of an environment which takes proper account of our embodied vulnerability and seeks to establish a degree of social justice and equality would be a good idea. It is certainly not that we cannot see how to make the world a better place, nor is it the case that we lack the means to do so. So why don't we?

We are, I would suggest, collectively very much in the same position as the individual client of psychotherapy whose predicament has become quite clear, but who still seems strangely incapable of doing anything about it. Why not just apply a bit of will power?

The answer, once again, is that there is no such thing as will power pure and simple. There is inside us no source of moral power which can be called upon at will to shape the material structures of the world. It *feels*, of course, as if there is, but in this case our feelings are misleading. I am not saying that we cannot act upon the world – quite obviously we can, and do. What misleads us into a conception of such action as volitional is that we cannot act without *experiencing* acting, i.e., having a feeling about it, and we take this feeling to be the *cause* of our action, when in fact it is just its necessary accompaniment.

In order to act we need the necessary powers and resources, and the impulse of such power comes most of the time from outside ourselves: we are, so to speak, points in social space *through which* power travels. There are, no doubt, simple acts which we can perform which originate within our biological structure and which we could loosely be said to be able to perform 'at will', but they have little significance: I can scratch my head, or cough, or walk down to the corner shop with the involvement of very little more than my bodily powers. But significant social action requires the contribution of powers considerably more distal than these, and they cannot be willed by me.

The illusion of will rests on the same phenomenon of 'proximality' as do many of the mistakes we make about the causes of our troubles. Any action we take involves our bodily complicity in and commitment to it, and so it is very hard to resist the impression that we are the causes of our actions. What we experience as 'will' is, however, nothing more than the subjective feeling of complicity and commitment in the *transmission* of powers which originate, either currently or in the past, outside us.

Right at the core of the mysteriousness of the reality which surrounds us is the fact that much of the time we cannot, and could not, possibly see what the reasons for our actions are, or what the consequences of them for that reality will be. We *cannot but* act in faith and hope. It is not just that so much happens beyond our power horizon or took place outside the span of our memory, though these factors make understanding difficult enough. It is also the case that, being ourselves part of the world we're trying to understand, we affect it materially in the very act of trying to understand it (Heisenberg's much-cited 'principle of indeterminacy'). So not only is 'free will' essentially illusory, but there is also no possibility of our being able to offer anything like a complete deterministic account of our actions either.

In some senses, this leaves us with little option but to *believe in* 'free will'. Since reality is at its heart an impenetrable mystery, and since we cannot in practice see what are the distal causes of our proximal activities, we are almost bound to become focused on the *experience* of the processes of action as we are bodily engaged in them. These processes are, furthermore, a *necessary* part of our experience, and cannot be disregarded. It is, in fact, not possible to be 'fatalistic' and to sit back as, so to speak, a spectator while the powers of determinism take over, pushing us around like puppets. For there is no entity 'inside' us capable of spectating; whether we like it or not, we are 'fated' to be actively complicit in our fate! While we cannot in effect pit our will against the distal powers which flow through us, we also cannot but experience them as the workings of our will.

It is only at times of acute conflict and distress that the paradoxes implicit in the idea of 'will' make themselves felt. We do not normally find it difficult to distinguish between actions we are happy to perform and ones which we feel constrained to carry out 'against our will', but there are times when actions of a kind which usually fit into the former category fall into the latter, and it is at such times that we may catch a glimpse of the inadequacy of our everyday ways of thinking about these things. There's nothing like trying to diet, or break free of an addiction like smoking, to demonstrate how fragile is the concept of 'will'. In the normal course of daily events, however, we are easily enough lulled into the belief that our co-operation with distal power (so long as it appears to coincide with our interests) is our own free choice.

*

We shall, therefore, not be able to change the world purely through an act of will, however clearly we might see the desirability of doing so. Even less shall we be able to make our lives any more comfortable through the cultivation of therapeutic make-believe.

What confronts us is a political programme in which an ethics built on reason and a knowledge of the world inspired by faith in its reality enable us to reconstruct 'forms' which can earn the assent of people secure enough to appreciate their worth. Even though our present social organization gives rise to enough distress to underline the desirability of such a programme, it may well be the case that the causes of such distress still appear too abstract and ideologically obscured to provide the necessary impetus for change.

When enough people hurt badly enough to be moved to act together against the roots of our troubles, one can only hope that they may be in a better position than has often been the case before to know what to do.

Appendix

What follows gives a summary of the theoretical position outlined in this book, relating particularly closely to the text of
Chapter Three (figure 3, page 74, in that chapter offers a
similar, though rather more simplified, summary in diagrammatic
form).

I have thus set out here what seem to me the principal features
of an 'environmental' approach to human distress in the form
of simple statements which I would regard as fundamental. Where
there is adequate explanation of these statements in the main text,
I have left them here unelaborated. Where there are points of
emphasis to be made, or where some further clarification may
be needed, I have added some brief notes.

FUNDAMENTALS OF AN ENVIRONMENTAL
APPROACH TO DISTRESS

1 A person is the interaction of a body with a world (environment).

The important point to grasp here is that there are no 'things'
involved in the construction of personhood other than bodies
and worlds. A person is not a thing, but an interaction; anything
material about a person is either body or world. There is no
particular harm in calling nonmaterial aspects of the person 'mind',
or even 'spirit'; difficulties arise only when such concepts are subtly
rematerialized and regarded as 'inside' the person in some
semiphysical sense (it is no doubt also confusions of this kind that
lead to conceptions of 'immortal souls' which are somehow
inseparable from mysteriously resurrectable bodies).

2 By 'environment' is meant, most importantly, social space-time.

3 The environment is structured by material power.

4 Power may be coercive, economic or ideological. These may be, but are not necessarily, positively correlated.

5 Ideological power is viable only to the extent that it can be rendered material through solidarity.

Statements 3, 4 and 5 attempt to express the idea that power is exerted *physically* on the world through human action, and that its operation can be inferred only through the observation of *material* change having taken place in physical structures. Ideological power can be effective only through its association with material force of this kind. 'Ideas', of themselves, have no power; what makes the difference between magic and wishful thinking on the one hand and ideologies like Christianity or Nazism on the other is that the latter are empowered through the association of large numbers of people able to *act* together.

6 The person's relation to the body is mainly one of sensation.

7 The person's relation to the environment is mainly through experience (intransitive reception of power) and action (transitive exercise of power).

A person is thus located in a field of power which s/he both absorbs and transmits, and from which s/he cannot be abstracted as an individual able somehow to choose or decide how to relate to the field of power independently of its influence. Our experience of being permeated by social power necessarily imparts the illusion that we *originate* action, but, in fact, we would more accurately be characterized as *loci* in social space *through which* power flows. (See 20 and 21 below.)

8 Both the experience and the exercise of power may be benign or malign.

That is to say, social influences may operate for or against the interests of the person they impinge upon, and s/he may in turn act for or against the interests of others. What a person believes about these processes (whether s/he perceives influences as malign or benign; whether s/he is 'sincere' about the 'motives' for his/her actions) is not essential to an accurate understanding of them, and may indeed be controlled by ideological powers of which the person has no knowledge.

9   Power operates at varying distance from the person – proximally and distally. It is always mediated proximally, but may well originate distally.

10 a From an objective perspective, the absolute magnitude of power is negatively related to its proximity to the person.
   b From a subjective perspective, the relative magnitude of power is positively related to its proximity to the person.

11 Each person operates within: a) a 'power horizon', and b) a 'memory span' which limits his/her ability to identify the reasons for proximal events and actions, including his/her own.

Between them, 9, 10 and 11 contain perhaps the most difficult and profound paradox of human experience. This is that, in trying to understand the reasons for social conduct, including his/her own, what are in fact the *least* accurate and satisfactory explanations are likely to be experienced by the individual as the *most* accurate and satisfactory ones. The person thus comes to live within a kind of illusory mythology which can be corrected only by a more 'objective' view, i.e., one which inhabits a much broader power horizon (it is just such a correction which the natural sciences attempt to perform for our understanding of the physical world). The 'truth' could, in any absolute sense, only be seen through the eye of God, but any version of it to which human beings can aspire, however extended their power horizon, can only be an approximation. It is essentially this paradox of human experience which makes the operation of ideological mystification – 'false consciousness', or simple 'bamboozlement' – possible.

12 Environmental influence becomes embodied (i.e., becomes a collection of biological assets and liabilities).
Whether environmental influence permeates the person intransitively or flows through him/her transitively, it is physically registered, materially changing physical structures such that learning can take place. Learning is thus inescapably a biological process and may well be irreversible.

13 There are no such things as 'inner worlds', but personal powers acquired (embodied) over time.

14 The extent to which a person can influence present circumstances will depend on the availability to him/her of material powers and resources, including embodied personal assets.

15 Powers and resources may be economic, cultural, educational, ideological, physical.

16 The degree to which the effects of the past can be influenced will depend on the nature and extent of their embodiment as well as on the person's access to resources.

17 A person's 'psychology' consists of the meaning systems through and with which his/her embodied experience of the environment is understood, interpreted and represented.
That we arrive at 'psychology' only at this point suggests some of its limitations. For psychology deals essentially with an abstracted *relation* of bodies with worlds, with that aspect of people which is neither body nor world, and which reflects their struggles to represent and talk about what it is like to be a body in a world. Perhaps this is why so many psychologists who pursue their speculations with any real tenacity tend to end up either as quasi-biologists or quasi-sociologists. The great temptation for psychology is, of course, to impute to its insights (into the systems

of meaning people develop to understand their world) a materiality they simply haven't got, and then to attempt to tie such *pseudo*material insights into *truly* material aspects of bodies and worlds. The most obvious example of this is to assume in one form or another the power of positive (or indeed negative) thinking, to try to make *direct* and *causal* connections between the way we see things and the way they are. *Of course* we cannot separate the way things are from the way we see them, but nor can we create a world just by imagining it. The importance of understanding a person's meaning-systems is for the clues it gives us to body-world relations; we change nothing of consequence by trying simply to manipulate those systems from within themselves. A more technical way of saying this is to point out that psychology confuses epistemological observations with ontological statements.

18 Such meaning systems may be, for example, idiosyncratic or cultural, implicit or explicit.
Even such simple distinctions as these, which may be represented on two orthogonal axes as shown, can give a theoretical coherence to psychological phenomena which if treated as entities in 'internal space' tend to multiply perplexingly. The schema here owes a great deal to the work of Rom Harré (see his *Personal Being*, Blackwell, 1983).

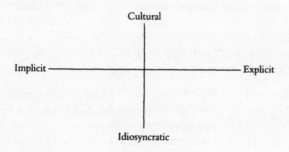

According to this schema, the character of a psychological phenomenon will be determined by its location relative to the two axes of meaning. For example a scientific production, and indeed language itself, would be found in the upper right quadrant, while some artistic productions (making explicit an idiosyncratic view) would be in the lower right quadrant; dreaming, and some forms of psychotic ideation, would be located mainly in the lower left quadrant. 'Symptoms' of distress which are commonly experienced but which people are at a loss to understand might find their place in the upper left quadrant. An example of one of these latter might be 'anorexia' (the meaning of self-starvation is almost certainly culturally determined, but remains mysteriously inarticulate; inasmuch as it becomes articulated as a form of protest – hunger strike – it moves along to the right of the horizontal axis).

By means such as these, the curious mixed metaphors of 'dynamic' psychology – for example, the hydraulics of 'internal' space in which 'mental contents' are pushed into and out of consciousness – may be replaced by *conceptual* distinctions giving, at a meta-level, coherence to phenomena which, insofar as they are purely psychological, are themselves conceptual (i.e., aspects of meaning-systems).

It is important to note that psychological phenomena are not necessarily unique or private to the individual in whom they occur (i.e., who provides a locus for them), but may be aspects of cultural 'forms' established independently of specific individuals.

19 Psychological operations may effect change only to the extent that they directly mediate, or facilitate access to, powers and resources.

20 The concept of 'will' derives from the *experience* of transmitting power, provided such transmission is congruent with the individual's wishes.

21 Freedom is proportional to the amount of power possessed by or available to the individual.

The idea that we have 'free will' thus derives from the experience most of us have had of being able to exercise a certain amount of power. Because we are especially intimately acquainted with the sensations of our own bodies (and may well be ignorant of the source and nature of the powers we sometimes transmit), we mistakenly identify the feelings which accompany the exercise of power as its origination, and we call this 'will'. Since we cannot choose not to have such feelings, it seems reasonable to suggest that 'will' is a *necessary* illusion.

22 A person's wellbeing (freedom from distress) is largely determined by current circumstances and the nature and significance of his/her embodied experience and exercise of power.

The interaction of the characteristics of power – whether it is benign or malign, transitive or intransitive – together with their mediation through the person's systems of meaning will determine whether the person feels pleasure or pain, love or hate, comfort or distress, confidence or fear, etc. For example, power exercised by the person transitively and benignly is likely to be experienced as loving, transitively but malignly as sadistic. Similarly, the intransitive reception of benign power is likely to be experienced as being loved, and so on.

The mediation of experience and action by the person's 'psychology' (meaning-systems) is important *not* because it can be 'therapeutically' manipulated to change distress into comfort (which in most cases would amount merely to ideological distortion or mystification), but because engagement with it offers opportunities for the clarification of previous distortions and mystifications (as well as, of course, for learning from the person what s/he knows about the world).

23 Clinical consultation ('therapy') operates only transiently within the person's proximal field and is therefore necessarily limited in its power to effect change.

24 Consultation consists of three main elements:
   (i) provision of comfort
   (ii) clarification
   (iii) encouragement in the use of available powers and
     resources.

How to Survive Without Psychotherapy

Preface

This book is the distillation of over thirty years' experience of talking to people in distress.

At the start of that period I had no reason to suppose that the received wisdom on questions of 'mental illness' would be in any way inadequate to the task of understanding and trying to help those I encountered. My naivety was quickly exposed. Working, as I then was, as an apprentice clinical psychologist in vast Victorian mental hospitals, I soon realised that we were not simply dealing with sick people whose illnesses needed to be diagnosed and cured by appropriate treatments before they were sent on their way.

Yet this was (as it still is) the ruling ideology. We worked in hospitals, with doctors, nurses, medical procedures and a suitably clinical vocabulary with which to describe our activities. The 'patients', though, somehow didn't seem to fit in with the model. Even the most severely disturbed didn't appear ill so much as confused and despairing, beside themselves sometimes with frustration, grief or rage; the less disturbed – the 'personality disorders', 'chronic neurotics' etc. – were at least profoundly unhappy. Though there were many whose case notes might have something like 'childhood uneventful' scribbled in them, there was, if you bothered to talk to them, not one whose life story did not abound with good reasons for their distress. To incarcerate people, drug them, patronise them with facile judgements about their 'adequacy', though one could see well enough how such procedures came about, was just to add insult to injury.

I quickly discovered that I was not the only one to find the orthodox approach to 'mental illness' unconvincing. Medicine wasn't infallible, science was full of uncertainty, the care of the 'mentally ill' was shot through with unexamined social and moral prejudice. And there were alternatives to the orthodoxy.

I changed my place of work to another vast Victorian mental hospital (Claybury Hospital in Essex), but this time one with a difference – a 'therapeutic community'. Here it was recognised that psychological disorder was a matter more of social experience than of illness, and the aim was to rehabilitate people through the experience of living together in a therapeutic environment (the hospital ward) where eccentricity was tolerated and difficulties in relationship reflected upon in daily meetings designed for that purpose.

For a short while the therapeutic-community movement, under the guidance of humane and to an extent charismatic figures like the psychiatrist Denis Martin at Claybury, flourished in the British National Health Service, and I am glad to have had the chance to play my part in it. But this approach, in essence anti-authoritarian in a way which presented an intolerable challenge to a hierarchical NHS bureaucracy as well as to entrenched medical power, was never likely to become the standard form of psychiatric treatment, and it passed its peak in less than a decade. Psychiatry retreated back into its medical/biological stronghold to busy itself with 'severe mental illness', and clinical psychology involved itself in the 'cognitive-behavioural' treatment of anyone whose problems could be seen as the result of their learned experience of life and relationships.

Even though liberated from the distortions and oversimplifications of the 'medical model', I found that there was still not a great deal of satisfaction to be gained from practising within the new orthodoxies of my profession. It was, true enough, a considerable and necessary advance to seek to understand people's distress in the light of their experience of life, but the theoretical background (such as it is) and practical toolkit of 'behavioural' and 'cognitive' approaches in clinical psychology, apart from having a kind of deadening banality about them, *just didn't seem to work*. In fact, *none* of the approaches to 'curing' people's emotional and psychological distress, whether derived from medical psychiatry, clinical psychology or the established approaches of psychoanalysis and psychotherapy, could make out a convincing case for its effectiveness.

Not that working with individuals in distress was itself unrewarding, but I suspect that, certainly in the earlier part of my career, I gained far more from it than they did. There was a huge amount to be learned from the fortitude and resilience with which people struggled with their difficulties, and their gratefulness for the crumb of comfort to be derived from talking to the likes of me about their predicaments was touching and warming. But only at my most self-deceiving could I have claimed that the 'therapy' I was dispensing was making any substantial difference to their lives.

In the early days I assumed that this was because I was simply not doing it as well as I should be. After all, the textbooks and the journal literature were absolutely confident about what could be achieved with the appropriate scientific scrupulousness. However, before long more reassuring and, I think, more likely explanations suggested themselves.

For a start, not *all* the confident pronouncements and scientific demonstrations in the literature could be right, because many of them contradicted each other. There must be another factor at work, and the most likely was professional self-interest. Doctors, behavioural scientists and so on are, sadly perhaps but absolutely inevitably, prey to the same need to justify themselves and earn a living as the rest of society. We told the stories the way we did mainly because that was the way we wanted it to be. That didn't mean that we were liars, charlatans or cheats, merely that we were human beings like everyone else. But it did mean that the very foundations on which our assumptions about mental health were built needed to be re-examined.

Another factor seemed to be that, closeted in our

consulting rooms, we were not taking enough account of what went on in the outside world to explain why our patients didn't get better in the way the theory predicted. It wasn't so much what the therapist did to the patient that made him or her better as what *everyone else* did when s/he returned to everyday life.

But it is really Margaret Thatcher I have to thank as much as anybody for opening my eyes fully to what I came to see as the absolutely fundamental and overriding importance of the social environment in the genesis of psychological distress. For it was the utter soulless, callous indifference in the Thatcher years to the welfare and security of ordinary people that finally made it obvious that what mattered to pyschological well-being was precisely not interior attributes such as the 'responsibility', 'self-reliance' and 'initiative' beloved of the New Right, but the provision within society of essentially *material* resources. In circumstances where these resources were stripped from whole sections of society and redistributed to another, no clinician with half an eye could fail to see the damage done to those deprived: they came to the consulting room in droves, mostly bemused and blaming themselves for what they saw as their own inadequacies.

Official psychology and psychiatry barely took societal issues into account in their approaches to the understanding and treatment of 'mental illness', and certainly nowhere were they made central to the field of enquiry. We had simply overlooked those factors that give society its dynamic force and most closely affect its members: the distribution, maintenance and embodied effects of *power*. What caused people distress was not so much their own mistakes, inadequacies and illnesses as the powers and influences that bore down upon them from the world beyond their skin.

This discovery was no real surprise. We all know it and enact its consequences in our daily lives: we struggle to wrest our livelihood and the means of our physical and emotional security from the social and material world around us, and the struggle involves almost the whole of our attention. It is only when we become significantly emotionally disturbed, it seems, that we lose sight of what we have taken life to be about and resort to the most abstruse and unlikely theories about what makes us tick.

In the light of this 'revelation', the focus of my clinical work shifted from the patients themselves to the worlds that they inhabited. I found myself spending more and more time trying to persuade people that there was nothing the matter with *them*, but quite a lot the matter with the past and present contexts of their lives.

Although many people find it a considerable relief to discover that they are not 'going out of their minds', not everybody is immediately receptive to this view. Despite its having a good deal to recommend it on the grounds of sheer common sense, the idea that circumstances rather than selves are 'to blame' for emotional distress has a formidable weight of cultural opinion against it, and it takes an unusual independence of spirit to reject institutionalised authority, even in favour of the obvious.

But the more I pursue this line, the more I am persuaded of its fruitfulness. Almost all the mystique falls away from the process of psychotherapy, and patients become equal partners in the conduct of an analysis not of their 'psyches' but of the predicaments that cause them distress. In this there is no need for professional mumbo-jumbo, secrecy or superiority, no necessity to disguise the theory or the therapist's thought processes from supposedly 'manipulative' or 'resistant' clients. And, given a clear enough understanding of the causes of distress – an initial liberating break from the mystifying production of a century of psychology – there is not a great deal of need for psychotherapy itself.

Hence the writing of this book. It attempts to cover the principal themes on which I have found it most useful to concentrate with people struggling to understand the roots of their troubles and to shape strategies for trying to deal with them. These themes – ideas about 'normality', 'responsibility' and 'will power', moral demands, change and, above-all, the use and abuse of power – are all closely intertwined, and hence recur throughout the book, but with each being given its principal statement in a chapter of its own.

The book is not intended as a do-it-yourself cure for psychological distress; indeed, its whole point is that such cure is for the most part not within the grasp of the individual sufferer, with or without psychotherapy. If the book can be said to have a 'therapeutic' aim at all, it is to remove from sufferers the burden of responsibility for their pain and to demystify as far as possible some of the ideas and practices that have grown up around psychotherapy during the course of this century.

A NOTE ON THE USE OF EXAMPLES

The use of 'case histories' presents a number of problems. They run the risk of either betraying confidences or straying into fiction, of including too much information or not enough. The more detailed and realistic one tries to make them, the more banal and pallid they seem to sound, or else luridly overdramatised, or (perhaps most often) subtly sentimentalised in a way that distorts reality. I know of no successful attempt to encapsulate people's lives in brief, 'clinical' snapshots of this kind (full-length biographies are problematic enough!). However, the provision of examples in some form is necessary to give shape and organisation to what would otherwise be an uncomfortably abstract discussion, and in what follows I have opted for a schematic oversimplification of types of distress and predicament which are so common as to identify no single individual, but may help to relate different strands of the argument to each other and to link themes that will recur in later chapters.

Inevitably, earlier examples anticipate subsequent discussion to some extent.

To make it easier to refer back to them, I have given the examples names in alphabetical order.

CHAPTER ONE

The Treatment of Distress: Current Approaches

Only the luckiest person gets through life without at some point suffering emotional distress to a degree which could be called 'clinical'. I'm not even sure that anybody is that lucky; if so, I haven't come across them myself. For the majority of us, the periods of our lives when we feel acutely emotionally distressed are usually fairly brief, or the distress itself not so intense that we think immediately of seeking professional help. But even so, there will probably be times in most people's lives when they feel at their wits' end and don't know which way to turn.

When a person does know which way to turn, it will probably be to someone in the family, a spouse or partner, a friend or perhaps a religious community. But sometimes – quite often, in fact – either there is no one immediately available, or those who are, are themselves involved in the problem in a way that makes it impossible for them to stand back and offer the kind of impartial concern necessary for effective support. At these times, the question of professional help may well occur to the person as something to consider.

Whether or not someone in distress consults a doctor (the GP usually being the first recourse), psychotherapist or counsellor, may well depend on a feeling that taking such a step would involve a tacit admission of 'abnormality', of having departed in a radical way from life's usual course. For many people consulting a professional constitutes in this way an expression of desperation.

On the one hand, it seems, there are unhappiness, upset, conflict, confusion, depression and distress (which we expect ourselves to deal with out of our own resources, so to speak), on the other, 'breakdown', 'mental illness', 'neurosis', 'psychosis', 'clinical depression' etc., which would mark us out as having departed normal company and in need of people in white coats.

Certainly, the people in white coats do little to disabuse us of the notion that there is a dichotomy between normal and abnormal, 'common unhappiness' and 'hysterical misery',[1] ordinary and 'clinical' types of distress. This is the received opinion, and one that gets endlessly circulated and recirculated via the media, eventually becoming 'common knowledge'. I do not think, however, that there is a great deal of convincing evidence to support it. In the end, what makes the difference between distress that the individual feels somehow able to cope with and distress apparently needing professional help is more a matter of quantity than kind: rather than splitting into a dichotomy, they lie on a continuum.

Usually, of course, it is events that upset us. However unbearable it may feel when it first overcomes us, the often very great pain events may cause us in the course of our lives is quite likely to fade with the passage of time, unless of course the events have effects that persist unchanged (as might be the case, for example, with having been made unemployed). No life could conceivably escape the occurrence of painful events, and, no matter how much we may hope to avoid them, most of us will not be so surprised at being overtaken by them that we feel outside the bounds of normal human experience. But even though painful events are common, most often relatively transitory, and only to be expected, how well we cope with them may depend on what we take to be the norm.

Interestingly, people rarely take their own experience as an indication of what is, so to speak, naturally human, but immediately look round at others to see how they handle similar eventualities. Rather than reflecting, when something painful happens to them: 'So *this* is how it feels when *x* happens', they tend to wonder: 'Am I reacting as people *normally* do?' Since, for a variety of reasons, it is often very difficult to establish what people *normally* feel in any given situation, it may often seem that what we are experiencing is significantly *unlike* what is 'normal', and when this happens we are likely to be overtaken by anxiety or shame, or both. This is a theme I shall be returning to in a later chapter. The point I want to make for the moment is that even quite common events that are likely to cause us distress in the course of a life – disappointments, betrayals, losses – may be frightening and isolating to the point where we may start to consider ourselves (and possibly even be considered by others) 'cases'.

It is not just our reaction to disturbing events that may cause us to worry about our normality. Even more problematic is the nature of our private experience. How do you know that the contents of your head from minute to minute, the ceaseless flow of thoughts and feelings which accompany your every waking (not to mention sleeping) moment, are acceptably similar to what's going on inside your fellow creatures? What is it permissible and what not permissible to think and feel? Since people almost never reveal exactly what they're thinking and feeling at any given moment, it is very hard to know whether our own flights of imagination might not be more than slightly crazy. In part, of course, it is precisely this worry that prevents us from revealing the private world of our imagination to others, and in situations where a person loses confidence in the soundness of his or her mental contents, something that is usually just kept to the self may become a source of great anxiety and distress.

In fact, we depend on a *culture* to establish the bounds of normality, within which we are able to feel at ease with our mind, and in this respect the culture may be more or less benign. The closing years of the twentieth century seemed to be one of those times when became less benign.

Cultures that become deformed by ideology tend to generate

a kind of policing of thought which attempts to regulate mental life. In some cases, for example under totalitarian political regimes or fundamentalist religions, this process may be quite overt, with secret police and vast bureaucracies for punitive control; in others it may be implicit and informal. Our own culture, driven principally by an ideology determined by commercial interests, offers us a view of mental life which is both impoverished and distorted. On the one hand we are invited to identify with the idealised picture of the happily adjusted consumer, socially perfectly balanced and of impeccable judgement in choosing the options life offers; on the other we are entertained by images of immense violence and sexual prurience, presented to us as features of a kind of alien fantasy world where savagery and madness reign. No wonder we become nervous about our own private experience, for nowhere outside ourselves can we find an indication of how ordinary, real people do actually feel (this, again, is a question I shall be returning to later in this book).

All of us, anyway, live a secret life of doubt and pain which we are quite likely to think is specifically ours. If people become sufficiently troubled by their experience to seek help from a doctor or other professional, they may well do so in fear and trembling that their difference from others will at last come to light and that they will be diagnosed as abnormal.

Some people will be aware that there are brands of psychotherapy designed less to provide solace for troubled minds than to offer the individual some kind of spiritual enrichment or 'personal growth' in the shape of deepened self-understanding and an enhanced ability to live life to the full. For such people, consulting a therapist may constitute more a privilege – even a kind of status symbol – than a badge of shame. It is not for those people that this book is written. Self-exploration, certainly, is a perfectly legitimate activity and may well prove rewarding to those who have the resources to pursue it, but my concern here is with people whose need to understand themselves and their predicament arises out of pain rather than curiosity. My focus is on the phenomena of emotional distress and the validity or otherwise of practices that claim to be therapeutic in relation to them.

PRINCIPAL SOURCES OF HELP

For the person in distress looking for professional help, the prospect is, to put it mildly, confusing and the likely outcome a lottery. If it seems simple and straightforward, either the person is very lucky or very unaware of the sea of complexity surrounding him or her.

There is, to be sure, a more or less standard procedure for seeking help with emotional or psychological problems, and this might lead the innocent to believe that the help they get reflects state-of-the-art treatment, but anyone with experience of the mental health industry will know how varied practices are and how little control people have over what happens to them.

Most often, people experience their distress as a form of illness (panicky anxiety, for instance, is often experienced initially as imminent physical collapse or even death), but even where they are aware that the core of their troubles is psychological rather than physical, the usual course is to approach the GP. Most GPs will treat the symptoms of distress by offering advice and prescribing the usual tranquillisers and antidepressants, but the pressures of their own job leave them very little time to listen to their patients, and they tend to vary quite markedly both in the way they are likely to view psychological problems and in their awareness of the specialist facilities that exist for treating them.

There are still many GPs of the 'pull yourself together' school and many whose only way of dealing with the mental is to translate it into the physical. These are not the best people to encounter if your distress is anything but temporary or superficial (if it is, on the other hand, these might be the best people to encounter!). Other GPs, an ever dwindling minority, may, in the best traditions of family medicine, use their knowledge of you and call on the wisdom born of years of observation and reflection to offer you sympathetic counselling and sound advice. Most likely, however, the GP will refer you to an expert whom s/he judges the most appropriate person to deal with the kind of problem you are presenting. GPs should have a good knowledge of the treatment facilities available locally (which may vary greatly from place to place), but this will by no means always be the case; there is, therefore, quite an element of luck about whom you may see next.

The options open to the GP for specialist referral are likely to be chosen from psychiatry, clinical psychology or 'counselling' in one or other of its forms. In some case, of course, s/he may wish to involve the social services or other specialist agencies, but probably only if there are obviously prominent factors of material or social deprivation or other practical difficulties involved.

The choice between psychiatry, clinical psychology or counselling is, however, not as straightforward as it may sound, largely because these are not unified disciplines offering standard approaches to treatment which have been tried and tested over time, but broad groupings of professionals who, while for the most part sharing a common and distinctive training, differ widely among themselves both personally (and in this field personality cannot be safely disregarded) and in what they believe about theory and practice. Which group the GP considers appropriate in any particular case is likely to depend on the view s/he takes of your difficulties.

If, for example, the GP considers that you are suffering from a form of 'mental illness', a degree of distress that can in some sense be considered 'clinical', the most likely referral will be to a psychiatrist, i.e. a medical practitioner who has specialised and obtained postgraduate qualifications in psychiatric medicine.

If, on the other hand, the GP considers your problem to be 'behavioural', i.e. arising from situational difficulties or the result of processes of learning that have in some sense been 'maladaptive', you are most likely to be referred to a clinical psychologist, who will have a degree in academic psychology and a subsequent postgraduate qualification, most probably these days as a (non-medical) 'doctor of clinical psychology'. The latter equips him or her to view your problems as having arisen from your experience of life and to treat them from, most likely, a 'cognitive-behavioural' standpoint which attempts to modify your attitude towards your difficulties as well as how you actually deal with them.

In those (frequent) cases where the person's distress seems to arise directly from his or her relations with others, possibly at work but more likely domestically, and where there is other-wise no hint of 'mental illness' or more deep-seated disturbance, there is an increasing likelihood that s/he will be referred to a counsellor. Counsellors may be attached to the GP's practice or may be located elsewhere in their own premises. Counsellors come from a variety of backgrounds. Some, like those who qualified originally as community psychiatric nurses, have professional roots in the mental health service and considerable experience of people in emotional difficulties. Others have no such experience, but may have received their training on one of the myriad counselling courses that have sprung into existence in recent years. Counsellors may be paid or voluntary and may subscribe to any of a range of theoretical approaches (the most likely being that of the psychologist Carl Rogers). Many counsellors will be without formal qualifications in one of the mental health 'core professions' such as psychology, medicine, nursing or social work, and though they may well have to conform to the standards of accreditation of the British Association of Counselling, this is not so in every case.

If this is already beginning to sound a little bewildering, it is, I'm afraid, even more complicated than I have so far made it appear. This is partly because, though most GPs are likely to refer roughly in accordance with the way I've indicated, there is in fact a wide overlap between the professions involved, and a lot may depend on who knows whom rather than upon any more reliable guidelines. There is also, as I have already suggested, a wide variation between practitioners within each of these fields, so that one cannot guarantee a standard product, so to speak. If, furthermore, one takes into account the provision of psychological help that exists in the private sector, the complications are greatly compounded and there is virtually no disinterested guidance for the individual to turn to. The major schools of psychoanalysis and analytical psychology (the respective creations of Sigmund Freud and C. G. Jung), for example, exist largely (though not entirely) outside the structure of public health services, as does a vast range of lesser-known approaches to psychotherapy and counselling which the individual may stumble across at some time more or less by chance.

Added to all this is the fact that the lay person has no way of judging the validity of the claims made by the various practitioners for the efficacy of their methods. For obvious reasons, people who depend for their livelihood on their ability to attract patients or clients tend not only to proclaim their wares with confidence, but also to believe their own rhetoric. And yet they cannot all be right. The variations in approach both between and within the broadly 'mental health' professions are not mere matters of emphasis, but are frequently mutually contradictory. This is not the place either to pronounce judgement or to try to reconcile these differences,[2] but it may be instructive to give an indication of some of the difficulties confronting the major approaches.

Psychiatry

Psychiatry is an interesting case in point. Despite having come under increasing, and in my view justified, attack in recent years as promulgating an inappropriate medical model of mental illness, psychiatry still wields considerable influence in the public provision of mental health services. The clinical head of 'community mental health teams' will usually be a psychiatrist, and though the teams themselves may involve a range of different professions – nursing, social work, clinical psychology etc. – the structure and content of their operations will be heavily flavoured by psychiatric ideology.

Psychiatry does of course have its uses. A society has to have some way of containing and, where possible, helping people who become so confused, disturbed, excited or frightened that they threaten the safety of themselves or others. Even if mental illness is a myth, as the American psychiatrist Thomas Szasz suggested over twenty years ago, there would have to exist a profession for dealing as humanely as possible with the extremes of human distress. There is, however, a difference between containing distress and curing it, and it is in the latter respect that psychiatry may be said to be found wanting.

Few psychiatrists would agree that mental illness is a myth. Psychiatry has become increasingly biological in its approach in recent times, and huge amounts of effort are put into classifying and diagnosing supposedly clinical conditions ('psychoses', 'neuroses', 'character disorders' etc.) which are taken to have their origins in various forms of genetic and/or biochemical disorder. Psychiatrists are trained according to the established procedures of medicine and their specialism is structured exactly like that of other hospital doctors. They compete for status and reputation with their colleagues in physical medicine, and their credibility would be destroyed if they drifted too far from their medical roots.

The standard psychiatric procedures of treatment and training mean that anyone who becomes a patient is likely to come under the care of a consultant psychiatrist who will be responsible for overseeing his or her 'case'. The doctor doing the actual treatment (most likely the administration of psychoactive drugs of one kind or another) will, however, probably be a more junior psychiatrist whose need to climb the promotional ladder, and so frequently change jobs, means that contact with the patient is unlikely to provide any continuity of care. Indeed, as in other branches of medicine, there is in any case no guarantee that patients will see the same doctor at each outpatient visit. In these circumstances, the patient will probably be treated as someone with an illness, and, though the time spent talking to the psychiatrist may be somewhat longer than that which the GP can afford to give, it is unlikely that a great deal of attention will be given to the social significance of his or her 'symptoms', i.e. the underlying traumas and difficulties in background and current circumstances which give rise to distress in the first place.

Of course, not all psychiatrists fit this picture, and there are those whose experience and compassion make them valuable partners in the exploration of patients' emotional pain. There are also psychiatrists who specialise in psychotherapeutic approaches (most usually derived from one or another variation of Freudian psychoanalysis), but they are relatively thin on the ground in Britain and there is no guarantee that the average patient will get the chance of a consultation with one.

Psychiatry has over the last three or four decades had to learn to share the field of 'mental illness' with a number of other professional disciplines and to modify the nature of its once monopolistic claims. It has also had to bend to political changes in the way psychological disorder and its treatment are viewed and funded (the closure of the old mental hospitals and the reliance instead on so-called 'care in the community' have made big differences to psychiatric practice). Always strongly prone to fashions in treatment (one thinks of the crazes not all that long ago for leucotomy and insulin-coma therapy, now mercifully extinct), psychiatry is nothing if not pragmatic, and it is now happy enough to redefine some conditions it might once, for example, have called 'neurotic' as concerns of the 'worried well' and to leave their treatment to various non-medical professions and voluntary groups of counsellors. These changes have not, however, resulted in psychiatry itself becoming any more liberal.

Increasingly, psychiatrists are having to develop and intensify their role as custodians of those who fall victim to the more extreme forms of distress our society gives rise to, often in very difficult circumstances dictated more by political constraints than by therapeutic concerns, and this, as noted, seems to result in a fortification of the biological approach. To read psychiatric textbooks, or indeed simply to attend to the received opinion reflected in the media, we could be forgiven for thinking that there is no doubt that serious mental illnesses like 'schizophrenia' and 'clinical depression' exist as entities established by medical science. It would seem that the future lies in the further identification of the genetic and biochemical processes underlying disturbed conduct and thinking, and the refinement of the chemical means of modifying them.

Knowledge, as the French philosopher Michel Foucault suggested so persuasively, is inseparable from power,[3] and it certainly seems to be the case that powerful interests within both psychiatry and the wider society have combined since the 1970s to paper over the cracks that critiques by people like Thomas Szasz and R. D. Laing had caused to appear in the notion of mental illness. An explosion of research in the sixties and early seventies which suggested that there could be important psychological causes for so-called psychotic thinking and behaviour has now been largely forgotten or summarily (and quite unjustifiably) discredited. Right-wing political regimes whose economic policies led directly or indirectly to profound psychological distress in whole swathes of the population, the enormously powerful drug companies supplying the vastly lucrative means of 'treatment', and, of course, the profession of psychiatry itself, all had a stake in presenting the concept of 'severe mental illness' as indisputably biological. Even the families of, for example, 'schizophrenic' patients, stung by what they experienced as the blame for their relatives' condition, formed associations to reinforce the indisputability of the illness model.

But disputed it has always been. There is a long tradition within psychiatry and psychology that has sought to establish that underlying even the more puzzling and apparently alien forms of psychological disturbance there are to be found social factors which have little to do with biological ones, except in so far as all thoughts, feelings and actions are mediated through and inseparable from our bodies. In my view, much of this work is far more intellectually convincing and empirically sound than the rough pragmatism of contemporary biological psychiatry, and yet its proponents are often barely heard of by present-day practitioners.[4] I can only account for this with the help of something like Foucault's notion of a 'discourse of power': only certain kinds of 'knowledge' are thinkable and sayable under a given power regime.

Modern psychiatry too has its critics,[5] but, again, their voices tend to be marginal and barely heard behind the chorus of orthodoxy. The view, for instance, that 'schizophrenia' can be called into question as a viable concept is now virtually irreceivable, despite its being one of the most muddled and empirically difficult to establish of all psychiatric diagnoses.[6]

What this means is that the sufferer falling into psychiatric hands cannot automatically expect to receive sympathetic, informed and intelligent help in understanding and alleviating his or her distress from the viewpoint of what it indicates about the nature of his or her world and what s/he can do about it. People in severe difficulties may of course be calmed down by appropriate medication, in some cases be given necessary if not always congenial asylum, and their families may receive much-needed respite. Psychiatry is far more about social control than it is about getting to the roots of psychological illness.

Clinical psychology

By contrast, clinical psychology is very much about understanding people's difficulties as the consequence of their experience of life (what's happening to them in the present as well as their 'learning history') and trying to devise ways of modifying their 'behaviour', as well as their attitudes and 'cognitions', so that the impact of these past and present events is lessened.

Clinical psychologists have nothing like the formal power of psychiatrists – they cannot interfere with or restrain their patients' *bodies* in any significant way – and so their influence over patients is reduced to the power of persuasion. Partly because of this lack of formal power, the kind of patronage or arrogance so frequently experienced with medical doctors is far less likely to be evident among clinical psychologists. They also spend much more time with patients than doctors do – consultations are likely to last for forty-five minutes to an hour at a time – and people are likely to be seen by the same person over the whole period of their treatment. A course of treatment may vary greatly in length, from just one or two consultations to over a hundred, but most will probably be between five and ten.

Although clinical psychology borrows liberally from related disciplines, in particular the various schools of psychotherapy (and practitioners may vary widely in their theoretical allegiances), it has its roots in academic psychology, where there is a strong emphasis on experiment and evidence. This has the advantage that there is always an element of pressure on clinical psychologists to justify their procedures according to whether or not they can be shown to be effective, and hence, at least indirectly, to respect the views of their patients in this regard. The disadvantage is that academic psychology itself is a curious patchwork of competing notions (often grandiosely called 'theories'), the superficiality and implausibility of many of which are pretty evident to all except those trying industriously to establish the evidence in their favour.

This means that the ruling dogmas of clinical psychology, usually referred to loosely as 'cognitive behaviourism', embody an, in my view, extraordinarily simplistic collection of ideas about how people come to be the way they are and what they can be expected to be able to do about it. For example, how people learn things, how they form and change 'attitudes', whether and how they can control their 'thoughts', are often dealt with in psychology according to models that have been constructed from a combination of everyday, common-sense (and occasionally contradictory) assumptions and simplified laboratory experiments which scarcely do justice to the complexity of human experience. Such ideas, acceptable enough perhaps to undergraduate students learning the experimental ropes, ring particularly hollow when they come to be applied in the clinical setting, where people's difficulties are often complicated and intractable. Since these issues form the main preoccupations of later chapters, I will not discuss them further here, except to note that, however simplistic, the typical notions of cognitive behaviourism do at least have the merit of treating people as if they exist as social beings in a world that affects them and on which they may, through their own conduct ('behaviour'), have a reciprocal effect.

It is important also to note at this stage that what a practitioner *thinks* about what s/he is doing (and this applies, of course, to all practitioners, not just clinical psychologists), what his or her theories about it are, need not necessarily be all that important to the patient. What matters from the patient's point of view is whether what the practitioner does is helpful. In fact, many studies have shown that, at least for the 'talking therapies', to which, of course, clinical psychology contributes, what counts most towards patients' recovery is precisely not the theoretical inclinations of the practitioners, but their personality, i.e. how far patients feel able to talk to them and to trust them – how likeable they find them.

This is not a particularly convenient finding for those bent on demonstrating that their particular therapy – or even therapy in general – is a *technically* valid form of 'treatment', and any demonstrable advantage for procedures over personalities, however slight, is quickly seized upon. But, time and again, it is so-called non-specific factors such as those mentioned that research throws up as principally important. This may mean that only personalities are important, but it may also mean that so far the active ingredients of successful therapy remain to be discovered. Given the simple-mindedness of many of the ideas about what is technically important in treatment, this latter possibility should not be discounted.

These speculations aside, we may conclude perhaps that what makes an encounter with clinical psychology more comfortable for many patients than one with psychiatry is as much as anything the time they will be given and the common sense and ordinary humanity with which they will be treated. Since counselling and psychotherapy share with clinical psychology a general lack of formal power (particularly in the case of non-medical practitioners), the same may be said, to a large extent, for them.

Psychotherapy and counselling

Although clinical psychology is a well-established mental health profession, there are still only a few thousand clinical psychologists practising in Britain, most of them in the National Health Service. There are undoubtedly many more counsellors and psychotherapists countrywide, though most of them practise outside the NHS. Like every other, the 'market' in psychotherapy and counselling has been largely deregulated over the past decade or so, and there has been a huge increase in the range of therapies available. Even staid institutions of the official health services may now be found offering alternative approaches such as aromatherapy or reflexology as part of their 'package of care', and the criterion of acceptability of therapeutic approaches in general has become one more of saleability than of demonstrable efficacy. It has also become extremely difficult to generalise about counselling and psychotherapy, and a virtual impossibility for the average 'consumer' to be able to make sensible judgements about what may suit him or her.

It would certainly not be possible in the space of a few paragraphs to give anything like a complete and balanced account of all the varieties of psychotherapy and counselling available, and in any case, as already remarked, the 'official' version of their procedures often differs quite radically from what therapists actually do. Anyone wanting to investigate how the various schools of therapy and counselling set about their business is probably best advised to start out with one of the available texts that attempt a general overview.[7] I would, however, like to highlight one or two issues that seem to me particularly important.

The most obvious person to hold responsible for the origination of psychotherapeutic approaches is Sigmund Freud. In the public mind, certainly, Freud's creation, 'psychoanalysis', has achieved a higher profile than any other approach, and many of the basic ideas of psychoanalysis have become part of our everyday thought and language. Freudian psychoanalysis, moreover, having spent, in Britain at least, some of the middle decades of the last century on the verge of, if not disrepute, then certainly neglect, has enjoyed a remarkable revival over the last twenty years. But it is important to realise that psychoanalysis is now only one of a vast range of 'talking' approaches to psychological distress, many of which have very little truck with psychoanalytic concepts.

All these approaches tend to differentiate themselves as clearly demarcated 'schools' with restricted entry, established procedures for training, and more or less strict criteria for accreditation. Psychoanalysis was no doubt very influential in setting this trend.

Freud, feeling himself and his colleagues a beleaguered band of scientific pioneers in a hostile and uncomprehending world of Philistines, was almost persecuted by the need to keep the strain of his ideas pure, and the structural development of psychoanalysis resembled more that of a fanatical religious group or a secret society than of a branch of knowledge. Similarly, those renegades who in the early days of psychoanalysis broke away from Freud to form their own systems, also took pains to differentiate themselves from others and to, so to speak, patent their ideas and give their approach a distinctive name. Alfred Adler, for example, developed his 'individual psychology', and C. G. Jung, rather more presumptuously perhaps, called his system 'analytical psychology'.

Throughout the twentieth century, ambitious and charismatic characters unable to toe the line of the therapeutic discipline in which they were schooled continued the tendency to develop a new and distinctive brand, so that now there are literally hundreds of them. They compete in a flourishing marketplace where there is no shortage of potential consumers, whose only problem is to decide which brand is for them.

There is absolutely no hard and fast evidence that any one approach to counselling or therapy is more effective than any other. This fact is hard to square with the often ferocious lengths a given school will go to to protect its boundaries and preserve the theoretical and practical distinctiveness of its approach. For, if there's nothing much to choose between them, why should they bother? The answer to this question must, I think, lie in the aura of authority which such tight regulation tends to impart. Careful vetting of candidates for training, scrupulous attention to teaching methods and requirements for clinical experience etc., and rigorous accreditation procedures, all of which tend to characterise the more established schools, give an impression to potential consumers that here indeed is a body of knowledge and a set of professional practices demanding veneration and justifying expense.

Psychoanalysis, largely through institutional practices of just the kind outlined above, has probably succeeded more than any other approach in developing a mantle of respectability and authority – with a strong dash of awe-inspiring mystique. The fact that many of its practitioners are medical doctors no doubt also contributes to its competitive edge in this respect. And yet it was precisely the shortcomings of psychoanalytic therapeutic technique – when it was without question the 'market leader' in psychological treatment – that led to the development of alternative approaches.

The psychoanalytic view is, essentially, that at the core of the patient's 'neurotic' difficulties lie the unconscious, wishful impulses of an illicit sexuality and aggression which have, through a process of 'interpretation' by the analyst, to be brought into consciousness and thereby under the disciplined control of the self.[8] The means whereby this was to be achieved, in orthodox analysis, involved an uncomfortably impersonal and distant relationship between patient and analyst, with the latter preserving a kind of neutral anonymity so that patients could 'project' onto him or her (as part of the 'transference relationship') the infantile desires and expectations which supposedly powered the unconscious mind. Quite apart from the fact that this procedure, when put to the test, didn't seem to work,[9] the coldly mechanistic nature of the therapeutic relationship did not endear itself to patients on the whole.[10]

It was probably the work of the psychologist Carl Rogers that did most to challenge the theoretical supremacy of psychoanalysis. Rogers, founder of the school whose 'brand name' is 'client-centred' (or sometimes 'non-directive') therapy, inspired a great deal of research around the mid-twentieth century which demonstrated that the relationship between 'clients' (as Rogerians prefer to call them) and therapists is crucial to the outcome of treatment. Far from preserving a 'neutral screen' for the 'projection' of fantasies by, as in psychoanalysis, sitting out of sight behind a patient stretched out on a couch, Rogerian therapists enter into a more recognisably human exchange with their clients.

In fact, the human characteristics of therapists – their 'warmth', 'empathy' and 'genuineness' – was shown by Rogerian research to be central to the effectiveness of therapy itself. Although, as with all psychological research in this area, these findings have not entirely stood the test of time, they do combine with others to emphasise the 'nonspecificity' of the more potent ingredients of therapy. As far as psychotherapy (including psychoanalysis) and counselling do have a beneficial effect, it is probably as much as anything the way the patient or client perceives the therapist as a *person* that makes the difference. To put it another way, it is solidarity with the therapist that lends heart to patients as they struggle with their difficulties.

Solidarity seems a rather mundane explanation of therapeutic efficacy to arrive at after so much effort and enthusiasm. If this is the conclusion to which experience, as well as the research literature, point us, it is a modest one, and one not easily accepted by either therapists and counsellors or their clients. Perhaps this is why so much energy continues to be invested by the ever-expanding schools of therapy and counselling in the development of distinctive and patentable *techniques* aimed at transforming the individual's distress into, if not happiness, then at least adjustment. And yet, though people's eagerness to believe in the magical promise of change implicit in so much of the therapy industry remains unabated, the evidence that such techniques can be found still stubbornly resists discovery.

The appeal of magic is extremely difficult to resist, and the idea that some kind of transformation takes place in the patient as the direct result of his or her interaction with the therapist is one that neither patients nor therapists find it at all easy to shake off. No less than with the 'mental illness' model of psychiatry, most forms of psychotherapy nurse a conception of the patient as someone to whom something is *done* through the technical procedures of the therapy: somehow or other, the *person* is changed, if only through having been moved to 'take responsibility' for his or her life.

This idea of the patient being inspired or transformed through association with an expert in possession of esoteric technical skills has a long history, and even in relatively recent times it is fascinating to see how the form as well as the content of the therapeutic consultation can be traced back to the practices of seventeenth-century magicians and astrologers.[11] So entrenched is this kind of notion in our culture that we can scarcely be blamed for continuing to insist on its validity, and it can probably be seen most clearly at present in the ubiquitous confidence placed in counselling as the antidote to life's commoner cruelties. It is as if anything that disturbs the smooth plastic surface of a 'normal' life, from problems in personal relationships to unexpected human-made or natural disasters, can be eased away with the unction of counselling.[12] It seems that we view psychological pain and emotional trauma as in themselves not only abnormal but unnatural, as something we have a right to have removed through the intervention of professional experts who can rearrange our feelings so that we are left unscarred by events. 'Post-traumatic stress' has thus become a 'disorder' rather than something we might reasonably expect as an entirely natural outcome.

Magic certainly lurks at the centre of a good deal of our thinking about counselling techniques. For example, the notion of 'positive thinking', in one or other of its guises, clearly maintains a widespread appeal. The injunctions of 'rational emotive therapy'[13] to see, and abandon, the folly of our 'irrational' assumptions about ourselves, or the emphasis in 'cognitive therapies' on changing the 'attitudes' that cast a gloom over our world – or even the popular inclination when times are bad to 'look on the bright side' – seem, perhaps, almost a matter of common sense. And yet they embody the profoundly magical idea that merely thinking about the world can change its nature. Noticing that the way we view the world can affect our experience of it misleads us into assuming that we can view it *how we like*: a psychological observation becomes a belief in magic.

THE SCOPE OF PSYCHOTHERAPY
Limitations of therapy

The idea that individuals are, at least potentially, in charge of their own fate lies at the very heart of therapeutic philosophy. Although this may seem at first sight a healthily optimistic, even necessary view, without which we would wallow in our misery as helpless victims, it is, I believe, an essentially destructive one. The way I have stated it – that people may be in charge of their fate – already, perhaps, begins to show up its inadequacy, but this is basically what ideas about 'changing attitudes', 'assuming responsibility', acting on 'insights' gained, 'cognitive restructuring' and so on, all boil down to. By working on the *self*, people can change their experience of the *world*, and the effects of ravages they have suffered in the *past* can be repaired by them (with, of course, the help of their therapist) in the *present*. This is, certainly, an optimistic view, and it is not one that holds water. Not only does it make very little logical sense, but there is also no convincing empirical evidence that it works in practice.

There are no magical solutions to the damage life inflicts upon us, and to place the burden of change on individuals, to be achieved through some kind of therapeutically mediated internal psychological process, is only in the long run to add to their troubles. For at the end of it all the world is still there, still doing its damage, and all people are likely to feel as the results of their therapists' ministrations is responsibility for their own misery.

What has misled us, I believe, is as much as anything else the environment in which psychotherapy takes place and in which psychotherapeutic theories have therefore been conceived. This is the environment of the consulting room. There are only two animate figures in this space: therapist and patient. In consequence, everything that happens in it comes to be causally attributed to one or the other of them.[14] Even the patient's past is made manifest in the consulting room in the present, so that description of events becomes, almost inevitably, confused with the events themselves. The consulting room becomes, almost by default, a kind of alchemical crucible in which the protagonists can transmute the inert properties of the 'beyond' (whether in space or time) through the passionate force of their intentions and their living interaction. The only thing that seems to matter is what passes between patient and therapist. If the patient improves, for example, it seems self-evident that this must be because of the healing intervention of the therapist – what else could it be, when there is no one else there?

And yet, however much it may be valued – or overvalued – by both patients and therapists, the environment of the consulting room is not the environment in which they live out their lives, and for patients in particular (except those clients of psychoanalysis who spend five hours a week, year in and year out, in the company of an analyst) the influence of therapy is of minute significance in contrast with that of all the other people and things in their lives. Any adequate account of psychological distress, what causes it and what might alleviate it, must surely include the totality of our lives, and as part of that process take due note of the powerful, often inexorable, forces that shape us in the world beyond the consulting room.

Psychological distress, I am suggesting, is not a problem *of* the person or *of* the 'self', but is a problem presented *for* the person by the world.

Even the currently popular notion of 'stress', which would on the face of it seem to suggest a force bearing down on the individual from outside, ends up being represented by most therapeutic approaches as something *inside* people which they have to learn to deal with or 'manage'. Programmes of 'stress management' are in this way directed at manipulating the internal processes through which people are supposedly able to handle stress, rather than at diminishing the stressors in the outside world which have come to make a misery of the lives of so many of us. Once again, it seems to me, this is little more than a disguised form of magic – the belief that we can alter the world by altering the way we imagine it.

It cannot be emphasised too strongly, however, that to suggest that therapeutic magic doesn't cure the ills of the world is *not* to sink into pessimistic resignation. To say that things cannot be changed in the way that most therapeutic approaches imply is not to say that they cannot be changed, nor is it to say that the therapeutic process achieves nothing at all.

The problem with most approaches to psychotherapy and counselling, in my view, is that the theoretical account they give of what they are doing bears very little relation to what actually goes on in therapy, and that, though therapists often *do* do things that are helpful to clients, they have failed to see what these are and to describe them accurately. This is because they have been so anxious to provide the kind of technical analysis of their procedures that would justify their professional stance. There are, of course, exceptions to this rule, and there have been several practitioners of psychotherapy who have had the courage and perspicacity both to take account of the essentially non-technical, personal nature of much of what they do and to write about the implications of this with power and clarity.[15]

What these writers achieve is to put psychotherapy and counselling in perspective (the perspective of the *relation* between patient and therapist), and in doing so – though this may not always be their main intention – they greatly reduce the grandiosity of its claims. Psychotherapy does not magic away the pains inflicted by the world, but, to some extent and in some cases, provides the patient with a way of understanding his or her predicament, and offers the solidarity of the 'therapeutic relationship' in trying to do something about it.

It is, I think, important to distinguish between three main components of psychotherapy: comfort, clarification and encouragement. These are present in different proportions in different approaches, and the effect of one easily becomes confused with the effect of another – a therapist may assume, for example, that a patient's improvement is due to the power of the 'insights' that have been derived from the explanatory model used in therapy, when it is simply the result of the comfort (solidarity) gained from the mere presence of the therapist.

Comfort

I suspect that it is principally the phenomenon of comfort that maintains the credibility of psychotherapy in the face of all the evidence that its efficacy is in fact only modest. The comfort to be derived from sharing your deepest fears and most shameful secrets with a 'valued other' who does not immediately heap blame or scorn upon you, but who instead listens patiently and sympathetically to what you have to say, is one of the most potently therapeutic experiences to be had. It is this experience that convinces patients and therapists of all persuasions of the validity of their enterprise. Indeed, some writers on psychotherapy, notably Ian Suttie[16] and Paul Halmos[17], have drawn attention to the absolute centrality of love itself to the therapeutic process, suggesting that the therapist's disinterested, loving concern for and acceptance of the patient is the curative factor in therapy.

But there are a number of important limitations to the provision of comfort[18] which must be noted. They are important not because they indicate that therapeutic comfort is somehow bogus, but because they do not square with the 'official' accounts which most therapists offer for the effectiveness of their procedures.

Comfort does not cure anything. Halving a trouble by sharing it does not somehow expunge it from the face of the earth, and when solidarity with the sharer finishes at the termination of therapy, the trouble becomes whole once again. In this way, it is the process of therapy itself that is experienced as therapeutic, and not anything the therapy brings about as a technical achievement.

Sometimes patients recognise the inadequacy of this state of affairs for themselves, especially with those varieties of counselling which consist almost solely of 'empathetic' listening ('it was all very well, but all she did was nod sympathetically'). Perhaps more often, however, they may become dependent on a relationship which, perversely from their point of view, is not intended to be available to them indefinitely: they will be expected to become 'better' at some point. It may well be the case, for example, that some people are sufficiently sustained by their relationship with their therapist to cope with life satisfactorily enough between visits, but it is the boost they get from the visits, rather than anything they have learned from the therapeutic process, that keeps them going. Once the visits have to stop (maybe because of the therapist's worries about 'dependency'), it is quite likely to emerge that nothing has really changed for the patient. The provision of therapeutic comfort of this kind is not unlike the administration of short-acting tranquillisers – it works, it is in a sense addictive, but it will have sooner or later to be withdrawn (with painful consequences).

This is not to say that therapeutic comfort is a bad thing, but it is to suggest that, if it is not to run the risk of becoming a bad thing, it has either to be available unlimitedly, or there have to be other components to the process which enable patients to benefit from it without becoming addicted. As long as comfort is not intended as an end in itself (which might be perfectly acceptable if there were enough comforters to go around), there should be other clear ends to which it may contribute as a means.[19]

Clarification

The component of what I call clarification is seen as essential by most therapeutic approaches. That is to say, it is usually considered necessary to furnish patients with an explanation of their distress – its history and antecedents. Certainly, when they first seek help, people often have no idea why they should be feeling so ill and distressed, and they may themselves attach considerable importance to being told by an expert 'what it is' that is troubling them.

Depending on the theoretical predilections of the therapist, accounts people get of the background to their problems may differ widely, as may the manner in which the information necessary for the construction of an account is extracted from them. It might, for example, take many hours of listening patiently to the sporadic free associations of a 'resistant' patient before a psychoanalyst feels able to lay bare the unconscious sexual wishes and fantasies thought to be at the root of the patient's present difficulties. An expert in 'behaviour modification', on the other hand, might, through a direct and matter-of-fact procedure of question and answer, arrive at a formulation of the client's 'learning history' in half an hour.

The most likely course, perhaps, would be for therapist and patient to collaborate in negotiating a view of the latter's difficulties that accords with the experience of both, so that the therapist will feel happy that the picture emerging of the patient's background and current circumstances is one that makes sense in terms of the kinds of events and relationships likely to give rise to distress, and the patient will feel that the explanations offered by the therapist do not jar too violently with what seems plausible from his or her own perspective. The therapist, in other words, checks the hypotheses that come to mind against the patient's experience.

It is, on the whole, probably not difficult for therapists who are reasonably intelligent, experienced and undogmatic to arrive at quite an accurate picture of what has been and is contributing to a patient's present distress. It may often be the case also that this picture is one which, though the patient eventually accepts it readily enough, came at first as a considerable surprise to him or her. It may be this element of unexpectedness that contributes to the mystique of therapeutic clarification – patients may be startled at what seems to them the almost magical perspicacity of the therapist in unearthing events and feelings in the past of which till then they had little inkling. Therapists are able to do this not because they have uncanny powers of insight (even if some would like to think so), but because they have seen many times before what the patient takes to be his or her utterly idiosyncratic experience. The answer to the question 'How could my therapist possibly have guessed that?' is that the same circumstance has been observed by the therapist in many previous cases.

There is, then, in principle at least, not a great deal of difficulty in arriving at an acceptable account of how people come to be as they are and what the origins of their distress are. Where difficulties do arise is in knowing what is to be done with this information. The idea that 'insight' leads automatically to cure, while figuring largely in many patients' expectations, has long been recognised to be problematic by therapists, even though in their hearts they find it very hard to abandon. Another temptation, touched on earlier, is to try magically to replace the account arrived at with one that offers a rosier prognosis. If we accept, as some 'cognitive' approaches do, that there is no reality beyond our interpretation of it (the way things are is the way we see them), then the possibility of altering history retrospectively becomes quite plausible. Cognitive therapists are fond of pointing out, for example, that a glass may be seen as half empty or half full, with the implication that a gloomy view of the past breeds a pessimism about the future and may be replaced by a more upbeat interpretation of our history.

It seems virtually impossible for almost any therapeutic approach to conceptualise the influence of the patient's past as anything other than something s/he must somehow *alter*, either by interpreting it as not so bad after all, or, having gained 'insight' into it, by deciding (presumably through an act of will) to be a different kind of person in the future; patients are required, that is, somehow to disregard or negate the effects of earlier experience.

Much of this book will be concerned with the impossibility of therapeutic ideas such as these, and with the intellectual and moral confusion which underlies them and which they generate in others. But this is not to say that the investigation of people's background and history is a waste of time. The point of establishing how you got to be the way you are is to disabuse yourself of mistaken explanations, not the least of which is that you are somehow responsible for it.

People are often mystified about the causes of their suffering, and an important aspect of their coming to understand what they can and cannot do about their predicament is to be *demystified*. Almost by its very nature (the expectation of magical transformation inherent in the therapeutic situation), psychotherapy is prone to mystify its clients further. For psychotherapy, along with all those approaches that see people's problems as *inside* them (as illnesses, 'character disorders', unconscious complexes, 'maladaptive' learning etc.), obscures the fact that there exists a world *outside* them in which the reasons for their distress are located. Psychotherapy, moreover, very often ends up by insisting, or at least implying, that the way out of their difficulties is up to them, and thereby makes matters worse by adding a moral burden to their troubles.

In this way, it seems to me, psychotherapy can easily become, and indeed frequently does become, a kind of disguised moral campaign which places colossal, and entirely unreasonable, demands on the individual. In suggesting, as many approaches to therapy and counselling do, that people ultimately accept 'responsibility' for themselves, not only do they betray a barely half-baked intellectual grasp of what could possibly be meant by 'responsibility', but they implicitly renounce any claim they could validly make to be offering a professional service.[20]

Encouragement

The third component of psychotherapy to be distinguished is encouragement. By this I mean any kind of influence brought to bear by the therapist on the patient to try actively to make a difference to the factors that are causing him or her distress. Therapies vary quite widely in the extent to which encouraging people to do things is seen as a legitimate role for the therapist. Some psychoanalytically inclined practitioners, as well as many counsellors, would not see it as any part of their business to give people advice or to intervene at all in the way they conduct their daily lives, though in fact there are probably few who can resist doing it at least in subtle ways. Others, like behaviour therapists, would see the prescription of action as an absolutely central plank of their practice.

For non-behavioural therapists and counsellors (principally those who belong to the 'psychodynamic' tradition of psycho-analysis and its derivatives), the giving of advice to patients is seen as creating dependency and undermining the kind of moral autonomy so important to 'taking responsibility'. Many no doubt slip from this somewhat severe impartiality into encour-aging and supporting their clients as the latter, following up on insights gained through therapy, struggle to make new adjust-ments to their world. But therapists of this persuasion have no developed ideas about what people should do or how they should do it: the theory offers no suggestions in this respect, and the practice, such as it is, is therefore likely to be haphazard, as much a factor of the therapist's personal experience – even whim – as anything else.

Behaviourists, as noted, are different, as are some of the more pragmatic 'cognitive' and 'positive thinking', rationalistic approaches. Courses of action may in these cases be prescribed with great confidence, perhaps even without its being felt necessary to give clients any explanation of why their behaviour is to be shaped in this or that direction. People, it is claimed, become different by acting differently, not by having insights or deciding to become responsible.

In some ways the behavioural view has a good deal to be said for it, and approaches of this kind, largely through the professional development of clinical psychology, have contributed a useful common-sense element to the practice of therapy and counselling. The realisation that insight gets nowhere without action is a necessary step forward. There are, however, difficulties with this kind of approach also.

These stem mainly from the extremely simplistic nature of many of the ideas about learning and change which underlie the cognitive-behavioural approach. These are frequently based on rather crude laboratory experiments in which captive groups of students or hospital patients are subjected to fairly obvious procedures of training or other behavioural manipulation, and the results generalised with little plausibility to the population at large. The intellectual sophistication of ideas about, for example, what constitutes 'learning' or the nature of 'attitudes' may not be great. Much of the earlier behavioural work was based on Pavlovian conditioning, giving rise to oversimplified ideas about positive and negative 'reinforcement' (reward and punishment) as the basis for human learning, and completely overlooking the importance of *meaning* to human beings. While a good deal of the more recent work on cognitive processes makes good this latter defect, it betrays, even so, a surprisingly unsophisticated view of 'cognitions' as things inside people which cause them to behave this way or that, and which can be worked on directly to change the way they behave. The logical mistake is made that, because reality is filtered through our minds, we can alter reality by changing our minds.

What this tends to mean for the patients of cognitive behavioural therapists is that, though they will certainly be encouraged to tackle difficulties in their lives which the process of clarification has identified, this may often have an unsatisfyingly superficial – and ultimately ineffective – aspect to it.

I have no doubt that it is possible for a person experiencing even severe psychological distress to be helped profoundly and permanently by someone else, whether or not that someone else is a professional helper. However, I do not think that there is so far any convincing indication that any of the orthodox approaches to professional help have a coherent explanation of what makes a relationship 'therapeutic', and in so far as people may at times be therapeutic, it is most often for reasons they do not themselves fully understand.

Frequently, as I have suggested, it is the solidarity with the helper that is found helpful, but this is likely to be a relatively transient phenomenon. There is no evidence that the kind of technical reasons therapists give for the effectiveness, such as it is, of their therapy hold water. Conversely, there is no reason why therapists should be able to say what makes their work effective – the fact that we are unable to give an account of something does not mean that we are unable to *do* it.

Therapists have, I believe, been hampered when trying to account for what they do by the blinkers which the enclosed world of the consulting room has placed on their vision. They have assumed that both the reasons for their clients' distress and the means of alleviating it are to be found within those walls, and they are wrong on both counts. Nevertheless, the experience that comes of trying to help people in emotional difficulties and the immense proliferation of conflicting ideas about therapy which this century has generated make it extremely unlikely that absolutely all therapeutic efforts are going to be in vain and that every theoretical position is vacuous.

There are indeed important lessons to be learned from the practice of psychotherapy, the clues to which are to be found in its three principal components. But, in contemplating the possible benefits of comfort, clarification and encouragement, we need a much more careful and precise analysis of what is really involved in these processes, and whether they could be achieved in other perhaps more effective – ways than through psychotherapy and counselling. For a further, more negative, but no less important, lesson to be learned from psychotherapy may be that it is possible to survive without it.

To appreciate this we need to see that much of what makes therapeutic intervention seem attractive to people in distress is precisely those elements of its mystique that cannot be fulfilled. Therapists are not the possessors of esoteric knowledge through which people may be transformed – on the whole, as I have suggested, they don't know what they're doing. Furthermore, the very process (the claustrophobic atmosphere of the consulting room) and some of the almost axiomatic beliefs of psychotherapy (e.g. about 'responsibility') militate against an adequate understanding of people's predicaments.

What I shall attempt to do in the remainder of this book is take what I believe can be learned from the practice of psychotherapy both to clarify some of the more common dilemmas people find themselves in and to point to ways of dealing with them which, I hope, may be found encouraging. In suggesting that psychological and emotional distress have their origin in the world rather than in the person, I hope also that there may be some comfort to be derived from these pages.

What I cannot engineer, of course, is a personal relationship with a psychotherapist. Although it is true that this is probably the most immediately potent element in all therapeutic approaches, I am not, for reasons I have already given, convinced that it is the most important one. Nothing will ever change the need for human solidarity, whatever form it comes in, and psychotherapy is only one of many. But the sheer confusion and mystification which still surround our basic notions of mental illness and emotional distress may perhaps best be attacked without the help of a therapy industry which, for the most part, does all too much to maintain them.

CHAPTER TWO

The Experience of Distress

It is not always easy for people in emotional turmoil to shift their attention from *self* to *world*, and yet, if they are to gain an understanding of the origins of their difficulties, that is the most important thing for them to do. We have learned, when in physical pain, to look for the cause inside our bodies, and perhaps that is why we tend to think that the roots of 'psychological' pain are to be found inside our minds. However, when it comes to understanding so-called clinical distress, the causes of our pain are likely to be found in the world beyond our skin.

Psychiatry's obsession with cataloguing the phenomena of distress into diagnostic syndromes of illness is rendered ultimately futile precisely because the supposed victims of such illness are not carriers of clear-cut cultures of disease, but in essence ordinary human beings struggling to cope with a disordered world. The continued efforts of psychiatry to define ever more tightly and exclusively the varieties of illness it thinks are to be discerned in emotional suffering borders, at the beginning of the twenty-first century, on farce. Psychiatrists seem to hope that if, like Victorian gentleman scholars sorting butterflies, they refine their descriptions carefully enough, they will identify species of disease which can be treated medically in the same way that, for instance, tuberculosis can. Widespread criticism of this approach,[1] not to mention its evident fruitlessness, has done nothing over the past hundred years to diminish the enthusiasm of those who engage in it, nor indeed to cast doubt on its viability in the public mind. There are all sorts of reasons for this, but the point I want to emphasise here is that we should not allow the apparent authoritativeness of the medical model to distract us from the search for a more satisfactory alternative.

It is of course possible to arrive at broad descriptions of the kinds of distress that human beings are prone to. As embodied creatures, we have only a limited number of ways to react to the blows life inflicts upon us: the way we express our thoughts and feelings will depend on the physical structure of our bodies. For example, I weep with sadness because that is how human beings are constructed to express the feeling we call sadness, but the physical process of weeping is not the cause of my sadness. On the whole we have no difficulty with the idea that, to understand the meaning of sadness, we need to look to the outside world to see what is making us sad. 'Meaning' points us outside ourselves. Similarly, we can talk about 'anxiety' and 'depression' reasonably comprehensibly because pretty well everybody knows how it feels to be anxious or depressed, and we understand, too, that people are anxious or depressed about something. When it comes to 'clinical' distress, however, we suddenly, and quite erroneously, abandon the quest for meaning and divert our gaze instead to the purely physical forms in which distress is given expression and the supposed interior 'pathogenic' process which, we assume, gives rise to them.

Psychiatry, of course, derives its plausibility from precisely those states where people feel anxious or depressed in the apparent absence of there being anything to be anxious or depressed about. It is in these circumstances, for example, that 'depression' may be characterised as 'clinical depression'. But the fact that you can't immediately tell why you're depressed doesn't mean that you have nothing to be depressed about, and that the depression is therefore simply a physical reaction which has got out of hand. It is, I believe, far more sensible and accurate to suggest that it is possible *not to know* why you are depressed than it is to maintain that you are suffering from a 'depressive illness'.[2]

The situation may seem more problematic in the case of the diagnostic labels psychiatrists have concocted to describe complex syndromes of feeling-states and behaviour, for example, 'schizophrenia'. The existence of a 'mental illness' corresponding to this label is nowhere near as well established as the orthodoxy would suggest, but, no doubt, its imposingly medical title deters the ordinary person from questioning it too profoundly. We may feel that our personal familiarity with depression and anxiety authorises us to talk knowledgeably about them, but how many of us would claim to feel schizophrenic from time to time?[3] In fact, there may well be ways for us to begin to understand the experience of 'schizophrenia': try, for example, to imagine feeling unbearably confused, excited and suspicious all at once and you should get quite a good idea.[4] There are times in most people's lives when they become so disturbed and distraught that a ten-minute talk with a psychiatrist could quite easily get them diagnosed as 'psychotic'.

The huge effort put by psychiatry into refining a set of diagnostic labels for the ways in which people exhibit 'signs and symptoms' of distress has become self-perpetuating: if you enforce a standard descriptive vocabulary and insist on similar methods of observation, you can indeed demonstrate a degree of consistency between observers. But the fact that people can agree reliably on a description of how someone is behaving does not say anything about the significance of that description. The fact that someone is showing signs of what psychiatrists have agreed among themselves to call 'paranoid schizophrenia' carries absolutely no implication that there is such a thing as 'paranoid schizophrenia'. This is the problem with psychiatry: there *are* no illnesses corresponding to the labels it has succeeded in agreeing upon.

However watertight and exhaustive a list of descriptions of distress can be made, it is bound not to throw any light on how those states arise, simply because it has nothing to say about the world in which they occur. The way we feel depends on a combination of our past experience and what happens to us in the present, both in the setting of our cultural expectations. We are in a continuous process of interchange with our social and cultural environment, so that the way we experience and express emotional distress depends on a whole range of factors outside ourselves and will also change significantly with the times.[5]

In fact, as I tried to show in *The Origins of Unhappiness*, it makes in many ways much more sense to diagnose the ways in which the *environment* can be damaging than it does the *people* who are damaged by it. I have no doubt, for example, that the radical shift to a 'business culture' which took place in Britain and elsewhere during the 1980s rendered whole sections of the population vulnerable to forms of distress that had touched them only minimally before, as well as creating forms of 'pathology', especially in the young, which are only now becoming evident. (I shall return to this later.)

What is important, then, is not to categorise individuals according to a descriptive typology of emotional distress, but to seek to understand how their distress, whatever form it takes, arises out of their interaction with the world and to identify the kinds of situation in the social environment that can be particularly damaging.

In the rest of this chapter, I shall try to relate some of the commoner ways in which distress is experienced to the kinds of predicaments typically giving rise to them. In order to simplify the discussion, I shall divide the latter into background and current predicaments. Both have their own distinct importance, and it is not really possible to say that one is more significant than the other in accounting for the distress a given individual experiences. Vulnerabilities people have acquired in the past may be brought to the fore by pressing difficulties in the present,[6] and when trying to understand the reasons for anyone's psychological pain it is probably wise to neglect neither the past nor the present.

I want to emphasise as strongly as possible that I am not trying in what follows to compete with psychiatry by setting out an alternative typology of 'mental disorder'. By seeking a structure in which to convey varieties of distress and the kinds of predicaments that may be underlying them, I want only to offer a framework in which they can be discussed without too greatly distorting reality. This is not, in other words, intended as any kind of definitive scientific analysis of the phenomena of emotional distress.

Nor is it intended to be exhaustive. In selecting the material for discussion and the particular examples which I hope may illuminate it, I have in mind a readership not unlike those I encounter in my role as clinical psychologist – people, that is, who have been unable to escape, or hide from themselves, the effect of some of the unkinder lessons of life, and who may perhaps have found the orthodox approaches to their difficulties not particularly helpful. I shall have less to say about the kinds of distress likely to be experienced by people whose fundamental predicaments have been so disabling that they are likely to need, at least occasionally, some form of institutional help. This is not because I regard the nature of such difficulties as qualitatively different from those I shall be considering, but rather because I can speak with confidence only from my own practical experience, which has, for the past twenty-five years, been outside the context of inpatient treatment facilities such as mental hospitals.

One further caveat: when looking, in this chapter, at 'background' and 'current' factors in a given type of predicament, I shall for the most part be doing so from the perspective of the individual occupying that predicament. I shall not, that is to say, be trying at this stage to give an objective account of how distress arises, but one that attempts to adopt the viewpoint of the person suffering it. It is of the utmost importance to distinguish between the way someone *experiences* their problems and what the causes of those problems are.

The importance of this distinction applies most strongly in

considering the influence of factors in the person's past, in particular the influence of the family. From the personal perspective, injuries suffered at the hands of family members, particularly parents, may very understandably – and in a sense even rightly – be seen as the responsibility of those family members. From an objective perspective, on the other hand, the individual's past was the family's present, and its members no doubt had at the time good reasons for conducting themselves as they did: reasons which they may, indeed, have been unable to resist. These are issues to which we shall return in later chapters, where I hope any apparent paradox will be resolved, but the point of distinguishing here between a subjective and an objective view of cause is to avoid as far as possible the apportionment of blame.

In my view, blame has no legitimate part to play in the objective, psychological understanding of people's conduct, but this is not to say that it is wrong for a person to feel aggrieved at the way, for instance, s/he was treated as a child. For the individual sufferer, that is to say, blame has a legitimacy that it does not have for the psychologist, and it is confusion over this issue that has led so often in the past to misunderstanding, offence and rancour at the suggestion that the nature of early family relations can contribute to later distress.[7] Let it be understood, therefore, that the adoption of the perspective of the sufferer in what follows does not imply an objective attribution of blame to those at whose hands s/he suffered. We all of us try our best, even though much of the time we don't succeed.

FORMS OF DISTRESS – THE WAY IT FEELS

The commonest reaction to adverse events and experiences is unhappiness or, if the events or experiences are severe or prolonged enough, despair. On the whole, people know why they are unhappy or despairing, and, though they may go to the doctor for pills to help them sleep or perhaps for practical advice, they tend not to consult professionals over feelings whose causes are clear to them. It is more when unhappiness takes forms that we cannot immediately understand, or has effects we seem unable to control, that we tend to turn to the experts for help. This is no doubt very largely because of a cultural expectation that suffering of unknown origin is likely to be the result of 'illness'. Freud's distinction between 'hysterical misery' and 'common unhappiness' would tend to bear this out.

In my view this is, however, neither the most productive nor the most accurate way of looking at things. It is not obvious why we should always be able to identify the causes of our feelings, and there is no good reason to conclude that our being unable to do so indicates some kind of 'neurotic' problem. Our disturbed feelings do not necessarily tell us *what* is wrong, but they do all tell us that *something* is wrong. In those cases where we cannot immediately see what is wrong, our potential for understanding may well have been diverted more by the misconceptions of our culture than by some kind of perverse impulse to hide the truth from ourselves. In my experience, people engage in the search for the causes of their unhappiness, when encouraged to do so, with seriousness and determination, and if they appear to be 'resisting' the enlightenment offered them by the so-called experts, that is for the most part out of an entirely healthy suspicion of the unhelpful mystifications they are being fed.[8]

There is, then, no difference in kind between distress caused by circumstances that are immediately identifiable to us and distress whose origins are obscure. The causes of distress may be out of our sight, situated in parts of the environment to which we simply do not have access, or perhaps out of the reach of our memory, having occurred at a time in the past we can no longer recover in words. However, human beings are not content simply to do without explanations, and if a person cannot see the reason why s/he is feeling unhappy or distressed, s/he is likely to invent one. The absence of a reason will be replaced by the most plausible reason that can be invoked. It is this phenomenon that is traded on by the professionals, who are only too ready to jump in with plausible explanations to account for their clients' distress – and plausibility here may be established more by the authority with which the professionals are ready to back their explanations than by any relation they bear to reality.

Establishing the truth of the matter – what the problem 'really is' – is by no means a cut-and-dried procedure, either in principle or in practice, but it does lie in examining precisely the relation between speculation and reality. Any hypothetical explanation for a given individual's distress needs to be validated against his or her experience of the world. In many ways, this is exactly what is meant by 'being scientific', but without any of the mystifying dogmatism and intellectual arrogance that have come to be attached to that expression. We need to be convinced of the truth of an explanation not because we have been impressed or bullied by the status or prestige of an authority, but because it makes sense to us in the context of our knowledge and experience of the world.

The mystique of authority derives at least in part from the notion that establishing the truth of the matter is not something people can do for themselves. It may certainly help to have a guide from time to time, but this does not mean that there is an esoteric access to 'truth' available only to a professional caste of experts. There is, of course, a constant struggle within society for certain professional groups to mystify and monopolise 'truth', but it is still perfectly possible to clarify the reasons for our unhappiness without recourse to a professional psychotherapist. In many respects, it may even be easier.

In those cases where the reasons for unhappiness are not transparent, the experience of distress itself is likely to include a feeling of loss of control – 'not knowing' *puts* one out of control. For the sake of discussion, I shall identify three kinds of loss of control: of feelings, thoughts and actions. This threefold distinction is to an extent artificial, and certainly not mutually exclusive – feelings, thoughts and actions are frequently bundled up inseparably together, and do not occur in neat sequences (one of the grosser errors of cognitive psychology is to assume that they do). I should stress that a feeling of loss of control is just that – a feeling – and does not imply that normally one is in control of what one feels, thinks and does. (The issue of control is one to which we shall return in Chapter Six.) Let me also emphasise again that what follows should not be taken as an attempt at a scientific categorisation of types of 'disorder'.

Loss of control of feelings

Being suddenly assailed by feelings of acute fear or panic out of all proportion to the situation in which they occur is probably the commonest form of distress prompting people to seek professional help. So inexplicable do these feelings seem at the time that they are not always immediately recognised as constituting fear, but may be thought by the sufferer to indicate some serious physical problem such as a heart attack. Certainly, the physical concomitants of 'anxiety states' can be extremely unpleasant and frightening in themselves: breathlessness, pounding heart, chest pains, sweating and trembling, faintness and dizziness, inability to swallow and sensations of choking can overtake the individual so rapidly and unexpectedly that the very possibility of a recurrence can itself become a constant fearful preoccupation.

Some people very quickly realise that the sensations they are experiencing do in fact constitute fear, even though it may not be at all clear what they are afraid of. Others may take some time to make the connection, perhaps arriving at this conclusion only after thorough medical examination has failed to reveal any serious physical pathology. Others again may never accept that their feelings have anything to do with fear and anxiety, and may devote years of their lives to the

ANN

Form of distress	Current predicament	Background predicament
Feelings of panic (dizziness, choking, inability to breathe, etc.) in public places like shops, restaurants, buses and trains. Only after a while does Ann begin to experience these 'symptoms' as fear, and a profound loss of confidence in the presence of other people.	After a messy divorce, Ann has married again, this time to a much kinder and more considerate man. However, the children of both their former marriages do not get on well together, and Ann and her new husband are experiencing friction about how to deal with the situation.	Ann's parents split up when she was fourteen, and she, as the eldest of three daughters, had to assume a good deal of responsibility for her sisters. Neither of her parents had taken much interest in her, being preoccupied with their own difficulties, and she had a very poor relationship with her stepfather. She married her first husband at the age of eighteen, thereby getting away from the family home as soon as she could.

quest for what they are convinced is the physical cause of their troubles.

Our culture certainly doesn't make it easy for us to grasp the relation between what we see as a mental experience, like fear, on the one hand, and physical sensations, like breathlessness and dizziness, on the other. We tend to compartmentalise ourselves into 'minds' and 'bodies', and we often take quite a bit of convincing that the two are not separate at all, but expressions of the same thing. We cannot, of course, feel anything without our bodies being involved in producing the feeling, but we still find it hard to shake off the idea that things are either physical events in the material world or are 'all in the mind', perhaps as products of our imagination. In this way, it becomes difficult for people to believe that the absolutely undeniable physicality of their feelings could be put down to anything as insubstantial and 'mental' as fear or anxiety, and they assume, not always wrongly, that an admission that what they feel is fear would be taken by others as evidence that they were 'imagining things'.

There is certainly nothing imaginary about the experience of acute pain and anxiety, though it is also true that it is not nearly as visible to others as the sufferer often fears. The discomfort and misery of such experiences are frequently compounded by the embarrassment the person feels at what s/he assumes is the obviousness of his or her condition to others. This can become a vicious circle, so that, for example, the feelings of shame attached to 'making an exhibition of oneself' – blushing perhaps – can in themselves become the object of phobic dread. The experience of anxiety consists of sensations that have enormous internal saliency but low external visibility: feelings which can be so overwhelming as to make the sufferer afraid s/he is about to faint or may even be dying are likely to go entirely unnoticed by casual passers-by. This is not to say that such feelings are not physical, but that they are mediated by bodily processes on the inside rather than the outside. What feels like a cataclysmic physical event may be externally observable, if at all, as no more than a barely perceptible tremor.

The fear experienced in 'anxiety states' may or may not become attached to specific objects, situations or events. Most commonly, fear of becoming socially conspicuous is what lies behind panic attacks, and the person comes to dread social occasions such as going out shopping or having to use public transport. Sometimes the fear becomes focused on particular situations, again usually in public space – for example, eating in restaurants (and making a spectacle of oneself through choking). Situations where one becomes for an instant the focus of another's attention (filling in forms, signing cheques or papers) can lead to sudden and terrifying panic.

The list of situations (open spaces, enclosed spaces, heights, thunderstorms, wind, snow, meetings, parties, flying, driving) and objects and animals (dogs, cats, spiders, bees and wasps, moths, types of food) to which fear and anxiety can become attached is virtually infinite. People may also fear loss of physical or mental control (often in the absence of any evidence that they have ever done so, or are particularly likely to do so). Dread of loss of bowel or bladder control, for example, may make people's lives a misery as every journey they take becomes a nightmare of planning and every unexpected invitation to go somewhere unfamiliar a cause for panic. Fear of going mad, 'going completely over the top', can often accompany and compound fears and phobias that are already disabling enough.

Most of us are afraid of *something* and could quickly be rendered to jelly by a confrontation with a tarantula, the edge of a steep cliff or an invitation to address a roomful of strangers. As long as such situations as these do not become anything more than rare events in our lives, we are likely not to be particularly troubled by them, and indeed if someone wished to get rid of, say, a fear of spiders, it is not particularly difficult to do so.[9] Sometimes, however, what look like relatively specific objects of fear constitute the visible part of broader or deeper anxieties which are not removed simply by tackling what they seem superficially to be about.

What unites practically all varieties of anxiety, phobia and panic that are not relatively superficial or trivial is a loss of confidence in oneself and one's ability to deal with and earn the attention and respect of others. Often this is a quite conscious part of people's distress, but sometimes, usually because of the kind of social role that is expected of them, it may be quite difficult and painful for them to acknowledge.

To sally out and deal with people in the world, to have 'presence', to appear to others in the way they appear to oneself, i.e. as of consequence, takes a degree of nerve and self-confidence which, when we have it, it is easy to take for granted. This, it seems, is how we are naturally, and to depart from that state is to have 'something wrong' with ourselves. And yet there is probably nothing natural about it. Indeed, I suspect that our culture greatly overvalues the kind of brash independence so many decently sensitive and shy people long to develop.

Be that as it may, there are times in most people's lives when their confidence is eroded to a point where they feel so socially incapable, or so conspicuously incompetent in the eyes of others, that they feel themselves wilting and shrivelling under their scrutiny. In many ways, this is the experience of anxiety, and this is what makes it so terrifying: we feel ourselves becoming nothing. We become, it seems, detached from the (social) world in which we are 'normally' rooted, our environment becomes uncannily distant and unreal and we are consumed by panic at the unfamiliarity, isolation and threat that are involved in the experience.

There can be few people who are not familiar with the state of depression. As with anxiety, it is probably when we can't see the reasons for it that it turns from a painful and unpleasant experience into a malign and threatening form of misery.

Being depressed about an event in the world (a loss or disappointment, perhaps) which can be clearly identified by the sufferer as well as those close to him or her is likely to be accepted by all concerned as a temporary phenomenon, and one that may even earn him or her a degree of comforting solidarity with others, which is itself healing. When, however, a black and deadening cloud of despair descends on the individual for no apparent reason, and stays there, perhaps, for weeks at a time, only to disappear as mysteriously as it came, not only does s/he come almost superstitiously to dread its return, but people around him or her are likely to get impatient with what they see as capriciousness. If people don't have a reason to be depressed, so the thinking goes, then they must be 'doing it themselves', so that persisting in being depressed must reflect some kind of wilful refusal to 'snap out of it'.

This virtually inevitable response from the family and friends of 'depressives' serves to compound a condition in which guilt

BRENDA

Form of distress	Current predicament	Background predicament
Periods of black depression when she cannot speak without weeping and spends most or all of the day in bed. Unable to go to work and overwhelmed by numbing misery. Only the presence of her small daughter prevents her, she feels, from killing herself.	Brenda seems to have almost no time for herself and no pleasure in life. Her work as a teacher is exhausting and demanding, and her husband sounds like a conceited bully (though she does not herself describe him as such) who constantly undermines her and lives his life entirely to suit himself.	Brenda's mother is a perfectionistic paragon who dominated the family as Brenda and her younger brother were growing up. Brenda felt she could never match her mother's virtue and capability, and it seems she was never able as a child to say how she felt or voice any criticism of anyone in the family. Her father was a weak, rather depressed man who drank a lot and died just before Brenda got married. Both parents, having always wanted a boy, clearly preferred her brother.

and self-loathing already play only too prominent a part. Depressed people know perfectly well that their state adversely affects those around them, but they are utterly incapable of cheering up to order, and the unhappiness they cause others simply becomes one more reason for self-reproach.

Depression, at its worst, is a hopeless, dulled despair from which all vitality has been drained, with a timelessness which abolishes, so it seems, all possibility of future redemption, all ties of love severed in a state of blank, black isolation. What is often striking about it is the degree to which it cannot be put into words: at its centre there seems to be, literally, something indescribable, a black hole impacted with meaning for which no language can be found. It is about something that cannot be said. Nor can it be touched by words of comfort: it is inexorable, and cannot be reasoned away.

There are, to be sure, usually some things sufferers *can* say, for instance concerning their personal worthlessness, and they may be consumed by guilt at what may seem to others imaginary misdemeanours. However, like the anxious person who 'hangs' his or her feelings on the most likely-looking peg available (even if, as in the case of some of the more outlandish 'phobias', it doesn't look very likely to others), the depressed person may simply try to find *something* to account for how terrible s/he feels.

Mercifully, depression lifts after a time, though not necessarily for any more obvious reason than its original descent. Sometimes it is replaced by a state of unusual energy and optimism. In its more extreme form ('hypomania'), this swing of mood can contain a degree of aggressive self-assertion and insensitive ebullience which can be more distressing to others (though not to the 'sufferer') than the previous state of abject depression.

There are, of course, other ways in which people's feelings can run out of control. These may or may not be associated with elements of anxiety or depression of the kind already discussed.

There is, for example, a form of guilt which haunts a lot of people's lives and is by no means always linked to depression. It may seem to be more an aspect of personality, a way in which the person characteristically responds to the implied, maybe even non-existent, demands of others. In many larger families there seems to be at least one person who takes on the cares of the rest, whose super-conscientiousness contrasts, perhaps, with the careless self-centredness of at least some of the others and is constantly made use of by them without hesitation or scruple. Furthermore, what started in the family often becomes extended to every other social situation the person occupies, including work. Even though people in this kind of role may be

CATHERINE

Form of distress	Current predicament	Background predicament
Most of Catherine's day is taken up with watching, testing and setting traps for her boyfriend. Once she detects (as invariably she must) the slightest sign of infidelity of thought or deed (he only has to look at another woman), she works ceaselessly both to get him to admit his guilt and to reassure her that he loves her above all. Needless to say, their relationship is strained to breaking point. She has always ended her previous relationships, often out of (never well-founded) suspicion and jealousy.	It is difficult to find anything wrong in Catherine's current life. She is clever, beautiful, and very successful in her job, and though his patience is tried to the limit, her boyfriend is loving and attentive.	Catherine's father deserted her and her mother when she was two. Her mother was an air hostess, who spent a lot of time away from home. First Catherine was looked after principally by her grandmother, who died when she was three. She then had a nanny whom her mother sacked when she was five. When she was eight, her mother married a rich businessman, and she was promptly sent to boarding school, where she remained, apart from sometimes exotic holidays with her parents, sometimes lonely ones without them, until she was eighteen. She hated school.

able to see perfectly well that they are being exploited by others, any attempt they make not to respond in the customary manner is likely to cause them unbearable guilt until they once again conform to expectations.

Jealousy can be a distressingly out-of-control emotion capable of wreaking havoc in the individual's personal life and relationships. Once again, it is the lack of visible justification that turns 'normal' jealousy into a supposedly 'pathological' condition needing professional attention. It is easy enough to empathise with, say, the jealous anger of a young woman whose boyfriend is flirting ostentatiously with someone else, but our imagination seems to fail us when, in the absence of such behaviour on his part, she harangues him for hours about his past relationships, ransacks his possessions in search of letters or photographs, and plunges into despair at what she is convinced is his disdain for her. In the first case, we are ready without hesitation to endorse the legitimacy of the emotion in relation to an event in the external world giving rise to it. In the second, we attribute her problem with almost equal conviction to a hypothetical internal pathology for which we actually have no evidence at all. It does not seem to occur to us to search her world a little more carefully and thoroughly. The banal assumptions of our culture, it seems, have made it more and more difficult for us to take an interest in each other's lives.

Loss of control of thoughts

For most people, most of the time, it seems that what they are thinking about is what they have chosen to think about. If invited to switch our attention from one line of thought to another, we can probably do so without too much difficulty, and even if we are not necessarily conscious of choosing to think this or that, the usual drift of our musings and associations – our 'stream of consciousness' – does not as a rule seem uncomfortably out of control.

There are times in everyone's life when, quite clearly, we are preoccupied with issues – or more likely an issue – that come to mind unbidden and are hard to shift out of. All of us know the feeling of not being able to stop worrying about a particularly pressing difficulty, or of not being able to concentrate at such a time on things we want to concentrate on, like reading a book.

Having thoughts or ideas imposed upon us without the involvement of our own will is also a common experience – it happens to us every night in our dreams. Again, the activity of writing frequently seems to generate ideas or narratives of which the writer had no conscious awareness – they seem to write themselves. On the whole, though, with the exception perhaps of nightmares, such experiences as these do not cause us any particular distress.

The kind of thinking that has come to be called 'obsessional', on the other hand, is most definitely distressing. This is not so much because obsessional thoughts seem to be imposed upon us as because they are bound up with feelings of tension and anxiety. They are also frequently bound up with a compulsion to do something – some repetitive or ritual action, perhaps – but since this is by no means always the case, I shall reserve discussion of compulsions for the next section.

Sometimes, as is the case with Craig to a considerable extent, the distress associated with obsessional thoughts seems to arise more from an uncertainty about how 'normal' they are (or, more strongly, a conviction that they are crazy) than from any direct association with anxiety-laden issues in the person's life. Especially for young people, it is not always easy to tell whether the thoughts and fantasies they find themselves engaged in are indicative of some kind of mental abnormality, quite possibly serious. It is rather as if we suddenly came to question the significance of our dreams for the state of our mental health – does their bizarre irrationality indicate that we are mad?

It is very hard to convince Craig, for example, that his speculations about existence have been the legitimate preoccupation of philosophers throughout their lifetime, and I have encountered many other young people who are disturbed by being unable to shake themselves free of thoughts or fantasies which, perhaps, contain elements of violence or other unacceptable impulses they fear may get out of control.

The intensity and frequency of obsessional thinking does often seem to fluctuate with the degree of stress in people's lives, though this may not always be obvious to them: as, again,

CRAIG

Form of distress	Current predicament	Background predicament
Craig is afraid he's going mad. At times when he should be concentrating on his work as a printer, he finds himself urgently preoccupied with 'silly thoughts' about who he would be if he were not himself, or about why a particular object in the room is where it is and not somewhere else. Such thoughts also seem to invade his mind unpredictably at other times of the day. Craig is also very worried that he may have contracted a fatal and contagious disease that he could pass on to his family.	There is a threat of redundancies at work, and though Craig is the most conscientious of his colleagues, he feels he is not 'one of the boys' and they may take the opportunity to get rid of him. He seems also to be under pressure from his rather possessive girlfriend whom he has known since schooldays, but from whom he is perhaps becoming a little distant now.	Craig's parents never got on particularly well, though they are still together. His father was a well-meaning but distant man, completely absorbed in running the small family business. His mother was an anxious, rather fussy and intrusive woman, ambitious for her son but somehow not entirely in sympathy with him. An only child, Craig had always been 'a bit of a loner' at school, though he had done well academically.

with some forms of 'phobia', the thoughts become a focus for anxieties which have their origins elsewhere. Indeed, the content of obsessional thoughts is often, though by no means always, linked to a dread that some feared event is about to take place or to a feeling – clearly recognised as irrational – that thinking about it systematically and intensely enough will somehow prevent its happening. There may in this way be a superstitious element in obsessional thinking (as there is more often and very markedly in the case of compulsive behaviour). On the whole, however, though there is undoubtedly *meaning* in obsessional thinking (it happens for perfectly good reasons, as

I hope will become clear in the course of subsequent discussion), in the majority of cases the person concerned is not aware of what the meaning is. This is not because of some failure of insight or intelligence on his or her part, but because there are no adequate cultural tools with which to get to grips with issues of this kind.

It is not only in 'obsessional states' that people may become painfully unable to direct the mind where they want it to go. This is also a feature of acute self-consciousness. If you become intensely aware of yourself as the object of the gaze of others, you may become locked into a kind of desperate self-monitoring which allows you to take account of practically nothing else in your social environment. It is almost as if you float above yourself, observing yourself going through the motions of talking to others, but excruciatingly aware as well that you can barely attend to what they say, and certain that they are as aware as you of your social incompetence. For shy people, something like this is a pretty common experience, and they may in time come to accept it as a more or less normal part of their lives, but the more shamefully inadequate people feel, the less they can forget themselves in their social encounters, and the more desperately fixed their attention seems to become on themselves.

One of the chief difficulties with all forms of loss of control over the direction of your attention is, of course, that the more you try to concentrate on something else, the more riveted you seem to become by the very preoccupation you are trying to escape.[10] This phenomenon in itself is a considerable cause of distress.

Loss of control of actions

Finding yourself unable to control your actions can be particularly distressing and alarming, not least because other people may become almost as involved in the problem as you are. This is particularly the case with the more serious addictions to drugs or alcohol, the results of which can at times be more devastating to families than to sufferers themselves,[11] but even with less dramatic forms of loss of control, it may be impossible for people to disguise from others the struggles they are going through, and the apparent irrationality of their conduct may become painfully exposed to bafflement or even ridicule. People who find themselves subject to so-called compulsive behaviour do their best to hide their difficulties from others, suffering agonies of shame as they perform their rituals in secret.

DAVE

Form of distress	Current predicament	Background predicament
Before leaving his room in the morning, Dave feels compelled to perform a number of safety checks on gas, water and electricity. These have become rituals which have to be performed absolutely precisely, and if any element is neglected (say, the order in which gas taps are checked), the whole procedure has to be started over again. If he doesn't do these things, he suffers unbearable tension and anxiety.	Dave is doing quite well on a postgraduate media studies course, though, because of his rituals, he finds it difficult to get to college on time. A couple of relationships with girls have ended rather messily and painfully, and he doesn't make friends easily, but otherwise there seem to be no great problems in his life.	Dave and his two younger sisters were brought up, as he sees it, lovingly and attentively by highly committed parents. They were devout, almost fanatical Methodists who laid enormous stress on conventional morality, any slight departure from which was punished by deep almost shattering disapproval. Both parents tried to protect their children from the evils of the outside world, and his mother in particular relied heavily on religious ritual to ward off threat.

'Obsessive-compulsive' behaviour can take a variety of forms, ranging from rituals of washing and cleaning to elaborate checking that some careless action, for example while driving, has not resulted in catastrophe. Almost always the conduct is aimed at the prevention of damage or injury, frequently to other people (Dave's worst nightmare was that, because of his carelessness, he would return home to find the house where he lived, and everyone in it, consumed by fire), or at reassurance that no such damage has already been incurred.

What is most puzzling and distressing for the sufferers is, of course, that the need for care or reassurance seems to go far beyond what is rational. The highly intelligent woman who takes fifteen minutes to select a packet of cereal in the supermarket so that she can be sure of not poisoning her family knows perfectly well that her infinitely tiresome precautions have no effect on the reality of the situation, but she knows also that she feels terrible if she doesn't take them.

Compulsive rituals are in this way acts of superstition, a form of magically controlling possible eventualities which are in fact uncontrollable. It is as if people in the grip of this kind of conduct find their lives dedicated to solving insoluble problems; the more insoluble the problem, apparently, the fiercer (and more exhausting) the effort put into solving it. It is often also the case that, if a problem does seem to be 'solved', it is almost immediately replaced by others even more difficult, until eventually a challenge is found that admits of no conceivable solution. Can you, for example, make absolutely sure by endless scrubbing and vacuuming that there is not a trace of asbestos dust in your house? Might it not have been introduced by someone's shoes or blown in on the wind? I remember a man in the town where I grew up, an inmate of one of the local asylums, who spent his waking life running between two clocks, perhaps 150 yards apart in the high street, trying to establish that they told the same time.

Difficulties associated with eating – 'anorexia nervosa' (self-starvation) and 'bulimia' (binge eating followed by self-induced vomiting) – are further examples of conduct over which the person is unable to exercise control. Most people who have ever tried to diet can understand how difficult it is deliberately to lose weight (though even here we are often unaware of the lengths we'll apparently go to in order 'not to notice' how much we're consuming), but it is less easy to empathise with the person who has starved herself to the point of death while passionately not wanting to die and trying all she can to eat. We can understand what we take to be weakness in the face of greed, but not, as with anorexia, when the reverse seems to be the case: involuntary abstinence from pleasure.

ELIZABETH

Form of distress	Current predicament	Background predicament
An intelligent and attractive woman, Elizabeth is painfully preoccupied with diet and exercise, petrified of becoming overweight. Every so often she binges secretly on very large quantities of, in particular, bread and butter spread with sugar, and chocolate. After each bingeing session she has to make herself sick to prevent digestion of the food.	Elizabeth feels pressured at work by new supervisory duties, particularly in respect of one or two women, previously equals, who she knows don't like her. Trying her best to be fair, she feels they take advantage of her. Her social life is limited, and her husband a little remote and lost in his own work problems.	Elizabeth's father was a clerical officer for the electricity board and her mother a socially ambitious teacher, not very happy with her lot or her husband's status. Both parents were remote, critical and rather stern, favouring both her older and younger brothers.

As with obsessive-compulsive behaviour, the preoccupations of people with eating problems often bear little relation to reality. 'Anorexics' seem, usually, literally unable to see the extent of their terrible emaciation, while 'bulimics' remain convinced of and anguished by their 'obesity' even though to an objective observer they are conventionally slim and attractive. Once again, it is the apparent irrationality, the clash with our normal understanding, that brings such phenomena into the field of psychiatry. Fat people, after all, though they may struggle with their diets, at least *know* that they are fat, and are trying to do something about it, while people with eating disorders seem to be trying to do something about imaginary difficulties. However, rather than concluding that there is something the matter with the sufferers themselves, it is more fruitful in my view (as will be elaborated in later chapters) to question the adequacy of our normal understanding and to begin to see that our everyday conceptions of rationality and will power are exposed as lacking rather than confirmed by the so-called pathology of compulsive behaviour.

Sufferers from these kinds of difficulties are not a race apart from the rest of us, but are as puzzled and pained as anyone else by the apparent inconsistencies of their conduct. They are neither unconscious schemers nor wilful architects of artful plans to seek attention or manipulate relations with others, but find themselves enacting, often with excruciating shame, patterns of behaviour which are as mysterious to them as they are irresistible.

Nothing could throw these issues into sharper relief than the predicament of the 'self-mutilator'. Beyond the immediate sense of relief it brings her, there is no secret satisfaction or manipulative intent, no 'secondary gain' for Frances in cutting herself. She understands no more than anyone else why she does it, and, though in many ways as ready as others (including the professionals) to accuse herself of various kinds of duplicity, she knows in her heart that it is not to be explained by the more obvious conventional hypotheses: it is not merely a question of 'attention-seeking' (for she does her best to hide it) or 'punishing herself' (it is a relief more than a pain).

For those fortunate enough not to have found themselves in

FRANCES

Form of distress	Current predicament	Background predicament
Every so often Frances finds the tensions and stresses of her life escalating to a point where they seem unbearable. The only way she has found to relieve these is to cut her arms and thighs with a razor blade. The sight of blood welling up through the cut calms her. Her arms and legs are criss-crossed with scars. Sometimes she has to get a cut stitched, but usually she hides her handiwork, and she has no suicidal intent.	Frances survives on casual waitressing jobs and has little social life. She has had a number of usually disastrous relationships with men, some of whom have been violent towards her. She tends to drink more than is good for her.	Frances comes from a large family where both money and parental interest were in short supply. Her mother had a vicious temper, and seemingly a particular dislike of Frances, whom she battered from time to time. For a couple of years she was sexually abused by one of her older brothers.

the kind of situation outlined in this section, the best approximation to understanding how it feels from the inside to be compelled to do something one desperately wants not to do may be to reflect on what it's like to be in a state of conflict over something. The problems facing the dieter have already been mentioned; there are other common experiences, like trying to give up smoking, in which the mind and the body seem to take different directions, with the body coming out on top. And yet it is not just a question of failure of mind over matter, of 'weak will', for the will is involved in achieving the body's bidding: the planning involved in buying a packet of cigarettes when we have vowed not to do so can be quite considerable. We get no further in trying to understand these dilemmas by moralising, by making them the conscious or unconscious responsibility of the sufferer. Instead, the role played by our notion of 'will' in the relation of mind to body will be considered in Chapter Six.

CURRENT PREDICAMENTS

Whatever the form in which distress makes itself felt, it occurs for a reason or, more often perhaps, a constellation of reasons. It is never the case that 'symptoms' simply erupt from within the person unbidden by events in the outside world. If someone has previously been leading a relatively untroubled life, feeling reasonably confident and optimistic, the onset of feelings of anxiety, depression etc. is an indication that something has become not right with his or her world.

People can seldom immediately identify the reasons for the distress they are experiencing, and there is a school of thought which claims that it doesn't particularly matter whether they do – it is more important, it is felt, to 'cure' the distress than to understand it. This is not as crass as it might sound, since there is certainly no logical connection between knowing why something is wrong and being able to do anything about it. The therapeutic assumption – that knowledge of cause, or 'insight', leads automatically to cure – has led to some oversimplified ideas about how to tackle emotional distress. However, rather than knowledge of cause being unnecessary for cure, it is more the case, I think, that cure may be impossible however much we know about the cause. Apart from relieving uncertainty, realising what the factors are in the outside world that are giving you pain is potentially 'curative' only if it is in your power to do something about those factors.

In what follows, then, it is important to remember that identifying factors in your environment that are giving rise to difficulty does not necessarily lead to a diminution of the resulting distress. But, for a whole host of reasons (not least to absolve yourself from 'responsibility' for your pain), it is probably better to know than not to know what they are.

Typical factors which lurk behind the development of distress can be viewed from two broad perspectives: the personal and the societal. Sufferers themselves are likely to be principally, and often solely, aware of the 'proximal' causes of their distress – the ones they experience, so to speak, up against themselves, in their immediate relations with the persons and events of their everyday lives. Viewed from the societal perspective, on the other hand, it becomes possible to discern the operation of 'distal' (remote) causes of which the protagonists may be completely unaware. In practice, it is impossible to discuss the kinds of predicaments people have to cope with in their daily lives without referring to both their personal, proximal perspective and the more distal factors affecting them. The significance of distinguishing between proximal and distal causes will be elaborated in Chapter Four.

The commonest causes of emotional distress and unhappiness are to be found, obviously enough, in the spheres of home, work and social relationships. Indeed, the most obvious are often overlooked by the professionals simply because they form such a familiar part of the experience of all of us. Financial deprivation and insecurity, unemployment (both actual and threatened), perpetual indebtedness – such factors as these form a backdrop of misery for a large, and increasing, proportion of the population, and their ubiquity should in no way detract from our recognition of the psychological damage they cause.

Sometimes precisely because of such material deprivations, people often also live in bitter and abusive relationships with others – most often women with men, children with parents from which escape is for practical reasons virtually impossible. Loneliness and loss are also a familiar part of the lives of all too many people, especially of course the elderly.

Little would be achieved by earnestly constructing examples of difficulties such as these. Their effects are obvious to anyone of averagely human sensibilities, and the only surprise – or perhaps rather absurdity – is that politicians, media people and social scientists should find it necessary to dwell on such questions as *whether*, for instance, unemployment causes depression. Only a rogue, a fool or someone with an *interest* in asking the question could, it would seem, possibly claim not to know the answer in advance.[12]

There are, however, many people who consult doctors and other experts in 'mental health' in genuine puzzlement about the causes of their distress, although their lives are blighted by deprivation and/or oppression of the kinds mentioned above to an extent which accounts easily for their feelings, often many times over. People seem to think that they should be able to bear such privations not only without complaining, but even without suffering, and if this proves not to be the case, they assume that something must be wrong with them. The notion that we should in all circumstances be able to smile through adversity is one of the mystifications that keep the mental health industry alive.

For many, if not most, of us, reality has in any case a distinctly adverse bias, and this sometimes makes it difficult to recognise that there are reasons outside ourselves for what seem to be our purely psychological troubles. It becomes hard to pick out from the general run of our experience anything that seems more than usually difficult to cope with; so used are we to struggling that we no longer recognise it as struggle, and are able to set no limits on what we think we should be able to cope with.

At the time when Gina married the first man who was kind to her, she had no conception of herself as an unusually intelligent and pretty young woman, nor did she recognise the disparity between herself and her husband in these respects; she was just glad to get away from home and to start building her own life.

Her husband, however, was always uncomfortably aware that he could have difficulty keeping up with Gina, and so he welcomed her basic lack of confidence in herself and lost no opportunity of increasing her awareness of the extent to which

GINA

Form of distress	Current predicament	Background predicament
Quite confident and outgoing as a teenager, Gina has become increasingly 'agoraphobic' over the years of her mid-twenties, and, though she pushes herself to go out, feels extremely uncomfortable in shops, on public transport and at social occasions where she doesn't know people.	Gina has two young school-age children for whom she bears the main responsibility. She married at eighteen a man who has become increasingly caustic and undermining of her, and occasionally violent. He is now out of work, while Gina does evening shifts cleaning at a local office complex.	Gina was one of four children. Her father drank heavily and rowed constantly, and often violently, with her mother. Neither parent was particularly occupied with the children, though Gina, as the only girl, was called upon to help in the home while her mother went out to work. She missed a great deal of schooling and obtained no qualifications, though she is very bright.

she depended on him to deal with the outside world (for example, because of her lack of schooling, Gina's literacy was not of the highest order). He was intensely threatened by her impatience with his relative slow-wittedness, and when they rowed he would occasionally hit her as the only counter he could find to her greater argumentative skill. Sexual attraction had not played a part in Gina's decision to marry, and her increasing distaste for sex became a bitter point of contention between them. All this, plus the principal responsibility for their children, who she was determined should not feel as emotionally isolated as she had done, and the added strain of having to work in the evenings, stretched her beyond the limits of her (very considerable) ability to cope, and the resulting loss of confidence in herself announced itself as anxiety: she herself could see her predicament only in terms of personal failure.

HEATHER

Form of distress	Current predicament	Background predicament
At forty-five, Heather has become virtually house-bound. Although always shy and sensitive, she had until a year or two ago been able to cope perfectly adequately in her role as wife and mother, but now she is overcome with crippling panic attacks at the prospect of having to leave the safety of the home for virtually any reason.	The third of Heather's children is about to take her A levels; the older two have already left home. Her husband, a self-employed businessman, works long hours and is impatient with Heather's difficulties. They seem to have grown apart over the years. Five years ago a brief affair with his secretary came to light.	Heather's mother was, and is, a vain, self-absorbed woman, openly contemptuous of her policeman husband, now dead, to whom Heather had been closer. Heather and her brother did not receive a great deal of attention from either parent, though their father did the best he could until he died when Heather was sixteen.

Some women still find as they start to enter middle age that their world as wife and mother is coming to a conclusion without any apparent alternative on the horizon, though changes over the last twenty years in child-rearing and the typical division of labour within the home have probably made this plight less frequent than it was. But, with Heather as with Gina, the dependency of women on men (regardless of whether the men abuse their position to become oppressors, about which there is no inevitability) remains an issue which causes a great deal of difficulty, surfacing usually as loss of confidence and consequent anxiety.

Having been a 'housewife' for fifteen years can be tantamount to spending time in a 'total institution', cut off from the changes and developments taking place in the outside world, gradually losing confidence in one's ability to cope with them. However sensitive to the situation the male partner may be, his greater access to and freedom in the outside world are almost certain to inject into the relationship elements of isolation, envy and resentment on the one side and frustration, impatience and incomprehension on the other. What is in fact the inevitable consequence of occupancy of different worlds (a pattern imposed by distal socio-economic factors well beyond individuals' control) is likely to be proximally interpreted by those involved as a purely personal predicament.

Difficulties of relationship confronting younger men and women who wish to form a settled partnership, combining companionship, sexual fulfilment and the building of a family, have undoubtedly been multiplied and complicated by social and economic developments over the past couple of decades. Not the least problem is how to maintain personal independence and freedom from the oppression of one sex by the other in a setting where the (frequently unequal) resources of both have to be pooled to maintain even basic standards within the family. Further, the competitiveness generated by at least an ideal of equality in the 'marketplace' has to be combined with the give-and-take of forms of sexual expression which are still deeply rooted in the traditions of earlier times (e.g. what it is to be male or female).

In these circumstances, it is proving difficult for many partnerships to achieve the desired goals within one relationship, which seems to have become a task no easier than squaring the circle. Attempts to solve the problem mostly seem to involve separating in some way the functions of sex and companionship. For example, a couple may form a childless liaison in order to embellish a home and fill it with consumer goods which establish an acceptable social image and 'state' an appropriate 'lifestyle', while conducting more or less casual sexual liaisons with third parties. Or a woman may marry a man she knows to be gay and who is therefore less likely to make 'selfish' demands upon her. Or couples with children may agree to live apart, though still sleeping together when the man visits, maybe quite regularly.

IAN

Form of distress	Current predicament	Background predicament
Ian has been off work for two months with mild depression. He is unable to concentrate on anything and has panic attacks when driving. He complains of irritability which he is afraid might get out of control, especially with his wife June, a 'lovely girl' who he is afraid will leave him if he doesn't get a grip on himself. Their sex life has come to a virtual standstill.	Ian is a middle manager in an insurance office. He met June as her supervisor when she was a management trainee. Since then she has joined another firm, becoming its marketing manager. She is often away from home on business, and now earns nearly twice Ian's salary. They have one little girl, whom Ian has been looking after since he's been off work.	Ian comes from a traditional working-class background. He feels close to his parents, though sees less of them than he used to, and he has grown a little apart from his brother and sister, though without animosity.

Again, it is obviously easier for a woman to play a bread-winning role more equal to her husband's (as likely, of course, to be a necessity as a matter of choice) if she can divest herself of some of the major responsibilities of traditional motherhood; these in turn have to be taken over by someone else, usually a childminder or nanny in a less advantageous social position.

Not infrequently, these 'solutions' are achieved only with a degree of pain, confusion or guilt which those involved tend to interpret proximally as the result either of their own inadequacy and in competence, or as the intransigence, malice or brutality of their partner.

Ian simply cannot understand why he should find himself becoming almost uncontrollably angry with June when he can't 'fault her' in any respect. She is clever, attractive, successful, a 'wonderful mother' and – so far – an extremely tolerant and affectionate wife. He has dredged his past, without success, for psychological traumata which might account for his 'illness'. Maybe, he thinks, it's a question of some kind of dietary allergy. He's consulted a hypnotherapist, with only temporary relief, and he now feels at his wits' end.

The high rate of divorce leading to the formation of second relationships involving children from the first introduces another set of pressures on all concerned. The absence of rules or established social patterns of conduct in such circumstances means that people have to invent for themselves ways of handling the inevitable difficulties. They are thrown back on purely personal resources to support conduct whose justification has to be constantly argued for, often in increasingly bitter family quarrels: there is no external criterion of what is or is not reasonable or acceptable in such situations, and the protagonists may end up frustrated and isolated behind a defensive wall of righteous indignation.

Jill feels that she has already put her children through enough without Kevin's nagging them, even though it is Jill's welfare he's concerned for. She feels he has no right to intrude in this way into her relationship with her daughter. Further, though she sees that he has a responsibility to his son, and though she is ashamed of her feeling, she finds the latter's presence in their already crowded house as practically intolerable – he is noisy, dirty and disrespectful, and she can't understand why Kevin, so ready to criticise her daughter, doesn't take a stronger line with his own son. In his turn, Kevin is similarly guilty about having deserted the boy in his teens, and does not feel it appropriate to 'go on at him' too much when he is already having such a rough time with his unstable mother. Jill's children, though they have little respect for him, feel torn in their loyalties to their father, who uses them as message bearers to his former wife, and to Kevin, whom they see as the more responsible and concerned of the two. They are puzzled and distressed by their mother's confusion and vacillation in disciplinary matters and by the tensions generated in the household. They quite like their stepbrother.

JILL

Form of distress	Current predicament	Background predicament
Jill was always an overconscientious 'worrier', but serious panic attacks started only after she had met her second husband, Kevin, and they have got worse now that they are in the fifth year of their marriage. Jill is riddled with guilt over having, as she sees it, deprived her two teenage children (a girl and a boy) of their father, and she encourages them to see him regularly.	Kevin is a much kinder, more tolerant and reliable man than Jill's first husband, and Jill also contrasts strongly with his first wife, who was extremely selfish and somewhat promiscuous. Jill can't stand Kevin's nineteen-year-old son, who is periodically thrown out of the house by his mother and so has to live with Jill and Kevin. Kevin is also, as Jill sees it, much too strict with her daughter, who he feels abuses her mother's good nature.	Jill's mother was an anxious, self-concerned woman whose husband devoted his life to ministering to her needs. Jill was left pretty much to her own devices, being also required to look after her two younger brothers when her mother was too 'ill' to do so.

The difficulties of young people too are given a distinctive shape by the times in which they grew up. The social revolution which took place in the 1980s[13] seems to have distracted a significant proportion of the 'parent generation' of the period (by which I mean all those having care of the young, not just their biological parents) from attending to the psychological needs of those engaged principally with the task of learning how to live. Furthermore, the social conditions since the 1990s have done little to welcome the young into the adult world. Especially perhaps for young men, there is virtually no assurance that they have a social value, that the world has need of them – a state of affairs reflected clearly enough in the dramatic increase in the suicide rate for this group.[14] Whatever one might think

KEITH

Form of distress	Current predicament	Background predicament
Keith feels depressed and without 'motivation'. He also has periods of quite extreme, anxious agitation when he can concentrate on nothing except a feeling that something terrible is about to happen. He quarrels a lot with his family and worries about 'not getting on' with people his own age, girls and boys.	A 27-year-old graduate, Keith got a good degree. He feels alienated from and irritated by his parents, both successful solicitors. He has no idea what he wants to do, at present taking occasional casual jobs. He has girlfriends, but does not feel involved with them – they tend to 'get on his nerves'. In relation to other young people, he 'doesn't feel real' – they seem somehow to have substance in a way he doesn't.	Both Keith's parents were preoccupied with building their careers as he grew up, and when they were at home together spent most of their time sniping at each other. From working-class backgrounds themselves, they were concerned that Keith and his brother should have a good education, and sent them as day boys to the local public school.

of its desirability, young women at least still have the option of fulfilling their biological function.

Keith appears to be profoundly uncertain not only about what he feels about himself and his life, but also about whether he feels anything much at all. It is difficult to trace within him any element of desire. He finds it literally impossible to think of things he would like to taste, to see, to feel, and there seems to be no particular gusto, even with sex. The world contains nothing he wants, and it appears to want nothing of him other than that he should have a satisfactory 'lifestyle'. He is puzzled about how to conduct his life in the directed way other people appear to. He only knows how to measure things as it seems to him his parents did – according to material success. For example, he is far more comfortable with choosing food on a

LUKE

Form of distress	Current predicament	Background predicament
Luke took an overdose when his girlfriend returned to her husband. He feels completely alienated from his social peers and workmates, is deeply in debt and is about to get evicted from his flat. He is cut off from his family and feels very isolated. Luke feels unlike anyone he knows; only his girlfriend seemed to understand what goes on inside him.	Luke left school with no qualifications, but subsequently got a diploma in catering. He has a very low-paid, part-time job which runs from week to week. Even so, he is in charge of kitchen staff who resent and tease him (he is unusually tall and thin). Luke has an acute, original mind, but finds no one to share his perceptions. He would like to 'go to college' but has no financial support and very little confidence.	Luke's parents separated early in his life, which was spent mainly with his father and seven-years-older sister. His father drank and gambled and his sister moved as soon as she could to another part of the country with a man now in prison. After leaving school Luke went through a difficult period involving drink, drugs and trouble with the police.

menu according to how expensive it is than to what he feels like eating. It is as if nobody while he was growing up tried to elucidate or explain to him what it is to *experience* the world, to make preferences in terms of pleasure and pain, good and bad.

Luke can see only one form of social existence open to him, which is to join the macho, petty-criminal network of socially, educationally, materially and vocationally disadvantaged young people whose only possibility to 'be something' is to develop the, so to speak, unofficial spaces left by a world totally preoccupied with individual success and survival and utterly indifferent to them. And yet the prospect is totally distasteful to him. Though incapable of seeing himself in this light (because nobody has ever given him the slightest indication that it is so), Luke has a kind of reflective intelligence and a sensitive appreciation of reality which set him apart from most of his peers and –

MARY

Form of distress	Current predicament	Background predicament
Gradually increasing loss of confidence in herself has led to Mary's developing panic attacks, especially when out shopping on her own.	Mary is a single parent of eighteen. She has a mixed-race baby two years old whose father deserted her after living with Mary for six months. Her mother is supportive, but 'interfering', and Mary is reluctant to leave her baby with her because she 'spoils her' and makes it more difficult for Mary to cope afterwards. Social services are involved, and though of some material help are also, she feels, 'on her back', not least in insisting that she concern herself with the baby's racial identity through attending classes, etc. She is also harassed by the father's family.	Mary's parents separated when she was thirteen and her mother remarried shortly afterwards. Mary hated her father and didn't particularly like her stepfather either, though she remains attached to, and slightly in awe of, her mother. To the disapproval of all concerned, she got pregnant and left to live with the father of her baby as soon as she could.

perhaps unfortunately – make it impossible for him to ignore an ideal of how he would like life to be.

Mary wanted a baby. She didn't particularly want to be a single parent, but she did want to become independent of the difficult and claustrophobic situation in her mother and step-father's home, to live her own life and to have 'someone to love'. With very little money, a lot of parental criticism and disapproval, no social life, harassment from her baby's father's family and intrusive surveillance from the social service department, she nevertheless managed to care for her child competently and devotedly.

BACKGROUND PREDICAMENTS

As soon as it enters the world, the infant has to start learning to deal with the immediate set of circumstances which fate has assigned it. Our successes and failures in this enterprise will during the course of the first decade or so of our lives form what we may choose to call, in shorthand, our character.

It is important to realise that there is a lot more to character than just the idiosyncratic personal foibles which make it possible for us to recognise each other as individuals. 'Character' also embodies the knowledge we have acquired of the world and the expectations this has led us to develop about how it is likely to treat us.

We do not invent these expectations – they are, more or less, imposed upon us by our experience of a real world. If, therefore, we wish to achieve a full understanding of why and how we react as we do to events in the present, we need to take into account, among other things, the influence of the past. The past, in other words, forms part of the *reality* of the present and is not to be dismissed lightly.

Issues concerning the influence of the past will surface several times in the course of subsequent chapters. For the moment, I want only to consider some of the more frequently encountered types of predicament shaping the characters – the knowledge and expectations of the world – of people whose later distress may lead them to contemplate seeking professional help. As indicated earlier, the constellations of early influence set out below are as seen from the perspective of the sufferer, and are not intended as 'the explanation' of their suffering. My concern here then, is, with the individual's proximal world, and does not stretch far beyond his or her view of it. The inevitability of that view's being distorted does not mean that it is 'wrong'; we may say, rather, that we are speaking of a limited truth – the truth for the individual concerned.

It is, of course, the family that looms largest in most people's consideration of their early lives, and it is with family – in particular parental – influence that we shall be mainly concerned in what follows. For the sake of convenience, I have once again divided what may be seen as damaging forms of family influence into a number of subcategories; as before, these are not intended to have special scientific validity, nor indeed to exhaust all the possibilities.

Oppression and indifference

Straightforward cruelty and physical abuse blight the lives of many children, and leave scars of various kinds – particularly, perhaps, an entirely understandable mistrust of people in later life and difficulty in forming close relationships with them. The child may, for example, become a kind of expert in violence – either in vigilantly detecting it so that it can be dodged in time (a kind of 'early warning' approach to relationships) or in learning its rules and applying it as vigorously as once it was suffered.

Violent abuse often does have the single advantage, if such it can be called, that it is easily recognisable and clearly attributable to its source. The drunken child-beater, for all the fear he instils and damage he does, can at least also be hated. Siblings who can form some kind of solidarity against their oppressor, perhaps also with their mother, experience a more benign world than do, for example, people who could not escape violence in their childhood, either because they were alone with their tormentor, or because violence was endemic within the family as a whole.

Mick's intelligence and sensitivity made it possible, certainly, for him to criticise his experience as he grew up, but he was not

MICK

Form of distress	Current predicament	Background predicament
In his mid-thirties and recently married with a small son, Mick has suddenly succumbed to panic attacks, especially at work. He also worries about his temper at home: though not violent, he often shouts alarmingly, and is very strict with his little boy.	Mick is under threat of redundancy at work, and stretches himself beyond his limits in trying to comply with the unreasonable demands of his job. He finds settling to the responsibilities of husband and father difficult, having previously led an extremely free, single existence.	Mick was a gifted and sensitive child, but his mother couldn't stand him, and regularly vented her rage upon him as a little boy, hitting him, pulling his hair, beating him with anything that lay to hand. Once she broke his arm. His father was not violent, but a cold, hard, narrow-minded martinet, whom, however, Mick respects as a 'fair' disciplinarian. His father viewed Mick's sensitivity with alarm, and made him join the army to 'make a man' of him.

lucky enough to encounter any real alternative to his world. His schools were in the deprived area where the family lived, with most teachers too harassed and demoralised to notice and encourage his talents – one who did was dismissed as 'a nancy' by his father. Mick knew that he wanted things to be different, and to be different himself, but he didn't know how, and veered between a compliant desperation to be liked and sudden flashes of violent anger.

The damage done by sexual abuse also includes the model of relationship it impresses on the victim, and at its most prolonged and violent simply wrecks, among other things, the possibility of the person being able to develop later trusting and tender sexual relations with others. Usually, however, it is more complicated than this, and its peculiar mixture of oppression and threat, guilty secrecy, mysterious (from the child's point of view) sexuality, and affection – the inappropriate crossing of family and generational boundaries – may have all kinds of consequences which, even though they may not prove catastrophic, are certainly likely to affect later life and relationships.

It is common for people to experience some form of 'sexual abuse' as they grow up, whether at the hands of other children, being groped by strangers on buses or being invited to view the equipment of local flashers. It is certainly possible to get unnecessarily strident and alarmist about such experiences as these, as also relatively transient and minor forms of abuse that might be committed by a dementing elderly relative or a drunken neighbour. But where the abuse persists, or occurs in an atmosphere of secrecy (often with the frightened complicity of other family members), in such a way that children cannot place their experience against a standard of what is socially acceptable or receive the support and validation of those close to them, their only recourse is to see themselves as responsible for what is happening (for that is the way we are taught to view pretty well all our conduct). This is the start of the feelings of guilt, dirtiness and self-loathing that are the well-known consequences of abuse.

The lack of security and failure of confidence which creates the kind of 'basic anxiety' so well described by Karen Horney[15] is often the result of forms of oppression or indifference less spectacular, but not necessarily less damaging, than those described so far. Rejection, abandonment, oppressive parental control and rigidity, may all serve to undermine the child's sense of itself as a character of substance or value, as may his or her awareness of having a favoured sibling.

Parents' actions may amount to rejection of their children even where this is the last thing they intend. Fathers or mothers feeling driven to desert the family because they can no longer bear the bitterness and frustration of living with a spouse they've come to loathe can easily forget that from the child's point of view it is *s/he* who is being abandoned. Such was the case with Ann, above. Her father's desertion of her at the age of fourteen served only to reinforce a view of herself (not, let it be noted, a *mistaken* view) that she was not the kind of person even a father would particularly want to stay with.

In the far from subtle way that psychoanalysis has of shifting the burden of responsibility from the more to the less powerful, the notion of 'sibling rivalry' suggests that difficulties involving brothers and sisters are due mainly to some kind of selfish struggle between them. In my experience it is more often the case that children defend themselves as long as they can from the painful recognition that a brother or a sister brings a light to parental eyes which go dull when they themselves come into view. Again, the conclusion such children arrive at is not that they are discriminated against, whether unfortunately or unfairly, but that they are unlovable in some way that their brother or sister isn't. An even more impossible situation to have to cope with – and one which seems to arise quite often – is where an older sibling died in infancy only to become for the parents a kind of idealised paragon with whom no living mortal could hope to contend.

The provision of love that is strictly conditional – powerful when present but desolating when withdrawn – presents the child with a world which has to be carefully watched, placated or manipulated. This was part of Dave's difficulties. The world he grew up in could go horribly wrong, not always predictably, though if he got it right, it was not without its rewards. His development of a kind of extreme superstitious caution may have looked pretty crazy at first sight, but it made a good deal more sense once one understood how he had spent his child-hood and youth tiptoeing through a minefield.

Parental indifference towards children, simple lack of interest in them (which may come about for a hundred reasons – at this point it is not our purpose to understand them), is probably the commonest cause of a level of self-confidence always vulnerable to erosion; there are several examples in the brief stories offered above. The feeling that you *matter* is not the innate heritage of every human being, but, if you are lucky, a gift from the social and familial world into which you are thrown at birth. In the absence of that gift, in circumstances, that is, where you did not particularly matter to those on whom you were most dependent, almost every social situation becomes laden with the threat that others will detect your fundamental lack of worth. As suggested earlier, becoming nothing is the experience of panic.

Intrusion and distortion

Abuse, neglect and indifference, whatever the evils they create, do not necessarily interfere directly with the child's perception of reality, though of course they might. They may *constitute* his or her reality, but they do not on the whole serve to distort the very processes through which s/he seeks to understand the world.

It has long been recognised by a thoughtful minority in psychology and psychiatry that one of the most difficult things for children to have to deal with is a situation where they are forced to abandon their own view of reality in order to conform to the emotional needs of the more powerful people around them, usually of course their parents.[16]

Some of the most damaging forms of intrusion on the child's ability to make *accurate* sense of the world are carried out in the name of love, though it is probably more correctly understood as anxiety. Many an anxious mother, driven by her own profound insecurity, has fussed over her child, imposing upon it a kind of fearful surveillance which inhibits, eventually, its every independent step. Parental anxiety of this kind, which is never acknowledged as such but presented to the child as a necessary protection from a terribly dangerous world, can prove quite crippling in later life. However, sufferers from anxiety who are able to acknowledge that their fears are a property of *their* world rather than of *the* world need not worry that they may somehow infect their children (perhaps genetically) with their own difficulties; it is only when parental anxiety focuses on the child, or else so dominates the family that everyone has, without drawing direct attention to it, to order their lives around it, that it is likely to create a real problem for others (Jill's mother was like this). I have known many very severely anxious and 'agora-phobic' women who have raised extremely self-confident and successful children.

Parental (again, usually maternal) anxiety about the world's darker aspect – its brutality, depravity, degradation – can lead to a superstitious censoring of reality and a prohibition of the expression of inevitable human feelings like anger which make it impossible for the child to face directly aspects of life that are in fact inescapable and to recognise and cultivate features of its character and experience that are part of every human being. This kind of background constellation seems often to lie behind the later development of 'obsessive-compulsive' strategies for dealing with the less acceptable sides not only of life but, more particularly, perhaps, of one's own character. Dave's example is again a case in point: unable to recognise, let alone openly acknowledge, perfectly normal feelings of anger and resentment, he experienced them as a potential danger lurking in the world around him which he had somehow to control and protect people from, for reasons he didn't at all understand.

Nadine had been taught by her parents' example to believe that love and duty were indistinguishable (even though her sister's relatively carefree situation seemed a puzzling exception to the rule). Though she tried her best to apply her considerable abilities scrupulously in every department of her life – her job, her role as wife and daughter – she never seemed fully to succeed, and her existence as a whole seemed always sadly

NADINE

Form of distress	Current predicament	Background predicament
Nadine is extremely worried about her inability to concentrate on her job as supervisor of a large secretarial agency; she is depressed, unable to remember things, and comfort eating has led to her becoming overweight, about which she feels very guilty. Having lost contact with her friends, she also feels isolated and lonely.	Nadine's job is demanding but unrewarding: she carries a lot of responsibility but gets very little thanks for her efforts. Her aged parents make very heavy demands on her spare time. She has recently divorced her rather feckless husband of fifteen years, who had been more like a spoilt child than a partner. She has no children.	Nadine's parents had never really been able to love her as they had her clever, pretty, older sister who had gone to university and realised all their ambitions. Instead, they had discharged their duty towards her. From Nadine's point of view this meant that she had for as long as she could remember been subjected to a kind of strict moral supervision aimed, presumably, at turning her general conduct into something of which her parents could approve. They never ceased to treat her as a rather stupid and irresponsible child.

lacking in satisfaction. The harder she tried, the more empty she felt. Her mission in life seemed to be to please, in particular, her implacable father. It never even occurred to her that she could try pleasing herself.

The inappropriate crossing of generational roles is another way in which parents may intrude on the lives of their children to shape their character for life. In some cases parents may draw a child as ally or accomplice into battles they are having with their spouse; in others they may become like dependent children themselves so that their offspring are forced into a parental role. Ann, Gina and Jill are all examples of this latter predicament. Possession by the kind of super-conscientiousness discussed above is frequently the result of having imposed upon one at an inappropriately early age responsibilities of parental proportions, usually for the care of younger siblings, but quite often also of parents themselves. Because the boundaries of responsibility are extended so enormously for a child placed in this position, s/he may never learn where the limits of his or her capacity to respond to demand lie, and in later life may continue to acquire duties and responsibilities to the point of breakdown (this theme will reappear in Chapter Five).

Parents may also compete with their children. Freud made the 'Oedipal' competition between son and father central to his theory of neurosis, but true to form, he saw the child as the instigator of the struggle for the love of the mother/wife. In fact, it is far more often the case that an essentially insecure and anxious parent feels compelled to ensure that s/he is not surpassed in any respect by a son or daughter. Brenda's mother, for example, could not allow her daughter to compare with her either morally or intellectually, so that there was a whole range of ways in which Brenda simply could not *be*. Daughters are also more easily undermined and rendered vulnerable to later anxiety by tyrannical fathers who do not allow their arbitrary (though not necessarily violent) rule over their timid wives and cowed children to be questioned. Boys in this situation may eventually grow big and rebellious enough to challenge the tyranny, or simply to leave.

Parental favour can sometimes be as damaging in the long run as disfavour. The blindly benevolent but nevertheless inflexible rule Norman's mother exercised over him prevented his developing any sense of having an independent will. Always in the back of his mind was the feeling that he could rely on her more than on himself, and so he was unable to develop any consistent direction in his life. In addition, any desires of his own which he did experience (but of which she would have

NORMAN

Form of distress	Current predicament	Background predicament
Mildly depressed and unable to motivate himself, Norman is also having difficulty controlling his drinking. He gambles compulsively and is squandering what little money the family has, mostly in secret. He is losing his temper at home more than he would like.	Norman was made redundant from his job as area sales manager for a furnishing business a year ago, and is still out of work. His third marriage, of eight years, is rocky, mainly because of his wife's discovery of his drinking and gambling.	In the eyes of his strong, domineering mother, Norman could do no wrong; she regarded his two older sisters with contempt. His father was a reasonably benign but distant figure who absented himself from the household as much as possible and consoled himself with other women.

disapproved) had to be indulged in secret and quickly became out of his control.

Parents' power to determine the nature of reality for their children may be used to represent indifference as love, neglect as solicitude, truth as wilful misconception. A child may, for example, quite easily be persuaded that its innocent perception of reality is a function of its own naughtiness, even wickedness. For there is nothing like the innocent perception of reality to rock the familial boat in situations where sources of pain or discord have to be denied and suppressed if the boat is to stay afloat. A comment on Heather's part, for example, that her mother seemed to have a particularly close understanding with the male neighbour who gave them lifts to swimming lessons, drew immediate outraged condemnation and punishment from both her parents in a way she couldn't possibly understand at the time and this contributed to a lifelong lack of confidence in her own judgement. Catherine, bombarded throughout her childhood, first by her mother and later by her stepfather as well, with messages about the sacrifices that were being made in her interest and guilty assurances about how much she was adored, took some time to see that the pain she felt at the loss of those who had loved her (her grandmother and a nanny), the bitter isolation of boarding school and the hollowness of parental assurances of love, were not somehow indications of her own social inadequacy and ingratitude, but sources of an entirely justifiable resentment and an all too well-founded anticipation of the likelihood of betrayal.

The single-minded concentration on material betterment of the 1980s, combined with a susceptibility to the dominant make-believe ideology of business, seemed to result in some, particularly middle-class, parents failing to nurture in their children any sense of what human beings are really like. Keith's parents were ambitious for him, certainly, and it was important that he should be a credit to them, but beyond that they had little time for or interest in him, so preoccupied were they with the construction of their largely separate images. From them as well as from the wider culture, he gleaned a knowledge only of the smooth outer surface of things. Under this surface was a world of quite bitter competition – his parents bickered almost continually – but the bitterness was always glossed over and denied, never dealt with directly in a language which could be used to take its measure. For Keith, it was as if the only true reality was that reflected in the world of advertising, and when internal experience failed to match up to external pretence, its rawness and untidiness, the inarticulateness of feeling, seemed chaotically alien, overwhelming and frightening.

Social disadvantages

Some factors of the social background work to erode the individual's self-confidence independently of specific figures such as parents. Social class is one such factor, and in my view probably still the most important. I have written about the phenomenon of 'class injury' in detail in *The Origins of Unhappiness* and I do not, therefore, want to repeat those observations here, but it is important to point out that a 'sense of worth' is not simply a matter of personal psychology and immediate family relations, but may also be an objective valuation which is placed on us at birth, and, if negative, escaped only infrequently and with the greatest difficulty.

The feeling of not being as good as some notional standard of, presumably, middle-class respectability may not only haunt individuals, but also set in train parental efforts to 'better' their children which, while unquestionably carried out with the best intentions, lead to damaging distortions of their reality. For example, the Methodism of Dave's parents had in part originated as a means of surmounting what was seen as the social degradation of the urban proletariat, but its principal effect was to render the family more or less incapable of acknowledging and dealing competently with the darker sides of life.

Although society is as riven by inequality as ever, and preoccupation with status was never more acute, it does seem that, at the beginning of the twenty-first century, traditional class divisions are less easy to discern than they were only twenty years ago. But it is still the case that for many people class is a significant factor of identity, and confusion over one's class background can lead to a kind of personal 'statelessness' not unlike confusion over nationality. Many middle-aged men who were able to realise their intellectual potential via a school system that operated across class barriers, but whose background was in the deferential working class which 'knew its place', have found themselves in jobs where they have both to compete and to socialise with middle-class colleagues who seem to move instinctively in a world which they themselves can never experience as other than essentially alien. The resultant feeling of being a stranger in what is in every other sense their own world can give rise to a considerable amount of anxiety.

The factor of *embodiment*, taken in a social context which fixes the body with an evaluative gaze, is again one that may

OLIVIA

Form of distress	Current predicament	Background predicament
For some time Olivia has been feeling uncharacteristically depressed, weepy and irritable with her three daughters. She has lost all interest in things, and gets anxious and panicky if she has to go out.	Married and with her first child at seventeen, Olivia has devoted her life to her children and her husband Tony. Now she is only in her mid-thirties, but her children are almost grown-up. Tony is a rock of dependability, though not as lively and bright as Olivia. Some of his family, she knows, abuse her racially behind her back. Tony is now out of work and the responsibility for managing the household falls on her. She enjoyed working part-time as a waitress in a local cafe, but the manager made constant allusions to her colour (e.g. 'You work pretty well for a coon'), and every so often she'd have to take racist abuse from customers.	One of several children from her mother's three relationships, Olivia was the only one of mixed race, her father being Ethiopian and her mother white. In looks, Olivia takes after him more than her mother. She is strikingly beautiful, tall and graceful. She never felt at ease with her step-relatives, most of whom made it clear that she was 'different'. Her mother, however, supported her lovingly throughout.

profoundly affect the individual's emotional well-being. Being fat, tall, short, or even having red hair, can for all too many children be a torment which makes their school life a misery of shame and isolation. There can be little doubt, too, that a commercially exploited male sexuality which fetishises the female body and makes it the object of relentless pornographic scrutiny, turns the simple fact of being a woman into a *problem* which cannot be evaded, even by the strategy of 'anorexia nervosa'. Men too, of course, worry a great deal about their personal attractiveness, and are by no means able to disown their bodies, but the difficulty for (particularly) young women is to be able to be *anything* but their bodies, and, whether beautiful or ugly, it is almost impossible for them to escape the awareness of embodiment.

Being black is of course another feature of embodiment that may render the individual socially vulnerable. Having lived with that vulnerability all their lives, and unable to escape a social background where racist attitudes are pervasive, many black people themselves find it difficult completely to shake off the idea that there is something inherently inferior about being black. Of all social injuries, this is the deepest and most cruel. Olivia, for example, for all her considerable intelligence and perceptiveness, felt that if she was kind enough to people she could 'make them forget' that she was black. In her mid-thirties, it came as a real surprise (and enlightenment) to her when a white friend pointed out that people abused her about her colour at least partly out of envy, precisely because they could find nothing else about her to criticise.

Background predicaments of all kinds, whether mediated within the family or imposed through more general social disadvantage, shape character and attitudes in a way that makes them a virtually ineradicable part of the person. We believe what we learn about ourselves, however unjust the lesson. The difficulty for psychology and psychotherapy (so far largely unrecognised) is that we cannot change our beliefs at will. The implications of this will form the substance of much of the rest of this book.

CHAPTER THREE

The Tyranny of 'Normality'

Many people (including many of its accredited students) come
to psychology out of a desire to understand themselves or those
around them better, assuming that psychology will provide
well-founded and reliable keys to the complexities and
mysteries of human mental and emotional functioning. This,
sad though it may seem, implies a very naive view of the nature
not only of psychology, but of knowledge in general.

Psychology is not simply a disinterested enquiry into 'what
makes people tick'. Like every other branch of knowledge,
psychology has aims and purposes that cannot be detached from
the fundamental interests of the society that defines, supports
and furthers it.[1] Human enquiry is not pursued through a gaze
of wide-eyed innocence, simply gathering 'facts', sorting and
storing them until a complete account of the nature of things
has been achieved. Our gaze is, on the contrary, always directed
by our needs and our wishes and the social powers which, in
turn, seek to control them. Absolutely 'disinterested' enquiry is
not just difficult to achieve, it is an impossibility, if only because
being human is inextricably bound up with having interests.

There is of course not just *one* psychology, and psychology
could presumably have taken many turns. Sadly, any expectation that it should consist principally in a kind of Socratic quest
to 'know ourselves' in order to make our living together in
sympathy and solidarity more achievable – the expectation that,
perhaps, attracts so many people to it in the first place – is
quickly disappointed. What psychology did principally become
is revealed with telling clarity in the standard definition of it

which held sway during its formative decades in twentieth century: 'the prediction and control of behaviour'.

It is not at all difficult to detect the kind of concern underlying this definition: it is obvious enough from the very meaning of the words. The behaviour to be predicted and controlled is of course that of people other than psychologists themselves. Psychologists stand apart from the subjects of their experimental investigations and observe them with lofty detachment. It betrays surprising philosophical naivety that behavioural psychology should have presented itself, as it so insistently did, as 'value-free', since the values implicit in this kind of 'objective expert' stance are so obvious: the psychologist becomes an instrument of social discipline, observing, reporting and advising on the ways in which the behaviour of others may be 'predicted and controlled'. At times these values became explicit (though still unacknowledged as values), as for example in a paper by H. J. Eysenck, the most influential psychologist in Britain in the 1950s and 1960s. He wrote of a 'technology of consent'

> which will make people behave in a socially adapted, lawabiding fashion, which will not lead to a breakdown of the intricately interwoven fabric of social life . . . a generally applicable method of inculcating suitable habits of socialized conduct into the citizens (and particularly the future citizens) of the country in question – or preferably the whole world.[2]

Psychology becomes revealed, not as a disinterested science trying to penetrate and unlock the secrets of the human psyche, but as a would-be technique of systematised power driven by aspirations of megalomaniac proportions. Of course, any programme as blatantly grandiose and unrealistic as that articulated by Eysenck could scarcely be taken seriously and in fact presents no great threat to human freedom, but the theme it overstates lies much more subtly at the heart of a whole range of psychological approaches, including most of those dealing with therapy and treatment.

As much as anything, the game is given away by the way in which the psychological expert is so often to be located apart from the objects of his or her interest. In many other branches of knowledge, the human enquirer's aims, interests and personal and social make-up are (almost) completely detachable from the object of study, but psychology cannot be like that.[3] Psychologists being of the same order of psychological complexity as their so-called subjects, their 'discoveries' must apply as much to themselves as to anyone else: they unavoidably become objects of their own study, and any attempt to escape this complication through a pretence that they can, by virtue of a kind of exclusive, esoteric knowledge, set themselves apart from the rest of humanity betrays a sociopolitical more than a scientific programme. It shows that what they are involved in is not so much knowledge about people as power over them.

It was above all Michel Foucault who exposed the essentially disciplinary nature of so much of psychology, psychiatry and psychotherapy.[4] It is of course not the case that mental health programmes and procedures for the psychological measurement and classification of particular 'disorders' and 'deficits' openly proclaim any socially repressive intent; indeed, there is no reason why those who carry them out should be conscious of any such intent, and the majority are probably not. To be successful, programmes and procedures of this kind must be conceived and executed within an ideology of *care*. It was Foucault's particular achievement to reveal how much of this care (of course not all of it) is really about control.[5]

When it comes to the specifically 'therapeutic' aspect of psychological approaches, one does not have to read far into the literature before becoming aware of their 'conquistadorial' concerns.[6] This is evidenced in, for example, the patronising superiority of the language used to describe patients; the obsession with 'diagnoses' which, inevitably, place a kind of moral distance between therapist and patient; the almost paranoid concern with exclusivity, in which an attempt is made to establish and, so to speak, patent a system which only a select few can practise.

The stance taken by the system-builders of therapy towards patients is in this way almost always one of omniscient superiority, the language, if not positively hostile, at best condescending. Where people are not sorted and labelled according to the essentially meaningless categories of psychiatric diagnosis, they tend to be characterised as 'neurotic', 'infantile', 'immature', 'inadequate', 'maladjusted', 'manipulative', 'attention-seeking' and so on. Patients are people who are incomplete or damaged in some way, therapists people who have the (exclusive and protected) knowledge and power to identify and make good the patients' personal deficits and render them worthy once again of the company of their fellow human beings.

Lying right at the centre of the psychological enterprise, the tacit if not explicit focus of everyone's concern, is the concept of normality. Establishing what is 'normal' has been the business of a huge investment in 'psychometry' as well as the core of the diagnostic programme in psychological approaches to treatment. 'Psychometric tests' have been developed and standardised on a vast range of human characteristics. Intellectual abilities (including, of course, IQ), 'traits' of personality, vocational interest and abilities, diagnostic factors, have all been identified and turned into measurable aspects of personal functioning, all of which in turn compare the individual with a statistically established norm. Even where no such systematic approach to measurement exists, the essential psychological judgement is one that pronounces on the degree of the individual's departure from the average.

Psychology has become the instrument of conformity, not the appreciation of uniqueness. Difference is interpreted as deviance. Although, in the 'clinical' area, it is probably 'better' to be 'normal', there are, of course, deviations from the norm that are regarded in a positive light. It is 'better', for instance, to have an unusually high than an unusually low IQ, but even in cases like this the dimensions along which we may vary are established according to the characteristics of a 'population'.[7] There is no room for uniqueness: whatever characteristic psychology is measuring in you, you have, if you are not 'normal', either more or less of it than the average.

The principal consequence of all this is that social life becomes a process of comparison, usually invidious, and to consult a psychologist or psychiatrist is like coming before a judge. Psychologists, as the arbiters of 'normal' behaviour and experience, function precisely as judges, and the majority make little attempt to disguise it (though many of them are not aware that this is their principal role).

Psychological judgement can be very comprehensive: not only may individuals' status be assessed from the material and moral aspect, but it is quite likely also to be considered from an aesthetic standpoint. 'Psychometry', for example, may place the individual relative to the norm on a whole range of abilities and aptitudes which are regarded as more or less unalterable and quasi–biological, IQ being the most obvious example. I have already noted how moralistic some approaches to psychotherapy (particularly psychoanalysis) can be: a judgement is made of the extent to which people are conceived to be driven by 'unacceptable' impulses of aggression and sexuality, possessed by 'guilty fantasies' and 'infantile desires', etc., and even though therapists may, through their 'interpretations', convey that their intent is neither to reprove nor punish, patients can scarcely help concluding that these are moral imperfections.

The aesthetic judgement nestling apparently innocently at the heart of so many 'humanistic' approaches to psychotherapy and counselling may in some ways be the most difficult to cope with. For, although the hope is held out that through 'personal growth', 'self-actualisation', etc., forms of experience and relationship far from the dreary norm may be achieved, the fact is that the clients of these particular brands of therapy are likely to find that, despite their investment, life continues to run along much as it always has, and may conclude therefore that they must be lacking in some vital respect. Most 'humanistic' therapies enshrine in this way an exalted notion of the potential of human 'being' which is beyond all but the most self-deceiving of ordinary mortals and which, if taken seriously, can only lead to a sense of personal disappointment and failure.[8]

In view of all this it is not surprising that so many people approach their first consultation with a psychiatrist or psychologist with trepidation, for trepidation is indeed the appropriate emotion for a situation in which such comprehensive judgements can be passed, where so much seems to hang in the balance.[9] For although in one sense people 'know' that the professional they have come to consult is there 'for their own good' and to help them with their difficulties (that is to say, they accept the ideology of care), they know also that they are likely to be on the receiving end of a 'clinical assessment' which will place them, very possibly unfavourably, in relation to a range of norms concerning their mental adjustment and their personal and social adequacy. And they are not wrong, for behind the ideology of care lies a much broader, if less articulated, concern to maintain a culture that lays the blame for psychological and emotional suffering squarely at the door of those who suffer.

But it doesn't have to be, and isn't always, like this. There are other ways of understanding distress than merely as deviance, and it is possible to think about personal suffering without its being interpreted as personal failure.

Rather than an apprehension of self, informed at its core by invidious comparison (where the best that can be said of one's self is, as H. S. Sullivan put it, 'at least I'm not as bad as the other swine'[10]), what is needed is an understanding of how person-hood comes about, freed of all the moralistic under- and over-tones which a century of psychology has managed to create. We need to abandon our fixation on the 'normal' and consider who we are, and how we came to be so.

THE MAKING OF PERSONS

The first thing that it is important to establish is that one does not *choose* to be the person one is. The issues of choice, freedom and responsibility are complicated and difficult, and our popular as well as our 'official' psychological understanding of them are probably more harmfully misleading than almost any other (we shall be considering these issues more directly in later chapters), but only the most wishful and unreflective thinking (of which, unfortunately, there is no shortage) could conceive of the individual person as self-creating. We cannot be held responsible for who we are, and the shame and blame of invidious comparison are therefore simply inappropriate.

We need to understand how 'the person' comes to be constituted not so much because we can necessarily do very much about our 'selves' but because we need to know what we can reasonably expect of ourselves and how we can influence the factors that shape personhood – if not for our own good, then at least for the good of others yet to become persons. Indeed, perhaps the most important thing to understand is precisely that we cannot do very much about our 'selves'.

Although psychology has been very much concerned with what it calls 'individual differences', the individuality concerned is always in relation to a norm, which leaves no room at all for individuality in the true sense. Indeed, individuality is a vexed question not only for psychology, but for philosophy and politics as well, and the way most systems of thought seem to try to solve it is to focus on one particular aspect of human nature in order to suggest, for example, that human beings are either *all* individuals or *all* part of a virtually indistinguishable mass. The thing is, we are both.

Embodiment

The very foundation of our nature as human beings is the way we are made – our embodiment. Everything we come, through the process of socialisation, to know, to think, feel, perceive, believe, imagine and desire, is conditioned by the kind of physical organism we are. Our interest in the world, the ways we approach, sense, handle and move within it, are given to us through the structures and capacities of our bodily organs. There is no experience, no passion, no *mind* without body.

We do not earn our embodiment, it is just given, and however much factions within society may attempt to colonise the body with power by endowing its superficial characteristics (e.g. skin colour) with indices of worth or by claiming that blood can be blue, in the end only fools and knaves can fail to acknowledge that in this fundamental respect we are all equal. Prick us, and we bleed. Cut us open, and we all look the same. There are, it is true, superficial differences between us in height, weight, colouring, and more important distinctions to be made in respect of sex and degree of maturity, but apart from these we are pretty well identical. In my view, it is our shared embodiment that lays the ground of our *community* and establishes thereby the fundamentally ethical nature of the relation between us.

For, being built the same way and sharing identical organs of sensation and expression, we cannot escape a knowledge of how we *feel*: knowing how *I* feel tells me also how the other feels. In this respect, and stripped of our social pretensions, we are all incontrovertibly equal. We cannot ignore the sympathy that gives us knowledge of each other's pain (though we can, and do, abuse it without mercy) because my nervous system stirs at the very sight – even the idea – of your injury.

Our embodiment determines our feelings of pleasure and pain, and makes it possible for us to read in each other the joys and sufferings which form the most essential stuff of our lives. There is no 'nobility' of suffering, no 'refinement' of feeling which would permit one person to claim greater value than others for his or her physical 'sensibility'. Raw sensation is the same for us all, and we can ignore its significance for others only by conceptually removing ourselves from the human race in the most basic act of bad faith. When it comes to the experience of pain, the most socially privileged are placed instantly on the same plane with the most deprived (this fact makes any kind of socially differentiated provision of health care fundamentally immoral).

Experience

In another respect, we are all absolutely unique. It is useful to reflect from time to time that, even on a globe teeming with animals outwardly distinguishable from each other in only the most superficial ways, absolutely nobody has been where you have been at the time you've been there and with the same people.

One of the greatest difficulties facing a 'scientific psychology' which can consider individuality only as different degrees of conformity is that no two people do share the same experience. Assumptions important for research in normative psychology for example about people sharing 'the same kind of background' – have to overlook the fact that, as far as people are concerned, there's no such thing as the same background. Many social scientists would no doubt see this as hair-splitting, probably claiming that people's backgrounds may be sufficiently similar for valid comparisons and generalisations to be made (e.g. that siblings share 'the same' familial environment). When it comes down to the individual trying to make sense of his or her own experience, however, the shortcomings of the normative approach become obvious. John and Jane's experience of 'the same' family background can be radically different, if only because John had Jane for a sister and Jane had John for a brother.[11]

This is no trivial matter. Only you know what your life has been like, what demands you have had to meet, what pains you have had to suffer. Throughout your life, only you have been occupying that space in the world which has been yours, and the angle from which you have experienced the world and the other people in it is utterly unique. Your relations with others have been shared with absolutely nobody else. Nonsense to pretend, to pursue the example above, that siblings share the same world or the same relations with their parents. Parental favouritism is a huge factor in shaping the experience of children, and just think, for instance, how different are the worlds of John and Jane where he has been bullying or sexually abusing her for years of her youth.

There can be no question of 'normality' when it comes to considering the significance of your private experience; there is no average to be calculated from a sample of one. There is in this way, at the heart of our existence, an aloneness of singularity, the terrible vulnerability of one against all, which (because we have all known it, all our lives) is easy to overlook but which we read easily enough in the faces of small children when they become doubtful of their safety in the society of others. Because of this, we depend for our well-being on the sympathetic support of at least some of those around us; we need to know the boat is shared at least with one or two, that we are not the only ones to be alone.

Right from the very start, the world is presented to you to organise and evaluate from a perspective which you share with no one. Your view of what is real and true, and your experience of pleasure and pain, are established from judgements only you can make. Those judgements may be supported, and indeed facilitated, by others, but ultimately you take your stand up against the world in utter solitude. Where you do get the help and encouragement of others, you are likely to develop a good degree of confidence in your own judgement, to feel that you have a secure understanding of the realities of the world, that you can move towards and within it without fear of unforeseen catastrophe or massive social rejection. For this, the help you get from others (particularly, of course, parents) needs to be centred on a knowledge of the uniqueness of your situation, to recognise that it is your shoes you're standing in, and not theirs.

There must be, I think, a crucial period of infancy where a competence to judge the world may become established, and no doubt a much more prolonged period of early life in which that competence may be extended and elaborated, or else threatened and undermined. The *courage* needed for a tiny, powerless organism to take a chance on the nature of its reality, to venture a first hesitant transaction with the all-powerful beings it encounters, must be colossal, and can only be acquired through a process of *encouragement*, in which a loving recognition of the uniqueness of the baby's perspective is central to the nurture and instruction offered.

Where this does not happen, where the infant is bullied or indoctrinated into a view of the world which has no basis in its own feelings and perceptions, it simply has to abandon any idea of its own competence to judge, to submerge its autonomy in a blind and ultimately inescapable obedience to the authority of others. (We shall return to this theme in the next chapter.)

Babies of course need the powerful support of their parents they cannot simply be left to their own devices to create a world for themselves. But the parental attitude needs to be one of, so to speak, informed tentativeness, as if the parent were to say: 'I think it may help you in the task I take you to be struggling with to conceive of it this way, to handle it like that. Let me know if I'm wrong.' This, of course, is what many parents do instinctively without the slightest self-consciousness. But not always, and where a parental view of the world is simply imposed, the baby is robbed of the very foundation of its capacity for autonomous thought and action, and becomes incapable of interpreting independently its own experience.

In this way, we need from the very earliest moment to become equipped with the means of making sense of a world in which there is no absolute confirmation of our judgement simply because there is no one able completely to share our experience. When it comes to assessing the significance of your experience, you are, ultimately, on your own. Rather like the 'good' parents, others can do no more than make suggestions which may help you articulate a feeling or intuition, or invite you to consider possibilities you may have overlooked. This is why the normative approach does such violence to the experience of the individual: by being compared to an average he or she is instantly dislocated from a personal biography, and the joys and sorrows of a unique lifetime are swept aside as irrelevant.

Culture

The fact that the location from which you have experienced your world is uniquely your own does not mean, however, that everyone's 'psychology' is totally different from everyone else's. As well as a private aspect, we have a shared, public one. Nobody else can have experienced what you have experienced because only you have been where you have been, but the ways in which you understand and interpret your experience are likely to be shared with a very large number of other people. These are the ways given by the culture into which you are born and bred; they are not chosen and developed by you as, so to speak, your personal creations or acquisitions, but impressed upon you impersonally.

Most obviously, the language you speak is not something you invent for yourself, but is culturally imposed. And language contains, of course, many of the tools of understanding and interpretation; it sets the limits on what you can talk about and establishes the concepts with which you make sense of the world. Furthermore, what you can talk about determines in its turn what you can think about. Language shapes and articulates our primitive, felt conceptions, and makes them manifest not only to others, but first and foremost to ourselves. We feel, of course, as if our thoughts are entirely our own, and in the sense that only we are having them at a particular time and place, that is indeed so, but the form in which we have them is shared with everyone else: we can think only in terms of meanings and assumptions we have in common with all those who share our culture, and we have no choice in the matter.

Culture imposes on its members far more than merely the language they speak and the way they think. Although our experience may be unique, culture defines its meaning. Just about all the evaluations we make of ourselves and others are shaped by the culture in which we live: we cannot step outside the network of common meanings which defines our very existence somehow to create a personal world (or, if we do, we will certainly be regarded by others as mad). For example, what it is to be male or female, adult or child, competent or incompetent, acceptable or unacceptable, good or bad in all the thousands of ways these judgements can be made, is determined always by reference to cultural standards over which the individual has no control at all – any more than s/he has control over the language s/he learns as an infant. In this way, our ideas about ourselves and our satisfaction or otherwise with the way we are will often depend heavily on cultural norms and standards which are far beyond the reach of any individual to change.

One important implication of this is that, contrary to what a lot of the psychotherapy and counselling industry would like us to believe, we cannot be self-creating, but can manoeuvre only in the room our culture allows us. We cannot create for ourselves alternative realities that liberate us from cultural constraints, perhaps by replacing them with more desirable inventions of our own. 'Stone walls do not a prison make' is a fine piece of wishful thinking, but in fact illustrates no more than the possibility of escaping *reality* into the *imagination*. Stone walls are precisely what make a prison, and if you're behind them you're a prisoner, however much you may fantasise about sunning yourself on a desert island.

A second important implication of the defining property of culture is that our sense of ourselves as persons is dependent on the integrity of the cultural forms of 'personhood'. If, for example, a particular cultural form starts to disintegrate – say the form 'masculinity/femininity' – individual people will begin to feel personally disintegrated in this respect. What is in fact a social phenomenon comes to be experienced by ordinary people as a personal problem.

Exactly this kind of thing has come about quite pervasively since the 1970s as, in the industrialised world at least, the amoral culture of business and the market has re-established the grip on society which was for a moment loosened by, in particular, the events surrounding the Second World War. Not only have conventional roles such as those of 'husband' and 'wife' changed radically, but the very conception of what it is to be a valuable and competent contributor to society has changed practically out of all recognition. This has meant that, quite apart from the bewildering redefinition of sex and gender roles many have found themselves struggling with, whole swathes of the middle-aged population, in particular, have experienced themselves as inadequate failures, anxiously grabbing at the opportunity trailed before them for early retirement.[12]

Because we do not have a popular psychology that recognises the dependency of the subjective experience of 'being a person' on cultural 'forms', the pain people feel in these kinds of circumstances is nearly always experienced in isolation, as a problem of personal inadequacy or 'relationship' difficulties. The example of Ian, in the previous chapter, shows how a man from a background where quite set and stable ideas of 'gender roles' were and to an extent still are the norm, becomes completely demoralised when he finds himself in a competitive 'market' of marital relations in which his wife not only challenges his traditional role but actually takes it over. Ian had no conception that society had changed, but just thought of himself as 'ill'. It took him a while to see that the pain he suffered was in fact not a form of illness, but a result of the experience of cultural disintegration. In other words, that's how people feel when an aspect of the culture on which they depend for their sense of self starts to disintegrate.

Jill's problems, similarly, had as much to do with the absence of any cultural norms about the proper conduct of second marriages (involving children from the first) as with any personal shortcomings of her own. Although her own background had no doubt to an extent sapped her confidence in herself and left her with a pretty punitive conscience, she was in fact a very able and perceptive woman, as sensitive as anyone could be to attending to the needs and wishes of others as a basis for social harmony; it was not knowing what the 'rules' were that made her life so difficult and potentiated her panic attacks.

In Keith's case the failure to acquire a workable idea of the relationship of inner experience to outer social behaviour seemed to be the result of having been brought up at a time, and in a particular class context of 'upward social mobility', where the principal cultural preoccupation was with the construction of an 'image' in which only the outer featured, and that in a particularly oversimplified and superficial form. One thing Keith had certainly not realised was that, among all those young people around him who he assumed were so much more 'together', there were many feeling exactly as disturbed and alienated.

In pointing out that the culture determines aspects of people that they cannot change – aspects usually regarded as 'personal' and 'psychological' – I am not arguing that they are unchangeable. The point is, rather, that they cannot usually be changed just by the individual in whose interest it may be to change them. They can certainly be changed through the operation of social power on a larger scale, as the examples above illustrate. It is also possible to negotiate cultural change politically. There seems little doubt that the women's movement has been influential in redefining gender roles, at least within some social strata, to an extent that has been concretely manifested in the lives of individuals (not always with their awareness, of course, and not necessarily either with their approval).

In relation to culture, we don't have much of a choice about whether we are 'normal' or not. If we are not 'normal', it may be either because we have for some reason been exposed to realities unlike those of others, or because the norms themselves are losing their integrity. Either way, there's not a great deal we can do about it as individuals, and to see 'abnormality' as some kind of personal lack or failing, perhaps to be put right by 'psychological intervention', sets up an entirely inappropriate framework in which to try to understand our subjective experience of ourselves and any emotional distress which may attach to it.

THE APPRECIATION OF CHARACTER

A particularly damaging effect of the obsession with normality which conventional psychology and psychiatry do so much to reinforce is to make us doubt the validity of our own experience. Many people, rather than being able to exist confidently at the centre of their own world, find themselves agonisingly conflicted over whether what they perceive, feel and conclude about things in their everyday dealings with others constitute *legitimate* perceptions, feelings and conclusions, or whether they are somehow reprehensibly unusual. 'Do other people feel, think, see things like me?' can become a question constantly posed to oneself in a kind of unremitting state of anxiety. Life may be lived in the secret dread that at any moment an unguarded comment will reveal the crazy eccentricity of one's perspective on life and/or relations with others.

This is, when one thinks about it, a very strange, not to say unfortunate, state of affairs. For the only certain knowledge you have of how human beings work is given to you through your own experience. Rather than asking yourself, via an apprehensive comparison with a mythical norm, 'What is it like to be human, and do I fit the description?', you could be realising through your own experience: 'So *this* is what it's like to be human.'

Confidence to believe one's own experience consists of a kind of boldness in which the individual takes himself or herself as the 'standard' of humanity and trusts his or her own subjectivity. This is not to suggest that everything one thinks or feels is necessarily true and real and genuine, but that the validity of thoughts and feelings, their acceptability, the claim they may have on the respectful attention of others, are *not* established in relation to their 'usualness' or 'normality'.

Anyone who abandons his or her own standpoint in order to reflect what s/he takes to be the 'normal' view (and all of us do this at least sometimes) risks losing the principal means s/he has for interpreting reality accurately and dependably (not, I should emphasise again, infallibly). Where this happens, people's ability to make judgements about the significance of their experience, to act spontaneously in their relations with others, etc., becomes tentative and vacillating, even paralysed, and decisions await the anxious, and quite possibly fruitless, reference to what is 'normal'.

We discover how it feels to be human by attending carefully to our own experience, and indeed (recognising that each person's experience is in one important respect unique) to the experience of others. To insist that only some kinds of supposedly 'normal' experience are in some sense valid or permissible is to commit an act of violence on all of us, since none of us is 'normal' in the singularity of our experience of life.

Breaking the anxious silence which dread of 'normality' tends to impose on people's revelation of their own experience can be tremendously reassuring. To discover that others are as eccentric as we are, that they too have unorthodox and unconventional thoughts and feelings, can be a huge relief, liberating us to think and feel what we like.[13] Great artists can perform this function. Listen to Tolstoy's account of his mother's death in his largely autobiographical *Childhood, Boyhood and Youth*:

I stopped at the door and looked but my eyes were too swollen with weeping and my nerves so unstrung that I could distinguish nothing. The light, the gold brocade, the velvet, the tall candlesticks, the pink lace-trimmed pillow . . . , the cap with ribbons, and something else of a transparent wax-like colour – all ran together in a strange blur. I climbed on to a chair to look at her face but there in its place I again saw the same pale-yellow translucent object. I could not believe that this was her face. I began to stare hard at it and gradually began to recognize the dear familiar features. I shuddered with horror when I realized that this was she. But why were the closed eyes so sunken? Why that dreadful pallor, and the blackish spot under the transparent skin on one cheek?

And later,

Having slept soundly and peacefully all that night, as is always the case after great distress, I awoke with my eyes dry and my nerves soothed. At ten o'clock we were called to the service which was celebrated before the body was borne away. The room was filled with weeping servants and peasants who had come in to take leave of their mistress. During the service I wept as befitted the occasion, crossed myself and bowed to the ground, but I did not pray in spirit and was more or less unmoved: I was more concerned with the fact that the new jacket they had dressed me in was too tight under the arms; I thought about how not to dirty the knees of my trousers when I knelt down, and kept stealthily observing all the people who were present. My father stood at the head of the coffin. He was as white as a sheet and obviously had difficulty in restraining his tears. His tall figure in a black frock-coat, his pale expressive face and his movements, graceful and assured as ever when he crossed himself, bowed, touching the floor with his fingers, took a candle from the priest's hand or approached the coffin were extremely effective; but, I don't know why, I did not like him being able to show himself off so effectively at that moment . . .[14]

Tolstoy was not a man to be terrorised by the norm. He does not ask himself what he ought to have been thinking and feeling as he viewed his mother's corpse, whether others' attention would, like his, have been drawn to the blackish spot under her skin. He knew well enough that his show of grief at the ceremony was merely outward and formal, and he does not hesitate to reveal his preoccupation with the tightness of his jacket or his reservations about his father's demeanour. In recounting with such candour what was after all his unique experience, he does not shock us with his eccentricity but reminds us what it is to be human.

What we know about the world is given to us through our unique experience of it. Even though we can only formulate and express that knowledge in terms shared with all the other members of our culture, nobody else can claim to know better than we what we saw, felt or thought about at any particular time. Nobody can judge our reality as somehow being less or more adequate than some notion of what is 'normal'. It is not our place to *judge* each other's realities, but rather to enquire into them sympathetically and respectfully.

Even where somebody's knowledge of reality seems to depart radically from our own, it makes no sense to conclude that somehow their experience is invalid or that the world they occupy is in some sense not as real as the average. People can, of course, misinterpret their experience, make mistakes or lie about it, but its *normality* is not the measure of its validity.

The fact that we share the same bodily structure is the grounding of our sympathy with each other and this in turn the basis of a morality which makes treating others as we would wish to be treated ourselves axiomatic.[15] Sharing a common culture, as well as providing much of the fabric of what we take to be our 'personality', is what makes it possible to understand, communicate and share our knowledge with each other. Our experience of life, on the other hand, is what gives us our knowledge and makes us the unique characters we are.

Rather than engaging in a continuous, fearful self-assessment to establish how far we deviate from what is 'normal', we would do well to regard ourselves as characters with an experience of life and a unique knowledge of the world which, far from hiding it in shamed silence, we should be ready to impart to those less expert than we. Only you have been where you have been and only you know what it felt like: you are indeed the expert in your own existence and it may well be the case that there are things others could usefully know which only you could tell them.

Catherine, for example (see Chapter Two), was an expert in betrayal and, having experienced it in various forms throughout her early life, spent much of her time trying to ensure that it didn't happen again. In this, it should be noted, she was remarkably successful: her vigilance meant that all her relationships were ended by her before any man got the chance to inflict on her the kind of pain she had experienced as a child. Normality and abnormality are irrelevant to an understanding of her predicament: she was, for very good reasons, a jealous character. She anticipated life in line with the lessons it had taught her, and though those lessons may have been uncommon, they were certainly not 'wrong'.[16] No doubt it was necessary for her to learn new and different lessons, but that did not mean that she could or should repudiate the old. Experience such as hers has a great deal to tell us about the injuries we do each other, often in the name of love; paradoxical as it may seem, her knowledge is actually valuable.

We seem to find it easier to pay attention to and learn from characters in novels than we do from characters in real life. *Madame Bovary*, for example, is no doubt a wonderful study of sexual passion and betrayal from which a huge amount may be learned by those whose lives have followed more pedestrian paths; but why dismiss similar insights as 'pathological' or 'abnormal' when they are afforded by the living characters we encounter in the course of our everyday existence?

Your knowledge of the world is hard won, carved in blood and bone and nervous tissue. Your character is in many respects the history of your embodiment. Perhaps it is because modern life is lived so much in the context of electronic technology on the one hand and pure fantasy, fuelled and exploited by commercial interests, on the other, that we pay so little heed to our embodiment. We like to think that painful experience can be erased and replaced like a magnetic recording or that, if we really, really want to, we can summon up the will to live in accordance with our wishes, unbound by the realities of our too solid flesh. But it is not so; the world imprints itself on our bodies and our bodies constitute the living, material record of our path through worldly space and time.

In the rawness of our experience, the chaotic jumble of our impressions, impulses and dreams, we are all eccentrics. Whatever the lessons of your life, there is nothing to be ashamed of or to fear about them. Fear and shame are introduced only through the process of invidious comparison set up by a mythical 'normality' and used in particular to disqualify the experience of those whose knowledge of the world suggests that all is not well with the organisation of our society. As the character you are, the embodied product of your times and places, you have a right to be taken seriously, for your knowledge to count. Truly shameful are those (usually more powerful) others who sit in judgement of your character and your knowledge and loftily discount them – perhaps by giving you a 'diagnosis'.

For the normalising eye – whether of the professional diagnostician or merely the everyday, defensive scrutiny of invidious comparison – is cynical, suspicious and unsympathetic. It looks past the patent reality of the individual person in search of inadequacy and duplicity. In contrast, the loving regard of the connoisseur of character – Charles Dickens is the supreme example – believes what it sees, wonders at and positively savours the diversity and complexity of our embodied efforts to solve the often tragic riddles life sets us.

Take, for example, the woman who, brought up as an orphan correctly but without love in a family of her dead parents' relatives, spends her adult life trying to please implacable men. She has no sense of herself as important, but uses all her gifts and all her (not inconsiderable) moral strength to try to make her successive marriages to two men (the first died) work. Both men are weak and abusive towards her; one of them verbally extremely cruel. How easy it would be for the therapist, whose efforts to 'normalise' her she steadfastly resists, to talk about 'personality disorder', 'masochistic needs' etc. and to dismiss her endurance of unhappiness as a form of weakness. But to do that one would simply have to ignore the reality of her sweetly tolerant, vulnerable courage. Her existence is in many ways a kind of lived enquiry into the mysterious nature of love, pursued with a gentle but inflexible stubbornness which, though one can see that it is doomed to eternal disappointment, is nonetheless moving and admirable for that. Hers is a character to be appreciated, not scorned.

It is above all important that you take *your own* character and experience seriously. It is the only firm anchorage you have in the world. This is, of course, not to say that you have nothing to learn from others, nor that everything you think and believe is right – far from it – but it is to say that the ultimate test of truth must, for you, be against your knowledge of the world. Sticking by what you know, maintaining respect for the lessons of your life, can be uncomfortable, and it is easy to be seduced by the blandishments of magical wishfulness or the security of authority. But in the end what is important is staying sensitively in touch with the real world of your experience, because that's the only way you will be able to influence the events that determine what happens to you and to others. It is essential to know when the emperor is clothed and when he is not, even though people will not always thank you for telling them.

The proper attitude of those seeking to help people in distress is one of appreciation and respect. The experience of suffering is not invalid, but has, as well as its reasons, its lessons. There is a great deal to be learned from people who know how a life can be derailed by misfortune or tragedy, and the lesson has usually very little to do with their own personal culpability. Denigration, probably the most widespread professional attitude (however subtly 'clinical' its packaging), has absolutely no place in any kind of psychiatric or psychological help. But neither, more surprisingly perhaps, has blanket approval.

I have already indicated, in the discussion of therapeutic comfort in Chapter One, that there seem to me to be difficulties with the idea that therapists can or should dispense a kind of loving concern for their patients. I do not mean that this does not sometimes happen, nor that it is necessarily wrong when it does; the point is that the provision of love cannot be professionally guaranteed. To undertake to love somebody for a fee must involve a form of deception if only because love cannot be willed.[17]

The same is true of the more technical-sounding 'unconditional positive regard' ('warmth' for short) of Rogerian counselling. Whether or not a therapist approves unconditionally of a patient is, even if it is something s/he can choose to do, irrelevant to their transaction. It is not the therapist's business either to approve or disapprove, but it is his or her business to treat people politely, kindly and with respect. As a matter of fact it is easy for therapists to *like* patients because of the balance of power between them: the commonest reason for disliking someone is being threatened by them, and the situation in which therapist and patient find themselves is one that protects the therapist from threat. But the fact that this is very often the case doesn't mean that it has to be. Psychotherapists would be very strange animals if at times they did not find themselves disapproving of someone they are trying to help.

The point is not how therapists should *feel* about people (for over that they have no control), but how they should *treat* them. I see no reason why you should not expect and require from your psychiatrist, psychologist or psychotherapist the same minimum standards of politeness and respect you would expect from any other professional person. Given that patients are, at the time of consulting professional helpers, often in considerable distress, we might further hope that they would be treated with kindness and compassion beyond the average.

It is, as well, a tremendous privilege to be taken into the confidence of so many different characters whose experience of life can be so revealing of the way the world looks. An element of gratitude, even humility, would not be misplaced in the professional response.

CHAPTER FOUR

Troublesome Worlds: People and Power

Emotional distress is not simply a personal matter. To understand why you are suffering – and to establish from that whether
there is anything you can do about it – it is necessary to extend
your enquiry far beyond the boundaries of your personal experience and relationships. Most conventional approaches to
psychotherapy, certainly the best known, have not only failed
to recognise the importance of this point but have actually made
it more difficult to grasp.

For, as was pointed out in Chapter One, the claustrophobic
setting of the therapeutic relationship naturally confines the
gaze of the participants to the psychological dynamics of the
consulting room. The therapist examines the patient for signs of
personal pathology and the patient looks to the therapist for
techniques of cure. The raw material of therapy becomes what
the patient can express, remember, imagine or dream, and the
main means of cure is limited to the influence the therapist can
exert over the patient's mental and emotional life merely by
talking and 'interpreting'.

To be fair, many psychotherapists have recognised that
outcome in psychotherapy is restricted to what can be achieved
through the non-specific factors involved in an essentially
personal relationship between patient and therapist, and that
evidence of profound, lasting improvement from psychotherapy is weak.[1] However, this (no doubt for sound commercial reasons) has on the whole not led psychologists and
psychotherapists to modify their theories about the causes and
cures of emotional distress, but rather to unleash ever more

sophisticated and intense research effort on the consulting room and its beleaguered occupants in the illusion that the holy grail of therapeutic effectiveness will at last lie revealed.[2]

The consulting-room model of human psychology which has developed over the last hundred years or so has had a profound effect on our idea of ourselves, reinforcing an emphasis within our culture on personal responsibility and autonomy in relation to psychological suffering. The effect of this has been to lift us out of the social environment and attribute to us not only a distinctly moral role in the acquisition of our own troubles but also the power to better our lot principally through our own devices (though perhaps needing a therapist to act as a kind of midwife to our efforts). The rest of this book will be taken up with an attempt to suggest alternatives to this model which are less illusory, and hence ultimately less damaging to our ability to cope with distress.

What the consulting-room model does above all is to inflate enormously, and grossly misleadingly, the power of individuals to take charge of their own fate. Rather than being one of two essentially autonomous agents able to negotiate profound personal change through consulting-room transactions, we are in fact infinitessimal social atoms caught in a vast and complex web of power which, among other things, permeates the consulting room through and through. Not only can we not choose our place in society, but neither can we select our personal experience, decide how to feel about it, nor determine the quality of our relationships through acts of will. It is not, as we shall see later in this book, that we are power*less*, but our powers are very strictly limited by the social environment in which we live, much more so than is envisaged by almost any approach to psychotherapy.

The issue of 'free will versus determinism' has tended to polarise opinion between those who take the view that human beings are entirely free to fashion their own fate and those who believe that every human action, no matter how minute, is determined by the inexorable play of cause and effect in a universe where everything is foreordained by the iron laws of science. In the field of the psychological therapies this split separates some of the wilder humanistic and existentialist therapists on one side from the hard-nosed, 'scientific' behaviourists on the other.

As I hope will become clear later (Chapter Six), I think this dispute is so difficult to resolve mainly because it poses the wrong question. It is not the case that *either* we are free *or* we are determined; some of us are a lot more free than others. The interesting question to ask is: *How* free are we in any particular situation to obtain what we want or need? Another way to approach this is to enquire into the amount of power available to a person to change things and the nature and extent of the powers that bear down on him or her to impede change, or indeed to change his or her circumstances disadvantageously.

What makes it possible to live a comfortable life, psychologically as much as materially, depends very heavily on the influences that impinge upon us at any given time within the social environment. Our freedom to change depends on the extent to which we can modify these influences. Much of the time, we may be able to do very little. Most approaches to psychotherapy take very little account of this limitation on our freedom – not surprisingly, perhaps, in view of the vested interest therapy has in the promise of change.

When you think about it, the language of therapy and the principal concepts it concerns itself with are extraordinarily unlike the main preoccupations of your everyday life. Whereas almost before you wake in the morning you are likely to be worrying about the rent or the mortgage, whether you'll keep your job or pass your exam, therapeutic language seems to have a lofty – at times almost contemptuous – disregard for such matters, as if they were merely distractions from the really important issues of your unconscious desires and fantasies and the ways in which, through them, you are supposedly creating your own problems.[3]

Therapy has to take this line, of course, because it has to concentrate on aspects of your 'psyche' and 'personality' which could plausibly be altered by you. The difficulty is, though, that once outside the consulting room the real world very quickly makes clear what it is and is not going to let you do. What 'makes us tick' (and loudly, at that) is not the ideas, wishes and plans inside our heads, but the pushes and pulls of the all too material forces which structure the social environment. The ideas, wishes and plans inside our heads are, to be sure, how we *experience* the material forces which press down upon us, but they are not identical with them, and in fact, taken on their own, have no power at all to alter anything.

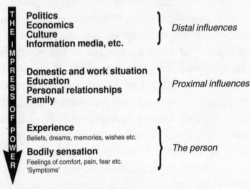

Figure 1: Influence of the social environment

THE STRUCTURE OF POWER

As suggested in Figure 1, what we most immediately *feel* are the influences of a world which stretches far beyond the individual person. These influences are mediated by our experience, filtered through our interpretations of the past and anticipations of the future as well as shaped and made sense of by all the cultural equipment we have acquired. The credibility of most approaches to psychotherapy hangs on the idea that we can work directly on our experience in order to change how we feel. But much of this experience – what one might call our psychological meaning-systems – is itself the result of external influence and has little, if any, power to change itself. There is no independent dynamic of experience that would allow us to detach *meaning* from the material reality which creates it and somehow mould it into an alternative reality where we can live more comfortably. We can try to live in our imagination, but the imaginary is precisely not real.

Our experience is acquired through the most proximal influences upon us: those which are transmitted by the people and things we encounter directly in everyday life. We are always, so to speak, up against a world which impinges directly on our senses, and anything at all that comes to be part of our experience does so via immediate personal contact. But this does not mean that the most proximal influences are necessarily the most powerful. For proximal influences are in turn shaped and held in place in the social structure by higher-order powers which act on them.

There is no great measure of agreement among sociologists on the definition of 'power', though pretty well all seem to agree that it is about getting other people to do things. For present purposes power could be defined as the means of obtaining security or advantage. Such means come in a variety of forms. Coercive, economic and ideological power seem to be the commonest types to be distinguished, most frequently encountered within such societies as ours in the form of military might, wealth and the ability to manipulate information and meaning. Different kinds of power often go together, but this need not always be the case – any adult, however poor and bereft of other forms of influence, has an ultimate recourse to brute force in some circumstances (probably exercised most frequently over children, unfortunately).

It is infrequent for really great power to be possessed by individuals, and even billionaires depend on large numbers of other people if they are actually to make their wealth count in the world to any significant extent. For most 'ordinary' people, what power they have usually stems from their association with others – being part, that is, of a relatively powerful organisation or group. But power certainly operates to the greater advantage of the few rather than the many: though the tyrant or dictator will be dependent on an army for the maintenance of his power, he will almost certainly be living a more comfortable life than his soldiers.

Although the levers of power are likely to be concentrated in the hands of a relatively small number of groups and individuals, its actual operation does not have to be a particularly conscious or self-conscious process. Like the working of Adam Smith's 'invisible hand', the distribution of power throughout society takes place without any need for deliberate, meticulous planning on anybody's part.

The principal medium of transmission of power in present-day Western societies is probably via the manipulation of self-interest. This is largely an automatic process, in which all the various official and unofficial institutions within society play their part, from big business, government and the media at one end to the black economy, the family and the school playground at the other. In order to 'hold people in place' by manipulating their interests, it is not necessary, as I have written elsewhere,

to maintain a very highly explicit, precision-engineered system; rather, the application of power would be a bit like tipping a bucket of water down the side of a hillock – by one route or another it will find its way to the bottom, facilitated by (and so deepening) available channels, cutting some new ones, swamping small obstructions, flowing round (and thereby isolating) little islands of resistance, and so on.[4]

THE EXPERIENCE OF POWER

What all this means is that the proximal events and relationships that loom largest in your experience of life, though they are certainly of the greatest significance as far as you are concerned, are not necessarily the most important causes of your joys and sorrows. The teacher who instructs you badly and fails your exam, the boss who makes you redundant, the husband who doesn't listen when you want to talk, the father who lashes out unpredictably, all have a pretty powerful effect on you, but a longer perspective might show that, because of the influences pressing down on them, they have very little choice in how they conduct themselves. The teacher may be following a politically determined curriculum, the boss transmitting the policy of a newly merged company, and so on. It may of course be in some theoretical sense that they *could* act otherwise, it's just that to do so they would have to act irrationally.

This is easily enough understood by most adults, but even so we rarely see beyond the actions of those who trespass against us to the reasons that might argue their forgiveness: emotionally, we live very much in the proximal world. For children, whose power is so minuscule in relation to that of their parents, it is even more difficult to get an objective perspective on what is happening. To a small child, it is likely to seem that power starts and stops with its parents, that they have absolute freedom to shape the world as they wish. Planted in the infant's head from the word go is a philosophy of which some aspects stay with most of us for the rest of our lives: the belief that beings with absolute power must have reasons for their actions which they have freely chosen.

A particularly poignant result of this philosophy for small children is that they are virtually bound to attribute parental displeasure, or even cruelty and hatred, to their own moral or material shortcomings – for what other reason could such powerful beings possibly have for behaving the way they do? 'If my mother hates me, it can only be because I am, in some respect at least, hateful.' Many are the fifty- and sixty-year-olds who seek still to earn the love of a parent who abused them throughout their childhood, as if they might still be able to uncover and make up for the faults or blemishes which so displeased.

The aspect of this philosophy that lodges stubbornly with pretty well all of us is the idea that the *causes* of actions reside in the *intentions* of those who carry them out. Even after we achieve a degree of sophistication which permits us to see that there may be reasons for what we do over which we have no control, we still habitually look first at the supposed intention – we still tend to blame others and ourselves as if they and we could have done otherwise.

I do not by any means wish to argue that we are all the victims of an inexorable determinism and that none of us can help what we are doing. The point is rather that we need to get sufficient distance from the immediate impact of our proximal experience and the passions it engenders to see that accurate explanations of our own and others' conduct involve much more than just intentions. And the point of doing this is so that we may achieve a more accurate understanding of ourselves. For example, my mother may have had other reasons for hating me than simply my hatefulness.

The way we experience and deal with the difficulties and pressures of life will always depend to some extent on lessons we have learned from the past, and our perspective on those lessons is always proximal. Enquiring into past experience, perhaps attempting to extend our perspective a little into the more distal causes of it, is often a good idea not because it leads to insights inspiring instant change, but because it can correct conceptual errors which obscure our view of reality. Realisation that, after all, the cause of my mother's hatred was not my hatefulness, though it won't lead instantaneously to my feeling better about myself, will at least perhaps give me reasons for believing that hatefulness is not just an inevitable and ineradicable part of my nature, and this may clear the path for action which I would not otherwise have been able to take. (There will be more to say about these issues in Chapter Seven.)

The impress of power, then, though in all probability origi-
nating at considerable distance from individuals, is inevitably
experienced by them proximally, through the mediation of
those with whom they are in daily contact. The infant's experience is impressed upon it bodily – 'wired in' – at least as soon as
it emerges from the womb. Experience is not provisional or
hypothetical, it cannot be picked over so that some parts can be
selected and others rejected: it is, so to speak, stamped on the
child's body as the indelible imprint of reality.

From the child's perspective, then, what all-powerful adults
around it do is of the first importance for its understanding of
the way the world is. The baby is thrown at birth (if not before)
into a predicament from which there is no escape and the
conclusions it draws from the experience are likely to stay with
it lifelong.

At first, the child has no words with which to organise and
think about what is happening to it; for the first year or two its
experience will be recorded in the form of feelings (and anticipations) of pleasure, pain, apprehension and excitement, and,
no doubt, various kinds of images associated with them. Only
gradually, with the increasing availability of language, will these
become differentiated into coherent ideas and thoughts.
Furthermore, the feelings and images in which our earliest
experiences are registered are not simply replaced or supplanted
by more 'rational', language-based modes, but rather provide
the foundation for them. Lying beneath the articulate ideas,
thoughts and descriptions we may have of our experience are
always inexpressible aspects of them which are simply felt or
pictured.

Nor is it just in early childhood that experience may be
recorded non-verbally – there are all kinds of circumstances in
later life (varying from simple unfamiliarity to extreme threat)
when words fail us not only in the expression but also in the
acquisition of experience.[5] It is again important to emphasise
that there is no question of choice over the impress of

experiences such as these: we cannot choose not to undergo them, nor can we opt for them to be different once we have undergone them.

The absence or unavailability of language is probably what explains the frightening quality of 'uncanniness'[6] that sometimes accompanies feelings, experiences or 'compulsive' actions in later life that seem to the individual involved profoundly irrational. What enables us to 'know' what we're doing is being able to rehearse our actions in words. Where words fail us, it may seem to us that we are losing our minds.

Both pleasure and pain experienced at a time before we could successfully attach words to them may well have a lot to do with, for example, difficulties such as 'eating disorders', in which sufferers find themselves quite unable to resist impulses to conduct which they know perfectly well to be self-destructive. Again, 'uncanny' anxiety may surround particular circumstances or activities in a way that strongly suggests the return of feelings, and sometimes indistinct images, from a time when they were simply raw, literally inexpressible, experiences of the imposition of adult power. The sexual abuse of small children before they have had the opportunity to develop a vocabulary which could make sense of what is happening to them seems often to leave them in later life with a painfully intangible sense of 'something' distressing pervading areas of their experience without their being able to say exactly what, but perhaps in the form of vague, dreamlike images.

Even though the acquisition of language may help make it possible for us to register events in a way we can subsequently make sense of, it still does not permit us, as children, to step back from our experience and criticise it. The child is locked into the perspective of its immediate environment – usually its family – and has no way of knowing, at least until it goes to school, that there are other perspectives. Moreover, it takes an exceptionally reflective person to question in later life whether the impressions of reality s/he received at various points throughout childhood were in any way unusual – and even if it is realised that they were, it doesn't make them any the less real.

Parental power can operate in all sorts of ways to shape experience, to reinforce autonomy or to undermine confidence. We have already seen in Chapter Two how Heather's observation of her mother's flirtation with a neighbour was greeted with immediate, punitive disconfirmation from the two people on whom she most depended for accurate information about the world. This event – no doubt the only one of its kind in her experience – significantly weakened Heather's confidence in what was, after all, a perfectly sound grasp of reality. She could neither abandon her view nor entirely trust it, and if she became aware of being oppressed or abused by others (as for example with her husband's affair) she could never quite believe in the validity of her judgement enough to take any kind of definite action.

Elizabeth's 'bulimia', experienced by her as simply a shameful, not to say very puzzling, form of greed, was in fact a fairly obvious extension of conduct she could scarcely have failed to acquire as a child. Sandwiched between two siblings favoured by her rather stern, ascetic parents, she could only by stealth obtain quite ordinary pleasures of life. Just as Heather hung admirably but fearfully on to her accurate view of her mother's sexual adventure, so Elizabeth had enough sense of self-preservation to acquire for herself the odd treat. But she could do so only in secrecy and with the ever present threat of the betrayal of her brothers and inevitable parental disapproval. This pattern became a way of life, an embodied part of Elizabeth's character, and she could not simply divest herself of it, even when she could see how she had come to acquire it.

The impress of parental disapproval is extraordinarily difficult to shift. Almost all Heather's often extremely insightful comments about others are prefaced by 'I expect it's me' or 'I know I must be wrong.' Elizabeth has not been able to sympathise with or approve of her healthy childhood stubbornness: her parents' imputation of badness (in the form of 'greed' etc.)

has become part of her own in-built make-up, and she is now the first to be disgusted with herself.

The whole of our lives can be shaped by the authorisation of parental power – what has and has not been permitted us during our formative years. Norman, for example, has throughout his somewhat erratic life always had an almost superstitious sense that something would turn up in times of trouble to bail him out of difficulty. In fact, something always has – in the shape of his mother. As a child he could have had no more powerful ally – even his father quailed before her – and he would have had to be extraordinarily self-denying (even had such a course been open to him) to turn down her support. But the alliance was not without its costs as far as Norman was concerned. He knew as a boy that some of his desires and activities would have to be concealed from his mother if he was not to test her loyalty too far, and so he developed the kind of double life which resulted eventually in his drinking and gambling running out of control. In fact, he had very little autonomy: while the conduct of his 'open' life was licensed by his mother, it was not underpinned by his own desire, and so periodically ran out of steam. The secret life of his desire, on the other hand, because it was not authorised, could not be given any kind of direction, nor be directly acknowledged even by himself.

THE REALITY OF POWER

There is nothing mysterious about the potency of parental influence: it is derived simply from the fact that, relative to their children, parents are so powerful. They hold all the levers that control the child's material as well as psychological development: not only is the infant dependent on its parents for its physical survival, the most basic sensations of pleasure and pain, but they also mediate its very access to reality through the discriminations of *meaning* which they encourage or discourage, permit or forbid. It is via parental influence that the embodied foundations of character are laid.

The irony is, of course, that though parents set the boundaries of the child's universe, they may in the wider scheme of things have extremely little power themselves. The less power available to parents, the less their room for manoeuvre in a possibly far from benign world, the narrower will be the options they are able to give their children (and the more uncomfortable the child's life will probably become). Indeed, relatively powerless though they are, children can in some circumstances become an outright threat to their parents.

For example, where a child starts to observe or conceptualise things that introduce elements of uncontrollability into the parents' world, issues they simply cannot, for one reason or another, handle, the parental response may be extremely – sometimes horrifically – punitive. It is likely, for instance, that Mick's mother's excesses were sparked at least in part by her gifted and sensitive son's ability to confront her with aspects of her own reality that were simply unbearable. I have certainly encountered people who were quite literally tortured as children (one with a flaming gas cigarette lighter) because they would not deny seeing things that threatened to destroy a parent's fragile hold on family life. The familiar phenomenon of a mother's silent complicity in her husband's sexual abuse of their child no doubt also has a lot to do with the necessities of the life in which she is caught.

For the most part, however, parental power is not exercised deliberately; indeed, because parents are often themselves so powerless, they may not have the slightest idea that they are wielding any influence at all. But parents are powerful in relation to their children simply because they are there, occupying the role society has accorded them. Nobody, for instance, could have felt less powerful than Jill's mother, whose whole adult life seemed to consist of one long demonstration of her incapacity and reliance on others (including her own children). And yet her anxiety constituted the controlling force around which the entire family had to arrange itself, shaping a reality from which Jill will probably never entirely escape.

It is necessary to dwell on the issue of parental power because of its importance for the formation of character. The physical machinery underpinning our relations with the world around us – the embodiment of our psychological meaning-systems – is unavoidably established under the shadow of parental influence. But this does not mean that early family life is the only, or necessarily the principal, source of later distress. Parental influence can be for good as well as for ill, and in any case we live our lives under the impress of powers that are mediated in many ways other than simply through the family.

I have already suggested in the discussion of 'current predicaments' in Chapter Two how much our emotional suffering comes about as the result of pressures in our everyday lives. If these are to be properly understood, it is important once again to emphasise that strains and stresses that seem to be a matter of essentially personal relations are likely in fact to originate in far more distal regions of the social environment. We experience them as personal merely because that is the only way in which they can be mediated – social influence is only ever transmitted by *people*, and it is the people we encounter in everyday life whom we tend to blame for the ills that befall us.

It would for example be very easy to see Gina's predicament as stemming almost solely from her relationship with her husband. This, certainly, was the way she experienced it herself, and it would have been hard for anyone listening to her story not to become indignant about the treatment she received at his hands. And yet her very attempts to 'solve' the problem, most of which eventually consisted of abortive alliances with other men (one or two of whom were indeed generous and kind), only served to demonstrate how much more complicated her situation was. Her lack of education and very low self-confidence rendered her both ashamed and dependent in a way which introduced painful complications into her relationships with any man, no matter how tolerant he might be, and yet the possibilities open to her of making good her deficits – for example, by 'going back to school' – were limited by all kinds of real material constraints. Similarly, the need for her to learn independence from men simply as protectors and providers was greatly hampered by the necessity of caring for her two children during out-of-school hours and holidays. She had very little money, and virtually all her family was out of work. Even while her marriage lasted it was so embedded in material privation that virtually any relationship would have been strained to breaking point.

'Society' does not consist of individual men and women picking and choosing what they would like to do and whom they would like to be with, constrained only by the amount of wealth they can scrape together through their own enterprise. Were things really like this, Margaret Thatcher would have been right – there would be no society, just a terrifying 'state of nature' in which everyone would be out for him- or herself. As social beings, we inhabit an environment structured by powers that *hold us in place*. How much room we have for manoeuvre will depend upon the extent of the powers available to us. For most of us, these are extremely limited.

Most of the time we cannot even see where the influences that we experience proximally come from. All we can see is what we take to be the intentions of others, and all we feel we can do is to resolve to alter our circumstances, get on our bikes. But the uncovering of intentions and the making of resolutions doesn't seem to get us very far; and not surprisingly, because all the resolution in the world is quite useless without power, and even the kinds of power that may be available to individuals are usually puny in comparison with the higher-order, distal powers which determine the social structure and our place within it.

One of the most disheartening experiences of 'doing psychotherapy' is to observe the tremendous courage with which people can tackle their problems and *still* fail to solve them. Gina, for example, was brave to the point of self-destruction in setting out to do something about her predicament, but the world which she came up against in the process was just too harshly unyielding, and over and over again her only recourse was to fall back on her one 'asset' – her attractiveness to men – to save herself and her children from complete destitution. And even that path was doomed, because she could not *choose* a man from the position of independence she lacked the powers to achieve; she had to persuade herself each time that 'this is the one' just as her original 'choice' of husband, though far from suitable, offered her just about the only way out of an intolerable situation.

Luke, similarly, resolved to lift himself out of the trough he found himself in by trying to repair the damage that had been done to his education when in his teens. There is no doubt that he had the necessary intellectual resources: he was very bright and had an original, perceptive mind which, in other circumstances, could have brought him considerable academic success. But nobody can act simply under their own steam, and the material and psychological hurdles were just too great for Luke. He had to support himself on a pitifully low income and he was deeply in debt. The insecurity of his job was a constant worry. In order to achieve his aim of studying social sciences at university, he would have first had to apply himself to the grind of preliminary qualifications. He received absolutely no support within the social stratum he occupied, which was geared to quite other means of survival: family members as well as acquaintances simply laughed at what they saw as his pretentiousness. Luke almost fell apart trying to keep his nerve long enough to get started on evening classes, but, inevitably, starved of any material and almost all emotional sustenance, it failed him.

It is, in my experience, not the case that people do not wish or do not try to tackle the difficulties, past and present, that beset them. Neither is it the case that when their efforts fail it can be put down to their 'resistance', their psychological weakness or their personal 'inadequacy'. It is because they lack the powers to make a difference. Sadly, however, this is rarely the way they see it themselves: having battled long and hard against impossible odds, even the bravest and most stoical souls are likely to berate themselves for what they see as *moral* failure. How well we have been schooled into blaming ourselves for our deprivation!

THE INADEQUACY OF THE CONSULTING-ROOM MODEL

Psychotherapy, of course, has been absolutely no help in this predicament. Although often very accurately establishing through a lengthy process of clarification exactly how past and present relationship problems and material difficulties have contributed to individuals' distress, psychotherapy proceeds then to burden them with the responsibility for their own 'cure', as if feeling and acting in new ways depended solely on their personal will. But though we may well come, or be brought therapeutically, to see the truth – even the error of our ways – putting matters right is not simply a matter of seeing things differently. Things happen to us in a real world structured by real powers, and though there may be some variability in the way we experience this process, we *cannot* experience it any way we like. Psychologically as well as bodily, we are held in place by influences over which, for the most part, we have absolutely no control.

Conditioned as we are by the consulting-room model and entrenched cultural ideas of personal responsibility and will power, this is likely to seem a bitter pill to swallow. Can I really be saying that very often nothing can be done about the kinds of emotional distress addressed by psychotherapy? Of course I am not saying that. What I am saying is that the types of solution offered by most approaches to psychotherapy are illusory. The first thing we have to do is understand and face up to the nature of our predicament, to take seriously the fact that the origins of our troubles lie not in the way we see things, nor even in the intentions of those with whom our lives intersect, but often in the distal powers which shape our social environment. If that involves disillusionment, so much the better. There is no virtue in labouring under illusions.

At the heart of human experience there lies a paradox which, as well as causing us endless difficulty, is a perpetual source of illusion and mystification. This is that what seem to us *subjectively* to be the most powerful influences on our lives are *objectively* the weakest. The fact that we can only directly experience life proximally means that we are constantly overwhelmed by the impress of power at the point where, just about literally, it impacts on our bodies. The evidence of our senses tells us what is causing us pain. It is very nearly impossible to doubt that what offends our eyes or ears, what stabs directly into our nervous system, is the cause of our problems. Seeing, hearing, feeling are believing.

The child who reels under his father's fist can have little doubt about who is the cause of his problems, and in a sense, of course, he is right. Talk to his remorseful father, though, and you are likely to find that he is aware of a whole host of pressures which led to his 'just not being able to stop' himself. Our difficulty is that we cannot by nature easily detach experience from explanation. What impinges most powerfully on our bodies looks incontrovertibly like the reason for our pain. But of course it is not so. The white snooker ball hitting a red can only narrowly be said to be 'the cause' of its movement, and hardly at all 'the reason' for it. If we are to understand why we feel as we do, we have to look beyond the people and things that simply mediate the distal powers which set things in motion.

But it is difficult to look beyond, if only often for the simple reason that we cannot see. It is as if there stretches around us a power horizon beyond which the chains of cause and effect mediating influential powers are hidden from our view. Our private experience, far from giving us privileged information about the reasons for our troubles, is actually misleading, for, overwhelming as it is, we are likely to attribute to it explanatory power it doesn't actually have. Certainly, only we can say *what* we are feeling (wherein, as we have seen, lies the source of our uniqueness), but when it comes to saying *why* we are feeling it, matters are very different.

For when it comes to the explanation of experience, the experiencing individual is in no stronger position than anyone else – indeed, it could well be weaker. This is obvious in the case of children. A child's power horizon is very close indeed, and, as has already been suggested, children are likely to attribute a degree of freedom to adults far greater than they really have; an adult observer of the child's predicament is, if reasonably unbiased, likely to have a much more accurate explanation of it than the child itself.

How far you are able to identify the reasons for what is happening to you will depend on the distance to your power horizon; that is, on the amount of accurate information available to you about the chains of influence that end up ultimately impressing themselves directly upon you. It is perfectly possible in any given situation that there will be others with a better view. People sharing a proximal world will be more or less in the same boat and so surrounded by the same horizon. Like children, we frequently attribute to each other more power than we actually have. It often happens, for example, that superiors at work, or bureaucratic officials of one kind or another, are thought by those dealing with them to have far more power than is actually the case to inflict difficulties or solve problems. A friendly word from the boss can carry a degree of reassurance out of all proportion to his actual power: however sincerely he delivers it, the board may at that very moment be planning to 'restructure' your job out of existence.

The difficulty that confronts us as we try to make sense of our lives and order our relationships is, then, that we are necessarily in ignorance of many of the factors that bear down upon us to influence our conduct. What we tend to do in this situation is search ourselves and each other for intentions and motives which might explain our actions. On the whole, I think, we are not very clear about what intentions and motives are exactly, nor about what is the difference between them. Motives are perhaps regarded as slightly more suspect than intentions – slightly dishonourable, often 'ulterior' aims which we are aware of but want to keep quiet about. Intentions are more upfront – the things we are trying honourably to achieve, though not necessarily always with success.

Motives, certainly, are at a slightly greater distance from us than intentions. Intentions seem personal, private, things that move us from the inside. Whether you could, plausibly, have the right to tell me what my intentions are is open to question – maybe you could suggest what they are, negotiate a view of them, so to speak, but not just tell me. Motives are a bit different, often seen as more external. My *Shorter OED* defines 'motive' as 'that which moves or induces a person to act in a certain way; a desire, fear, reason, etc., which influences a person's volition'. So motives are not just personal, internal things. It would be perfectly plausible for you to tell me what my motives are because what moves or induces me to act may be just as open to your inspection as to mine – quite possibly more so at times.

'Motives' fit in better than 'intentions' with the idea of our being moved by distal forces over which we have little, if any, control, but still there is a suggestion, even in the dictionary definition of 'motive', that what *really* causes our behaviour is 'a person's volition', and the examples of motives given ('desire, fear, reason') are on the whole also very internal things. Once again, it seems to me, we are having trouble escaping the immediacy (what I have called the proximality) of our experience. We are, I believe, confusing *the experience of being influenced* with *the cause of our conduct*: we *feel* ourselves doing things, and then take that feeling to be the cause of what we are doing.

Because of its central importance to our whole understanding of therapeutic change and how we can alter our conduct, I shall be returning to these issues in greater detail in Chapter Six, where I shall also give more concrete examples of how they affect us. For the moment I want just to underline the paucity of our understanding of what 'makes us tick', the inadequacy of the consulting-room model, and the severe restriction on the depth of our vision of the causes of our conduct. As we try to understand the reasons for what we do to each other, we are all for the most part relatively in the dark, unable to penetrate the gloom of motivation beyond the confused ideas and feelings we and those closest to us are able to divine and articulate.

As long as we limit the search for the wellsprings of action to the 'person's volition' and assume also that it is only through personal volition that changes can be made and human distress relieved, we shall continue to be confused. We have to shake ourselves free of the intense sense of conviction that the almost overpowering immediacy of our personal experience gives us about our motivation and see that, like children, we have only the vaguest notions of why we act as we do. Like the red snooker ball, all we register, most of the time, is that we have been hit by the white, and we have no idea of what the general strategy of the game might be – or even that we are in a game at all.

THE ROLE OF SOCIETAL POWER

It is not just our ignorance of distal power that makes it so difficult to resolve the 'paradox of experience' we have been considering – the subjective attribution of importance to events in inverse proportion to their actual, objective importance. Many of the more powerful elements in society have a strong interest in our continuing to believe in the consulting-room model. This must be so in a society that distributes power (and therefore advantage) pyramidally, with the most powerful being at the apex and the least at the base. The powerful few can only preserve their advantage over (i.e. exploit) the relatively powerless many through the use of, among other things, mystification. As long as the many believe that their greater privations are the result solely of their own actions and of those with whom they are immediately in contact (also members of 'the many'), the question of the distribution of power itself is not going to arise.

Already well prepared by our experience as infants of the impress of power in the family to conceive of ourselves as personally responsible for the errors of our ways, we do not take much persuading in later life that the troubles which beset us are largely of our own making. When, therefore, government ministers (actual or would be) talk of 'irresponsibility', failure of 'duty' and lack of 'values' as *causes* of joblessness or homelessness or general social disintegration, or of 'criminality' as a cause of crime, they are using a language that we are already more than half inclined to accept. Similarly, almost all media comment on the sometimes desperate actions of the most deprived and despairing members of our society ('sex-crazed monsters' etc.), all the revelations of 'evil' in the tabloids, the musings of television pundits and weekend-supplement feature writers on how we might tackle the discomforts of our lives, are couched in terms of what we as individuals are guilty of, or should have resolved or might yet resolve to do.

What this completely diverts attention from, of course, is the apparatus of power (so well analysed by Foucault) through which our conduct is held in place and which controls the possibilities and choices open to us to better our lot (and which, for example, government ministers are in a far better position to influence than we). Rather than extending our gaze distally – out into public space – to try to discern the operation of the forces that serve to constrain our freedom and blight our lives, the cultural trend is increasingly to persuade us to turn it inwards into that private domain where, supposedly, we examine our motives, form our intentions and make resolutions (even if, to do so successfully, we are advised to have a 'counsellor' at our side).

Apart from anything else, the consulting-room model simply doesn't work. The comforting warmth of the therapeutic presence soon wears off once the patient leaves the consulting room and re-enters the chilling embrace of all those influences that caused distress in the first place. Just as New Year resolutions start getting difficult to keep on 2 January, so the simple realisation that something needs to be done, no matter how convincingly it is made, is not enough to undo the past or reconstruct the future. The same character walks out of the consulting room as walked into it, and the same world awaits him or her as was there before. Therapists are not sorcerers with magical powers to transform either the person or the world; their influence is minimal, limited for the most part to the simple solidarity they can offer to people in distress.

In order to escape all the distortions of our understanding that the paradox of subjectivity/objectivity brings about, it is necessary to remind ourselves constantly that neither we nor the vast majority of the people who occupy our proximal world have anything like the power we think to make significant differences to our circumstances. There is therefore very little point in our berating ourselves for our lack of courage or failure of will, or in imputing 'evil' to others, or even in blaming them particularly strongly for the wrongs they seem to do us. Much more to the point is to try to get as clear a view as possible of the intricate networks of power which press down upon us all, to unravel as far as we can the infinite complexity of the ways in which they entangle us, and to use whatever powers may be available to us to free ourselves of their grip.

Certainly in the long run, but possibly also in the short, this is not so much a 'therapeutic' as a political undertaking. The conditions of our lives are determined by the state of the world we live in – in particular, of course, its social organisation.[7] We will not bring about real improvements in the former until we address ourselves seriously to the latter. It is no accident that the political role of ordinary people has dwindled almost to vanishing point and that the function of citizen has collapsed into that of consumer of counselling – it is in the interests of the powerful and privileged minority that this should be so. In order to rebuild the possibility of citizenship (which is in part to see that the principal form of power available to those of us at the base of the social pyramid is solidarity), we may first have to become clear about what is and is not possible for individuals to do to minimise the distressing effects of the world they live in. It would be hard to do without psychotherapy if we did not first disabuse ourselves of the illusions that the consulting-room model creates.

CHAPTER FIVE

What Should We Do? Moral Demands

A large component of the felt suffering associated with psychological distress has to do with 'feeling bad' – not in the sense of feeling ill (though that may of course be present as well) so much as in the sense of feeling unworthy. Feeling ashamed, feeling guilty, feeling 'different', feeling undeserving of the love and respect of others, form a significant part of most of those 'conditions' that tend to get labelled anxiety, depression and so on, and indeed for many people are experienced as the cause of their suffering.

As we saw in Chapter Three, patients frequently approach their doctor or therapists with apprehension, expecting to be found 'abnormal' in a way that places them outside the company of ordinary, decent people. This may well be more than just a fear of statistical abnormality and may encompass an expectation of *moral* condemnation. You're not merely unusual, you are *bad*.

This phenomenon is not limited to the area of psychological distress. The social life of all of us is inescapably bound up with moralistic judgement. We all spend a great deal of time in the moral evaluation of our performance in relation to others and theirs in relation to us. Eavesdrop on any reasonably intimate conversation and it won't be long before you encounter justifications of self and accusations of others. We need, it seems, to maintain a good opinion of ourselves and to make sure that this is reflected in the eyes of others. It is comfortable to be in the right, painful to be in the wrong. We all worry about what people think of us, and the attribution of blame is one of our principal social concerns.

So preoccupied are we as a society with blame that we often overlook the importance of explanation, even where it would be particularly important to maintain the distinction between the two. Whether we're dealing with the actions of individuals, with collective problems like poverty or urban rioting, or with tragic accidents like aeroplane crashes or other public disasters, the first question we ask is: Who's to blame? We are not happy, it seems, until we have located the reasons for events such as these *inside* a person or a group in the form of an intention for which they can be held morally responsible. We watch each other with a kind of unremitting vigilance, ready to pounce with a damning accusation at the first available opportunity.

However, though they seem to have become fused in our minds as equivalent, blame and explanation are clearly not the same thing. Blame is about apportioning moral responsibility; explanation is about finding the reasons for things. Blame and self-justification are, perhaps, necessary features of a proximal existence in which we have to negotiate our relations with each other on the basis of what we can see (which, as suggested in the previous chapter, is not very much). Explanation, on the other hand, reaches further out to the causes of things, operating within a distal perspective which renders the intentions of individuals largely irrelevant.

The difficulty facing the person who is wrestling with feelings of shame, guilt and unworthiness is that the conceptual framework, the whole vocabulary of thought and understanding available to him or her, offers no escape from the 'blame dimension'. It seems that the only way to absolve ourselves of moral condemnation is to shift the blame elsewhere, most likely onto the shoulders of somebody else. This is exactly what happens in the acrimonious debates about who is to blame for so-called mental illnesses like 'schizophrenia'. Practitioners and research workers who point out that family relations and communications may result in the acute disturbance of more vulnerable members (particularly of course children) are immediately pilloried for 'blaming the parents'.

We seem in fact to have made for ourselves a world in which we move in a kind of minefield of recrimination, where we scrutinise each other constantly for indications of culpability, gingerly tossing each other unpinned hand grenades of 'responsibility' as in general we become more and more suspicious and defensive. It is scarcely surprising in circumstances such as these that guilt and shame – 'feeling bad' – should constitute so central a part of the more pronounced forms of distress. This is pretty well bound to be the case so long as we remain incapable of separating blame from explanation.

I would certainly not want to maintain that the apportionment of moral responsibility – 'blame' – has no valid part to play in the conduct of human affairs. In the proximal sphere in which we are fated to play out our lives there is almost certainly no way we can escape moral judgement, and indeed moral judgement may be an essential way of ordering our relations with each other in some respects. But we do allow it to spread beyond the confines of its proper field of application, and we need to be more aware than we are of where blame is appropriate and where it is not.

One place where blame is certainly not appropriate is in the psychological process of trying to understand why people feel and act as they do. Even in posing these questions, the importance of explanation as opposed to blame immediately becomes apparent. For a psychologist to assert that someone is unhappy because 'it's her own fault' would be transparently inadequate. What one requires from a psychologist is an explanation that transcends banal accusations and imputations of blame and reaches out to the chains of social cause and effect in which the person is entangled. When it comes, therefore, to your understanding the reasons for your own distress, it is important to remember that *you are your own psychologist*.[1] Although it may well be impossible to resist feelings of guilt, of 'being different' and so on, there is no way in which such feelings could conceivably contribute to an explanation of your problems, and in this latter respect they have simply to be ignored.

Although very obviously aware of the problem of moralistic judgmentalism, therapeutic psychology has not really itself succeeded in escaping the 'proximal' prejudices of our culture, and its most significant failure in my view is not to have developed a language that avoids our common moral assumptions, our habitual concern with issues of responsibility and blame. For while it is true that most therapists, from psychoanalysts to Rogerian counsellors, stress the importance precisely of *not* blaming patients and clients for the psychological predicaments they find themselves in, this is achieved largely through a suspension of moral judgement rather than through a recognition of its irrelevance.

Indeed, as already noted, psychoanalysis constitutes a quite extraordinarily moralistic approach to 'neurotic' suffering in which all kinds of 'badness' are attributed to the personal unconscious of people who can be redeemed only through a kind of morally cleansing process of rational rebirth ('where id was, there shall ego be'). The whole language of the 'humanistic' approaches to therapy positively drips with uplifting precepts and blueprints for life on a higher moral plane,[2] and even Carl Rogers's advocacy that therapists maintain 'unconditional positive regard' for their clients avoids blame only by prescribing its opposite.

But it is in my view utterly inappropriate for people in distress to have to approach their therapists as, so to speak, penitents whose best hope is for tolerance or forgiveness. It is not just the case that therapists should forbear from moral judgement, but that we should see that psychological explanation has nothing to do with moral judgement at all. Occasionally one hears therapists agonising over their moral sensibilities in relation to, say, sex offenders or abusers of children, as if they might be tainted, corrupted or somehow emotionally damaged by professional contact with such people. This seems to me a particularly silly form of preciousness. The point is that trying to understand people's predicaments simply has nothing to do with judging them. I have heard people say, for example, that they would draw the line at trying to 'treat' Adolf Hitler. I don't see why. Hitler and a potential therapist might not have got very far even had he felt like consulting one, but the attempt to understand him would have harmed nobody.[3]

THE ORIGINS OF SHAME

Those who suffer from feelings of moral inferiority, which may at their worst constitute a bitterly pervasive self-loathing, do not as a rule find it difficult to see that such feelings cannot have any real justification. Even those who experience themselves as irredeemably culpable because of their difference from others in some respect, are usually quite ready to acknowledge that this would not be a reasonable way to evaluate anyone else – what is felt so strongly to apply to the self does not extend to the judging of others. This is frequently the case, for instance, with people who suffer from shyness: if you stand in a corner at a party 'not knowing what to say' to people, you feel yourself to be an object of contempt, but the last thing you would do is feel contemptuous of a fellow sufferer. In the place of the person who you feel must despise you, your heart would actually go out to yourself!

In trying to understand how we could be possessed of apparently unshakeable feelings of unworthiness which are at the same time so obviously undeserved from any objective standpoint, we need to consider once again the impress of power under which they are acquired.

It is impossible to overemphasise the vulnerability of the small child to the power of the social environment into which it is launched. Every tentative step it takes in trying to understand its world, every judgement it makes about the nature of things, every interchange through which it negotiates its relations with the all powerful adults around it, is fraught with terrible possibilities of rejection and derision, if not worse. Even the most fortunate child whose courage is consistently built up through the loving approval of others is certain at times to come painfully unstuck.

For most of us, the route to gaining some kind of influence within our childhood world is through the love and approval of our parents: the main powers we can acquire are those which are accorded us. It is the conditional nature of this approval that presents us with the problem of shame. This is not a bad thing: it would be no worthy pedagogical aim to try to bring up children who are shame*less*, and children who are so brought up – either because they received no love at all or because they were 'spoilt' with a kind of blanket approval disguising indifference – tend not to make the most attractive adults (even if they are free of the curses of shyness and self-doubt).

Shame, then, arises from the experience of being denied (temporarily) the love or approval of people on whose good opinion one depends in order to maintain an emotional, intellectual and social grip on the world. As children, we have no way of telling whether the suspension of approval we suffer at any given time is justifiable or not (we are almost bound to believe that it is), and the manipulation of shame in children is a weapon which adults can all too easily abuse. An experience that may come about in inevitable but small doses as part of a necessary process of socialisation may also come in massive overdoses where parents (and possibly others) use it as the principal way of controlling their offspring. But the child knows nothing of the injustice of this: it will conclude simply that, instead of being 'out of order' some of the time, it is being really bad most of the time, and its movement around the emotional minefield of its life will become increasingly uncertain and expectant of sudden pain.

It is, then, a central aspect of the child's powerlessness that it cannot see into injustice: it is quite likely that the only source of information available to it concerning the validity of the actions and views of those who oppress it comes from the oppressors themselves. As Alice Miller so compellingly shows, there is likely to be no ground from which the child can question whether the emotional torture it endures really is 'for its own good'.[4]

Sometimes escape is possible. One of the bravest women I've met had throughout her childhood and adolescence been abused physically, mentally and sexually, almost unremittingly, by whole ranges of adults in and outside her family. As far as I could see, the only reason she had not been psychologically destroyed by her experience of life was the fact that she was one of a large group of sisters and stepsisters who maintained an inspiring solidarity (for example, two of her sisters came physically to the rescue when she was being abused sexually by a neighbour). As I have already noted, consistent ill treatment is in some ways easier to cope with than the capricious use of punishment or shame: I can think of another utterly admirable woman whose early life was so terrible that she was actually rescued in part by Hollywood – she learned 'from the films' that people actually could love each other (one could scarcely say that her adult life has been 'normal', but her courage and her totally uncompromising honesty make her an extraordinarily positive force in the world).

But where parents don't, so to speak, blow their cover by being just so awful that the child concludes there *must* be a better world outside the family, the only logical conclusion available to it is that the cause of their displeasure must be its own badness. Being excluded from parental love or approval is the first, prototypical experience of feeling 'outside the pale' – which is the form in which it is likely to recur in later life.

Parents do not usually tyrannise their children for the pure sadistic fun of it. Children have powers of which they themselves have no knowledge, particularly the ability to spot the emperor's nakedness, and it is frequently out of fear of these that parents feel, consciously or unconsciously, that they have to exercise 'control'. Children do not realise that the adults around them are also still children inside, and that they too live apprehensively under the critical moral gaze of a society obsessed with blame. Quite apart from anything else, the child's very innocence in relation to the social pitfalls of life make it a danger to those around it who are struggling in more ways than one to 'keep up appearances'. The trouble starts for the child once parents' anxieties get out of control and they can no longer use the art of shaming in the child's interest, but instead as a weapon with which to defend their own self-image.

Truthfulness and trust

It is hard not to conclude from listening to the accounts people give of their childhood that, far from being (as in fact they are) spectacularly powerless in relation to adults, children are often perceived as dangerous. Certainly, much of the activity of parents and others charged with the care and instruction of children seems to be concerned with finding ways of limiting what little power they have got. Children quickly learn, for example, that truthfulness is an essential component of their claim on love. It seems that, in order to earn the affection and respect of the adults around them, children are discouraged from developing a truly private life: their thoughts, feelings and motives must be open to the inspection of adults at all times, and they should be ready at any occasion of cross-examination to give as honest an account of themselves as they possibly can.

This heavy emphasis on truthfulness in childhood translates later into our extraordinarily self-contradictory notion of 'sincerity', in which a profound knowledge of the treachery of words is matched in intensity by a kind of desperate need to *believe in* sincerity. The whole of political and commercial life, for example, is pervaded by a vast enterprise dedicated to manufacturing the appearance of sincerity in circumstances that virtually ensure its impossibility. All of us know this, and yet hardly any of us can credit the irrationality of it all, so strong is the yearning for true 'credibility' which has been stamped upon us at our most impressionable age.

But whatever the later societal consequences may be, we are certainly likely to learn as children that it is shameful to have a private life which we are not willing to expose on demand to the most powerful people around us. Since the development of a private life, a personal world of thoughts, feelings, ideas and images, is an absolute inevitability – is indeed something over which we have not the tiniest element of choice – and since there are certain to be elements of that private life which we are unwilling to discuss with others, we are almost bound to carry round with us from our earliest moments of self-reflection a sense of shame which is literally in-built.

There probably are cases where a child does feel able to share with an unusually indulgent (not to say intrusive) parent absolutely everything that courses through its head (a circumstance no doubt boding ill for later relationships), but most of us need to be able to cast a decent reticence over much of what we detect buzzing around inside us, and the adult demand that this be open to inspection is likely to cause us continuous difficulty as children. We all of us feel that we have things inside us that would make us unlovable if only people knew.

As with truthfulness, so, often, with 'trust'. Instead of constituting a loving, liberating belief in someone, 'trust' can become the anxious parent's way of extending control into the very heads of their children. Truly to trust someone is to credit them with having good reasons for what they do even if we cannot see or understand what they are. In the biblical story, Abraham trusted God to have good reasons for insisting that he sacrifice his son Isaac.[5] It would be asking a lot of the rest of us to take risks on quite this scale, but it is a necessary risk of parents' love that they do not always use their power to prevent their children from doing things that seem incomprehensible, reprehensible or even dangerous. However, for parents unable (usually because of the extent of their own anxieties) to take such necessary risks, trust becomes something quite different: a form of remote control.

For example, for Nadine's father, unable to get out of his head that, unlike her (in his view) prettier and more talented sister, Nadine could not be *trusted* to conduct her life sensibly and productively, his measure of 'trust' as she grew up became the extent to which she conformed to his wishes when out of his sight. Whereas he and her mother would spectate passively and approvingly as her clever sister surprised them with her talent and her boldness, opening up for them worlds of which they had no previous conception, they could scarcely bear to let Nadine think a single thought for herself, and when she did escape their attention for any length of time, they would set little traps for her to see if she was toeing the line.

It was not until much later in her life that Nadine was able to grasp what had been (and still was) going on. As a child, she had perforce to interpret her father's intense concern with her every move as love, and her own repeated inability to meet his requirements as a kind of congenital stupidity or moral weakness which made it all the more remarkable that anybody could love her at all. Even long after she had moved away from home, her life, far from being liberated, was almost completely controlled by her father's 'trust'. Almost her every action was determined not by what she herself wanted, but by whether her father, if he knew, would approve. 'Trust' was a kind of leash which prevented her from living any kind of life truly her own, or from developing any needs or wishes of her own which she could satisfy or enjoy.

Nadine's life, like the lives of so many people whose childhoods were characterised by the anxious moral supervision of at least one parent, was lived conscientiously, indeed selflessly. She accumulated duties at work and, having married a man who had an almost limitless need to be looked after, also at home (she divorced her husband only after his third bout of infidelity). She paid endless attention to the needs of her ageing parents. She was unable to say no to almost any demand made on her and so became involved in a whole range of out-of-work community and charitable activities. None of these gave her any pleasure; indeed, she had no clear idea of what pleasure was. Even her comfort eating was no healthily enjoyable greed, but rather the secret and guilty snatching of a little illicit sustenance (and she always made sure that when she did binge it was on basic food-stuffs which could in no way be seen as luxurious – no boxes of chocolates for her).

Where the best approximation to love a parent can provide is supervision, insistence on truthfulness and the use of 'trust' as remote control, it is common for people's lives subsequently to be dutiful but empty, for the notion of 'want' to be totally submerged in the insistence of 'should'. People who have had to shoulder inordinate responsibility (for their siblings, for a parent) at an early age have a similar problem. Frequently not knowing how to refuse others' demands, combined with the inability to acknowledge or even recognise their own wishes and needs, means that people from this kind of background go on shouldering responsibility to the point where they simply collapse under the strain. This is not because they are 'inade-quate' – they are most often superadequate – and the 'depres-sion' to which they may eventually succumb is probably best understood as the mute rebellion of an abused nervous system.

For most of us, the impress of parental power in childhood, in the form in particular of moral control, is neither so great nor so relentless as to result in a near-total loss of self, but rather leaves us vulnerable to the conviction that there are inside us wishes and impulses, feelings and thoughts, that are uniquely shameful. If we have bought the parental line that it is wrong to tell lies, that to be 'trusted' means to act only in ways of which the powerful would approve, we are quite likely to have an uncomfortable feeling that we are the possessors of guilty secrets which make us people who should not be trusted, that our outer aspect is a sham which people would quickly see through if they caught a glimpse of our 'real selves'.

The 'need to please', 'need to be liked', which people so often sense as a particularly contemptible part of their make-up, is something that virtually all of us share, and it has a great deal to do with the necessity of, so to speak, shoring up the external impression we make on others in order to render the penetration of our defences, the discovery of our shameful interiors, a little more difficult. Though the contrast between how we feel inside and how we wish to appear to others is universal and causes most of us many an uneasy moment, the extent to which we suffer in this way depends probably on the degree to which we were allowed as children to develop private lives without the threat of adult censure.

'Feeling a fake'

People who are truly at ease with themselves, if they exist at all, are extremely rare, but there may be more who are lucky enough to be able to avoid, most of the time at least, the kind of precariousness of subjectivity – the uncertainty about one's private 'self' – that leads one to think of oneself as a fake. 'Feeling a fake', feeling more or less perpetually 'to blame' for anything and everything of which one could conceivably be accused, is, even so, a common experience, and a frequent accompaniment of social anxiety. It arises, of course, from the awareness, which surely cannot entirely escape any of us, that our private selves are very different from our public personas. Where the anxious or disapproving surveillance of power has stamped upon us as children a conviction that privacy is almost by definition 'wrong' (but not gone so far as to prevent our developing any), we will as adults always carry an awareness that the face we present to the world is not really 'telling the truth'.

It is quite easy for people to live an entire life of moral impeccability and high achievement, earning the respect and affection of nearly all those they encounter, while convinced subjectively that the whole thing has been a sham. Their excellent exam results were achieved because their teachers did not realise that their ideas were not their own or that they had just been 'lucky with the questions'. Their success at work came from a series of fortunate accidents or from their having been unfairly privileged by superiors who hadn't been clever enough to see their faults. Their personal relationships, despite every indication to the contrary, were really hollow, and nobody who could see behind the mask could possibly like, let alone love, them. The only possible circumstance that could redeem such a person, s/he feels, would be if outside appearance and subjective sense of self were to match perfectly.

The official psychologies and philosophies of the twentieth century have, if anything, only served to increase the vulnerability of our subjectivity. Jungian psychology's disapproving assessment of the overdeveloped 'persona', Sartrean existentialism's positive valuation of 'authenticity', Freudian psychology's mistrustful vigilance for 'unconscious motivation', and so on, have all done their bit to contribute to what has become the banalised craving for 'sincerity', an urge to collapse the public into the private and to publicise the private by turning it inside out. It is as if the only person we could trust, including ourselves, would be one who is completely transparent, outside indistinguishable from inside.

But, however inconveniently complicated it may make our lives, we are three- not two-dimensional creatures. We have depths hidden not only from each other but also from ourselves, and if the waters are at times murky, it is simply in their nature to be so.[6] Mistrust of and shame at our privacy merely turns us into cardboard cut-outs colluding in the pretence that what you see is what you get, but secretly agonised over the certain but incommunicable knowledge that there is more to us than meets the eye.

This virtually universal, in-built propensity to shame and

guilt renders us ripe for exploitation by any power prepared to make cynical use of it. Any parent, colleague, competitor, boss or politician with an interest in our toeing a particular line can play on our fearful sense of our own hypocrisy to make us drop like a hot potato any objection to his or her plan we might be tempted to raise on the basis of our subjective instinct. Because our subjectivity is so precarious, to take a stand on a *subject* – to 'stick our neck out' on any particular issue – is for most of us a frighteningly risky business. The moral battle of our right to interpret the world from our own subjective standpoint is joined from the moment of our exit from the womb, and once our privacy has become infected by shame, the powers that be are well on the way to winning.

At a trivial level, it is this lack of trust in a subjective self that lies behind the phenomenon of always being in agreement with other people's arguments. Many of us will be familiar with the feeling that there seems to be a curious unassailability about the arguments of anyone with any claim to authority (seen, that is, as possessing a certain form of power), even when those arguments are quite contrary to our own beliefs, or are contradicted by other 'authoritative' arguments (which seem equally compelling!). 'Whatever he says, I always seem to agree with him' or 'I always feel there must be something wrong, but I can never think what it is' or, less drastically perhaps, 'I can only think what I should have said hours afterwards' are the common experiences of those of us who live in a subjectivity-sapping culture in which our confidence in our own judgement has been eroded from the earliest age by the intrusive moral scrutiny of power.

More seriously, our precarious subjectivity renders us vulnerable to manipulation by anyone in power who can confidently and convincingly appear to 'know best'. The entire institutional apparatus of a society that is constructed first and foremost to maintain an unequal, pyramidal distribution of security and advantage, is saturated through and through with an ideology of benign parenthood, instilling at every possible opportunity the idea that, like Mummy and Daddy, people in power are there for your own good. All too frequently, Mummy and Daddy are themselves caught up in this apparatus, dutifully reproducing the ideology at the very point that serves most effectively to maintain it.

Nearly all of us have succumbed to this ideology to some extent. We turn our faces to power with the innocent openness of sunflowers following the sun, unable to believe that our elders and betters, bosses and leaders could be motivated by anything other than an intention to do their best for us. There can in my view be no explanation other than the innocent trust of the 'sunflower mentality' for how whole societies can be turned willingly and well-meaningly into bureaucracies for the achievement of diabolical ends, as in, at one extreme, Hitler's Germany and Stalin's USSR or, at the other, Thatcher's Britain in the 1980s.

The point, of course, is that the intentions of those who direct us may well be benign, but we have already seen that intentions count for very little when it comes to understanding why people do things. We have not yet learned to look beyond the proximal world of intentions to the play of the more distal influences which hold us all in our place. In order to do that, we need no doubt to learn first how to arm ourselves against the exploitation of conscience in our private lives.

COUNTERING THE 'MORAL' IMPRESS OF POWER

The distinction between public and private is crucial to a proper understanding of morality. Moral rules are about how we conduct ourselves in relation to each other, not about the propriety of what goes on inside our own heads. You can't *do* what you like, but you can certainly *think* what you like; social disapproval may legitimately be used to constrain your actions, but is utterly irrelevant to your feelings.

There are some unfortunate religious ideas about its being as wrong to commit a sin in imagination as in practice, but these, it seems to me, are best dismissed as attempts at extending an intrusive and illegitimate form of parental 'remote control' into the individual's private space. For the point about trying to introduce rules to control psychological processes like thoughts and feelings is that *it simply cannot be done*. Rules can apply only where there is the possibility of choice, and you can't choose what to think or to feel at any given moment.

Even the standard ideas about the nature of morality embedded in our culture, inadequate as they are in many respects, recognise that moral precepts cease to be valid in situations where the person's power to choose is for one reason or another diminished. A whole range of extenuating circumstances, from insanity to lack of knowledge of cogent facts, may be invoked to soften social condemnation in any particular case. What is important when people do something wrong is to determine whether they had the power to do otherwise: was any other course of action open to them?

If we're not careful, we stray here into notions of 'will power', which, as I shall argue in the next chapter, can be very complicated and misleading. But though we might debate in any given case whether someone could have done otherwise, or whether, for example, s/he was in the grip of powers beyond his or her control, it is clear that rules can be made that do in fact have the effect of controlling the conduct of large sections of the population (usually because they are linked to sanctions). Yellow lines on the road give me a good reason for not parking there. And if I do, it would be absurd for me to tell the traffic warden that I 'couldn't help it.' Moral rules about how we should behave, where they work, are not all that different.

The impossibility of mind control

When it comes to consideration of what's going on inside your head, the situation is very different, and in some ways much clearer. For it is not at all obvious that you can help what you're thinking and feeling. 'Whatever you do, don't imagine the colour red' is not an instruction you can reasonably be expected to obey. Similarly, admonitions that it is wrong to think about murder or sex are about as silly as telling someone not to feel cold. For, of course, there comes a point when we have no choice at all about the contents of our consciousness, and this is because we are not beings who can choose to be conscious of this, that or the other, but are beings who simply *are* conscious. There is no non-conscious part of us which can, so to speak, choose what to fill consciousness with.

Of course we can, while awake, give some direction to our mental activity, we can 'concentrate' on this or that task – make a shopping list or add up a column of figures – but even here we cannot always switch concentration on and off at will (as anyone who tries reading a book while feeling depressed will know). And in any case, in the background even of our conscious existence, there runs along a continuous process of uncontrollable mentation – thoughts, feelings, impulses, images – over which, like dreams, we have no control at all. It would be the ultimate absurdity to attempt an extension of moral control into the area of dreaming, and yet that is, in a sense, precisely what the 'privatisation' of morality tries to do.

The anxiety about what might be going on inside our heads, which powerful interests have stamped upon so many of us at an early age, has created a culture in which it seems practically impossible for people to be honest about the contents of the continuous, dreamlike stream of consciousness which accompanies our every waking, not to say sleeping, moment.[7] And for some people whose experience of censorship in childhood was particularly strong, detection of 'immoral' thoughts and feelings can become almost shatteringly worrying (we have already seen that this was the case with Dave). The same may be true for people whose subjective experience as children simply received no endorsement from respected powers, their nascent feelings and perceptions having been not so much condemned as discredited or overlooked as worthless. Large areas of Brenda's 'self', for example, were simply wordless blanks because they had been left untended, unelaborated and unarticulated as she grew up. It is often the case with people vulnerable to depression that there are large parts of themselves they feel to be 'bad' without quite being able to say what they are.

We all of us live in a profoundly eccentric private world, much of the contents of which would have us in deep trouble if acted out publicly. The fact is that not only is a good deal of our stream of consciousness completely unique, but there are also no guarantees about its moral purity. I remember a man telling me with real agitation that sometimes he felt like reaching out and touching the breasts of women who passed him in the street. The answer, of course, was that he could feel like anything at all, but if he did it, he'd end up, quite rightly, in court.

Not only can one not prevent oneself from wishing that a troublesome neighbour, a bumptious colleague, an unsympathetic teacher, would 'drop dead' at the precise moment one utters a polite 'good morning', but it is quite useful and satisfying that one has such a harmless freedom to vent one's feelings. One can indulge daydreams of murder and mayhem on quite a spectacular scale without causing the least damage, and the wildest forms of sexual fantasy, kept to oneself, cause offence to no one.

It may of course be the case that rapists and murderers spend quite a lot of time musing about rape and murder, but this is not to say that the imagination causes the act: there is no *necessary* connection between them. It is not as if our dreams, daydreams and fantasies somehow constitute an indication of what we are 'really like' or adumbrate some enduring, secret project which may eventually burst forth from us in reality. The point is that as a matter of fact we are all far, far, less civilised in our private world than in public and it is absolutely not a matter of concern to find ourselves engaged, for example, in violent, vengeful fantasies, disloyal thoughts or imagined infidelity.

This is not to say that the life of the imagination is without interest. There may well be, for example, *reasons* for our imaginings which it could be useful to discover. Catching yourself in a daydream that, let us say, your spouse and children have been demolished by a mad axeman may at first be acutely disturbing, but if you can bring yourself coolly to examine the possible reasons for it (perhaps, for instance, your fantasy provides a simple solution to the burden of responsibility you are feeling for your family), you may learn quite a lot about the raw primitiveness of some of our psychological processes and the indirect way they sometimes manifest themselves. There is more to wonder at here than to worry about. At times, indeed, it might be quite important to be able to picture in the privacy of your own head scenes of rage, frustration or desire for which there can be no permissible external outlet. But in any case, the least freedom we can reasonably insist on as a right is the freedom of our imagination.

Morality, then, belongs in the real, social world in which we interact with others and where our actions can have concrete significance for the way others feel, for example whether we cause them pleasure or pain. That's why we need moral rules. The world of the imagination carries no such rewards or penalties; it really doesn't matter what goes on in the privacy of our own head. Even though speech cannot always (in fact, if we are to lead a reasonably quiet life, can hardly ever) be unconstrained, freedom of thought really is something we can claim without risking injury to someone.

When it comes to the guilt and shame which so often pervade our feelings about ourselves, what we need to do, then, is first to try to establish whether they should be taken seriously – whether, that is, they stem legitimately from our actual social relations with others, or whether they are merely the censorious echo of, for example, parental injunctions about what we should think and feel which we have internalised from the past. If the latter, we should pay them no attention (much easier to say than do, though some suggestions will be given in Chapter Seven). If the former, we need to give some thought as to what our obligations in relation to others really *are*.

Determining the limits of obligation

The policing of the imagination by powerful influences can lead to significant later distress, but the imposition of real responsibilities and duties can also lead to the individual's becoming overburdened to the point of breakdown. Both Ann and Jill, for example, had had to shoulder responsibility for their siblings at a time when they were only children themselves (Jill had also had to adopt a largely maternal role in relation to her own mother). Nadine had, as we have seen, been schooled from the outset in a kind of soulless obedience to duty. Many children have to grow up fast in order to compensate in one way or another for the difficulties and inadequacies of their own upbringing, and in the process they frequently fail to develop any idea (a) that their own needs and wishes have any legitimacy, and (b) that there is any limit to the difficulties they can be expected to handle and the responsibilities they can take on.

In predicaments like these it is as if moral duty is an open-ended demand that can be laid on people at the whim of those who have power over them. Superconscientiousness thus grows out of a response to a *personal* power, as though to a jealous and demanding authority able to make seemingly arbitrary rules and impose any conditions it requires (this, of course, is exactly how an unreasonably and unreflectingly demanding parent will appear to a child).

In fact, moral rules are not simply the creation of the personal authority of powerful individuals. What you should do is not determined capriciously by what God or your father think you should do at any particular time. Morality is evolved by the social community of which you are a part. Moral rules are not particularly clearly stated, codified or written down, but nevertheless we have a general understanding of what it is and is not reasonable to expect in particular situations. This understanding is precisely what the superconscientious have been prevented from developing, usually because it was not in the interests of those who had power over them that they should.

The particular mark of superconscientiousness is that it is underpinned by a non-reciprocal moral law. 'Do as you would be done by' informs every action of the superconscientious person, but it never seems to occur to him or her that this is a rule which should apply to anyone else, so that 'others should treat me as I treat them' simply doesn't enter the frame.[8] This is not a reasonable or practicable basis upon which one can lead one's life, which is why it becomes very important to establish the limits of our obligations to those among whom we live our day-to-day lives.

Where the matter of obligation gets so far out of hand as to cause persistent distress and perhaps breakdown (by which I mean not 'mental illness', but literal collapse under an impossible load), it is usually because the common-sense moral rules attaching to particular social roles are being overlooked, if not grossly flouted. Typical examples are where parents come to expect a daughter (less often a son) to devote herself to their welfare almost from the moment she leaves school (if not before); husbands expect their wives to wait on them as their mothers did even when both are working full time; older relatives, or superiors at work, abuse their power in pursuit of sexual gratification. Even in less obviously dramatic and abusive cases, superconscientious people are almost bound to become chronically overburdened, if only because they make such wonderfully easy targets for others (that is most of us) who find it hard to resist the opportunity of exploiting a willing slave.

In any case, the important questions to raise are usually those concerning what are the normal rights and duties attaching to the role of parent, child, spouse, lover, employer and employee, and so on. For example, parents (except in old age) are expected to look after children and not vice versa; married partners should share responsibility equally for most tasks and difficulties that arise in the domestic sphere; employment should be governed by some form of explicit contract; sexual interest should be expressed only in situations free of any significant duress.

Most important of all, where one party fails to deliver their side of the bargain, the other may legitimately be expected no longer to regard themselves as bound by the moral conventions of *their* role. Obedience is not owed to an unjust or repressive authority; children cannot be expected to submit to parents as well as look after them; sexuality forms a legitimate component of some types of relationship but not others; women no longer defer to men by virtue of their sex alone.

In fact, of course, we all of us know that the operation of moral rules should be marked by reciprocity and fairness. Even those who habitually find themselves being exploited have some awareness that it shouldn't be happening, but their sense of injustice, the resentment which simmers in the background, hardly ever boils up to the point of being expressed openly. There seems in many situations to be far more at work than simple transgressions of the moral code which could, presumably, be settled easily enough through normal procedures of argument and debate.

What makes the difference is the impress of power. Exploitation is probably only rarely carried out mistakenly, to be corrected as soon as the error of the exploiter's ways are pointed out. On the contrary, exploiters usually have an important stake in the success of their exploitation, which means that it is backed with all the persuasive force they can muster. Whether the exploiters are, for example, parents who need for the preservation of their own self-esteem to prevent a child from seeing their feet of clay, or perhaps a husband whose masculine pride would be destroyed by his wife's being seen as cleverer than him, the pressure brought to bear is likely to be ruthless. In personal relationships, this usually includes heavy doses of emotional blackmail and too often the threat of violence.

What this tends to mean, especially for people who have learned their obedience to unreasonable power as children, is that any challenge to authority in later life is likely to be over-shadowed by a dread of retribution which, though once entirely justified, is now out of all proportion to the reality of the situation. In the adult world (at least of the Western democracies), any legal challenge we make to authority is unlikely to be met with such terrifying punishment as that risked by the rebellious child, and even the father whose rage could once be a shattering experience has probably become an arthritic old man who couldn't hurt a fly. But the painful reality of powerlessness becomes embodied in the child who, once oppressed by parental violence, disapproval or anxiety, later finds it very diffi-cult indeed to be able simply to act on the recognition that, as an adult, all s/he has to do is 'stand up for' his or her rights. And even the now powerless parent may still find ways of intimi-dating a potentially disobedient offspring into submission (by 'getting upset', becoming ill or even, *in extremis*, dropping dead).

'Love,' 'loyalty' and duty

The mixture of oppression, dependency and emotional black-mail – a lethal cocktail usually referred to as 'love' or 'loyalty' – which too often characterises parent-child relationships is prob-ably one of the most difficult issues to confront for those who become significantly distressed in later life. Power protects its abuses not only by insisting that they are 'for your own good', but also by mystifying the parent-child relation as necessarily one of love and insisting that the child's only proper response to all kinds of terrifying treatment is one of *loyal* acceptance. I have listened countless times to stories of quite appalling brutality and/or mental sadism which end up 'but I do love him/her; s/he is my dad/mum after all'.[9]

Whatever may once have been society's reasons for reinforcing family loyalties at all costs, there can surely no longer be any justification for people being forced to maintain within them such deep emotional schisms. For not only do some people spend pretty well all their lives trying to discover and testify to a love for a tyrannical parent they absolutely don't feel, but, convinced that a parent's failure to love them must be 'my own fault', others may devote their existence to trying, fruitlessly, to earn the love they take to be, at least potentially, the birthright of all.

Perhaps we hang so much moral weight on the apparent necessity of love and the maintenance of loyalty precisely because parenthood is such a lottery. Who your partners are is one of the very few relationships in life over which you have absolutely no choice. There is nothing about parents that entitles them to unconditional respect: anybody can be a parent, no matter how stupid, cruel, sadistic, immature, irresponsible, frightened, anxious or incompetent. Indeed, it may well be that 'good' parents are in a minority, and, whatever else may be the case, there can surely be no shame in having lousy parents.

Even if the kind of superstitious compulsion children seem inevitably to acquire to 'love' and respect those who have power over them is practically irresistible, at least perhaps we should try to rid ourselves of the moral complications of the parent–child relationship. Your parents did not fail to love you because you are *bad*, nor is it *bad* not to love people whose influence upon you was largely negative, if not positively damaging.

It remains true, no doubt, that love between parents and children is the most sustaining and positive force in the lives of those fortunate enough to experience it, and it is very hard to envisage what more satisfactory unit than the family could form the basis of society. Love, moreover, is demanding, and being a parent can be at least as difficult as being a child: tolerance and forgiveness must of course play a large role in the struggles of any family to maintain its integrity, and even the most loving will cause each other hurt.

In view of the immense warmth and lifelong security that can be gained from a loving family, it is extremely sad for those who did not fare well in the lottery to recognise that, for instance, they were not loved. But it is not more than sad. It does not reflect on their moral worth, and there is no obligation to love those who have failed to give love. You do not owe allegiance to tyrants, and there's no reason why a tyrannical parent should not be the object of a healthy hatred.

In the struggle against oppressive power and authority it is essential to recognise not only what is the legitimate sphere of morality, but, within it, what are and are not reasonable moral demands. Moral rules, as we have seen, simply do not apply in the realm of feelings, if only because feelings cannot be switched on and off at will. You cannot, if you do not, love somebody just because you are in some sense 'supposed to' (this is as true for parents as it is for children). Agonising about 'sincerity' or 'authenticity' is irresolvably pointless because, on the one hand, it is just not possible to force your feelings into line with how you wish to appear, and, on the other, it would be equally impossible to run a day-to-day life – let alone a society – in which honesty about your feelings was unswervingly observed.[10] Further, moral rules are not incontrovertible edicts handed down by some unquestionable authority, but can only reasonably be observed in a context of justice and fairness. The issue of 'telling the truth' is an interesting case in point.

Where respect and trust exist between equals, breaches of honesty are obviously likely to constitute a particularly malign form of betrayal. It cannot be right, for example, to manipulate the open, loving trust of someone by lying in order to obtain an advantage for oneself. On the other hand, childlike obedience to the injunction of power always to tell the truth simply places you at the mercy of that power for all time and robs you of one of the principal means of challenging it (through being able to dissemble your motives).

This is by no means a matter of mere academic speculation. Where survival in a setting of abusive power becomes paramount, lying can become almost the only defence available to the abused. Tyrannical parents and brutal husbands are just two of the groups whose intrusions may need to be resisted by lying, but there are many other situations in which power is abused (including the unfair and illicit manoeuvres sometimes adopted by employers over employees) where the victim's only recourse is to subversion of the truth.

One of the factors which led during the 1980s to there being so many psychological casualties among the middle-aged occupants of responsible jobs, particularly but not only in the public service, was that such people had often been brought up to believe in the essential benignity of power. They simply could not conceive that the business revolution which swept through all our lives could be in the sectional interests of only a small minority towards the top of the social pyramid, and struggled unsuccessfully both to understand and implement the changes forced upon them, eventually cracking under the strain. Had they had a conception of resistance that included disguised disobedience to unjust power, they would have fared much better.

When it comes to the kinds of problems in relationships that concern so many of us in our private lives, we would do well, I think, to rehabilitate the concept of duty. Rather than drowning in guilt and shame about what we think we should – but are not able to – *feel*, we would do better to engage in a cool calculation of what is and is not required of us to *do*.

Nadine, resigned for years to 'popping in' to her parents' house almost daily and ferrying her mother (who, though old, is able-bodied and clear-headed) around the shops twice a week while feeling guilty that she could not do it with better grace, at last begins to consider what might reasonably be expected not only of her, but also of her mother. For one thing, there is not the slightest sign of gratitude from her mother or consideration of life's other demands on Nadine; on the contrary, she spends most of the time admonishing, criticising and 'advising' her. Both Nadine's parents, in fact, seem intent on maintaining the fiction that she is dependent on them, when in truth the boot has long since been on the other foot. One day, trying to absorb a diatribe from her mother while driving her and a large load of washing home (her parents have no machine of their own), she snaps, draws up outside the local launderette, dumps the washing on the pavement and tells her mother to get on with it on her own. (Unfortunately, this is only a momentary rebellion, and Nadine is racked with guilt for days afterwards; nevertheless, it is a start.)

We do not have to feign a love or loyalty we do not feel, nor, when it comes to duty, do we have to perform it willingly. It doesn't matter how you feel about your duty, as long as you do it. For example, where the balance of power between parents and children becomes reversed, and the parents develop an unavoidable dependence on their children, it may well be the case that, even where the parents discharged their own duties badly, the children may consider themselves bound by a duty of care. But that's all it is. Love is a bonus which comes unasked, and cannot be bidden.

The qualities of love and loyalty, like mercy, are not strained. Where our early relations with each other have been conducted from the loving fullness of the hearts of those involved, we may well find depths of confidence and security which stand us in good stead throughout our lives. But such happy circumstances cannot be willed, and their absence is an occasion neither for blame nor for shame. Nor is the presence of more negative emotions. You can no more banish hatred from your heart than you can summon love into it, and the wisest course is to accept that, whatever you feel, you probably have good reasons for it.

It may, of course, help to try to understand how difficulties in families arise, but that is far easier to do for someone who has not been involved in the bitter struggles for and abuses of power which are likely to have taken place. It is asking a lot – I think often too much – to expect people who have, for instance, been viciously physically and/or sexually, or indeed emotionally, abused throughout long periods of their childhood, to stand back and see that their parents had understandable reasons for acting as they did. It may sometimes be possible, and indeed comforting, to do so, but often it is more important for the individual to accept and justify his or her own hatred and resentment and to untangle the mystifications of 'loyalty' than it is to be understanding towards those who inflicted the damage.

A great deal of distress could be avoided, then, if we could learn to withdraw 'morality' from the private world of our feelings and to concentrate instead on the rights and wrongs of our *conduct*. For of course it is important how we use the powers available to us in our relations with each other. You may not be able to pick and choose your feelings, but there almost certainly will be choices open to you in the courses of action you can take towards those with whom you live in closest proximity, and the greater your power is relative to theirs, the more choice you are likely to have.

The calculation of duty cannot be performed according to some absolute code of proper conduct, but only in relation to what is possible. And what is possible for any given person will depend on the powers and resources afforded him or her by the social environment in which s/he lives. We can deploy only the powers we have. This is why, when trying to understand why people act in the ways they do, a psychologist must look beyond their private subjectivity, beyond even the proximal world of their immediate relationships, and examine the influences that bear down on them from much more distal regions of the social environment. What you *should* do, in other words, is utterly dependent on what you *can* do, which is what will be considered next.

CHAPTER SIX

What Can We Do?
The Problem of Willpower

The idea that we *will* those of our actions that are not very obviously forced upon us by deliberate coercion or overwhelming circumstance is absolutely central to our view of what it is to be an autonomous person. It is, so it seems, through the exercise of will that we push ourselves into doing things: we survey the possible field of action, weigh up the pros and cons, 'decide' what to do and then 'will' the appropriate activity. There seems to be no problem about this; it is part of everyone's experience, and to suggest, as of course determinists have over the centuries, that actually our actions are governed by forces over which we have absolutely no control seems to be an affront to what we unquestionably *know* about ourselves.

This is all very well as long as *wanting* to do things and *willing* them go hand in hand. You identify the course of action you want to take and then you will yourself into taking it (you 'decide', 'make up your mind' to do it, and you do it through the appropriate act of will). Everything goes smoothly. Or maybe there are a few obstacles to your achieving the desired outcome: it's not quite as easy as you thought and the process takes longer than you had anticipated because people tried to divert or prevent you from reaching your goal; maybe you failed once or twice and had to persevere through adversity. But you won through in the end. A triumph of the will, perhaps: it is particularly the cases where we persist through obstructions and difficulties that convince us of the validity of the concept of will, for what else would sustain us and give us the necessary impetus to keep going?

What's more, the successful exercise of will, especially where achieving your aim has not been easy, brings with it a strong sense of satisfaction. Even if modesty forbids drawing attention to it, there is something praiseworthy about trying and trying again if at first you don't succeed. We admire Robert the Bruce for his moral fibre (forgetting, perhaps, that the source of his inspiration – the web-weaving spider – could scarcely qualify as a *moral* teacher and might in fact point up quite different lessons). It may seem to us that the strength to persevere, 'will power', is drawn from some internal moral source of which we can be quietly proud and which we should seek to inculcate in those for whose development we are responsible.

Things get rather more problematic when you find that wanting to do something is not smoothly linked with the process of willing it. You identify the desired course of action all right, but all your best efforts come to nothing, and what you find yourself doing is actually something quite different. This is a familiar part of everyone's experience. New Year resolutions, determination to give up smoking or to go on a diet, quickly demonstrate that seeing that something needs to be done, even really wanting to do it, is not enough to spark the application of the requisite amount of will.

In circumstances such as these, we would probably talk about 'failures of will', chastise ourselves for being 'weak-willed', maybe indulge ourselves with a tolerant admission that we 'just didn't have enough will power'. We can afford to be fairly lenient with ourselves because defeats such as these are the everyday experience of all of us: no one really expects us to keep New Year resolutions, and being able to stick to a diet is, as we all know, a rare achievement. It would not occur to us, simply on the basis of these apparent exceptions to the rule, to question our whole notion of 'will', nor indeed to regard ourselves as particularly morally defective.

When we come to supposedly clinical forms of distress, however, the situation becomes far more serious. For in many of these it seems that the will has broken down so badly that not only can people not perform the most ordinary volitional acts, but they seem – to themselves certainly, and very possibly to others as well – reprehensibly deficient in moral fibre.

Nothing simpler, you'd think, than going through a super-market checkout, driving your car down the motorway (as you have hundreds of times before), taking a lift to the second floor, signing your name on a cheque, getting on a bus, looking at the view from a high building, feeding the pigeons in the city square. And yet all these simple, everyday activities, and many, many others, can be so taken over by anxiety that the exercise of 'will' becomes a complete impossibility. Anxiety, it is true, is probably most often experienced (more accurately) as a failure of confidence than a failure of will, but in any case, as many sufferers know to their chagrin, even the greatest 'effort of will' is unlikely to overcome the panic.

And what of the situations where the 'will' is insufficient to stop people from doing things they clearly don't want to do but nevertheless are unable to resist? What, for example, does the predicament of the 'obsessive-compulsive' person tell us about the nature of will? Why cannot Dave simply will himself to cut short his morning safety rituals? If this represents a failure of his will, what is maintaining the ritualistic conduct itself? Is Dave willing it, secretly or unconsciously, or is it in some strange way 'unwilled' behaviour? How, similarly, can we account for the profound, bitter distress of the anorectic girl dying from starvation, unable to will herself to eat, but able, apparently, to go to elaborate lengths to avoid the ingestion of food; is she engaged in some extraordinary game of deception – of herself, of us?

So long as we can regard such cases as these as instances of 'disorder', as pathological departures from the norm, we may not feel that their predicaments should lead us to revise our notion of will. But if they are to be taken seriously as instances of the way human beings can *be* in regard to the control of their own conduct, they throw enormous doubt on our ordinary conception of 'will power'. And they are not, I think, different in kind from the dilemmas all of us may experience in situations *where we are in the grip of powers we do not ourselves control and whose influence we do not like.*

The simple concept of will is just not sufficient plausibly to account for how we come to act in any given situation, and quickly becomes incoherent as soon as we find ourselves at odds with what we're doing. Take, for example, the young wife and mother of firm moral convictions who suddenly finds herself involved in a passionate love affair with the next-door neighbour: it is likely to take her months just to get over the shock and bewilderment of finding that she has 'no will power' and trying to understand what has taken her over.

These issues need to be addressed not just because of the interesting philosophical questions they raise about the nature of will, but especially because of the distress which is attendant upon the 'breakdown of will'. People who find themselves unable to perform actions that other people seem able to do without a moment's hesitation or reflection are not only frustrated at being out of control of their own conduct, but feel humiliated and ashamed at what seems to be their deficiency in moral strength. It is in this area, in my view, that psychotherapy has failed its clientele most seriously.

PSYCHOTHERAPY AND 'WILL POWER'

Despite being faced with countless examples of people who are desperately struggling to will conduct over which they have no control, no brand of psychotherapy that I know of has taken up the implicit challenge to reconsider the popular notion of 'will power' which is embedded in our culture. While it is true that most are ready to recognise that sufferers can't pull themselves together by a simple act of will, it has not occurred to them to doubt the validity of the concept itself,[1] and, as far as therapy is concerned, it is in the end always up to the individual to will the necessary personal changes that will lead to an improvement in his or her condition.

Not all brands of psychotherapy refer directly to a concept of will – many never mention the word – but it is always implicit in their ideas about how change comes about. Furthermore, these ideas, where they have not been simply incoherent, have always been troublesome for psychotherapy.

The notion of 'insight', for example, is really nothing but a lightly disguised version of generally accepted ideas in our culture about how we come to decide, or 'make up our minds', to do things. We survey the options, weigh the pros and cons, decide on the course of action we most favour, and then do it. The trouble is that it is precisely in *doing* it that the clients of therapy often have their greatest difficulty. Psychotherapy has always worked focally on the *background* processes leading up, through 'insight', to a supposed act of will, and though it has not failed to notice that the problem for patients is indeed most acute at the moment of *acting*, it certainly has failed to take the implications of this seriously.

The fact that 'insight' – whether intellectual or emotional – doesn't necessarily lead to changes in conduct has long been a theoretical and practical frustration for psychotherapists of all persuasions, but that has not stopped them from persevering with the idea, albeit unexpressed, that clearing the ground for decisions to be made (the essential work of therapy) leaves it up to the individual to make them – all that is needed is the appropriate act of will, and if the patient doesn't choose to make it, that's his or her responsibility. Psychotherapy doesn't question the concept of will, it simply tries to restore the processes through which it might operate. If, having supposedly done so (by providing all the necessary 'insight'), it finds that patients still fail to take appropriate action, it is likely to change them with (precisely!) *wilful* recalcitrance, perhaps in the form of 'resistance'.

The difficulty for psychotherapy is, of course, that it literally cannot *afford* to recognise what stares it in the face every day: no matter how much people may *want* to change, despite their excellent understanding of the reasons for their previously 'maladaptive' behaviour, however simple it may seem to an outside observer for them to put the required changes into effect, desperately hard though they may strive to change, they simply cannot do it.

The answer to this conundrum is in fact relatively easy to find: it is not that people in this kind of situation are *unwilling* to change, but rather that they haven't got the *power* to change. The reason why psychotherapists cannot see this is that their practice depends for its credibility on the assumption that anyone able to become a client of therapy will be able to put into effect necessary life changes once s/he can see a good reason for doing so. If the *means* of changing conduct turn out not to be within the individual's grasp, the whole point of therapy is vitiated. In this way it is much more profitable for psychotherapy to cling on, however inexplicitly, to a notion of 'will power' than it is to countenance the idea that the powers requisite for change are likely to be beyond the patient's reach.

For 'will power', shadowy and unanalysable concept though it is, seems to be something available to any individual who has or can be given the strength to reach down inside him- or herself into a kind of interior moral space where, supposedly, the source of will resides. It seems as if all of us are born with a kind of moral fuel tank inside us containing the power we need to turn our projects into action. There seems, indeed, to be something humane and equitable about the idea that no one is entirely disqualified from being able to save themselves from adversity if they really, really want to, or if outside encouragement, exhortation or inspiration are strong enough.

If it really were like this, the psychotherapeutic enterprise would make perfect sense, for its procedures clearly are directed at smoothing the path for the successful operation of will, and there would be no obvious reason why they wouldn't work. Psychotherapy is very good at solving puzzles over and exposing the reasons for the problems people experience and the pain they feel: if there were a fuel tank within full of 'will power', psychotherapy would certainly enable them to tap it.

But the power to act is not a kind of in-built resource to which all of us, potentially, have access. It is something afforded us from outside. It may indeed be the case that we can – to pursue the metaphor – 'store' power we have acquired from external sources as in a kind of tank, but it is certainly not the case that the tank is full to start with. Whether or not we are able to realise our desires, put our plans into effect, do what we know to be right, will depend on our access to powers and resources which we need to acquire, or to have acquired, from the world around us. And this is something psychotherapy can help us with hardly at all.

THE PROCESS OF DOING

Before going on to consider the kinds of external powers and resources we need in order to be able to realise our aims, a little more needs to be said first about why it is often so difficult to achieve goals we *do*, on the face of it, have the power to reach. Once again, this has a lot to do with our conventional assumptions about how action comes to be taken.

What could be easier, for instance, than opening the front door and walking out into the street, or, as you have done thousands of times before, going into the kitchen to prepare a simple meal? You are, let us say, healthy and in good working order and there are no new powers you need to carry out routines long practised – what's to stop you, then, from simply doing what needs to be done? Difficulties like these are, as already pointed out, the common experience of, among others, people suffering from so-called obsessive-compulsive disorders or depressive illnesses. The man who has failed to check the gas taps and electric switches at the right time and in the right order finds it simply impossible to leave the house; the woman conscious of the need to prepare the evening meal for her family suddenly finds that she just cannot bring herself even to go into the kitchen, and instead goes to bed and pulls the blankets over her head. It can easily seem here that what we have is a serious failure of 'will power' – and that is exactly how it often seems to the sufferers themselves.

This is because we normally think of the exercise of will as rather like having an executive director, or perhaps a general, somewhere inside our heads who assesses the options, marshals the troops, and then 'decides' on a particular course of action. We have a sense of, as it were, launching ourselves into action, or perhaps rather being launched into action, by an executive decision after the pros and cons have been weighed and our 'minds' have been 'made up'. For people who find themselves experiencing difficulty over doing things they were once able to do without any problem, it often seems as if it is this 'executive director' who has suddenly disappeared. They can see well enough what's needed and there seems to be no lack of desire to do the things that have suddenly become impossible. It just seems that the decision itself cannot be made – it is the will that has failed.

Failure of courage is another form in which difficulties of this kind are often experienced. 'I just haven't got the guts to . . .' is the despairing view of many people who find themselves unable to perform apparently simple everyday actions like getting on a bus or going shopping. Contempt for oneself, even self-loathing, are the frequent accompaniments of supposed failures of will, and not having the courage to do things that everyone else seems able to perform without even thinking seems particularly shameful. 'Courage' tends to be thought of as a kind of moral resource very much like 'will' – something people are responsible for dredging up from an interior source and if they cannot locate it, this reflects on their worth as human beings.

In one way or another, then, it seems that when 'will power' fails we are no longer in charge of ourselves in the ways we take to be normal. The decision maker has disappeared, courage has drained away, the internal fuel tanks have run dry, we are no longer masters of our own actions.

Not the least problem with the ideas surrounding will – that we have an executive director in our heads or that we depend for successful action on adequate inner supplies of courage – is that they are so mysterious. *Where* within us are these things? On what organs do they depend? How can we access, augment, replace them? As we have seen, the strategy of pretty well all therapeutic approaches had been to ignore the problem in the hope that this is not the part of the putting-into-action process that really matters, and that if we concentrate on the weighing-up procedures of clarifying reasons and surveying pros and cons, somehow decisions will get made automatically. So-called cognitive approaches are no exception to this: if people cannot do the things they clearly want or need to do, it is because the 'cognitions' (attitudes, assumptions etc.) on which their behaviour is based are somehow faulty – it's because they're looking at things the wrong way.

The mystery of how plans get willed into action is thus no better understood by therapists than it is by those who find themselves unable to do the willing, and indeed is actually ignored. Therapy has come up with absolutely no better ideas about how people come to be 'in charge' of themselves than those embedded in the popular culture, whose inadequacy is shown up so obviously by the very difficulties of which the clients of therapy complain. It is, therefore, high time that we began to consider the possibility that our notion of will is so mysterious mainly because it is wrong.

In fact, the difficulties experienced by people supposedly suffering from 'clinical' conditions, far from compounding the mystery, may actually be pointing the way out of it. What their experience demonstrates may not so much be that they have lost charge of themselves in some pathological manner as that *we are none of us as much in charge of ourselves as we think*. The exercise of will may be an illusion.

WILL AS ILLUSION

The point is, I think, that we cannot help observing ourselves act, and it is easy to confuse observation with the execution of the act.[2] It may not so much be that we are *doing* things as that they are happening *through* us. Maybe we're not so much *willing* our actions as *witnessing* them.

As things happen to us and as we respond to them, we cannot but be consciously involved: we both *feel* the events (and our responses) as they impinge upon us, and we represent them to ourselves through the media of imagery and language – we *think* about them. All the time, we are, inescapably, intimately bound up with the constant interchange between ourselves as embodied creatures and the environment that surrounds us and the powers that flow through us from it and back into it. There is absolutely no way we can step outside this experience and view it objectively – it is our subjective experience of being in the world, and, among other things, we keep up a kind of constant running commentary to ourselves on what is going on.

This running commentary, if only because of the structures of the language in which it is necessarily couched, splits our experience up into logical stages, assigning to it sequences and causal chains which in fact have much more to do with the characteristics of thought than they do with the nature of the events they are trying to describe. As the influences that shape our actions flow through us, we commentate on them to ourselves by describing the processes they arouse in us in as orderly and comprehensible a manner as we can. For example, we characterise the process of being pushed and pulled in various directions as 'weighing the pros and cons' – indeed, we may often succeed in imposing an element of order on this process by actually looking for influences pro and con which we can submit ourselves to, in which case our conviction that we are somehow 'in control' will be heightened.

If all goes smoothly, we will experience the process of being influenced to act as 'making up our minds', and if we actually do find ourselves performing the appropriate action, we will tell ourselves that we have 'carried out the decision'. What is happening here is that the 'commentator' is attributing to the complex process through which we respond to the influences which bear down upon us a degree of subjective direction and deliberation which doesn't actually exist. It is not that, in performing an action, we are simply responding passively to some kind of coercion, but rather that the neat process we describe to ourselves – of cogitation and weighing up leading to executive decision – doesn't accurately represent the way we come to do things. This inaccuracy is likely to be revealed only when the 'commentator' is surprised to find things not turning out as neatly as expected.

Certainly *I* do what I do, but not under the guidance of some kind of inner executive director. Sometimes – most of the time, perhaps – what I do runs along in harmony with what I expect and wish to be doing, and with what other people consider is broadly all right and reasonable for me to do. At times such as these the commentator is perfectly happy and attributes to me a high degree of autonomy and 'will power'. Sometimes, however, I do things that run counter to my own or others' expectations, in which case the commentator's way of seeing things breaks down. In these latter cases the commentator wrongly attributes failures (of will, of courage, etc.) to me which are more accurately represented as inadequacies of 'his' descriptions.

Failures of will are not so much the sudden absence of the executive power as the commentator's inability to make sense of what we are doing, mainly because the theories 's/he' subscribes to are inadequate to the task. The point is precisely that I am not in control of my actions in the way my running commentary assumes. Rather than being able to stand apart from my activity to deliberate over and direct it, all I can really do is describe what happens. Rather than having 'intention' based on my 'will', I am really limited to finding out what my intentions were *after* the event. It would be much more accurate, though probably still far from completely adequate, if we saw will and intention as something we infer from our actions rather than as something we need to activate *before* we actually do things.

The trouble is that it seems to us that we *own* the events that take place inside us as our activity is shaped by the influences upon us – and in a perfectly good sense, of course, we do. But our subjective conviction of ownership goes far beyond a mere recognition that we are the hosts of processes over which we have but little control: almost irresistibly, we feel we own them in the sense of being responsible for them, even of inventing them. After all, we only feel them, they are only truly alive for us, when they form a part of our embodied experience. If the sunflower could speak its feelings as we do, it too would no doubt claim that it is *willing* its face to turn to the sun.

Contrary to what is popularly thought to be the case, being able to introspect on what it feels like to be engaged in one's own activity may actually be a disadvantage when it comes to trying to understand the reasons for our actions. We may in fact be less misled when trying to work out the reasons for other people's actions than when reflecting on our own. This is because when looking at others we are not so easily distracted by a 'commentator' who, so to speak, thinks 's/he' has privileged access to what is going on inside the person; all we can see is the way others respond to the events that seem to be affecting them from outside.

Certainly the whole edifice of behaviourist psychology was

built on the observation that introspection is a highly untrustworthy route to accurate knowledge of the self, and 'dynamic' approaches to therapy also recognise the unreliability of the 'commentator', frequently preferring to read off people's intentions from their 'unconscious' impulses and preoccupations.[3] The fact, also, that small children cannot say why they have done things until *given* the explanation by an adult (until, that is, both action and experience have been given meaning within a culture) also suggests that being the agent doesn't necessarily give us privileged insight into the reasons for the act.[4] When we insist, especially with children but also to an extent with adults, that they 'tell us the truth' about why they did something, as if the agent's introspection is the only certain source of knowledge, we actually risk introducing distorting aspects of internal commentary which we could well do better to avoid.[5]

The two essential points that I am trying to establish in this discussion are (a) that human beings are not the initiators of conduct in a vacuum; we cannot will things out of nothing, and (b) that when trying to identify the wellsprings of our conduct we are not necessarily in any better position than anyone else (it is equally essential to note that they are also not necessarily in any better position than we); our motives are identified, if at all, from the influences upon us – quite possibly more apparent to others than to ourselves – and not from some kind of privileged inward view.

The causes of our actions are best understood as *powers* which flow through us and *resources*, existing in or originally acquired from the outside world, to which we have access. The feeling that we are in control of these powers and resources is largely illusory, and will be strongest when there is no conflict between what we do, on the one hand, and what we or others wish us to do, on the other. This does not at all mean that our conduct is, or is in danger of being, 'out of control', but merely that it is not under the control of an 'executive director' in our head. Our conduct is in fact directed and socialised by all kinds of influences, some of which will have, so to speak, become part of our personhood, and some which will be located outside our skins, possibly at distal regions of the social environment of which we need have no awareness at all. The fact that we can observe and commentate upon what goes on inside us does not enable us in any automatic manner to direct it, and is in fact more likely to mislead us about its origins.

When it comes to understanding what we are up to, then, we are probably best advised to take a stance towards ourselves as we would towards others, and to try to 'read off' from our actions what must be the nature of our intentions (or, more accurately, our motivation). Quite apart from the 'commentator' being misled by the overwhelming immediacy of experience into wrongly attributing proximal explanations to distal phenomena, 's/he' also has a moral partiality which makes 'him/her' a particularly unreliable judge of motivation. This is an assertion anyone can test for themselves: just think of the last occasion when you were in some kind of moral dispute over your conduct (with a spouse or partner, perhaps). Almost certainly you will have recounted the incident to yourself over and over again until you thought you'd arrived at 'the truth' – a truth which in all probability will put you in the most favourable moral light!

The advantage of looking at yourself as a kind of way station for external influences is that it makes sense of a whole range of phenomena, particularly many so-called clinical phenomena, which cannot be accounted for by the notion of 'will'. Far from being incomprehensible, 'pathological' or morally defective, the difficulties so commonly experienced by us when we become anxious, depressed and so on become explicable in the same terms and at the same moral level as conduct we take to be 'normal'. The disadvantage of doing away with 'will' is that it may appear to dehumanise us and render us morally unaccountable. I shall consider the advantages a little more before trying to show that no such disadvantage in fact threatens us.

THE MEANING OF 'SYMPTOMS'

Psychological theories that lay emphasis on the importance of 'unconscious' motivation have long recognised that apparently 'irrational' conduct – the kind of thing thought to constitute 'symptoms' of 'neurosis' etc. – almost always has a *meaning* in the context of the individual's world. Such theories have, however, failed to draw the radical conclusion from this insight. People have, certainly, *reasons* for doing what they do even when their actions may seem at first sight incomprehensible to themselves and/or others. But the motive force of these reasons is not to be found in an unconscious *intention* (which simply shifts the concept of will, together with all its confusions and inconsistencies, from the conscious to the unconscious sphere) so much as in influences from which, for one reason or another, the illusion of control has been stripped. The 'commentator', being unable to describe accurately what the person is doing, is unable to maintain the fiction that s/he is 'in control' (and is thereby confronted with an uncomfortable truth about the 'self' of which more fortunate people remain in blissful ignorance).

For example, when Brenda gets depressed she experiences a total collapse of will, and it seems to her that, though she has a thousand things to do, she simply cannot summon up the energy – the 'will power' – to do any of them. And yet her conduct is still fairly clearly directed to certain ends, most of which have to do with a kind of necessary (and in the context of her life as a whole very unusual) self-protection. For a while she goes on strike – goes to bed when she 'should' be cooking her husband's meals, doesn't go to work, doesn't answer the telephone, and so on. She is unfortunately not able to enjoy her periods of rest, and indeed experiences them with an intensity of despair only too evident, but nevertheless they do constitute a form of rebellion and a break from the joyless routine of service which her life has become and without which it could not continue at all.

When she is depressed Brenda simply *hasn't the power* to go on. This is not a matter of her will, but the inevitable result of the unremitting drudgery of her life which her character (her embodied experience of the past) makes it impossible for her to criticise. The impress of power (in the form particularly of her mother) simply didn't allow her to develop an idea of herself as *counting* or as able to *please herself* and these were not concepts her 'commentator' could in any way take seriously. Thus, when the time came that she could just not go on any longer, she had no way of representing to herself what was happening other than to view it as yet another indication of her inadequacy as a wife and mother.

Dave's rituals of checking are a way of protecting the world from destructive forces that he is afraid might get out of control. Given his experience as a child, when parental power impressed upon him that there were indeed in the world as well as in him potentially catastrophic forces of aggression and evil which could be dealt with only by a combination of denial and religious superstition, it is scarcely surprising that his 'symptoms' take the form they do. It is particularly noticeable, for instance, that Dave's rituals increase in frequency and intensity when things are happening in his life that would, if he were a different kind of person, make him angry. What this teaches us is not that he is the victim of an irrational pathology, but that the impress of parental power has real consequences in shaping our subsequent conduct. Dave knows, of course, that most people don't act like him, but that doesn't make it any easier for him not to be himself. Where such powerful influences are common to the culture, no indications of irrationality are visible: priestly rituals and conjurings are viewed with uniform equanimity by the congregation.

Failures of confidence of the kind so characteristic of 'anxiety states' demonstrate as clearly as we could wish that action may become impossible where certain essential resources are missing. Even so, the demonstration is lost on many – too often the relatives of those who have succumbed to anxiety. For it is one of the more unfortunate aspects of our popular understandings that, as well as blaming ourselves for the absence of powers over which we have no control, we also congratulate ourselves on their presence. The husband of the 'agoraphobic' trembling with terror on the threshold of the supermarket is all too likely further to undermine her with his cold impatience because he cannot conceive of not being able to do what she finds impossible: all she needs is to 'push herself', to apply some of the 'will power' which he so ably taps whenever necessary. Understanding may dawn, perhaps, when a couple of years later he suddenly finds himself sweating with fear at the prospect of having to drive his car down the motorway to a neighbouring town.

The wife's confidence runs dry as a combination of past deprivation and current difficulties. She can cope with the vulnerability created by the lack of encouragement she experienced as a child, by the fact that no one had much confidence in her, just so long as there is enough support and recognition in her current life. When this fails – because of her husband's waning interest in her, her children growing up, her friends moving away – her resources are no longer sufficient to keep anxiety at bay.

The husband's situation is a little different, less a consequence of vulnerabilities created in childhood. Like many men until recent times, he had a belief in himself sustained by having a valued role outside the home, giving him a certainty of his own worth and ability which made it particularly hard for him to understand his wife's problems. But suddenly his firm is taken over by a large overseas concern intent on 'rationalisation'. Redundancies are in the air, assets about to be stripped. His technical role is devalued in favour of marketing and image. Meetings become an ordeal of competitive scrutiny, and his reputation is on the line before people who are fundamentally unsympathetic. Powers that he had felt to be safely part of him are suddenly revealed as subject to the whim of others. He feels so weak that he no longer has the aggression and competitiveness needed to cope with motorway driving, and business trips become a nightmare.

For confidence, or 'courage', are precisely not things we can summon up from inside when we most need them, but are powers accorded us by the social environment. You gain confidence from having, or having had, people being confident in you. Courage comes from en*courage*ment. A certain quantity of confidence or courage is not the birthright of us all – we are not born with full tanks, and how much we are able to call upon will depend upon our experience as children as well as our current circumstances. We are as vulnerable to being over-confident as we are to lacking in confidence, though the latter is likely to be far more painful for the subject.

For people struggling to get to grips with the deprivations their anxieties impose upon their lives, nothing is to be gained by moral self-reproach or searching their interiors for the springs of 'will power'; something has to be done about making the social environment a less confidence-sapping place (more will be said about this in the next chapter). Confidence comes from outside.

THE ILLUSION AS INESCAPABLE

If we are just the passive recipients of outside influence, reacting like snooker balls to the play of forces over which we have no control, would this not render all our views of moral conduct meaningless, reducing us to dehumanised puppets of fate? Would such a view not justify a cynical fatalism which simply claimed not to be able to prevent socially destructive and selfish behaviour on a massive scale, repudiating all sense of responsibility? Would we not be able to excuse any kind of antisocial behaviour by shrugging it off as the unavoidable result of, for example, an 'unhappy childhood'?

It is important first to emphasise that I am *not* suggesting that everything we do is simply in passive response to outside forces. After all, we ourselves are forces within the total environment, albeit often far from powerful ones. To greater or lesser extents we do have powers to make a difference to the social world of which we form a part, however minuscule. We are by no means as inert as snooker balls: there is a complexity about us which makes our direction of travel after being struck by outside influences extremely difficult to predict. My point is rather that *we are not in control of the processes of influence in the way that our popular moral understandings imply*. We are much more the hosts, mediators and witnesses of the play of power than we are the executive directors. There is indeed no such thing as 'will power', but that does not mean that our conduct is necessarily chaotic, immoral or without direction. What direction it has is, however, an *aspect of the conduct itself* rather than imposed by our 'will'. The direction is, in other words, revealed in what I do, not by what I intend, would like, or think I ought to do.[6]

If it were possible to step outside the arena of human behaviour, experience and understanding into some scientifically complete, cosmic view of cause and effect, it might indeed be possible to give the kind of total, deterministic account, able to predict every minute event and action, which has at times been so attractive to some thinkers. God, viewed as a kind of omniscient scientist possessed of all the facts, would presumably be able to tell whether you were going to buy apples or oranges, scratch your nose with your finger or with your thumb. In circumstances such as these, questions of morality would become as senseless as it would be for us now to charge cabbages with the moral responsibility for their growth.

But we are not, and never will be, in such a situation. We are all, whether we like it or not (and however much 'scientific psychologists' might wish to distance themselves from the objects of their study), inescapably human. We have access to no cosmic view which could remove uncertainty and unpredictability from our dealings with each other. We can sense only with human bodies and think only with human concepts. We are necessarily involved in the processes of our own conduct in ways that make agonising about its morality absolutely inevitable.

The experience of struggling to keep control of our actions, of needing to do what is right or feeling guilty over doing what is wrong, of trying, and failing, to predict our own behaviour as well as that of others, is not something we can avoid even if we can recognise that, from the cosmic perspective, all such factors may be determined in advance.

We are indeed possessed by powers which we did not originate and which we do not direct, but that does not permit us to abandon our sense of responsibility, for our sense of responsibility is the sensation of being possessed by such powers. Even where our conduct is to a large extent the result of an 'unhappy childhood', to disclaim that conduct as having 'nothing to do with me' would be totally in bad faith, not only because we cannot escape the sense of responsibility which stems from being an agent, but also because the conduct itself *has* 'to do with me'. The challenge facing psychologists (among whom I count anyone who wishes to understand the origins of his or her own distress) is to show *in what sense* conduct has 'to do with me'.

I am suggesting that my conduct does not necessarily have 'to do with me' in the sense that I will it, that I am in executive control of it, or that I am to blame for it. I am responsible for my conduct in as much as it is I who do it, but that does not necessarily mean that I can 'help it'. But the fact that I may not be able to help it cannot free me from the struggles and dilemmas I experience in the course of acting, for those struggles and dilemmas are *the inescapable concomitants of being the host of powers and influences, whether or not I am in control of them.*

There is no such thing as 'will power', but the subjective conviction that we have 'free will' is inescapable, because *that is how it feels* to be an active human being. 'Will' is given in the experience of doing. We are in the grip of a necessary illusion. For the purposes of our everyday social lives, our ordinary ways of understanding these issues are probably effective enough, and it is far from my intention to suggest that we should abandon or reform our usual moral language. When it becomes important to understand how far we can be expected to control or to change ourselves, as it does in the case of emotional distress, we need, however, to be more precise. We need to see, for instance, that talk of 'will' leaves too many quite familiar phenomena of everyday experience unexplained and serves only to obscure our understanding. To turn our attention instead to the play of power upon and within us, and the availability of resources to us, proves in my view far more fruitful.

How free you are to do things depends on the powers and resources available to you. Beyond those you may have acquired from the past, some of which will have become embodied as part of your character, together with those which are available to you in your current environment, there are no further moral reserves of 'will power'. The extent to which you can do things that need to be done – and however clearly you can see that they need to be done – will depend on whether you have access to the requisite powers and resources. 'Freedom' is directly correlated with power. The more power you are able to wield, the more freedom will be available to you. However morally distasteful some people may find this, it is obvious from the way our society is organised as well as from our daily preoccupations that nearly all of us struggle to maximise our access to power and resources in the awareness that this will give us more room in which to move and exercise choice. Freedom is being able to choose.

How much you can do to alleviate distress depends, then, not on moral reserves of will to be called up from inside yourself, but on the extent to which you can bring influence to bear on the essentially *external* factors that are, or have been, bearing down on you. If there are no powers or resources you can call upon, there is nothing you can do about your predicament other than grin and bear it. On the other hand, there may be powers and resources of which you are unaware. Maybe, for example, it had simply never occurred to you to look at things in this light, so that vain attempts to tap a nonexistent internal reservoir of 'will power' had distracted you from looking outside yourself for the necessary motivation. We need to consider in a little more detail what kinds of external resources are important.

POWERS AND RESOURCES

The powers and resources that make it possible for us to choose between different courses of action in order to make some impact on the world vary greatly in the degree of their proximity to the person. Broadly speaking, the extent of their potency is correlated positively with their distance from the person: the more distal the resources to which you have access, the more powerful they are likely to be.

Resources of embodiment

Nobody is born without the potentiality of possessing in-built means of bringing influence to bear on the world in some degree, however slight. Although we are all constructed virtually identically, we are clearly not born equally in terms of the gifts nature confers upon us. Some are cleverer than others, some more beautiful; some are equipped to become athletes, some musicians; more debatably, some may be extrovert and some introvert. However much one might argue about the details, there can be little doubt that genetic differences in physical structure interact with established cultural values in numerous ways to give some people a degree of social advantage right from the outset.

None of these can be legitimately seen as *moral* advantages. You do nothing to deserve the gifts you may be born with, and you have no reason to congratulate yourself on those you have: it is merely a matter of luck. What makes the difference is not your embodiment itself, but the valuation placed upon it by society. Being unusually intelligent, for example, is as a rule an advantage, but in a social revolution where intellectual leaders are regarded with fear and suspicion, it could result in summary execution. Being black is pretty obviously a disadvantage in such societies as ours, but its irrelevance to any question of human worth is obvious to all but fools and bigots. Even though bodily resources are the only ones that can plausibly be said to be 'internal', they are thus still heavily dependent for their effectiveness on external validation.

Another important point to note about embodiment is that in most important respects it is, so far, beyond our control – out of reach of our 'will'. This is clearly something that irks us, and the importance to us of embodiment is easily discernible from the emphasis given in contemporary culture to health clubs, gyms, beauty salons, cosmetic surgery and genetic engineering. But for the most part you cannot significantly improve your IQ, turn black into white or change sex without considerably straining credulity, spending huge amounts of money and risking mutilation. The vast majority of us are stuck with the bodies we've got.

Bodily resources can be very important within the sphere of the individual's proximal world. For example, the issues of both beauty and intelligence can be deeply preoccupying, not to say intensely painful, for people who feel themselves lacking in either of these respects. Psychologists can be very nervous about facing up to the implications of people's worries in these two areas because, quite rightly, they recognise that (as much more obviously in questions of race) such considerations are easily corrupted by moral/political overtones that have a distinctly fascist flavour. By objectifying beauty or intelligence into some form of measurable trait we risk the beginnings of a morally illegitimate discrimination between people on the grounds of inherent personal worth.[7]

However, while acknowledging that no such discrimination would be legitimate, it is important to recognise that, albeit in some ways unfairly, it is possible for people to make advantageous use of embodied resources, and that sometimes they may be almost the only resources they have. Female beauty, for example (particularly though not solely), is made a commodity by our culture in a way which gives it distinct market possibilities, even if often these bring with them an oppressive element of exploitation. Muscle power may, rather similarly, give some (usually but not exclusively) men an option for violent influence where no other form is available to them. Brain power undoubtedly offers possibilities of more far-reaching influence.[8]

Money

Financial resources are of vast importance to us, and in this respect it is quite extraordinary that psychology and psychotherapy have paid them so little serious attention. With the possible exception of violent coercion, as through the use of military power, the quickest and most immediately effective way of influencing people is through controlling the means of their livelihood.

Money may not be able to purchase happiness, but it can probably buy just about everything else, including, in some circumstances, love. Worry and insecurity over finance are a familiar part of most people's lives, and the greater part of our daily activity, not to mention our sleeping nightmares, are concerned with getting enough money to stay alive and maintain a degree of social respectability. People who have a great deal of money are not only cushioned from forms of insecurity to which the rest of us are frequently prey, but they are able to exchange their wealth for practically all other forms of influence.

No doubt it is because of its absolutely fundamental importance to our lives that money – income – has become, so to speak, the ultimate repressed in our social intercourse. It is no longer indecent to discuss our sexual activities in public – even members of the royal family show little reticence in this regard – but it would not be regarded as proper to enquire into the extent of someone's financial resources. The heir to the throne as well as his spouse, happy enough to reveal marital indiscretions to television interviewers, would no doubt be utterly affronted if asked to display to the camera the balance sheets of their estates. As we saw in Chapter Four (see note 3), even the great architect of repression himself seemed blithely unaware of the extent to which his own professional preoccupations were guided by financial considerations. Psychology has more to do with money than with sex.

No doubt our vulnerability to financial power is precisely what leads to our being, on the whole, so secretive about how much money we have. There is a strategic element to the manipulation of power which makes it only prudent to keep your cards close to your chest, but when it comes to considering the choices you have in being able to influence your circumstances, there is no shame in acknowledging, at least to yourself, that financial resources are of the first importance.

Education, class and cultural capital

Education, of course, provides very real access to distal forms of power which make it possible for people to obtain social and financial advantage as well as an understanding of – and hence an ability to manipulate – the way the social structure around them works. At the very lowest level, literacy confers enormous advantages over those who have not achieved basic skill in reading and writing (life can be a torment of confusion and shame for the illiterate); at higher levels education is one of the most important resources for acquiring vocational or professional security and status as well as giving the possessor a purchase upon the apparatus of social influence.

Throughout the scale of educational achievement people may seek to differentiate themselves from each other, for example on the grounds of taste, in ways that establish social advantage. The French sociologist Pierre Bourdieu has documented the importance of various kinds of 'cultural capital' to the establishment and preservation of social power.[9] These are forms of power that, though not necessarily directly related to financial resources, may be possessed by people who are themselves quite unaware that they have acquired them from outside – they may, for example, experience them as personal qualities or marks of distinction that are somehow in-bred. The markers of class membership are closely bound up with various forms of cultural capital.

Although Bourdieu's work has particular relevance to French society, where intellectual and cultural achievement are in every sense more highly valued (and hence more effective forms of power) than in Britain, nobody can beat the British in the art of class distinction, and his treatment of the way indices of superiority can be established and maintained independently of mere vulgar money is particularly illuminating. For the most painful thing about class as a social valuation of people is that it is hard to shake off: you can't easily buy your way out of it, and the signs of class membership are often either embodied characteristics (e.g. regional accent) or early-established patterns of conduct (e.g. the manners and vocabulary of mealtimes) which it requires a prodigious effort to change in later life. Furthermore, the ideological option of taking pride in lower-class membership, even though based on undeniably positive values (e.g. courage and solidarity), cannot disguise the equally undeniable and all too material disadvantages of working-class status.

However, class membership pure and simple is probably no longer the vicious obstacle to social achievement that it was only a few decades ago, and while middle-class status can, for all the obvious reasons, certainly be counted as a valuable resource, being born into a working-class family does not on its own absolutely preclude people, as it once did, from entry to and acceptance in a wide range of social and professional circles. It just makes it much harder.

Home and family life

I hope that by now the crucial importance of parent-child and sibling relations in early life to the formation of character will be abundantly apparent. Those personal attributes that give us the courage to tackle the inevitable obstacles and setbacks of life (in particular the all-important factor of 'confidence'), however much they may seem to be congenital aspects of our personality, are acquired from our experience of the success or otherwise of our first tentative engagements with the social world outside ourselves.

The resources of character are thus the embodied constituents of early experience. Given the current structure of our society, there can be no doubt at all, I think, that the degree to which children are able to acquire skill and confidence in their dealings with the world and with others as they grow up plays a vital part in later vulnerability to emotional distress. And whether or not they are able to acquire such skill and confidence will depend on the readiness of the significant adults around them to afford them power and encourage their early efforts.

There are, of course, other important resources connected with family life. Solidarity with other members of the family – the more extended, the better – provides an important source of proximal power. Parents, children, sisters and brothers, aunts, uncles and cousins may provide comfort, collaboration and support at times of distress or difficulty. Membership of such families (an important feature contributing to the solidarity of the traditional working class) is becoming increasingly rare, and there is no guarantee that being one of a large family will automatically bring such benefits – indeed, family disunity can be as big an emotional liability as family solidarity an asset.

The colossal weight placed in modern society on 'relationships' – by which is usually meant love relationships with spouse or partner – means that more and more frequently they break under the strain. But where long-term relationships are established in which sex and companionship strike a successful balance, there is no doubt that they do provide an enormously positive resource in people's lives. The difficulty is not in understanding why such relationships are so valuable, but in being able to make or maintain them. The greater the desperation with which we seek love, the harder it seems to get to find. A little more will be said about this in the following chapter.

Social life

Friends in whom we can confide (and whose confidences we are ready to receive in return), on whom we can call at times of crisis or acute distress, with whom we can eat and drink, play games and so on, are at least as valuable a resource as good love relationships, and probably quite a bit easier to find.

Belonging to societies, joining political groups, signing up with evening classes for interest or further education are often helpful both in acquiring or extending personal powers and in establishing a degree of communality and solidarity with others, making friends, etc.

The power of association is probably the principal way in

which 'ordinary people' in the modern world can hope to
extend their influence beyond the immediately proximal.
Reduced to the absolute singularity of the private individual,
we have little hope of influencing the world beyond appeals
to the charity of others on the one hand or brute force on
the other. It is by being *part* of something (usually at work)
that people acquire status, respect and influence. The potency
of association is well recognised by those political influences
that seek to 'individualise' and 'privatise' the life of the
ordinary citizen (hence, for example, the enormous
ideological effort put into discrediting the trade unions). The
lone couch potato browsing through electronic shopping
malls or lost in virtual reality is scarcely likely to threaten the
political status quo.

The social context

Our lives are dominated by a social environment over which
we have very little if any control but which may accord us or
deprive us of crucially important resources.

The general economic situation may determine whether or
not you have a job, and hence not only your financial power
and security, but also, in all probability, the degree to which
you can regard yourself as having a worthwhile part to play in
society. What kind of job you have, where you figure in the
hierarchy of power, how creatively you are able to work or
how repressed and restricted you are, will all contribute to your
level of confidence and sense of freedom.

The quality of the physical environment in which domestic
life is lived can be as important as the emotional relations
between those in the home. Overcrowding, poor housing,
bleak, dangerous neighbourhoods can quickly crush the spirits
and extinguish the optimism of those who have to suffer them.
Indeed, the emotional, 'psychological' or 'spiritual' qualities
that are supposed to sustain us in times of trouble are often

fatally weakened by the very material conditions that they are supposed to buttress us against.

We do not, of course, ordinarily think of ourselves as split up into powers and resources of the kinds I have sketched above. If we think about it at all, we are likely to see ourselves as *agents* who consider what we want to do, survey the alternatives and decide on the most appropriate course. In the process of so doing, it seems that we are constantly drawing on resources inside us and enacting our will to achieve our aims.

What we can do, however, is limited to what can be achieved by use of the powers life has afforded us, and when we find ourselves unable to do things we want to do or feel we should so, there is little to be gained from self-reproach. We need to look not at what ails us, but at what we lack, and nothing is likely to make that clearer than when we come to try to change ourselves.

CHAPTER SEVEN

What Could We Do?
Learning and Change

The twentieth century, on many counts the bleakest on record (certainly the most violent and destructive), could also be called the most optimistic. For, as the century of psychology, the last hundred years have established in the Western mind expectations of the banishment of distress through therapy far greater than is justified by the actual lessons of experience. Not only do we expect to be able to overcome, with the help of psychotherapy, 'symptoms' of emotional distress seen essentially as forms of illness, but we hope also that psychology may instruct us in possibilities for 'personal growth' which could lead to our becoming unusually adequate or even excellent specimens of our kind.

There is of course nothing unusual about such hopes and aims. As I pointed out in Chapter One, psychology is in many ways continuous with practices of magic which go back as long as recorded time, and it is perhaps only to be expected that our aspirations and longings should, through psychology, seek a suitably 'scientific' garb for themselves in the technological age. And yet there is something incongruous about the existence side by side of the kind of uncompromisingly realistic intelligence that can send space probes to Jupiter and the wildly unrealistic fantasy that human beings can be changed from the inside out in accordance with their wishes. Our wishfulness, it seems, is detached from our intelligence so that each in its own way threatens to run out of control.

Something of the flavour of this split was already apparent early in the century as Freud and Jung juggled their esoteric psychological mysteries while barely casting a glance at the wars and revolutions which erupted around them – as if Psyche, contriving an ostrich survival, dared not contemplate the terrifying realities of human society.

Not that striving for moral purity, mental balance or personal development are unworthy aims, nor that staring straight into the mouth of hell is somehow a bracing form of intellectual discipline to be recommended for its own sake. My point is rather that our hopes of what we can do to better our psychological lot need to be tempered by a sober assessment of the restrictions placed on our room for manoeuvre by the world in which we live. The lesson of history is that, with the best will in the world, we inevitably fall well short of perfection,[1] and perhaps it is time we realised that, rather than each of us being the centre of a psychological universe which somehow we can find the secret to manipulate, we are atoms in a social world which we must learn to control *collectively* if we are to make a noticeable impact on our own suffering. Furthermore, if we are to avoid, on the one hand, the fanatical imposition of our views on others and, on the other, unnecessarily crushing disillusion in our personal lives, it is probably important for us to remind ourselves how modest even our collective achievements are likely to be.[2]

By establishing the idea that happiness, emotional balance and mental adjustment are the norm, psychology and psychotherapy serve only to add an edge of despair to the distress most people encounter at least sometimes in their lives. The contrasting view of life as tragic, reflected in particular in the greatest artistic and literary works throughout the ages, is probably not only more accurate than the cosy smugness of so much therapy and counselling,[3] but is actually a solace to those who value the discovery that they are not alone in the boat.

It is almost inconceivable that anyone can live a life without repeated and significant experiences of loss, disappointment, failure and pain; and for millions of people on the globe life is a continuous experience of toil and privation. Death finally punctuates the whole experience with an ironic question mark whose import can be overlooked only by dwindling numbers of resolute optimists and the most steadfastly religious.

If we really knew how to escape the tragic elements of life through the cultivation of therapeutic (or any other) techniques, we would no doubt long since have perfected them, and the endless labours of research workers seeking the demonstrable benefits of psychotherapy would be unnecessary. As it is, we know perfectly well that the best – if far from infallible – insurance against the worst of the world's unkindnesses is the social and economic advantages which give us a measure of ascendancy over others and choice about the conditions of our lives. Global society is structured accordingly.

The whole lesson of life is that change is not easily achieved, and certainly not from the inside out in the manner promised by therapeutic magic. Closing our ears to the woolly rhetoric of psychobabble, we can very quickly see that no one is transformed through psychotherapy, and that making even modest changes to our being-in-the-world is almost always extremely difficult and demanding. Even if we can understand the influence of the past on the formation of character, we cannot step out of the embodied person we have become. Image and make-believe may contribute to a collective delusion that anyone can do and become anything, but the impress of power is in fact not so lightly to be escaped, and Norma Jean inhabits Marilyn to the end.

Above all, the stability of character is what defeats the more sanguine hopes of psychotherapy, but it also makes the world an interesting – not to say bearable – place in which to live. Just imagine how terrible life would be if we really could be therapeutically engineered into clones of some kind of norm of 'adjustment', and how inevitably therapeutic technique would become an instrument of tyrannical repression. As it is, nothing convinces us more of our indelible individuality than watching people struggling to change aspects of themselves that cause them distress.

For better or for worse, the impress of power stamps upon us strategies and projects which we pursue lifelong, as if fated like characters in Greek tragedy. And indeed it is the case that we struggle to appease the powers we first encounter as if they were the gods of Olympus. It may on every rational count be crazy for, say, this harassed and lonely middle-aged woman to strive unremittingly to please the implacable mother who neglected and abused her from infancy, and yet it seems that no argument and no exhortation can divert her from that aim. It seems that we are indeed born as sunflowers, programmed to turn our faces to the most potent force in our environment, dependent for our very sense of existence on the endorsement of power.

We are social creatures and cannot exist independently of the influences that structure our world, and if the most powerful of those influences, when we encounter them as defenceless infants, should turn out to be the overwhelming proximal relation with an adult who hates us, we will nevertheless seek endorsement through it, not out of masochism but because, quite literally, we could not exist without it. For all too many people there is no power beyond the cruel or indifferent parent, or later perhaps the abusive spouse, from whom they may seek the affirmation of their being. It is this kind of circumstance which 'therapy' needs to address in order to understand the limits of its enterprise.

Seeing how we need to be different, wanting, no matter how passionately, to change in accordance with obvious goals, may or may not be necessary precursors to tackling our predicament, but they are certainly not of themselves sufficient for overcoming it. Psychotherapy trades on the excitement experienced by people on seeing for the first time that there are comprehensible reasons for the way they feel and the conviction following from this that the solution is at hand. But if they are not in possession of the powers they need to change, therapeutic insight of this kind may lead only to even greater pain and frustration. As we have seen, 'cure' comes about neither as the automatic consequence of insight nor through the most determined efforts of 'will power'.

Many people recognise this, at least implicitly, by seeking salvation not through any inside-out attempts at self-transformation but rather through intimate relationships with others. To young adults in particular it may seem that many of their most painful difficulties would be alleviated by finding someone with whom they can share their lives. Change will come about not through self-transforming efforts of will but through the redeeming power of love. People search for, form and maintain such relationships as their own personal barriers against adversity. 'Relationship' becomes a kind of commodity to be acquired, exchanged or hoarded as the minimal solidarity needed to survive in a harsh world.[4]

The difficulty with this is that the relationship ceases to be about anything but itself. Friendships as well as love relationships (and of course, more basically, sex) become things to have rather than relations through which something is made or achieved. We thus become possessions of each other, with the burden, if we are not to be summarily discarded and replaced, of providing a whole range of satisfactions: sexual, companionable, even 'therapeutic' levels of comfort and understanding. No such burden can be borne for any length of time by one individual, even if 'in a relationship' with another individual bearing a reciprocal burden.

The impossibility of the demand placed upon relationship is what often makes its attainment ultimately disappointing. The commodified nature of 'relationship' as an end in itself – epitomised in the existence of dating agencies and singles clubs – could not distract us more effectively from an understanding of what does make relations built on love the source of strength that they sometimes are. For example, love is often more about forbearance, the tolerance of difference and acceptance of inevitable aloneness than it is about the constant supply of warmth, understanding and satisfaction. It is certainly true that loving relations with another person, friendships in which appreciation and sacrifice are freely given and received, can constitute an enormously important 'resource' to those both fortunate and strong enough to take part in them. The sobering fact is that they are really quite rare.

There are those, I am sure, who will see my dwelling on the difficulties of personal change as an almost destructive erosion of hope. But it is only false hopes that I wish to destroy. To discover that your best efforts to escape from distress or despair are vain not because of your own inadequacies but because it simply isn't possible to do it all on your own may indeed be disillusioning, but in a way which is, I believe, reassuring rather than disheartening. To bring about change you need access to power. You cannot change your 'self', but you may be changed by shifts in the powers and influences which structure the social world around you.

CHANGING THE WORLD AND NOT THE 'SELF'

It would be impossible for a normally cheerful person to make a New Year resolution to be unremittingly miserable for the coming twelve months. On the other hand, if our normally cheerful person loses his job in January, suffers a major bereavement in February and is severely injured in a road accident in March, one would have no difficulty understanding or explaining his misery. Your mood depends on what is happening to you, not on what you decide to feel. The obviousness of this observation may seem to make it hardly worth making, and yet it is surprising how difficult people in distress often find it to grasp.

If you want to know why you are unhappy, look into the world around you, and if you want to change how you feel, look to see if the world can be changed. As an individual, this is just about all you *can* do. And yet many people don't even get this far: instead of looking into the world, they look into their 'selves'. 'It's *me*,' they say (encouraged by a century of half-baked 'psychology'). 'I know it's my fault really.' 'I know there are thousands worse off than me.' 'I feel so stupid.' Shame and self-blame are the commonest reactions to feeling distressed, but, as we have seen in earlier chapters, are singularly inappropriate as strategies for identifying the causes of distress and seeing whether anything can be done about them.

It is about as sensible to seek the reasons for distress inside the 'self' as it would be to see feeling cold as a matter of personal responsibility. It should be no mystery to you why, standing lightly dressed in a field in midwinter, you suffer from the cold. You are unlikely to say to yourself: 'I wonder why my body is shaking and my teeth chattering – there must be something very strange the matter with me.' And in order to cure your problem you are likely to institute an environmental change – put a coat on, or go indoors and light a fire.

It is exactly the same with depression, anxiety and so on. Although the causes of such feelings as these may not be so obvious as in the case of feeling cold, part of this lack of obviousness is because we have become so mystified by the popular culture, by 'psychology' and by powerful ideological (political and commercial) interests which are eager for us to construe our miseries as of our own making. Things are made more difficult by the fact that the causes of our problems are often out of sight, in distal regions of the social environment we might not even know about, and possibly also distant from us in time – perhaps having occurred in the past beyond the reach of our memory. But to start with the idea that it is not you but the world that is 'at fault' is the first essential step in tackling those aspects of your difficulties that can be tackled.

CHANGING POSITION

Psychological distress is unlikely to be just a matter of the influence of the past. We may be shaped as characters in many ways, some of which no doubt render us particularly vulnerable to certain forms of noxious influence, but unhappiness is highly likely to be to a significant degree a consequence of things that are happening in the present. Some of these things may be avoidable by changing our position in the world.

Escaping the causes of distress is, however, in all probability not going to be as easy as walking in out of the cold. It is likely that sufferers will already have tried just about everything they can to improve their lot, and indeed it is often the very irresolvability of the conflict they find themselves in that gives rise to the distress in the first place. Difficult marriages are a good case in point: it may be obvious to one of the partners that s/he is profoundly unhappy, but what to do about it is precisely the problem. Wives may be financially dependent and have nowhere else to go; emotional damage to children may seem to either partner too high a price to pay for separation, and so on.

Again, a change in the physical environment – moving out of bleak, noisy, overcrowded or otherwise distressing domestic accommodation – can often bring about a huge reduction in the degree of psychological distress suffered, but anyone with the means to do so would probably have taken the necessary steps before their living circumstances became a significant problem.

Similarly with changing jobs, improving our opportunities through further education, finding someone to love or developing a social life: if these were easy, it would be simple enough to avoid distress in the first place.

People whose distress would be greatly alleviated by a change in their position in the world could do two things. The first is to consider carefully what their powers and resources are; the second is to grasp the nettle of change.

By 'grasping the nettle' I mean recognising that, if they are to *feel* differently, something will have to be *done*. They must abandon trust in the magical blandishments of the various kinds of marketed make-believe which promise painless transformation. There are some situations in which change, though perhaps extremely difficult, is at least possible. This applies particularly in the area of relationships. For women in particular, it is all too possible to get caught up in relationships that do take a terribly destructive toll on their personal development and happiness (Gina is a case in point). Children may certainly be affected by the break-up of a marriage, and finding somewhere else to go may be very problematic. All the same, it is often possible for a woman in this position to be much stronger and more resourceful than she thinks (especially after years of having been undermined by her partner) and to discover that there is in fact more support available to her in the social environment than she had thought possible.

Similarly, challenging parental power, once the victim of it has grown up, is a possibility, even if putting it into practice can seem shatteringly risky. In every case where I have known a grown-up child challenge a tyrannical parent, the tyrant has backed down surprisingly meekly. I have never yet known an aged parent die of apoplexy if his or her daughter has at last refused after thirty years to mow his or her lawn, prepare his or her meals or do his or her shopping at some precisely ordained (and extremely inconvenient) time, but I suppose it's always possible that one might. But that would be the price of tyranny, not of filial rebellion.

However, as I have already argued, determination on its own is not enough to change your position in relation to the rest of the world: to be successful, you need more material powers or resources on your side.

Assessing available powers and resources

In thinking about the forces we may be able to muster in our struggle with life's difficulties, it may help to develop a rather more systematic view of the kinds of power and resources that were considered in the previous chapter and to present them in the form of a diagram.[5]

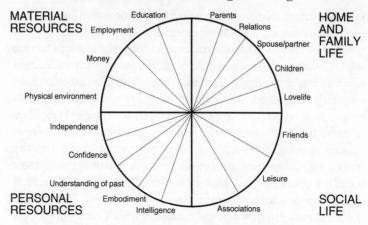

Figure 21: Possible availability of powers and resources

The segments that go to make up each of the four main quadrants of Figure 2 are not to be regarded as constituting a definitive or exhaustive, 'scientific' analysis of available resources, but rather an indication of the areas it may be worthwhile surveying when trying to identify what you may have going both for and against you. The more a given segment could be regarded as 'filled', the more possible it becomes for that particular area to be used as a positive resource; the relative 'emptiness' of a segment would indicate not only the lesser availability of the resource in question, but the possibility also of greater pressures and demands in that area.

For anyone suffering significant distress, *home and family life*, for example, is likely to be as much a source of difficulty as it is of strength. Almost all the examples in Chapter Two indicate how problems in relations with others – parents, spouses or partners, children and stepchildren – have a part to play, if not in directly causing distress, then certainly in stirring up vulnerabilities acquired earlier in life. For obvious reasons problems are more likely to be caused by the absence than by the presence of a lover in the individual's life, but there is no shortage of difficult and destructive relationships which are probably better ended than persevered with.

Consideration of this quadrant is probably as useful for understanding the nature of our difficulties as for indicating what might be changed. Individuals can expect to be able to do very little single-handedly to alter the quality of the family relationships in which they are embedded. Even 'family therapy' or 'marital therapy', which do provide a form of intervention backed by a degree (albeit limited) of power not available to the individual, cannot escape the fact that the families and their members are held in place by environmental and historical powers not amenable to the influence of therapists. Therapies of this kind may provide a useful forum in which family members (particularly parents and children) can reflect on unhelpful 'habits of relating' which may have established themselves, and therapists may play a more or less educational role in clarifying problems and suggesting alternative strategies. As with individual therapy, however, the benefits of 'insight' should not be overemphasised, and difficulties in families are often the consequence of more than just misperceptions or faulty habits.

Married couples or partners may well find marital counselling or therapy helpful in clarifying what they feel about the relationship and each other, and where there is a strong bond of affection between them, having a neutral 'referee' with whom to air difficulties, grievances and sources of pain may quite possibly result in their finding it easier to live together. But there is no way in which counselling of this kind can guarantee to repair difficult relationships, and, depending on what they were hoping for from it, partners are as likely to find the outcome negative as positive. The world has a way of reasserting its influence once the couple are away from the consulting room, and understanding the nature of the problem does not necessarily point the way to a 'cure'.

As indicated in the last chapter, *social life* is a resource of the first importance. Solidarity with others is both one of the most significant and, all things considered, the most available forms of power for 'ordinary' people.

Once again, it is of course extremely difficult for people who find themselves socially isolated to whip up out of nowhere friendships or other forms of association with congenial or influential individuals or groups. But it is often the case that the very people who *feel* most unlikeable, and are therefore particularly vulnerable to emotional distress, are those whom others would take to most readily. The kind of social diffidence that early brushes with power so easily instils tends also to make its victims adaptable and attentive to others, and free of objectionable bombast, so that they are potentially very good (and, if they're not careful, exploitable) friends. It may therefore be possible, at least in principle, for such people to discover that they can make friends much more easily than they had thought.

In times of trouble, when people most need the friends they do have, just such diffidence may make them reluctant to burden people with their problems. Many people *will* burden anyone who cares to listen to the point of ultimate desperation, but these are *not* the people who feel diffident about it. In other words, if you do feel you would like to talk to your friends about urgent or pressing difficulties but really feel reluctant to trouble them – and if, especially, you usually find yourself listening to *other* people's problems – you should almost certainly take the plunge. It would be very surprising if you don't get a sympathetic and helpful response.

As suggested in Chapter Five, it is sometimes helpful for the shy person, who would like but is terrified to approach people who seem congenial, to remember that s/he is 'other for others', and that they are likely to respond to him or her in exactly the way that s/he does to them. In other words, their likely reaction to being approached would be pleased and sympathetic. In order to discover this, of course, there is no alternative to taking the necessary action.

Most forms of broadly cognitive therapy depend very heavily

on challenging the assumptions seeming to underlie difficulties that, from every practical aspect, look quite easy to overcome, and it may well be the case that encouragement from a therapist could be a useful source of solidarity in propelling people to take apparent risks it would be very difficult for them to take on their own. As will no doubt be apparent by now, my own view is that while such approaches can be helpful, they do tend to overlook the problem of embodiment – of how deeply 'wired in' are apparently quite superficial ways of conducting oneself – and people should not feel too despondent if they find therapeutic instructions very difficult to follow.

Again, in considerations such as these it is as important as ever to beware of the tyranny of the norm. It is simply not the case that, if we were to expose ourselves to the requisite therapeutic regimen, we would all become averagely sociable human beings, nor is there any particular reason why anyone who wants to shouldn't become a recluse. One aspect of character frequently to be encountered in socially diffident people is that no amount of demonstration of friendship or affection is sufficient to convince them that they are in the least lovable, and while this may in many ways be a painful characteristic, it is certainly not one that makes those who embody it less than human.

It is, however, often the case that making the effort to engage in social activities of some kind leads to great improvement in people's lives and, consequently, considerable mitigation of their distress. Mobilising interests in order to do things with others (hobbies, sports, evening classes, religious or political convictions – pretty well any form of association providing a focus in activity for doing things with people) is probably the best way of developing friendships or deeper relationships. To this end, it may be a good idea, if you wish to widen your social life, to consider what resources you have (of interest, ability or previous knowledge) that could be drawn on or in some way initiated to reposition yourself alongside others.

When it comes to considering *personal resources* it may once again be more a question of taking stock than of immediately identifying ways of increasing the amount available. For most people suffering from emotional distress it is highly likely that their stock of confidence will be very low, and, as we have seen, there is no way it could be increased directly by a determined act of will. It is, however, helpful sometimes for people to recognise how much lack of confidence is contributing to their predicament, rather than, say, 'neurotic illness' or moral cowardice. It may also be helpful to note how confidence may sometimes be increased precisely by *not* focusing on it directly, but through the acquisition of powers and resources in other areas.

Both embodiment and intelligence are, again, not aspects of the person that can easily be altered. Quite often, however, these resources are overlooked, especially by people who are feeling depressed or unhappy about themselves. Particularly in the case of intellectual ability, it may be possible to make use of untapped resources to acquire skills or qualifications that can make a very significant contribution to a material increase in power. There are also many people whose education was impaired or interrupted for one reason or another, and who have wrongly concluded that they are 'thick' because, perhaps, they have difficulties with literacy. Although it can be very difficult to walk into adult literacy classes all on your own, without the backing and encouragement of family or friends, it can, for those who somehow manage it, open up worlds almost undreamed of. I have met many highly intelligent and perceptive, but educationally deprived, people who had no idea of their exceptional talents.

Acting on the recognition that they have unrealised potential maybe by 'going back to school', doing an Open University course, taking evening classes or entering further education by any other available route – may introduce people to a *social* world whose existence they hadn't previously been able to envisage. There are many people who have an unrequited love of truth which they feel as a purely personal pain, and are astonished and overjoyed to find that not only are there others who share their passions and their interests, but that a whole world exists in which such interests are regarded as perfectly normal and in which friends are quite easily to be made.

Much more difficult to swallow (and, happily, in my experience very much less frequent) is the situation in which people need to recognise that their intellectual ability is being stretched beyond its capacity. There are obvious costs to status and self-esteem in acknowledging that, for instance, they are not up to their job, and there may be circumstances in which these costs are not worth paying. On the other hand, there may be times when people find it an enormous relief to retrench to a position in which less is demanded of them intellectually.

Understanding of the past is, on the other hand, something that can be increased relatively easily, and is certainly, through the process of 'clarification' discussed in the opening chapter, one of the main things psychotherapy can help with. Confusion and bewilderment over why we are in the grip of distressing 'symptoms' can often be assuaged quite quickly through a process of relating how we feel to the influences that are affecting and have affected us in a real world over which we have and have had virtually no control. But, as I have emphasised throughout this book, 'insight' of this kind is of limited usefulness, since in and of itself it changes nothing of real significance. It may be, however, that for some people 'knowing the reasons' for things provides a necessary degree of incentive to do something about them. The therapeutic process of clarification, in this way, works best with people who are already in possession of the necessary powers to make changes to their lives: seeing that something needs to be done is fine if you have the wherewithal to do it but may be cruelly frustrating if you haven't.

Independence – most often from some kind of oppressive

authority or personal relationship – is again something that may, at least theoretically, be within our power to increase. Those adults I have encountered in life able to be most honest with themselves often say that they still feel like four-year-old children, and for many of us it can easily seem that, like children, we are surrounded by 'grown-ups' who seem to have a handle on the world (i.e. access to powers) well out of our reach. For people (often, of course, those who are most socially oppressed, like working-class women) who find themselves overshadowed or undermined by others in their proximal world, it may be important to recognise that the 'power horizon' of their oppressor is in all essential respects the same as their own, and that, if challenged, he (usually) will back down.

The principle of challenging power in personal relationships should, however, not be turned into some kind of fatuous therapeutic nostrum. While it is very often the case that people who *feel* powerless have, through their normal rights as adults and citizens, much more power than they think they have (or know about) and may, if they can discover it, use it to great effect, it is also true that those whose power relative to those around them is restricted (children, women, ethnic minorities etc.) may if they step out of line find themselves at the receiving end of some shattering punishment.

The possibility of exercising our rights as citizens to use the social institutions that offer advice and support in battles with adverse powers is not evenly or fairly distributed among the population. Not only, for example, do we need money to pay for legal advice (except in increasingly rare circumstances), but the knowledge (and hence confidence) to approach authorities, tackle bureaucracies, and so on, is acquired principally as part of a middle-class upbringing. Professional people in official buildings are often bearded with great trepidation, if at all, by people who have been brought up to fear and respect power. It can, for example, be very difficult to persuade those who would most profit from their services even to step inside the excellent Citizens' Advice Bureaux.

Increasing independence need not only be a question of relations with others: there are also relations with the world. It is, for example, surprising how often an extension of mobility, perhaps by acquiring a car and/or learning to drive, can result in a very significant increase in someone's freedom and, consequently, feeling of confidence. Quite literally, someone may be able to change his or her position in the world and open up new horizons of power simply by establishing the means to move around it. Here again, it is quite obvious how increasing independence in this way is not simply a 'psychological' procedure, but depends on very real material resources.

It is precisely the acquisition of *material resources* that makes possible the ability to influence our world in practically every other respect. Apart from the fairly routine assessment in research work of people's 'socio-economic status' and the observation that the middle class (in particular those of its members who are 'young, attractive, verbal, intelligent and successful'[6]) tend to profit most from 'treatment', psychotherapy has almost totally disregarded the significance for psychological well-being of material advantage.

Money can't buy happiness, but then neither can happiness be assured through psychotherapy. It is easy to highlight the vulgarity of money and to scoff as the crude materialism of the *nouveau riche*, but far more difficult, it seems, to acknowledge that many if not all of what we regard as our most refined virtues and spiritual accomplishments are also acquired through the judicious use of, in the end, financial advantage. When it comes to trying to understand the origins of emotional distress, it helps to realise that what cushions us against the cruelties of the world, what enables us to relax in each other's company, to avoid spiteful competition and invidious comparison (and hence many of the forms of relationship that result in psychological damage), is a degree of material comfort.

This insight, though, as already pointed out, far more the subject of repression than sex and hence rarely openly discussed, lies nevertheless at the very heart of our social structure. At the very moment we adjure each other to 'count our blessings', 'accept responsibility', 'tighten our belts' etc., we scrabble as hard as hell for the most materially advantageous perch we can find.

In view of this, there are not likely to be very many people who have not already, very sensibly, done what they can to maximise their material resources. Nevertheless I want to underline what an important factor the material situation is. So much emphasis has been placed in the general literature in psychotherapy on the idea that 'it's all in the mind' that people often actually overlook the most appalling deprivation in their living circumstances when trying to account for their distress. For anyone who can, it often really does help to move house, change job, invest in further education, have a holiday or even get away for the weekend (all things that affluent people may do as a matter of course – and without reflecting that their ability to do so is what keeps them sane).

LEARNING TO BE DIFFERENT

In order to change our position in the world under our own steam (as opposed to being put by powerful forces in a different position, which is a more frequent occurrence), it is often necessary to learn to do things differently. To 'be' different, we may have to alter our characteristic ways of acting in some important spheres.

Challenging unreasonable power in our proximal relationships, or taking the risks involved in making social overtures to others, is often extremely difficult, not least because it is likely to involve going against the grain of deeply embodied habits of personal conduct. Even therapeutic approaches that stress the importance of changing the way we *do* things – like those derived from behaviourism – usually overlook how difficult this is actually to achieve. There tends to be – as usual – a tacit assumption that once the need to change has been established, actually doing things differently is merely a matter of performing the necessary acts of will.

Because we acquire our characteristic ways of conducting ourselves effortlessly (or so it seems), we assume that all that we need to be able to do things differently is a 'good reason'. This overlooks the fact that we can only do things we know how to do. I do not do what I do just because I have good reasons to, but also because I know how to. It may certainly be true that I seem to have acquired that knowledge without even trying, but that doesn't mean that I also know how to do things *differently*.

Speaking a language is a good case in point. I know how to speak English without being conscious of ever having learned to: it seems that I 'just can'. But I do understand clearly why it is that I can't speak Chinese, and I can of course grasp conceptually the fact that I must have learned to speak English as an infant just as, if I wanted to speak Chinese now, I would have to *learn* to do so.

The case is not greatly different, in my view, with other aspects of conduct that people appear to perform effortlessly, including activities that enhance or detract from confidence or cause emotional distress. 'Being confident' is, at least in part, a matter of knowing how to act in particular ways in particular circumstances, and for many people the only way to acquire that knowledge may be through a relatively long and arduous process of learning.

Unfortunately, the view of change implicit in the 'learning model' – already considerably more difficult and demanding than the promise of magical transformation implicit in so many non-behavioural approaches to therapy – is still far too simplistic as a basis for the 'treatment' of psychological and emotional difficulties. For what people can learn is not simply a matter of what they can see as a good reason for learning: they need also an environment that will support their learning.

The learning environment

Learning something new is not simply a matter of deciding to. For example, in order to 'decide' to learn Chinese, you would probably need to have a fairly pressing interest in doing so: an economic, educational or social motivation exerting pressure on you. In addition to this you would need access to books, libraries and teachers, which would cost money. You would also probably need the support and understanding of people close to you: your family would have to be prepared to give you the time to learn and not hinder or ridicule your attempts. In order to keep going, you would almost certainly need a lot of encouragement from people who mattered. You would require the time and space for regular work and revision. For most people, the idea of learning Chinese just for the sake of it would be more than extremely daunting, it would be impossible, and this because they are not inhabiting an environment that makes the learning of Chinese a sensible undertaking.

When you think about it, a great deal of effort is put into our official procedures for teaching people things they are not otherwise highly motivated to learn. Ask any conscientious schoolteacher on a Friday evening how s/he is feeling and you will get some idea of the expenditure of energy necessary to teach even the rudimentary skills of our culture. In order to learn, children need years of intensive effort on the part of others.

Consider also that we make it as easy as we can for children to learn (or as difficult as we can for them not to!). We set up special institutions for them in which to do so, and, while they are learning, we tolerate their making mistakes – we expect them to be ignorant and inexperienced in many respects. As far as we can, we organise the lives and the social environments of children to take account of the fact that they are supposed to be learning.

With adults, things are on the whole very different. The world is not set up for them to learn, especially aspects of conduct and relationships that 'normal' people are supposed to have acquired by their early twenties, and there is unlikely to be anything like the intensity of instruction and tolerance of mistakes that official learners like children are afforded. It is true, of course, that adults may be expected to be more self-motivated than children and that therefore they should not need a similar input of resources, and this is indeed the case with mature students who are, as teachers will often affirm, 'such a pleasure to teach'. But even with willing learners, there is still a need for the material media of their instruction and a lengthy commitment to study and practice, not to mention the social support and encouragement of others.

In comparison, the kind of learning necessary for people to alter their position in the world so that it will become for them a less distressing place receives practically no such support from the social environment. In diagnosing people, in segregating them no matter how subtly as 'abnormal', there is virtually no sign of the provision of the kind of context in which learning to 'be different' could be practised and encouraged. Even in offering 'therapy', the emphasis tends to be more on moral regeneration than on analysis – let alone provision – of a context that would make change possible. And even in those approaches to 'treatment' which do stress learning, it is of course far beyond a therapist's powers to affect any but the most proximal aspects of the person's social environment in ways that would *facilitate* learning.

It is necessary to stress these constraints on 'learning to be different' in order to avoid falling into a kind of narrow 'thera-pism' which once again suggests that if sufferers don't improve, this time through their own strenuous efforts of learning, it is all their own fault. Having made this point, which cannot be emphasised too strongly, it is possible to make one or two suggestions that might make the process of change, if not easier, then perhaps a little more comprehensible to anyone who has been disappointed by the promises of 'therapy' or who is dismayed by the prospective difficulties of having to learn to behave uncharacteristically.

Doing precedes feeling

For someone to feel differently, something has to happen. Things may of course happen to people, in which case they may not have very much control over what they are: uncontrollable events usually lie at the root of emotional distress in the first place. If, on the other hand, you want to feel differently as the result of your own efforts, it is important to recognise that you will have at first to take action (probably to change your position in the world in the way already discussed) while still feeling distressed. Many people expect somehow to 'feel better' *before* undertaking the task of reorganising their lives, whereas in fact 'feeling better' is only likely to come about once the process of 'learning to be different' is well under way.

Most of us recognise that, as in speaking a language, we enact our characteristics effortlessly, and this gives us a sense of who we are. In other words, we are what we know how to do best and most skilfully, even if we would rather be doing something else. Peacemakers who do anything for a quiet life (and hence get unmercifully exploited by others) are likely to say that 'it's not like me to lose my temper'. In order to learn to become more assertive, it is therefore necessary for such people to go through an uncomfortable period of behaving uncharacteristically, during which they may feel horribly false. If they persevere, however, the requisite conduct becomes part of them in a way that feels, and is, perfectly genuine.

You could not 'feel like' a footballer or a concert violinist if you'd never played the game or touched the instrument. It is the same with many psychological characteristics: we do not come ready-made, so to speak, and we only feel like what we are after a long process of learning. The difference between the usual course of character formation and a programme of self-change is that in the first case the learning process is informal and in the second formal. What happens naturally in the case of character formation has to be set about artificially in the case of learning to be different.

It would be dishonest to pretend that there are no important differences between these two processes. For example, therapeutic learning does not simply produce a 'new' character; newly learned characteristics (say, of being 'assertive') do not *replace* old ones, but are superimposed on top of them. This is rather like the difference between naturally speaking with a particular accent and having learned (as an actor, perhaps, or through elocution lessons) to speak with it deliberately. Therapeutic approaches to learning often seem to make a tacit assumption that the client to be changed is a *tabula rasa*, the therapist a Pygmalion sculpting character from virgin materials. This, of course, is far from the case. The client is already a character with a range of embodied dispositions which are not simply wiped out by new experience.

Someone trying to learn to behave differently in some key situations may have a tacit awareness that the old ways of responding are indeed not far away, and this may contribute to a sense of ungenuineness. It would be a shame, however, if this put them off the process of learning, for learning to be assertive (say) is no more 'ungenuine' than learning Chinese. It may not be, so to speak, your first language, but becoming expert in it is none the less useful for that.

'Walking the plank'

In order to get launched on the process of learning to be different (and thereby to give ourselves the possibility of discovering that acting differently will lead to feeling differently), there is no mediating procedure that will make it easier. By this I mean that there is no procedure the individual can interpose between seeing that action is necessary and carrying it out. There are no 'decisions' to be-waited for, no 'courage' to be scraped up out of some illusory internal reserve. Certainly, we may receive encouragement from outside, but in the end the only motto is: Just *do* it.

Going against the grain of embodied experience entails a frightening unfamiliarity which no one should make light of. Behaving in radically new ways challenges deeply embedded certainties, contradicts everything we have learned to expect and undermines an 'expertise' which we have built up perfectly validly over the years. That this expertise no longer serves us as it used to can be discovered only through an act of faith, for otherwise we have no evidence at all that doing things differently will result in anything but the catastrophe which seems most likely.

There is very little in our culture to support the idea that it is sensible or even possible to take the plunge in this way, and most people consult a counsellor or therapist precisely in the expectation (fuelled most enthusiastically by the profession itself) that making changes will somehow be rendered relatively painless. It is true that the solidarity offered by a therapist may provide useful support in walking the plank of change (i.e. in 'just doing' things differently), but reliance on therapeutic tricks and gimmicks is likely to be disappointing.

For the shy person who wishes to become more sociable, for example, there is simply no alternative (other than the passage of time and the inevitable lessons of life) to making an approach to others. It would, of course, be sensible to think about the easiest and least threatening circumstances in which to do so, and there is absolutely no virtue in making the initiation of change any more difficult than it has to be – one of the merits of behaviour therapy has been to emphasise the value of taking it gently. But in the end the first step has to be taken in fear and trembling, with no guarantee that there will be a positive outcome. It is only after the event, and most likely after a considerable period of practice, that things will start to feel different.

Asking people to challenge through their conduct the very thing they are most afraid of – suggesting to someone who suffers from agoraphobia that she should go out for a walk, for example – may seem impossibly demanding, and the active support (the solidarity) of sympathetic others is probably the most helpful way of bringing about the desired result. Otherwise, we can only attempt to strengthen the person's faith that nothing terrible will happen and indeed that in the long run they may 'feel better'. Faith, again, is not an internal resource, but the *assurance of power* that something is so.

The need for practice

Learning through our own efforts to be different requires a huge amount of effort. This is again in stark contrast to the magic-infused promises of so many approaches to therapy, and almost no one is prepared for the amount of hard work and practice that has to be put into doing things differently.

To understand this, I think it is helpful to reflect on the processes of learning necessary to acquire forms of skill or knowledge that are more obvious and concrete than those underpinning habits of feeling and relationship. Nobody expects to be able to learn a language or to play a musical instrument, for example, without a great deal – sometimes years – of arduous practice. All the difficulties encountered by people trying to learn to 'be' different, which may often seem to them insuperably disheartening, are familiar enough – and frequently much more easily tolerated – in the acquisition of more clearly defined skills.

For example, the pain of shaping our body to unfamiliar

movements in learning musical or sporting aptitudes, the despair of the novice at 'not being able to do it', the embarrassment at our halting attempts to speak another language, the initial clumsiness and inevitability of stupid mistakes – all these are equally to be expected by someone trying to act in new and unfamiliar ways.

Similarly, there is a need to establish a discipline of practice. Many people embarking on some kind of behavioural programme to challenge anxieties or establish uncharacteristic ways of responding to others fail to appreciate the necessity for practising regularly, whether or not they 'feel like it' (and however 'weak' their 'will'), and the temptations to take a line of lesser resistance are exactly as strong – indeed probably much stronger – than they are for the child desperate to evade homework or piano practice.

KEEPING CHANGE IN PERSPECTIVE

In trying in this chapter to give an indication of some of the factors that need to be kept in mind by people struggling to get to grips with their own predicament, there is a danger once again of making personal action the core of 'cure', 'taking responsibility' the road to salvation. The possibility that *perhaps*, if s/he has the necessary resources, the individual can do something to modify the forces that cause distress, does not mean that this is all there is to do, nor that personal action is likely to be the most effective approach to psychological suffering.

All the possible measures I have considered in this chapter are necessarily only applicable in the individual's proximal world. The trouble is that, as we have seen, the powers at work in this world, even though they loom largest in individual experience, are nearly always only mediating much more potent influences which operate at a much greater distance. In relation to these distal powers the individual's possibilities for influencing even those people and events closest to him or her are puny indeed.

The whole point of this book has been to emphasise the fact that we are all in boats not of our own making, and hence that there are other ways of understanding personal distress than merely seeing it as the kind of failure to cope with, or 'manage', our personal life and relationships which is best addressed by some variety of therapy or counselling. It is not only far truer, but also, I think, more productive, to see psychological distress as an indication that there is something wrong with the world than it is to interpret it as a sign of some inadequacy or deficiency of the self. This is not a cop-out, and in no way absolves us from struggle. It just indicates that our struggle should be directed at other targets than our 'selves'.

The proximal world which absorbs so much of our effort and attention is held in place by powers that there is no possibility of our influencing as individuals, and we will make no significant impact on personal distress until we find ways of modifying distal power. The bitterness, fear and exploitation so often poisoning our relations with each other, the defensive blunting of sensitivities which characterises our everyday social intercourse, certainly do give rise to individual distress, but they are not the ultimate cause of it.

The civilised values, freedom and unselfish love which provide the context for truly benign 'personal growth' and psychological stability are built on a foundation of material comfort and freedom from threat which is almost completely absent from our society. For even the most affluent and privileged minority cannot be free of anxiety that its advantages may all be taken away. Indeed, probably the single most destructive factor in our social relations is the fear of loss of power and advantage. From the brutal racism of the least privileged, through the proverbial mean resentment of the petit bourgeois to the paranoid secrecy of the very powerful, we are all haunted by the possibility of slipping from our perch.

I have made a lot in this book of the abuse of parental power within families. Such an emphasis is unavoidable if we are as individuals to make sense of our experience of a proximal world. But it is even more important to see that the shape given to our relations with each other is not simply a matter of personal likes and dislikes, random loves and hates, but is given principally by our need to survive in a difficult and often cruel world and our perception (frequently, of course, imposed upon us by greater power) of the advantages we need to cling on to and the threats we must, if we can, arm ourselves against.

We will not significantly reduce the prevalence of emotional pain in the world through psychotherapy, which sees it essentially as a personal matter, but rather by coming to accept that it is a function of social organisation, which is a political matter. It is distal, not proximal, powers we will have to modify before we 'feel better' to any noticeable extent. As things are, the hugely unequal distribution of power works against the vast majority of people being able to live a life in which insecurity, anxiety, confusion, ignorance and pain are kept to an unavoidable minimum. For things to improve for this majority, power would have to be redistributed.

We have not reached 'the end of history'. Indeed, we must hope that, from a longer perspective, we are still feeling our way in a dark age, gradual emergence from which may yet take inestimable time. Psychotherapy is an irrelevance to the political task of making a more equal society in which 'all the social hierarchies will have to be overthrown, not merely those of money or state power, not only social privilege but the uneven weight of the past and of culture' (see note 2). Perhaps it will never happen. But given intelligence, knowledge, solidarity, unending perseverance and the kind of moral strength and commitment to others seen most clearly in those who suffer most, you never know.

Notes

Chapter One

1. A frequently quoted distinction of Freud's, which he made very early in his career (1895) before he substantially revised his ideas in such a way as to place far more emphasis on 'hysteria' than on unhappiness. (Pelican Freud Library, Vol. 3, *Studies on Hysteria*, 1974, 393.)
2. I considered this issue in a little more detail in my book *The Origins of Unhappiness*, HarperCollins, 1993.
3. See, for example, his *Power/Knowledge*, Harvester, 1980. This is a selection of interviews with and writings by Foucault over the period 1972–77. Some are more accessible than others.
4. To give but two examples: the ideas of the psychiatrist H. S. Sullivan, though influential in American psychiatry around the mid-twentieth century, are virtually unknown today, and yet his view of the development of psychiatric disturbance within the social context was highly sophisticated and brilliantly expounded (see his *The Interpersonal Theory of Psychiatry*, New York: Norton, 1953). Similarly, the psychoanalyst Karen Horney's analysis of the 'neurotic personality' in the context of 1930s American society was not only extraordinarily penetrating, but remains as fresh and relevant today as it was then (her *The Neurotic Personality of Our Time*, New York: Norton, 1937, gives as good an account as one will find of the nature and origins of the kind of basic anxiety underlying a range of 'neurotic' problems).
5. Two who spring to mind are Lucy Johnstone, whose book *Users and Abusers of Psychiatry* (Routledge, 1989) provides a cogent view

of the psychiatric scene in Britain, and Peter Breggin, whose *Toxic Psychiatry* (Fontana, 1993) contains telling, indeed at times courageous, criticism of psychiatry's heavy and unjustifiable reliance on drug treatments.

6. See, for example, Mary Boyle's *Schizophrenia. A Scientific Delusion?*, Routledge, 1990.

7. A good, accessible starting point would be Joel Kovel's *Complete Guide to Therapy: From Psychoanalysis to Behavior Modification*, Penguin, 1978.

8. It is hard to overestimate the complexity, variety and sheer abundance of psychoanalytic ideas, not to mention the stupendous confidence and authority with which they tend to be stated in the vast literature they have generated. I know of no better critical account of psychoanalytic thought and practice than Ernest Gellner's *The Psychoanalytic Movement*, Paladin, 1985.

9. A famous study by the psychologist H. J. Eysenck, published in 1952, indicated that people treated by broadly psychoanalytic methods seemed to recover no more quickly than people not treated at all. Although Eysenck's work was flawed in its methodology, the findings have been modified only slightly by subsequent research. Therapies of a variety of descriptions can be shown to improve on controls where no treatment was given, but differences are not great, and the various forms of therapy cannot be reliably differentiated from each other. An extremely good source of insight into the controversies surrounding psychotherapy and its efficacy is W. Dryden and C. Feltham, *Psychotherapy and its Discontents*, Buckingham and Philadelphia: Open University Press, 1992. Coming to my notice (with thanks to David Munck) only just in time to include in this note before going to press, a swingeing critique of the adequacy of research into psychotherapy, and the claims which rest upon it, has been made by William M. Epstein, *The Illusion of Psychotherapy*, New Brunswick and London: Transaction Publishers, 1995.

10. Not all psychoanalysts adopt the orthodox approach to the 'therapeutic relationship'; indeed, there is plentiful evidence from Freud's writings that he himself often departed very far from the

kind of neutrality so strictly observed by some of his less imaginative followers.

11. See Keith Thomas's *Religion and the Decline of Magic*, Penguin, 1973, for an extremely instructive account of this process; some of the parallels between practices in former centuries and those current in recent years are astonishingly close.

12. An excellent overview and critique of the counselling scene is to be found in Alex Howard's *Challenges to Counselling and Psychotherapy*, Macmillan, 1996.

13. The 'brand name' of Albert Ellis's contribution to the therapy industry.

14. Some psychotherapies have, of course, extended their sphere of operations to groups or even 'systems', but that does not alter the fact that virtually all the most influential theoretical notions of therapy were born in the context of private individual treatment.

15. I think, for example, of Peter Lomas's books *The Case for a Personal Psychotherapy*, Oxford University Press, 1981, and, more recently, *Cultivating Intuition*, Penguin, 1994. R. F. Hobson's *Forms of Feeling. The Heart of Psychotherapy*, Tavistock, 1985, is another rewarding source of insights into the process of psychotherapy. Miller Mair's *Between Psychology and Psychotherapy*, Routledge, 1989, is one of the most honest accounts available of what is involved in the practice of therapy from a clinical psychologist's point of view. My own *Psychotherapy. A Personal Approach*, Dent, 1978, was an attempt to address the implications of therapy as a personal undertaking.

16. L Suttie, *The Origins of Love and Hate*, Penguin, 1988.

17. P. Halmos, *The Faith of the Counsellors*, Constable, 1965.

18. I prefer the term 'comfort' to 'love' because it seems to me that, with the exception of a tiny minority of exceptionally dedicated therapists, to talk of 'love' overstates the case. Though the therapist's attention to and concern for patients may be concentrated, intense, and genuine enough, it does not in most cases stretch far beyond the fifty minutes or so that they are in the consulting room together, and does not really match the commitment we might expect of one who can truly be said to love another.

19. There is, of course, also the issue that the professional provision of comfort is a poor substitute for the social solidarity in public life and loving generosity in private life that one would hope to see in the kind of 'sane society' which, for example, Erich Fromm writes about in his book of that title (*The Sane Society*, Routledge & Kegan Paul, 1963). Not the least difficulty about the 'professionalisation of love' is that it gives those who dispense it, i.e. therapists, a financial stake in maintaining society's sickness. These are questions which I consider at some length in my book *Taking Care*, Dent, 1987.

20. Criticisms of this kind form the subject matter of Jeffrey Masson's important book *Against Therapy*, Collins, 1989.

Chapter Two

1. Thomas Szasz's *The Myth of Mental Illness* (New York: Harper & Row, 1974) remains the classic text in this respect, and is still well worth reading.

2. Dorothy Rowe has been a relentless critic of the medicalised view of depression, as her several books on the subject will testify. See, for a concise discussion, the chapter on depression in her *Beyond Fear*, Fontana, 1987.

3. The idea of schizophrenics as having a 'split mind', which is sometimes reflected in popular usage, bears no relation to the way in which the psychiatric label is used. 'Clinical schizophrenia' is much more about being confused than it is about being in two minds about something or torn between two incompatible states of feeling.

4. In *The Interpersonal Theory of Psychiatry* (see previous chapter, note 4), H. S. Sullivan provides a masterly account of the ways in which a variety of clinical phenomena, including those associated with schizophrenia, can be traced back to the social ('interpersonal') context in which the individual acquired them. For example, lack of 'consensual validation' (i.e. the failure of crucial figures in the child's early environment to provide a consistent

interpretation of reality) may result in a situation in later life in which the absence of such internalised consistency makes it impossible for the individual to grasp the 'reality' which seems so obvious to others.

5. It is a commonplace to observe that the nature of so-called neurotic symptoms has changed quite markedly in many respects from the time when, say, Freud was writing. Our culture sets limits on how we experience and what we are able to say about ourselves. The iconic language of 'hysteria' is, for example, no longer viable as one in which we can attempt to give form to our distress – one does not these days encounter people who are rendered deaf or blind by their troubles.

6. It is common in the language of the 'illness model' to talk of 'precipitating factors' in the present which somehow trigger a slumbering 'predisposition' to breakdown. Although it is easy to see how this manner of thinking can arise, it is, I think, neverthe-less misleading as it once again diverts our attention from damaging worlds to supposedly constitutional weaknesses within individuals.

7. The writings of R. D. Laing are often cited as an example of the unacceptable blaming of parents for the subsequent schizophrenia of their offspring. In fact, I do not believe that a careful reading of Laing's work substantiates this criticism, but it does seem that a whole range of (extremely interesting) research work implicating family relations in the causation of 'psychosis' in the 1960s and 1970s ran into difficulty because of the slur that seemed to be cast on, in particular, parents, and much of present-day research carries a kind of pious disclaimer of any intention to implicate family relations. It is interesting in this context also to note Jeffrey Masson's argument, in *The Assault on Truth* (Penguin, 1985), that Freud abandoned the idea that, for example, his female patients' neuroses were based on the sexual misdemeanours of their fathers, largely because of a failure of moral courage in the face of the outrage he stirred up.

8. The phenomenon of 'resistance' – another psychoanalytic creation – is commonly invoked to explain patients' unwilling-

ness to accept their therapists' interpretation of their free associations. This is a good example of the moralism that runs deep in so much psychoanalytic and therapeutic thinking: as if the patient is a naughty or recalcitrant child bent on rejecting the sweet reason of adult supervision. Much more often, however, it is a case of patients' being entirely reasonably reluctant to accept without evidence (solely on therapeutic authority) the often highly charged sexual allegations with which the analyst seeks to establish their motivation. In contrast to this supposed battle of wills, patients have in fact a particularly strong and obvious interest in uncovering the reasons for their difficulties and more often than not will readily accept accurate explanations.

9. The kind of procedures beloved of behaviour therapy are particularly suitable for the 'treatment' of 'mono-symptomatic phobias' such as specific fear of spiders, winged insects etc. Gradual introduction of the feared stimulus in doses the person feels comfortable with perhaps first as a photograph, or even as a word, then as graduated specimens in glass jars, and finally as living examples wandering around the room – usually does the trick. It is important that the person is allowed to go at his or her own pace. Many entirely wellmeaning amateur 'therapists' have turned an otherwise perfectly helpful approach into trauma by deciding that it's time for their charges to 'go for it' head on.

10. Cognitive-behavioural psychology has, certainly, tried to invent techniques of 'thought-stopping' and other diversionary tactics, but, though they may work up to a point, their plausibility depends on the notion that our attention is indeed ultimately under our own control, that we have a kind of mental director sitting in our heads deciding the direction of our awareness. How far this may be so is debatable. Is there, for example, another director sitting in that director's head?

11. Because of the special difficulties they pose in terms of both physiological involvement and medico-social management – sometimes necessitating hospital treatment – I shall not consider drug and alcohol addiction here. However, the problems of control and the exercise of 'will power' which such addictions present

are, I believe, not different in kind from – indeed are virtually prototypical of – the phenomena I shall consider in this section.

12. This is not to say that there is no value in documenting the manner in which social evils such as unemployment cause damage. An excellent article by David Fryer, for example, shows how unemployment and job insecurity have a whole range of adverse effects on victims and their families (D. Fryer, 'Benefit agency?', *The Psychologist*, **8**, 1995, 265–72).

13. An extended analysis of this is to be found in Chapter Four of my *The Origins of Unhappiness*, HarperCollins, 1993.

14. According to official government figures published in 1991, the suicide rate in England among men aged 20–24 increased by 71 per cent during the 1980s.

15. See Chapter One, note 4.

16. H. S. Sullivan's work is again of central relevance in this regard (see Chapter One, note 4). The work of Theodore Lidz and others in the USA and of R. D. Laing and others in Britain during the 1960s, together with the writings of Gregory Bateson (on the 'double bind'), Jay Haley and Paul Watzlawick, all focused in one way or another on the way communication may distort experience.

Chapter Three

1. This fundamental point was articulated most fully by Jurgen Habermas in his highly erudite (if for most readers difficult and often obscure) *Knowledge and Human Interests*, Heinemann, 1972.

2. H. J. Eysenck, 'The technology of consent', New Scientist, **42**, 1969, 688–90. My attention was originally drawn to this quotation by Professor John Shotter.

3. Any credible psychology must be *reflexive*, i.e. must include the psychologist in the scientific equation. Don Bannister ('Psychology as an exercise in paradox', *Bulletin of the British Psychological Society*, **19**, 1966, 21) offered the following neat little parable to illustrate the point:

The master chemist has finally produced a bubbling green slime in his test-tube, the potential of which is great but the properties of which are mysterious. He sits alone in his laboratory, test-tube in hand, brooding about what to do with the bubbling green slime. Then it slowly dawns on him that the bubbling green slime is sitting alone in the test-tube wondering what to do about him. This special nightmare of the chemist is the permanent work-a-day world of the psychologist – the bubbling green slime is always wondering what to do about you.

4. See in particular his *Discipline and Punish*, Penguin, 1979, for a brilliant and persuasive account of how psychiatric and psychological approaches which could naively be supposed to be 'for the good of humankind' can only be coherently understood once we take into account the purposes of *social control* which underlie them.

5. Foucault was of course not the only person to concern himself with this issue; there is a reasonably large constituency of social critics and historians who have documented and analysed the ways in which psychiatry, psychology, education, social work etc. are intimately associated with the exercise of powers of social control. Andrew Scull and David Ingleby in Britain and Christopher Lasch in the USA are prominent examples of those whose writings are illuminating in this respect.

6. Writing in an unguarded moment to his friend Wilhelm Fliess, Freud even self-consciously described himself as a 'conquistador', and 'actually not at all a man of science, not an observer, not an experimenter, not a thinker' (J. M. Masson, ed., *The Complete Letters of Sigmund Freud to Wilhelm Fliess 1887–1904*, Cambridge, Mass., and London: Harvard University Press, 1985). No doubt Freud meant by this to represent himself as a bold explorer and conqueror of unknown territory, and yet – as he himself could be the last to deny! – our words can reveal more than we realise or intend; the ruthless subjection by the conquistadores of the hapless populations they encountered was surely not an irrelevant aspect of their purpose.

7. Psychology's claim to be a science rests principally on its insistence on the objective measurement of the phenomena it addresses, and for this it is heavily reliant on procedures of statistical analysis. Population sampling, frequency distributions, measurements of central tendency (means, modes, medians), significance testing etc. lie at the methodological heart of academic, experimental psychology, and many of the most influential figures in the development of, in particular, Anglo-American psychology were first and foremost statisticians. It tends to be forgotten these days that the preoccupations of these gentlemen ofen had very centrally to do with social engineering and control, particularly where it was felt that significant departures from the norm threatened social stability. My late colleague and friend Richard Marshall was fond of pointing out that, for example, Karl Pearson, one of the revered founders of British academic psychology, enthusiastic eugenicist and inventor of statistical approaches still bearing his name, expressed his admiration in an after-dinner speech at University College London in 1934 for 'Reichskanzler Hitler and his proposals to regenerate the German people'.

8. See for example John Rowan's *Ordinary Ecstasy. Humanistic Psychology in Action*, Routledge & Kegan Paul, 1976, for a classic example of an account which is stuffed from end to end with aesthetic judgements about human nature and being. The title is itself revealing enough.

9. Probably the most terrifying situation of all is the psychiatric 'case conference', where a roomful of doctors, psychologists, social workers etc. will gather to scrutinise and ultimately pronounce upon the hapless patient – a procedure which R. D. Laing once aptly characterised as a 'ritual degradation ceremony'.

10. H. S. Sullivan, *The Interpersonal Theory of Psychiatry*, New York: Norton, 1953.

11. This kind of observation renders at least dubious a great deal of research in psychiatry which has sought to establish a genetic component to 'mental illness'. Such research has relied on the argument that different degrees of genetic endowment (as between

identical and non-identical twins) can be assessed in relation to constancy of environment (as in the same family) and diagnosis of 'illness' be shown to vary significantly between the two groups.

12. Better than any psychological, or indeed sociological, text that I have come across is Eric Hobsbawm's historical account of the 'cultural revolution' we have endured over recent times. See his *Age of Extremes. The Short Twentieth Century 1914–1991*, Michael Joseph, 1994, especially Chapter Eleven.

13. Sigmund Freud was probably as guilty as anyone of trying to submit the imagination to moral judgement. His *The Interpretation of Dreams*, full of insight and creativity though it is, is also a *tour de force* of disciplinary moralism. In the course of this work Freud takes the appreciative enthusiasm of his precursor K. A. Scherner for the workings of the imagination and develops in its place a disapproving analysis of the 'irrational' sexual and aggressive impulses he takes to lie at the centre of what he calls 'primary processes' such as imagination and dreaming.

14. Translated by Rosemary Edmonds, Penguin Classics, 1964.

15. This is also, of course, the basis of our immorality. Knowing that others hurt as we do is what gives torturers their power.

16. The 'personal construct' psychology of George Kelly is the most carefully and illuminatingly elaborated theoretical approach to take seriously the ways in which people structure and organise their anticipation of life in accordance with their experience of it. Kelly's *The Psychology of Personal Constructs*, Vols I & II, New York: Norton, 1955, is his major work. His influence on British clinical psychology has been considerable, mediated particularly by Don Bannister (see, for example, D. Bannister and F. Fransella, *Inquiring Man*, Penguin, 1971) and most prominently represented now by Miller Mair (see his *Between Psychology and Psychotherapy*, London and New York: Routledge, 1989) and David Winter (whose *Personal Construct Psychology in Clinical Practice: Theory, Research and Applications*, Routledge, 1992, is a specialist volume, but indispensable for the serious student of the subject). In the field of education, Phillida Salmon is an influential Kellyan – see for example her *Psychology in the Classroom*, London and New York: Cassell, 1995.

17. I have discussed the similarities in this respect between psychotherapy and prostitution at greater length in my *Why Therapy Doesn't Work*, part I, Robinson, 2001.

Chapter Four

1. Anyone wishing to study this evidence in detail can do no better than consult the compendious *Handbook of Psychotherapy and Behavior Change* edited by A. E. Bergin and S. L. Garfield, Wiley, 1994.

2. If this seems unduly cynical, consider a recent account of the significance of conducting research within the British counselling organisation Relate. 'Client (consumer)-dependent evaluation', it is suggested, 'has both facilitated development and suggested clients think well of the organisation for considering their views important. Ultimately this can only increase confidence for all stakeholders associated with counselling practice.' Again, through 'research and development activity', the authors enthuse, a 'counselling agency can harness the skills and methods of psychotherapy research to maintain its place in the market and improve the quality and effectiveness of its services'. (J. Mellor-Clark and D. A. Shapiro, 'It's not what you do . . . it's the way that you do it: the inception of an evaluative research culture in Relate Marriage Guidance', *Changes*, **13**, 1995, 201–07). Research is thus conducted in pursuit of market advantage for 'stakeholders' and not of truth; whether or not psychotherapy works has become an irrelevance.

3. It is fascinating to see how, throughout the correspondence with Wilhelm Fliess which chronicles the development of his theories about the unconscious sexual origins of neurosis, Freud naively reveals (and utterly fails to notice) how his own preoccupations and worries, not to say motivation, are shaped by more mundane matters. Like the rest of us, he is most concerned by the ability to make a living. On 21.9.1899, for example, Freud writes:

My mood also depends very strongly on my earnings. Money is laughing gas for me. I know from my youth that once the wild horses of the pampas have been lassoed, they retain a certain anxiousness for life. Thus I have come to know the helplessness of poverty and continually fear it. You will see that my style will improve and my ideas will be more correct if this city provides me with an ample livelihood.

(J. M. Masson, ed), see Chapter Three, note 6.

4. D. Smail, 'Psychotherapeutic theory and wishful thinking', *Changes*, 10, 1992, 274–81.

5. It is of course to this kind of process Freud meant to refer in his concept of 'repression'. It is unfortunate that, in Freud's writing as in the subsequent development of psychoanalysis, repression came to acquire a *purposive* aspect, as though the individual deliberately strips experience of words so that s/he may not be held morally accountable for it. Repression, in my view, is much better understood as what is done to people than as what is done by them.

6. I have borrowed this term from H. S. Sullivan. His account of the development of the child's conceptual and social understanding is highly relevant to this discussion. For example, his outlining in *The Interpersonal Theory of Psychiatry* (see Chapter One, note 4) of the development of 'prototaxic', 'parataxic' and 'syntaxic' experience constitutes one of the best accounts I know of the phenomena we are considering. His framework has not, however, been widely taken up in psychology and psychotherapy.

7. For anyone trying to understand the causes of, and possible cures for, much of our distress in the past decade or two, Will Hutton's *The State We're In*, Jonathan Cape, 1995, is worth libraries full of therapeutic literature.

Chapter Five

1. That we are all psychologists is a particularly unpalatable fact for a discipline that attempts to monopolise and, as it were, 'patent'

psychology as a professional pursuit. In the end, that attempt must result in obvious absurdity. Psychology, to survive as an intellectual or practical undertaking, needs in my view to cultivate a very strong sense of professional modesty and to strive continually to make clear what the limits of its possibilities are.

2. At times, as for example with the work of O. H. Mowrer (*The Crisis in Psychiatry and Religion*, Van Nostrand, 1961), psychological distress has become linked directly to religious concepts of sin. Ever since C. G. Jung there have been those who see strong connections between religion on the one hand and psychopathology and psychotherapy on the other, and there are several 'pastoral' approaches to psychiatry and psychotherapy which again equate 'cure' with redemption.

3. In fact, Alice Miller achieves precisely this in her illuminating study of Hitler's childhood in her *For Your Own Good. The Roots of Violence in Child-rearing*, Virago, 1987. In this book, as in her *The Drama of Being a Child* (also published by Virago in 1987), there is much to be learned from Alice Miller about the adult abuse of power over children.

4. See note 3 above.

5. Kierkegaard's meditation on this theme in *Fear and Trembling* makes the point powerfully.

6. The most penetrating statement I know on the complexity of 'motivation' comes from the political scientist and philosopher Hannah Arendt (*On Revolution*, Penguin, 1973, 96):

. . . not only is the human heart a place of darkness which, with certainty, no human eye can penetrate; the qualities of the heart need darkness and protection against the light of the public to grow and to remain what they are meant to be, innermost motives which are not for public display.

She goes on to point out that the insistence on dragging motives out into the light of day leads inevitably to profound and widespread mistrust which sees 'intrigue and calumny, treachery and hypocrisy everywhere'. We develop procedures of 'motivational research' which become 'an eerie sort of filing cabinet for human vices, . . . a veritable science of misanthropy'.

7. 'Political correctness' can easily become an additional factor making it hard for people to be honest with themselves about what they think and feel. There is a fine line between stipulating what people should be able to say and trying to prescribe what they should think. Regulating conduct offensive to others is one thing, trying to police the contents of our heads, quite another.

8. In this way, for the superconscientious person, Kant's 'categorical imperative': 'So act that the maxim of your will could always hold at the same time as a principle establishing universal law' (*Critique of Practical Reason*) becomes applied to the self with no universality at all. 'Act always for the good of others without expecting, requiring or even wishing that they should do the same for you' is more the superconscientious code.

9. This is poignantly exemplified at the time of writing by the court testimony of the stepdaughter of Rosemary West. West is accused of murdering ten girls and young women, one of them her own daughter and another the witness's sister. Violently sexually assaulted by her stepmother and raped by her father at the age of eight, the witness 'recounted years of abuse and degradation at [their] hands. [She] said she was told that "all loving parents" subjected their children to such treatment as she had experienced in the cellar. At fifteen she had run away from home, but *she had always remembered to send a Mother's Day card to Mrs West.*' (*Guardian*, 19.10.95 – my emphasis.)

10. A preoccupation with 'authenticity' probably came into mid-twentieth-century philosophy ('existentialism') at least in part as a counter to a kind of institutionalised hypocrisy which *pretended* a harmony between outer act and inner motive. But *insisting* that they be harmonious is in the long run no more satisfactory than pretending that they are, mainly because it is only relatively rarely the case that they can be.

Chapter Six

1. At first sight it looks as though the Freudian notion of 'psychological determinism' does indeed constitute a challenge to the received view of will, but closer examination reveals a surprisingly confused account of what could be meant by this. For example, modestly claiming 'a triumph for the interpretative art of psychoanalysis' in revealing the origin of 'parapraxes' such as slips of the tongue, Freud wrote that such events were 'strictly determined' and 'revealed as an expression of the subject's suppressed intentions' or 'a clash between two intentions, one of which was permanently or temporarily unconscious' (from the first of Freud's 'Two Encyclopaedia Articles' in Vol. 15 of the Pelican Freud Library, *Historical and Expository Works on Psychoanalysis*, 136–7). All that seems to have happened here, however, is that Freud has transferred the processes of will from the conscious to the unconscious mind; 'unconscious mental acts' come about in exactly the same way as conscious ones, apart, of course, from the individual's not knowing about them.

2. The best account I know of the process I am trying to describe here is in Jean-Paul Sartre's *Being and Nothingness*, even if not always expressed in the most accessible terms. Gilbert Ryle's classic *The Concept of Mind* (Hutchinson, 1949) is another work which, in an altogether drier and more Anglo-Saxon mode, still constitutes an illuminating critique of our usual ways of representing the causes of action to ourselves.

3. Although one might credit the considerable perspicacity of both behaviourism and psychodynamic therapy in recognising the limits to be placed on the person's own account of his or her motivation, both also abused this insight by claiming that only the trained expert was in a position to offer an accurate account – the behaviourist, or the psychoanalyst, 'knew better' than the subject what lay behind the subject's actions. In this way, professional psychologists placed themselves in a position of intransitive power in relation to the subject or patient. Intransitive psychologies of this kind fail to recognise that psychologist and subject are in the

same position when trying to understand motivation, with neither being especially privileged.

4. The work of the Russian psychologist Lev Vygotsky has been seminally important in demonstrating that the child's 'inner world' is actually a projection from external experience. See for example his *Thought and Language*, Massachusetts Institute of Technology, 1962.

5. An extremely funny article pointing out the dangers to psychotherapy in, among other things, not considering the potential inaccuracy of self-report has been written by Simon King-Spooner: 'Psychotherapy and the white dodo', *Changes*, **13**, 1995, 45–51.

6. This view is argued at much greater length, and with matchless subtlety and profundity, by Jean-Paul Sartre in *Being and Nothingness*.

7. The eugenics movement between the wars provides a cautionary lesson concerning the way 'scientific' measurement can be used to attempt legitimation for profoundly dubious sociopolitical programmes (see Chapter Three, note 7).

8. The question of how far 'intelligence' is genetic is of course far from settled in psychology. Much of the controversy which has raged in this area centres on the means that have been used to 'measure' intelligence – tests of so-called IQ. It seems to me to stretch credulity to suppose that genetically inherited physical structures are irrelevant to many of the intellectual gifts and abilities that are necessary for some kinds of human achievement. This does not mean that we know what these structures are. It has been amply demonstrated that their 'measurement' is fraught with difficulty to the extent that, for example, educational discrimination between children on the basis of 'tests' is not rationally justifiable.

9. See his *Distinction*, Routledge & Kegan Paul, 1984.

Chapter Seven

1. In his wonderfully instructive but now unfashionably titled *The Perfectibility of Man* (Duckworth, 1970), John Passmore surveys the principal ways in which, since Greek times, we have sought to achieve the kinds of solutions to our predicament for which we look now so hopefully to psychotherapy and counselling. This work is still extremely well worth reading for the insights it gives into the forerunners of contemporary thought, showing once again that there is nothing new about either our preoccupations or the proffered answers to them.

2. The most healthily sobering observation I know in this respect comes from Fernand Braudel at the end of his magnificent survey of the socio-economic history of modern times (*Civilisation and Capitalism 15th–18th Century*, 3 vols, Fontana, 1985). Quoted at greater length in my *Why Therapy Doesn't Work*, part 2, Robinson, 2001, some of what he says is worth repeating here:

   Jean-Paul Sartre may have dreamed of a society from which inequality would have disappeared, where one man would not exploit another. But no society in the world has yet given up tradition and the use of privilege. If this is ever to be achieved, all the social hierarchies will have to be overthrown, not merely those of money or state power, not only social privilege but the uneven weight of the past and of culture.

3. There are, of course, exceptions to this. One notable one is Roy Schafer, whose book *A New Language for Psychoanalysis* (New Haven and London: Yale University Press, 1976) elaborates a 'tragic view' of psychoanalysis.

4. I discuss the business of 'relationship' at much greater length in *Why Therapy Doesn't Work*, part 2, Robinson, 2001, .

5. I am very grateful to Dr Teresa Hagan for permitting me to borrow her notion of 'power mapping' in order to construct Figure 2, which is based essentially on her work with people whose distress is the direct upshot of powerlessness. From work

currently in progress, Dr Hagan and I hope to develop a more formal mapping structure in which to consider the extent of available powers and resources and relate it to various forms of psychological distress.

6. These qualities, forming the acronym YAVIS, were first identified in 1964 as characterising the kind of patients psychotherapists preferred to deal with (W. Schofield, *Psychotherapy: The Purchase of Friendship*, Prentice-Hall). Very little has changed since.

Index

abnormality 245–6, 248, 348, 377, 456
  distress defined as 19, 245–6
actions
  doing precedes feeling 457–8
  loss of control of 285, 297–303, 419
  power and resources as causes of 418, 426
  and will power 415–19, 421
Adam Smith Institute 211
Adler, Alfred 36, 261
adolescence 122, 190
advertising culture of 1980s 108–9, 118
advice: as tool in power structure 41
agoraphobia 85–6, 306, 307, 321, 422, 460
alcohol addiction 298, 470n
anarchism 197–9
anger 92
'animas' 59
anorexia nervosa 218, 232, 299–300, 328, 408
antidepressants 249
anxiety 247, 279, 280, 286, 288, 289, 290, 296, 303, 306, 318, 320, 323, 326, 362, 365, 377, 385, 388, 393, 408, 422, 442
  parental anxiety 320–1
anxiety management 187
Arendt, Hannah 477–8n
aromatherapy 260
art: 1980s social depression 127
assertiveness 457
assertiveness training 187
association, power of 433–4
attention-seeking 301
attitudes
  forming and changing 258, 265
  nature of 274
authenticity 389, 401, 478n
Ayer, A.J. 214

background predicaments 241, 281, 282–3, 287, 291, 293, 296, 298, 300, 302, 306, 307, 309, 311, 312, 313, 314, 315–28
Bannister, Don 471n, 474n
Bateson, Gregory 471n
beauty 428, 429
behaviour modification 270
behaviourism and behavioural therapy x, 12, 60–1, 62, 64–5, 71, 82, 183, 184, 259–60, 273, 274, 470n, 479n
Bellah, Robert, *Habits of the Heart* 104
betrayal 348, 349, 401
Bible 219, 385
biological psychiatry xxi
black people 327, 328, 428
blame 283, 377–8, 379, 380
  and explanation 378, 379
bodily resources 427–9
Bookchin, Murray 197
Bourdieu, Pierre 431
  Distinction 43
bowel or bladder control, dread of loss of 289
Boyle, Mary, *Schizophrenia: A Scientific Delusion?* 20n, 466n
Braudel, Fernand 481n
breathlessness and fear 286, 287
Breggin, Peter 466n
British Association of Counselling 251
bulimia 33–4, 300–1, 363, 387
Burkitt, Ian, *Social Services* xiin
business
amoral culture of 342
  Business Revolution of 1980s and Business Culture 98–110, 116–30, 158, 166, 197, 202, 281, 402
  counselling as business 111–16

business *(contd)*
    growth of consultancy 105–10
    health care industry 120–1, 123
    links with politics and corruption
        76, 96, 200, 201, 207
    marketing of sex 'fulfilment'
        114–15, 119–20, 122–3
    power of 76, 77, 79, 96–8,
        117–18, 180, 196, 202, 228

care in the community 254
care, ideology of 331
case conference, psychiatric 473n
case histories
    aimlessness 140–5
    childhood and power 29–31,
        32–3, 34–5, 133, 135–8, 147,
        181–2
    depression 150–1
    eating problems 34–5, 175
    failure of 'forms' 89–90, 139–40
    fear 130–5
    frustration at distal power 40,
        66–7, 75, 176–7
    privacy and interiority 85
    professional disillusionment 155–9
    religious aspects 49, 50
    sexual problems 48, 147–9, 182
    social degradation 45–7, 48–51
    use of 242–3
    violence 29–30, 49, 136, 146–7,
        181
change 242, 274
    keeping in perspective 461–3
    and learning 436–63
    limitations on freedom to 'walking
        the plank' 458–60
changing position 442–53
changing the world and not the 'self'
        441–2
character 315–16, 438, 448
    appreciation of 344–52
    formation of 366, 432, 438, 458
    formative habits of 1980s 128–30
    need to respect individuals 9,
        71–2
    resources of 432
character disorders 253, 272
children/infants 316–18, 399
    abuse of 18, 48, 54, 115, 147,
        316–18, 359, 362, 365, 370, 383

competence to make judgements
    339
exposure to power 26–31, 35–6,
    39, 52–3, 136, 175, 179, 192,
    359, 359–60, 361, 365, 371,
    381–2, 387–8, 399
intrusion and distortion 320–5
learning 455–6
love, loyalty and duty 399–401
and marital relationships 306, 308,
    309, 310
oppression and indifference
    316–20, 382–3
parental/family influence 283,
    316–28, 359–60, 363–6, 397–8,
    432–3
rejection of 319
relationships with parents, target for
    counsellors 115
and shame 382–4
sibling rivalry 319
social disadvantages 325–8
toys as introduction to consumerism
    118
truthfulness and trust 384–8, 419
    see also adolescence
Chomsky, Noam 197–8
Christianity 9, 49, 81–2, 200, 219, 220
    see also religion
Church of Ireland 39
Citizens Advice Bureaux 452
clarification, therapeutic process of
    166, 170–8, 191–2, 233, 270–3,
    276, 450
class
    'classless' society 44, 103
    'consuming' class 125–6
    embodied characteristics 431
    issues 40–1, 42–5, 49–51, 97
    mediating class 126, 127
    middle class 40, 41, 44, 52, 126,
        326, 432, 452
    patterns of conduct 431
    underclass 97
    upper class 43, 220
    working class 40, 41, 44, 51, 97,
        124–5, 326, 432, 433
class distinction 431–2
class injury, phenomenon of 44–5,
    49–51, 326
Claybury Hospital, Essex 238

client-centred (or sometimes 'non-directive') therapy 12, 15, 60, 262
cognitive behaviourism x, 238, 251, 258, 274–5
cognitive restructuring 265
cognitive therapy 12, 172, 173, 264, 271–2, 286, 447–8, 470n
comfort, therapeutic 17, 165–70, 191–2, 233, 268–70, 351, 467n
commentary, internal 415–16, 417, 419, 420
compassion: as social reality 221
'complexes' 59
compulsive behaviour/rituals *see* obsessive–compulsive behaviour
conditioning, Pavlovian 274
conduct and will power 422–3, 424
confidence 45–6, 83, 129, 423, 452
children in parents 28
loss of 289, 320, 422, 449
Confucius 219
consensual validation, lack of 468–9n
consultancy, business: rise of in 1980s 105–10
consulting-room 266, 276, 353, 354
inadequacy of 369–73, 375
consumerism 97–8, 102, 116–18, 120–8
conviviality 118
corruption: links with politics and power 76
counselling *see* psychotherapy and counselling; therapy
courage 83, 139, 148, 413–14, 423
failure of 413–14
crime: links with power and corruption 76
cruelty and physical abuse 316–18, 399
cultural capital 431
culture
disintegration of forms of 342–3
and normality 247–8, 340–4, 347
Cupitt, Don 201
current predicaments 281, 282, 287, 291, 293, 296, 298, 300, 302, 303–15, 306, 307, 309, 311, 312, 313, 314, 366

decency 24–5
demystification 272
dependency 168, 170, 269
depression 52–3, 89, 122, 150–4, 255, 279, 280, 290–2, 305, 312, 394, 420–1, 468n
clinical depression 279
Derrida, Jacques 100
despair 245, 283, 290, 413, 421
deviance 332–3
Dickens, Charles 350
Hard Times 214
distress 239, 275, 277, 278–328, 353, 376, 404, 436, 437, 441, 462, 476n
background predicaments 241, 281, 282–3, 287, 291, 293, 296, 298, 300, 302, 306, 307, 309, 311, 312, 315–28
and changing position 442–53
current approaches to treatment of 245–77
current predicaments 281, 282, 287, 291, 293, 298, 300, 302, 303–15, 306, 307, 309, 311, 312, 313, 314, 366
distal causes 304
experience of 278–328
forms of 283–303
ideological obscurity 8–9, 22–3, 115, 225
ordinary vs. clinical 246
origins in childhood 27–9, 52–3, 175
as pathology 19, 60, 90, 93, 94
personal responsibility and autonomy 354
principal sources of help 249–59
product of society 1–3, 19–20, 23, 36, 38–9, 47–8, 88, 90, 104, 160–1, 170, 194
proximal causes 304
remembering the origins 174–5, 223, 229, 232
scope of psychotherapy 265–77
and will power 407–9
divorce 310
dizziness and faintness 286, 287
doctors
as businessmen 103
as providers of comfort 169–70, 191, 250

doctors *(contd)*
  supposed superiority   49–50, 78,
    257
doing precedes feeling   457–8
drama: 1980s social depreciation
    127
dreams, daydreams and fantasies   295,
    394–5
drug addiction   298, 470n
drug companies   255–6
Dryden, W. 466n

eating disorders   33–5, 124–6, 175,
    232, 299–301, 362, 363, 387,
    408
economy/economics *see* business
education   430–1, 474n
  biological process   230
  counterforce to distal power   66
  dispensed with by business   97,
    101–2
  the learning environment   455–7
  new class of mediators   102–4
  source of ideological power 78, 86,
    180, 188
  see also universities
egos   59, 62
Ellis, Albert   15, 467n
embodiment   326–8, 349, 448, 449
  and normality   336–7
  resources of   427–9
empathetic listening   269
encouragement   166, 183–92, 233,
    268, 272–5, 339, 423
enjoyment: as social function   125–6,
    128
Enlightenment   199–200, 201, 203
environment
  nature of   65–8
  need for therapists to consider
    57–8, 162–3, 183–7, 194–5
  need to restructure   94, 185,
    188–91, 195, 202, 211–13, 222
  pathology of   93–4, 228
  people as product of   61–5, 71–2,
    73–4, 82–4, 87–9, 176, 185–6,
    227–8
  reality of   209–12
  see also power; society
epistemology   212, 213
Epstein, William M.   466n

equality and inequality   219–20
ethics
  misuse of truth   221
  to guide knowledge   212–15, 222
existentialism   389, 478n
experience
  explanation of   370–1
  non-verbal   361–2
  and normality   337–40, 345, 347,
    349
  of power   358–69, 374
  of social environment   356, 370
explanation   370–1, 378
  and blame   378, 379–80
Eysenck, H. J.   330, 466n, 471n

family influences   283, 316–28
  and experience of power   359–60,
    362–4
  intrusion and distortion   320–5
  oppression and indifference
    316–20
  social disadvantages   325–8
  see also parental influence/power
family life   432–3, 445–6
family therapy   446
fear   286–9, 349
  case history   130–5
  of loss of power and advantage
    462
  see also panic
'feeling a fake'   388–91
feelings, loss of control of   285,
    286–94
Feltham, C.   466n
feminism   88, 218, 221
Flaubert, Gustave, *Madame Bovary*
    349
Fleming, Ian   76
Fliess, Wilhelm   472n, 475n
food
  'addictification'   124–6
  eating problems   33–5, 124–6,
    175, 218, 232, 299–301, 362,
    363, 387, 408
  'forms' of society   87–92, 101, 117,
    130, 139–40, 196–7, 200
  need to reconstruct   203, 211–12,
    225
Foucault, Michel   255, 331, 374,
    465n

Foucault, Michel *(contd)*
  Discipline and Punish 8, 37, 78,
    180, 198, 205, 472n
free will 163, 164–5, 223–4, 232–3,
    426
  vs determinism 354–5
  see also will, will power
freedom 232–3, 355, 426
Freud, Sigmund 252, 260, 261, 284,
    389, 437, 465n, 466n, 469n,
    472n, 474n, 475n, 476n, 479n
  disciplinary moralizing 13, 14, 57,
    59, 179
  psychoanalytic theories 2, 14, 15,
    18, 50, 58, 171
  transference concept 33
friendships 440, 441, 447
Fromm, Erich 36, 468n
Fryer, David 471n

Gellner, Ernest 460n
gender roles, redefinition of 342–3,
    344
General Practitioners 245, 249–51,
    254
generational roles, inappropriate
    crossing of 318, 322–3
genetics 64, 473n
Gestalt therapy 12, 14
Godwin, William 197
good: defining concept of 213–14
Goodman, Paul 197
guilt 35, 75, 89, 91, 113, 138, 139,
    292–3, 309, 310, 318, 333, 378,
    379, 390, 395, 402, 425

Habermas, Jürgen 8, 212, 471n
Hagan, Teresa 481n
Haley, Jay 471n
Halmos, Paul 268
Harré, Rom, *Personal Being* 231–2
Harvey, David, *The Condition of
    Postmodernity* 95
health care industry 120–1
Heisenberg, Werner 224
helplessness of the individual xi–xii
Herzen, Alexander 197
Hitler, Adolf 381, 391
Hobsbawm, Eric 474n
Hobson, R. F. 467n
Horney, Karen 36, 318, 465n

Howard, Alex 467n
Hume, David 213–14
Hutton, Will 476n
hypocrisy 18, 116, 390
hypomania 292
hysterical misery 246, 284
  vs common unhappiness 284

ideology
  of advertising and consumerism
    108–9, 116
  ideological power 41–2, 45–6, 72,
    73, 75, 78, 180–1, 205–9, 228,
    230
  of social systems 99, 102, 105, 230
ids 59, 62
Illich, Ivan 118
independence 450–1, 452
indeterminacy, principle of 224
indifference 318, 319–20
individual differences 335
individual psychology, Adler's 261
individualism viii, 63–4, 82–8, 108,
    116, 140, 193–4, 216, 335–6
infantile desires 333
influence, transitive and instransitive
    65
Ingleby, David 472n
inner resources 82–4, 188
inner world x–xi
insecurity *see* security and insecurity
insight(s) 69–70, 173, 271, 272, 303,
    410, 446, 450
instinct 62
insulin-coma therapy 254
intelligence 428, 429, 449, 450, 480n
intelligentsia
  of postmodernity 99–101
  theorizing preserve 5–6, 203
intentions 372
  and motives 372, 391
  unconscious 420
interiority 86, 201, 208–9
interpretation technique 33, 163,
    171
introspection 417–18
intrusion and distortion 320–5
IQ tests 332, 333, 480n
irrational conduct 420, 421

jealousy 293–4, 348

Jenkins, David, Bishop of Durham, *Free to Believe* 8
Jenkins, Rebecca, *Free to Believe* 8n
Johnstone, Lucy 465n
Jung, C. G. 13, 14–15, 122, 171, 252, 261, 389, 437, 477n

Kant, Immanuel 219, 478n
Kelly, George: 'personal construct', psychology of 474n
Kierkegaard, Soren 477n
King-Spooner, Simon 480n
Klein, Melanie 36
knowledge
    1980s redefinition 101
    for effective psychotherapy 193
    need to pursue 203–4, 208–13
    and power 180, 183, 206, 255
Kovel, Joel 466n
Kraepelin, Emil 93
Kropotkin, Prince Peter 197

Laing, R. D. 35, 36, 255, 469n, 473n
language
    of 1980s business 98–9, 103, 106, 108–10, 117–18, 180
    difficulties of union leaders 44–5
    and experience 361–2
    inability to describe experience 90, 211
    learning/speaking 455, 460, 461
    of power 75, 78
    product of environment 63, 86–7, 180, 232, 340–1
    regional accents in class fugitives 44, 51
Lasch, Christopher 472n
    The Minimal Self 104, 197
learning
    and change 436–63
    doing precedes feeling 457–8
    a language 455, 460, 461
    learning environment 455–7
    maladaptive 272
    nature of 274–5
    the need for practice 460–1
    to be different 453–61
    'walking the plank' 458–60
leucotomy 254
liberalism 198, 201

Lidz, Theodore 471n
literacy 431, 449
literature, 1980s social depreciation 127
Lomas, Peter 467n
loneliness 194
loss of control
    of actions 285, 297–303
    of feelings 285, 286–94
    of thoughts 285, 294–7
love 319, 321, 323, 325, 399–401, 403–4, 429, 440–1, 467n
    Christian precept 219, 220
    conditional love 319
    impress of power 31
    and parent–child relationships 399–401
    professionalisation of 468n
    self-depreciation 34–5
    and shame 382
    source of comfort 17, 268, 351
    and truthfulness and trust 384–8
    see also comfort, therapeutic
loyalty 30, 399–401
lying 401–2
    necessary skill 183
Lyotard, François 00

MacIntyre, Alasdair, *After Virtue* 104, 214
madness 90
magic 78, 198, 201, 206, 209, 221, 263, 264, 265, 267, 299, 436
Mair, Miller 467n, 474n
Major, John 96
making up our minds 416
maladaptive learning 272
management
    1980s problems 97, 104, 105–10, 132–5, 157–8
    growth of consultancy 105–10
    need to discard unwanted methods 178
    political 96
    power of 40, 66–7, 75, 106–7
    see also business; professionals
manipulation of self-interest 358
Marcuse, Herbert 205
marital relationship difficulties 305–10, 342, 366–7, 443, 444
marital therapy/counselling 446

marriage, debasement of 120, 139–40

Marriage Guidance Council *see* Relate

Marshall, Richard 473n

Martin, Denis 238

Marx, Karl 198

Masson, Jeffrey 469n
  Against Therapy 18, 59, 161, 169, 171, 192, 468n

material resources 240, 445, 452

media
  power of 75, 78, 80, 109
  radio phone-ins 91

medicine 62, 170
  see also doctors

mediocracy: established in 1980s revolution 103–4, 106–10

memory: remembering origins of distress 174–5, 223, 229, 232

mental illness 246, 250, 251, 253, 254
  genetic component 473–4n
  medical model 253, 254
  orthodox approach to 237

Miller, Alice 383, 477n

mind control, impossibility of 392–6

money 429–30, 452–3
  instrument of power 25, 43, 188
  transfer from public to private hands 109–10

mono-symtomatic phobias 289, 470n

Monroe, Marilyn 438

Moore, G. E. 213

moral demands 242, 377–405
  countering the moral impress of power 360–1, 391–405, 398–9
  determining the limits of obligation 396–9
  impossibility of mind control 392–6
  love, loyalty and duty 399–405
  the origins of shame 381–91
  public *vs* private 391, 394

motives, motivation 372, 479n
  definition 372
  Hannah Arendt on 477–8n
  and intentions 372
  unconscious 389, 420

Mowrer, O. H. 477n

National Health Service (NHS) 238, 259

nationalism 200–1, 202

'naturalistic fallacy' (Moore) 213–14

neuroses 93, 253, 465n
  Freud's theory of sexual origins of 323, 475n
  symptoms 420, 469n

Nietzsche, Friedrich 203, 205

nonbehavioural therapists 273

normality 242, 295
  appreciation of character 344–52
  concept of 332
  and individuality 335–6, 338
  the making of persons 335–50
  tyranny of 329–51, 448
  vs abnormality 245, 246, 377

obligation, determining the limits of 396–9

obsessional thinking 295–7

obsessive-compulsive behaviour 98–9, 321, 408, 413, 421

Oedipal competition 323

old age: modern predicament 120–1, 126

Open University courses 449

oppression 316–20, 398, 399, 451

The Origins of Unhappiness (Smail) 281, 325–6

pain
  result of society 'forms' 89, 94
  solidarity of 215–16, 337

panic, panic attacks 26, 27–8, 50, 135, 137, 139, 286, 288, 289, 290, 307, 309, 311, 314, 317
  see also fear

parental favour 323–4, 338, 383

parental influence/power 283, 316, 320–5, 339–40, 359–60, 363–4, 365–6, 385–6, 462–3
  and cause of distress 28–30, 35–6, 39, 45–6, 52–3, 136, 192
  challenging 444
  love, loyalty and duty 399–405

parenting skills 115

Passmore, John 481n

past
  influence of the 315, 316, 360, 438, 442
  understanding of the 450

pathology
  casualties of 1980s revolution
    107–8, 281
  distress defined as   19, 60, 90, 93,
    94
  of the environment   93
Pavlov, Ian   60
Pearson, Karl   473n
persona   59
  overdeveloped   389
  private *vs* public   388, 391
personal resources   445, 447–52
personhood, the making of persons
    viii, 335–50
  character   344–52
  culture   340–4
  embodiment   336–7
  experience   337–40
philosophy
  relevance to everyday life   6, 82,
    186, 211–12
  and truth   205, 206, 208
phobias   288–9, 292, 296, 470n
physical abuse   316, 317, 404
Plato, *Republic*   87, 186–7
political (in)correctness   218, 478n
politics and politicians
  of the   1980s 95–101
  attitudes towards distress   19
  extolment of family unit   79
  feminism and power   88
  manipulation of statistics   109
  power   25, 55, 69, 73, 76, 88, 96
  and truth   204
pop music   126–7
positive thinking   264, 274
post-traumatic stress disorder
    112–13, 264
postmodernity   99–100, 198, 201–2,
    205, 206
  The Condition of Postmodernity
    (Harvey)   95
poststructuralism   100–1
poverty   47, 48, 216–17
power   xxii, 354, 355, 381–2, 383–4,
    402, 418, 427, 462
  cause of distress   23–33, 65–9, 174,
    178–80, 240
  challenging   444, 451, 453
  childhood experience   26–30,
    35–6, 39, 52–3, 80, 175, 179, 192

and class   40–1, 42–5, 49, 220
coercive power   42, 67, 69, 72–3,
    77, 99, 197–8, 217, 228, 357
of psychiatry   3, 60, 61
concept ignored by psychologists
    24–6, 36, 37, 42–3
countering the 'moral' impress of
    60–1, 391–405, 398–9
definition of   357
'discourse of power' (Foucault)
    37, 39
economic   42, 43, 72, 91, 96–105,
    196–7, 228, 230, 357
embodiment and disembodiment
    216–24, 230
experience of   358–69
exploitation   398–9
faith as assurance of   460
fear of loss of   462
gained through association   76–7,
    79, 80–1, 188
ideological   41–2, 45–6, 72, 73,
    75, 78, 180–1, 205–9, 228, 230,
    357
influence of distal power   37–42,
    45–6, 53–5, 66–9, 75–7, 88, 91,
    98–105, 176, 187, 223–4, 228–31
and knowledge   255, 256
of media   75
mediation of   77–9, 98–107, 160,
    178–80, 211, 219–20, 223–4,
    232–3
nature of   26, 31–3, 53–5, 65,
    72–7, 192, 198–9, 217, 228–9
political   25, 55, 69, 73, 76, 88, 96
principle of challenging   451
proximal power and power horizon
    37–40, 42, 45, 66, 67–9, 75–7,
    88, 90, 176, 223, 229, 451
reality of   364–9
in scientific community   207
societal power   373–6
structure of   356–8
of therapists   161–6, 167, 185, 187,
    192
unequal distribution of   463
use and abuse of   242, 402, 404,
    462
see also parental influence/power;
    society; will/will power
practice, the need for   460–1

predicaments *see* background predicaments; current predicaments
private life, privacy   385, 388, 389
　lack of 84–5, 113
　public vs private   388, 391, 394
　see also mind control
private sector, provision of psychological help in   252
professionals
　case history   155–9
　irreverence towards   101
　new men of 1980s   102–6, 108, 132
　urged to discard unwanted fashions   78, 194
　see also management
prostitution and psychotherapy   475n
Proudhon, Pierre-Joseph   197
psychiatry   238, 240, 250, 252–7
　clinical shortcomings   9, 12–13, 87–8, 93, 161, 193–4, 238–9
　coercive power   3, 60, 161
　medical model   238, 253, 264
　and schizophrenia   19–20
psychoactive drugs   253–4
psychoanalysis   252, 261, 319, 333, 380
　1980s popularity   100–1
　exclusivity   11, 14–15
　Freudian   2, 260, 261
　Harré schema   231–3
　interpretation technique   33, 163, 171
　psychodynamic tradition of   273
　'repetition compulsion'   191
psychodynamic therapy   12, 27, 57, 188, 479n
psychological determinism, Freudian notion of   479n
psychological meaning-systems   357, 366
psychology
　Adler's individual psychology   261
　analytical   252, 261
　basic methodology   57–8, 71, 84, 230
　clinical   250, 251, 257–9
　definition   329–30
　flaws and shortcomings   9, 13, 16, 20–3, 36, 58–60, 69–70, 82, 177, 230–1

　fragmented nature of   59, 186
　growth industry   11–12, 16, 19
　importance of environment neglected   186–7, 194
　Kelly's 'personal construct'   474n
　make-up of personal psychology   73–4, 82, 186, 231–3
　misinterpretation of 'forms'   87–8
　neglect of consideration of power   24–6, 36, 37, 42–3
　and normality   332
　received expectations   4–5, 7, 13, 19, 72, 178
　reflexive   471n
　as a science   472n
psychometry, psychometric tests   332, 333
psychopatholgy   1, 90, 93
psychoses   93, 246, 253, 280, 469n
psychotherapy and counselling   vii, x 250, 251, 254, 257, 259–65, 267, 269, 273, 333, 351, 475n
　clarification process   167, 170–8, 191–2, 233
　class issue neglected   42–3
　component of mediocracies   104–5, 110–16
　credibility problem   18–19, 161–5, 185–6, 192–5
　disaster counselling   112–15
　environment of consulting room   266
　giving encouragement   183–95, 233
　humanist   201
　limitations to efficacy   2–3, 8, 15–16, 20–3, 58–60, 69–70, 168, 174, 233, 265–8
　misinterpretation of 'forms'   87–8, 117, 189
　provision of comfort   17, 165–70, 191–2, 233
　received expectations   4–5, 7, 72, 167–8, 192–5
　relationship between 'patient' and therapist   16–19, 32, 36, 57–60, 162–5, 166–70, 187, 194, 241, 262–3
　scope of   265–77
　societal influences   36–9, 113–14, 171–2, 208

psychotherapy and counselling *(contd)*
  therapeutic comfort   17, 165–70,
  191–2, 233, 268–70

racism   327, 328
rational emotive therapy   12, 14, 15,
  264
reality management   xxi
reality, nature of   199, 205–6, 207–8
reason, nature of   199, 205–6, 207–8
reflexology   260
reinforcement, positive and negative
  (reward and punishment)   274
rejection   319
Relate *(formerly* Marriage Guidance
  Council)   114
relationships, commodified nature of
  440
religion
  in case histories   9, 50
  failure as socially cohesive force
    199, 200–1, 204, 205, 209, 214
  fundamentalism   49, 81, 92, 200
  Jung's fascination   14–15
  means of controlling society   78,
    391–2
  persistence of Christian ethics   8,
    219, 220
  power of Church of Ireland   39
  Religion and the Decline of Magic
    (Thomas) 22
  source of associative power   49,
    81–2
repetition compulsion   191
repression   171, 174, 178–82, 430,
  476n
resistance, phenomenon of   469n
resources   418, 427–35
  assessing available   284, 444–53
  of character   432
  education, class and cultural capital
    430–2
  of embodiment   427–9
  financial   429–30
  home and family life   432–3,
    445–6
  material   445, 452–3
  personal   445, 447–52
  possible availability of   445
  social life   433–4, 446–7, 448,
    449–50

responsibility   xii, 68, 163, 264, 273,
  276, 303
risk economics   116
Robert the Bruce   407
Rogers, Carl   15, 17, 60, 163, 251,
  262–3, 380
Rorty, Richard   100, 205
Rowan, John   473n
Rowe, Dorothy   468n
  Wanting Everything   25, 78
Runciman, W. G., *A Treatise on Social
  Theory*   72n
Ryle, Gilbert   479n

Salmon, Phillida   474n
Sartre, Jean-Paul   389, 479n, 480n,
  481n
Schafer, Roy   481n
Scherner, K. A.   474n
schizophrenia   20, 254, 255, 280,
  378–9, 468n, 469n
  paranoid schizophrenia   780
science and scientism
  disciplinary   198, 201, 204, 205,
    206–7
  need to reconnect with faith   209,
    210
  in therapy   57–61
Scull, Andrew   472n
second marriages   310, 311, 343
security and insecurity   26, 201,
  296–7, 318
self-confidence, loss/lack of   45–6,
  289–90, 307, 318, 320, 422, 449
self-consciousness   83, 297
self-control   82–6
self-help   vii
self-justification   378
self-loathing   291, 318, 381, 413
self-mutilation   301
sex and sexuality   308, 328, 333, 397,
  428, 430, 470n, 475n
  abuse of children   18, 48, 54, 115,
    147, 316–18, 362, 365, 383
  Freud's view   18
  accepted topic of conversation   24,
    430
  dangers in Church of Ireland
    doctrines   39
  debasement of marriage   120,
    139–40

sex and sexuality *(contd)*
  emotional problem attributed to
    patient   171
  eroticism as escape from modernity
    205
  feminism   88, 218, 221
  marketing 'fulfilment'   114–15,
    119–20, 122–3, 126
  masculinity–femininity form
    87–8, 118, 217–18, 342
  pimp-prostitute relationship   77
  plight of women in middle age
    122–3, 307
  pornographic scrutiny   328
  power exploitation   217–18, 397
  problems in case histories   48,
    147–9, 182
  separation of sex and companion-
    ship   308
  sex roles, redefinition of   342
  wishes and fantasies, unconscious
    270
Shakespeare, William, *Merchant of
  Venice*   218
shame   288, 297, 335, 376, 378, 379,
    383, 395, 400, 402, 442
  'feeling a fake'   388–91
  manipulation in children of   382
  origins of   381–91
truthfulness and trust   384–8
Shotter, John   471n
shyness   290, 297, 381, 447, 459
sibling rivalry   319
sincerity   389, 401
  self-contradictory notion of   384–5
single parents   314–15
Smith, Adam   358
social context   xix, 434–5
social control   257, 472n
social disadvantages   325–8
social environment, influence of
    xxii, 254, 354, 355–6, 434, 434–5
social life/activities   433–4, 446–7,
    448, 449–50
social space–time   viii, ix
society
  1980s revolution and mediocrity
    96–128
  accessibility to privacy   84–6
  cause of distress   1–3, 19–20, 23,
    36, 38–9, 47–8, 88, 90, 104,

    160–1, 170, 176, 225
  community as core of moral system
    214–18, 222
  counselling as social interference
    13–16
  distress blamed on individuals
    19–20, 22–3, 171
  enjoyment as social function
    125–6, 128
  erosion of social cohesion   54–5,
    91–2, 99, 117, 128–30, 196–202
  influence of 'forms'   87–92, 101,
    117, 130, 139–40, 196–7, 200,
    203, 225
  influence on individuals' behaviour
    73–7, 93–4, 117–20, 194, 200–2,
    228–31
  majority interests ignored   40,
    129–30, 219–22
  means of controlling   77–9,
    97–105, 218–21
  middle aged and adolescents in
    market place   121–3, 190
  need to seek new values   202–16
  network of dependencies   168
  predicament of the old   120–1
  social degradation   38, 45–53
  see also class; consumerism; envi-
    ronment; power
sociology and power   25, 75–6, 207
solidarity
  between family members   432–3
  between 'patient' and therapist
    16–17, 166–70, 177, 187, 190,
    194, 263, 268, 269, 275, 459
  ethical   215–18, 221–2, 228
soul   62, 68, 201
space and time in environmental
    power structure   viii, 65–7,
    69–71, 95, 185, 228
Stalin, Josef   391
statistical analysis procedures   473n
stream of consciousness   294, 393
stress   266–7, 295
  post-traumatic   112–13, 264
stress management procedures   267
subjectivity/objectivity, paradox of
    70, 373, 375
suicide   141, 145, 311, 471n
Sullivan, H. S.   36, 90, 334–5, 465n,
    471n, 476n

Interpersonal Theory of Psychiatry 90n, 468n
superconscientiousness 292, 323, 396, 397
superstition 92, 296, 319, 321, 364
suspicion 92
Suttie, Ian 268
symptoms, the meaning of 420–3
systematic desensitization 187
Szasz, Thomas 253, 255, 468n

'talking therapies' 258–9, 262
terrorism 221
Thatcher, Margaret 96, 99, 116, 238, 367, 391
therapeutic relationship 268–70, 275, 353, 466–7n
therapeutic-community movement 238
therapy
  choice of therapies available 12, 14–16, 172–3, 183
  component of mediocracies 104–5, 110, 114
  effectiveness questioned 19–23, 36, 57–60, 70, 161–5, 174, 233
  humanistic approach 380
  ingenuousness of counsellors 110–11, 115, 183–4
  ingredients 165–6
  power of therapists 161–6, 167, 185, 187, 192
  relations between client and counsellor 16–19, 57–60, 162–70, 351–2
  see also psychotherapy and counselling
Thomas, Keith, *Religion and the Decline of Magic* 22, 467n
thoughts, loss of control of 285, 294–7
time *see* space and time
Tolstoy, Leo 197
  Childhood, Boyhood and Youth 346–7
trade unions 44–5, 79, 97, 99, 434
tranquillisers 249, 269
Transactional Analysis 12, 14
transference concept (Freud) 33

Tressell, Robert 73
truth
  abused by terrorists 221
  casualty of 1980s revolution 100–2, 204
  establishing 285
  need to rediscover 204–13
  truthfulness and trust 384–8, 401, 418

unconditional positive regard 351–2, 380
the unconscious x
unconscious complexes 272
unconscious minds 59, 62
unconscious motivation 389, 420
unemployment 38, 97, 99, 115, 116, 304, 305, 471n
unhappiness 246, 283–4, 285, 350, 443
  hysterical vs common 284
universities 5, 101, 103, 180, 207, 212
upward social mobility 343

violence: case histories 29–30, 49, 136, 146–7, 181, 316–17
Vygotsky, Lev 480n
  Thought and Language 179

'walking the plank' 458–60
Watzlawick, Paul 471n
'weighing the pros and cons' 416
West, Rosemary 478n
will, will power 62, 68, 163, 164–5, 222–5, 232–3, 392, 406–35, 426, 440, 470n
  failure of 407, 408, 413, 414, 416–17
  as illusion 415–20
  the illusion as inescapable 423–7
  the meaning of symptoms 420–3
  powers and resources 427–35
  the process of doing 412–15
  and psychotherapy 409–12
Winter, David 474n
women's movement 344

young people, difficulties of 311–12
'yuppie' culture 44, 97